Septimius Severus
THE AFRICAN EMPEROR

Septimius Severus
THE AFRICAN EMPEROR

ANTHONY BIRLEY

DOUBLEDAY & COMPANY, INC.

GARDEN CITY, NEW YORK

1972

ACKNOWLEDGMENTS FOR ILLUSTRATIONS

*Acknowledgments and thanks for permission to reproduce the photographs
are due to G. D. B. Jones for plates 2a, 2b, 5a, 5b and 13b; to Richard du
Cane for plates 3, 4a, 4b, 11a, 14c and 16; to the British Museum for plate
4c; to the Staatliche Museum, Berlin, for plate 6; to the German Archaeolgical
Institute for plates 7 and 11b; to C. M. Daniels for plates 8 and 9; to the
British School at Rome for plate 10; to the Museum of Antiquities, the University, Newcastle for plate 13c; to James Walker for plates 14a and 14b;
and to Felbermeyer, Museo Nuovo, for plate 15.*

To Suzanna

CONTENTS

ILLUSTRATIONS

MAPS

PREFACE

The last biography of Septimius Severus in English, by Maurice Platnauer, was published over fifty years ago, in 1918. It was followed three years later by Johannes Hasebroek's *Untersuchungen* into the *vita* of the Emperor in the Augustan History. These two works have remained standard up to the present moment,[1] and Platnauer was reprinted in 1965, which implies a demand. Much new evidence has turned up since 1918, a lot of work has been done on the sources, especially on the Augustan History, and a new biography is needed. 'Biography offers the easy approach to history,' Sir Ronald Syme has remarked.[2] Lives of Roman Emperors are no exception and they are quite numerous. I make no apology for adding another.

Interest in Septimius has cropped up in unexpected places: his racial origin and his qualities as Emperor were the subject of exchanges in the U.S. House of Representatives in the summer of 1963.[3] I have devoted a fair amount of space to the first of these questions – not because of what was said in the U.S. Congress (I did not learn of it until I had finished writing: but the Congressmen's remarks perhaps demonstrate the need for further investigation). However, the Severan period has not been much studied in English-speaking universities. Mainly because the sources are poor or at least peculiar; perhaps also because the events themselves have been judged insufficiently uplifting in comparison with earlier periods of ancient history. Still, not least because it was an era of upheaval and change, it deserves attention at this time.[4]

---

[1] Hasebroek wrote without knowledge of Platnauer: cf. chapter 1, esp. p. 5, n. 1.

[2] *Tacitus* (1958), p. 91.

[3] See *Congressional Record for 1963*, pp. 11498, 12122f., 12198 (remarks by Reps. O'Hara, Illinois and Waggonner, Louisiana). Garbled versions of what was said seem to be current still.

[4] It has in fact already begun to receive this attention, as may be judged from the bibliography to this book.

This book is only a biography, of course, not a history of the period; and I have tried not to exaggerate the importance of the man. Emperors were autocrats. But their capacity to mould the course of history was very limited. I do not pretend that Septimius was an attractive personality – few autocrats, least of all Roman Emperors, ever have been – but he was not particularly odious either. It is admittedly difficult to penetrate deeply into the personality of a figure from so remote a past. There are a few exceptions – Cicero, Marcus Aurelius, Julian the Apostate, St Augustine, for instance – but only a few. I have just had to do the best I can with what evidence has survived. I have aimed above all at setting him in his context, and for this reason have devoted half the book to his life before accession. The evidence for this is scanty, but a good deal is known about many of his contemporaries and friends.

Through the accident of birth I spent about seven years of my childhood a stone's throw from the fort of Vindolanda built in Septimius's reign for the *cohors IV Gallorum*, and the name of the Emperor was almost a household word at an early stage in my life. But I do not want to claim any special insight thereby gained. My serious acquaintance with the period began under the supervision of Professor Syme. His first advice to me was that I should read Hermann Dessau's epoch-making paper on the Augustan History in *Hermes* for 1889. Since that time (1960) Professor Syme himself has contributed a great deal to the better understanding of that strange work. I owe him a great debt for his guidance while I was writing my dissertation – and subsequently. I am also greatly indebted to Professor Johannes Straub for inviting me to attend three of the *Colloquia* on the *Augustan History* held in the Rhineland. I gained enormously from debate and discussion there, and it was at the 1966 *Colloquium* that M. H. G. Pflaum suggested to me that I should undertake a biography of Septimius Severus. He should not be blamed for the result; but I am grateful to him for providing the stimulus.

Personal experience of places that were important in the life of his subject is not indispensable for a biographer. But it has given me some satisfaction to have spent some time at Lepcis Magna, Septimius's birthplace; Athens, where he lived in enforced retirement; Carnuntum, where he was proclaimed Emperor; Rome itself; Viminacium, where he made his son Caesar; Lyons, where he crushed Albinus (and where he had been governor); Carpow on the Tay, where he campaigned against the barbarians of the Scottish Highlands; and York, where he died. Few Emperors, however, had so wide an experience of the Roman provinces as Septimius: the list of places to which he journeyed and where I have been unable, so far, to follow is much longer – Sardinia, Spain, Syria, Sicily, much of Asia Minor, Byzantium, the Euphrates and the Tigris, Egypt. In 1961 my brother Robin Birley discovered the Severan date of the fortress at Carpow. The many weeks we spent excavating together, both there and elsewhere, have been valuable and have given me a lot of pleasure. I am indebted also to my friend Charles Daniels, whose invitation to join the Fezzan Expedition in 1965 gave me the chance of spending some days at Lepcis, as well as to investigate, under his direction, the Garamantian sites in the Wadi el-Agial.

I have incurred many other debts. First and foremost to my father Eric Birley for his ever ready advice and encouragement. My friend Dr Géza Alföldy has discussed many of the problems with me and with characteristic generosity has made available to me a number of his forthcoming publications in typescript. This has been a tremendous help to me. Four other friends, at various times, have discussed par-ticular *quaestiones Severianae* with me: A. J. Graham, G. D. B. Jones, J. B. Leaning, J. F. Oates. I am most grateful to them. They, together with Robin Birley and Sir Ronald Syme, have helped me to eradicate errors and to improve the book in various ways: the faults that remain are my own. I began the book at Leeds, but more than half was written at Duke University, Durham, North Carolina. During my year there I was able for the first time to teach the Severan period in detail. My thanks are due to the participants in my graduate seminar, for their patience, industry and perception. My other obligations can best be gauged from the Bibliography and notes – except that to my wife Suzanna, whose help has been the most valuable of all.

Throughout I have used the name Septimius, rather than Severus, to avoid confusion with various kinsmen. And, perhaps perversely, I have preferred the names Bassianus and Antoninus successively for Caracalla (except in ch. XVII). Various delays in the publication have enabled me to make use of at least some of the fairly numerous relevant works published recently. In the notes, I have cited author's names only, with a date in brackets where necessary, and page references. Fuller details are given in the Bibliography. To avoid overloading the footnotes with prosopographical detail, I have reserved discussion of various key figures to the Appendices.

A.R.B.
Leeds

15 January 1971

SEPTIMIUS SEVERUS
the African Emperor

I

INTRODUCTION

'The contemporaries of Severus, in the enjoyment of the peace and glory of his reign, forgave the cruelties by which it had been introduced. Posterity, who experienced the fatal results of his maxims and example, justly considered him as the principal author of the decline of the Roman empire.' This was the verdict of Edward Gibbon, at the end of the fifth chapter of *Decline and Fall*. No one any longer treats the decline and fall of the Roman Empire as does a detective investigating a crime, pursuing the forces responsible for it, to arraign them before the bar of history. Nor indeed was Gibbon himself so simplistic. But it is remarkable to find him apparently giving an outright answer to the question that he had set himself. His book is a classic, and for this reason alone the personality of the 'principal author of the decline', the villain of the piece, is of more than passing interest. Lucius Septimius Severus was Emperor for nearly eighteen years, from 193–211. It was the longest reign of any Emperor between the death of Marcus Aurelius in 180 and the accession of Diocletian in 284. The dynasty he tried to establish did indeed survive him, and lasted until 235. The fifty years that followed the death of its last member have always been characterised as a half century of crisis and anarchy.[1]

The changes in the Empire are mirrored, in a very real sense, by the identity of its rulers. First came the Julio-Claudian dynasty, of noble and patrician stock. After the interlude of confusion in 68–9, the

[1] On the third century the *Cambridge Ancient History* XII (1939) is still the most comprehensive account. The number of separate reigns between Severus Alexander and Diocletian, 235–284, amounts to eighteen on the lowest estimate. The longest was that of Gallienus, sole Emperor for less than nine years, 260–268; but his authority never extended over the whole Empire.

Flavians ruled for twenty-seven years, representatives of the Italian *bourgeoisie*. Then, after two years of Nerva, came the accession of Trajan and the entrenchment of a dynasty sprung from the colonial aristocracy of Spain and Gaul, Baetica and Narbonensis. By the time that Commodus was murdered, it was the men from Africa who dominated. Their representative – in a sense – was Septimius Severus. Septimius's wife was a Syrian, and it was members of her family who ruled from 218–35. Later in the third century, and in the fourth, the other areas of the Empire were to have their turn.[1]

The origin of Septimius Severus is of some importance therefore. Just how important is a question that has been hotly disputed. Early in the twentieth century the voice of Alfred von Domaszewski was powerful, damning Septimius in sweeping terms. His attitude is naturally present in the monograph by his pupil Johannes Hasebroek, published in 1921: Septimius's purpose (in the bloody purge which followed his victory at Lugdunum in 197) was 'the complete annihilation of the existing social order, the destruction of all property, the fanatical rooting out of the last remaining elements of Greco-Roman culture, the place of which was taken by the barbarism of the provinces'. The battle of Lugdunum marked the final, decisive struggle between Roman culture and barbarism: 'the decline of the ancient world begins in truth with the sole rule of Septimius Severus'. Maurice Platnauer, whose biography of Septimius, published in 1918, was not available to Hasebroek, took a very different view: 'Such statements [by Domaszewski] as that Septimius planted "the despotism of the East in the soil of the West", or that "it was his fault that the empire was handed over to a pitiless soldiery who in self-devastating strife destroyed the culture of the Mediterranean", are little more than nonsense.' Platnauer ignores Septimius's origin as a significant factor. But others preferred to follow the views of Domaszewski and Hasebroek. In volume XII of the *Cambridge Ancient History*, published in 1939, S. N. Miller emphasised that 'cruelty as well as perfidy was commonly

[1] The rise of the provincials is a key theme of Sir R. SYME's *Tacitus* (1958). 'Other areas': for example, Maximinus the 'Thracian', the Gordians (probably from Galatia or Cappadocia, cf. A. R. BIRLEY (1966)), Philip the Arab, and the 'Illyrian' Emperors Decius, Claudius II, Aurelian and Probus. Gallus, Valerian and Gallienus were – curiously enough – Italian.

attributed to the race from which he was sprung, and there were some who called him a "Punic Sulla". . . . His consciousness of his origin and his race is proclaimed in his coinage and is evident in his policy. To such a man the Roman tradition was alien.' A. Piganiol declared that Septimius 'did not possess Roman patriotism; and was to restore the tomb of Hannibal'. E. Kornemann wrote darkly of 'Hannibal's homeland wreaking belated vengeance on Rome'.[1]

At the same time, efforts have been made to minimise the alleged non-Romanness of Septimius. Mason Hammond, in an article published in 1940, argued that he was a typical product of the imperial civil service. In 1951 Julien Guey emphasised, in his paper on the grandfather of Septimius, that his family, while doubtless of native extraction, was thoroughly typical of most senatorial families of provincial origin. To those who have seen Septimius as alien to the spirit of Rome, it is a natural corollary to suppose that he favoured his native land at the expense of the rest of the Empire, or at least that it received exceptionally favourable treatment. This conclusion has indeed been reached by the majority of scholars, whether or not they saw Septimius as a new Hannibal on the throne of the Caesars. But in 1940 R. M. Haywood sought to dispel the idea: 'The emperor was born in Lepcis. It is not correct to say, as a means of indicating the direction of his patriotic sentiments, that he was a native of Africa. . . . The assumption that Severus must have favoured all the African provinces because he was born in the city of Lepcis runs through all discussions of the subject, and in many it has led to distortion and misinterpretation of the evidence.' G. Barbieri, in an article of 1952, based on his collection of the evidence in *L'Albo senatorio*, sought to show that in the choice of men for high office Septimius in no way favoured Africa and the east at the expense of Italy. M. G. Jarrett argued in 1963 that the same applied to the imperial equestrian service. In 1967 T. D. Barnes reiterated the conclusions of Haywood, Barbieri and Jarrett, and sought further to demonstrate that the Septimii of Lepcis were possibly not

[1] Cf. J. HASEBROEK (1921), p. 99, and e.g. A. v. DOMASZEWSKI (1909b), II, p. 256. – M. PLATNAUER, p. 162 (referring to Domaszewski, p. 262). *CAH*, XII, pp. 19ff. (the quotation is from p. 24). – A. PIGANIOL, p. 356. E. KORNE-MANN, II, p. 178. – Cf. further G. WALSER, p. 7f. and G. ALFÖLDY, *Senat*, p. 112, n. 4.

'Punic' at all, but a family of immigrant – Italian – stock.[1]

From this rapid examination it is clear that there is a wide discrepancy of opinion. It is the aim of the present work to cast more light on the origin and background of Septimius and his associates. It is, however, strictly a biography and not a comprehensive history of the period. Study of the life of an Emperor forms only one of many elements from which an estimate of his times can be made. It is now rightly emphasised that 'the significance of the individual ruler declines steadily' during the second century A.D. Nonetheless, an Emperor did retain some individual importance, and the nature of the evidence dictates that more is known, in most cases, about Emperors than about any other single person in their reigns. It would be nothing less than wasteful to abjure biographies of Emperors completely.[2] But it must be emphasised once again that a biography of an Emperor is not a substitute for a history of the Roman Empire during his reign. In this biography political and military history occur, indeed at times dominate the narrative. But that is because at times politics and war dominated the life of Septimius Severus. There is a rider to this statement. Sir Ronald Syme observed thirty years ago that 'in all ages, whatever the form and name of government, be it monarchy, republic, or democracy, an oligarchy lurks behind the façade; and Roman history, Republican or Imperial, is the history of the governing class'.[3] In the

---

[1] M. HAMMOND (1940), *passim* (but cf. T. PEKÁRY, p. 473, n. 220, for a critique of H.'s description of Septimius as a typical 'Roman bureaucrat'). – J. GUEY (1951a), esp. p. 184 and n. 2 (but his views on the rank of Septimius's grandfather are not here accepted; cf. p. 36 below and A. R. BIRLEY, *HAC*, esp. pp. 75ff.). – T. R. S. BROUGHTON, pp. 153ff. is a typical representative of the view that Septimius favoured his native Africa. In spite of R. M. HAYWOOD (1940), P. ROMANELLI (1959), esp. p. 435 and n. 3 continues to belief in special favour to Africa. – G. BARBIERI (1952), *passim*; M. G. JARRETT (1963), pp. 215ff. – T. D. BARNES (1967a) (his views on the origins of the Septimii are criticised by A. R. BIRLEY, *HAC* pp. 63ff., and cf. ID. [1969], pp. 253ff.). See further pp. 34ff., below.

[2] The quotation is from R. Syme, *Classical Review* 53 (1939), 79. Note the comments of F. Millar, reviewing F. GROSSO, in *Journal of Roman Studies* 56 (1966), pp. 243ff., where he asks 'whether Imperial biographies, or histories of individual reigns, should be written at all' – and answers in a more or less negative sense.

[3] Sir R. SYME (1939), p. 7.

biography of an Emperor, particularly one who seized power in a *coup d'état* and spent four years of civil war in disposing of his rivals, investigation of his associates is as important an aspect of his life as any.

The last detailed studies on Septimius Severus were written some fifty years ago, by Maurice Platnauer and Johannes Hasebroek. Platnauer's book was of orthodox type, an account of the life and reign of the Emperor: one chapter devoted to 'Early Life' and nine chapters to the reign. Hasebroek's work was totally different. It was in effect a commentary on the *vita Severi* in the *Historia Augusta*, with useful appendices assembling coin-legends and inscriptions. The nature of the sources dictated the balance of the book: fifteen pages on 'early life', ninety-five on the wars of 193–7, and forty on the rest of the reign. (In 1947 G. J. Murphy published a study of the reign only, based on 'the evidence of inscriptions'. But this cannot be said to have marked any real advance in knowledge.)[1]

But in the meantime there has been a great increase in the body of available evidence and great progress in the study of previously known sources. These sources must now be examined. They are broadly divided into two categories, literary and archaeological. In the first category belong the three main historical works from antiquity that cover the period: the *Roman History* of Cassius Dio, Herodian's *History of the Empire after Marcus*, and a number of *vitae* in the *Historia Augusta*. These three are supplemented by the writings of contemporaries such as Galen the physician, Tertullian the Christian apologist and theologian, Philostratus, the biographer of the Sophists; and, of course, by the excerpts from the jurists, and from the imperial rescripts, preserved principally in the *Digest* and *Code* of Justinian. Later chroniclers such as Aurelius Victor and Eutropius also have some use.

---

[1] Note J. HASEBROEK, p. v, n. 1, revealing that he had first heard of PLATNAUER's book while his own was in the press (but had not seen it). On G. J. MURPHY, cf. the review by M. HAMMOND (1950). The article on Septimius in Pauly-Wissowa, *RE* 2A (1923), cols. 1940–2002, by M. Fluss, is based largely on Hasebroek (cf. 1942) and though useful in its way has little independent value. Note the comments by T. FRANK, p. 78, n. 39: 'Hasebroek . . . did much to penetrate the sources; Platnauer . . . gives a eulogy'. Cf. G. ALFÖLDY, *Senat.* p. 113, n. 4: '*Die grundlegende Arbeit über Septimius Severus ist bis heute das Buch von J. Hasebroek. . . . Im Gegensatz dazu idealisiert das Bild des Herrschers M. Platnauer.*'

The second category, archaeological sources, covers a wide range: as well as material evidence for military and civil structures of all kinds, and the objects of trade – archaeological evidence in a narrow sense – there is the material discovered by archaeologists, coins, inscriptions and papyri. Besides these, there are the historical reliefs, some of which have of course remained visible since they were first set up (as indeed have some of the inscriptions).[1]

The work of Cassius Dio can now be much better understood, thanks to the monograph by Fergus Millar, published in 1964. Millar has placed Dio firmly in his context: 'What Dio represents – and with him a whole class, or series of classes, of men – is the fusion of two traditions, of Greek civilization and Roman government. . . .' He shows how Dio 'took as his own the political and national traditions of the Roman state, while retaining unimpaired the cultural outlook of the Greek world in which he was born'. However, Dio's text has not survived in its original form for the period of Septimius's life, 145–211. What has been preserved consists of excerpts from that text, or abbreviated versions of it. The most important of these is the *Epitome* of Books 36–80, covering the period from Pompey to Severus Alexander, made by the eleventh-century Byzantine monk John Xiphilinus of Trapezus. His work 'is not so much a précis of Dio as a rather erratic selection from his material, substantially, but not invariably, in Dio's order and often keeping very close to Dio's wording'. The great value of Dio's account lies in the fact that he was a contemporary and a senator. As an informed eye-witness of much of what he described, he was in a superb position to impart an accurate and vivid picture. 'In spite of its fragmentary condition, Dio's account of his own time still occupies nearly 200 pages in Boissevain's edition and is thus the longest and fullest contemporary narrative we have of any period of the early Empire.' Dio was of course biased. But at least, unlike Tacitus, he makes no pretence of writing *sine ira et studio*.[2]

In the course of his work Dio makes frequent personal asides, which

[1] F. GROSSO in his recent (1964) work on the reign of Commodus has a detailed discussion of many of the above sources, pp. 1–93 – in so far as they are relevant to his own subject. His conclusions are not always accepted here.

[2] Quotations from F. MILLAR (1964), pp. 2, 119, 190, 191. – 'Biased': cf. Millar, ch. iv, pp. 119ff., esp. p. 173.

allow the main course of his life to be reconstructed in some detail. He was born in 164, a native of Nicaea in Bithynia. His father, Cassius Apronianus, entered the Roman Senate soon after Dio's birth, and Dio may therefore have spent some of his early boyhood at Rome. He was certainly in the capital for most of the reign of Commodus; and he notes explicitly that from the return of Commodus to Rome in autumn 180 onwards, his account is based not on what he has got from others, but on his own observation. As a senator's son he will have been entitled to attend meetings of the Senate before his quaestorship. Apart from a few years when he was away with his father, while Apronianus was governing Cilicia, he had ample opportunity to observe the behaviour of Commodus at close hand – sometimes uncomfortably close. He had personal dealings with Didius Julianus, whom he successfully prosecuted in court on more than one occasion; and was designated to the praetorship by Pertinax.[1] He himself records the genesis of his *History*. He wrote a pamphlet describing the dreams and portents which told Septimius that he would become Emperor. Septimius responded warmly when given a presentation copy. Dio had a dream the same night, in which 'the Divine Power' ordered him to write history. He

---

[1] Cf. e.g. Dio 75.15.3, 72.7.2, 72.4.2, 7.12.2, etc. See F. MILLAR (1964) pp. 5ff., esp. 13ff. But I see no reason why Dio must have spent the first seventeen or so years of his life in Bithynia, as Millar assumes, p. 13f. Since his father presumably entered the Senate soon after Dio's birth, if not before, Dio is likely to have spent a good part of his boyhood in Rome, while his father went through the quaestorship, tribunate (or aedileship) and praetorship. For one thing, senators needed special permission to be out of Italy (except for visiting Sicily and Narbonensis) – cf. Dio 52.42.6. Dio may even have been born in Rome. The dating of his career after praetorship in 194 is still not settled, but I follow Millar, pp. 204ff. in assigning the first consulship to ca. 205. G. BOWERSOCK (1965) p. 473f. prefers the later date, ca. 223. The question is important as it affects the interpretation of Dio's attitude to Septimius. Bowersock argues that the curatorship of Pergamum and Smyrna should be praetorian (normally). But it should be remembered that Macrinus, who appointed Dio (79.7.4) was singularly inept over senatorial appointments, cf. Millar, pp. 161ff., discussing Dio 78.13.1ff., 78.22.2ff., 35.1, etc. On another – related – point, the African post, which on the view here followed must have been the proconsulship, Bruttius Praesens is not really the latest example of a man governing an imperial province *after* Africa (or Asia), cf. now G. ALFÖLDY, *Reichsbeamte*, p. 40f., on Aufidius Victorinus. On Dio 76.16.4, where he refers to his consulship, cf. p. 237, below, and P. GARNSEY, p. 56.

7

therefore began an account of the wars and civil wars that followed the murder of Commodus. This also won approval. The success achieved by his first two works encouraged him to undertake a complete history of Rome. He spent ten years taking notes, covering the period from the foundation of Rome until the death of Septimius. The work of composition took a further twelve years: the *History* finally covered everything from the beginning down to the year 225. The earlier narrative covering Septimius's wars was incorporated into the larger work, with some changes. The precise dating of the various stages is not completely clear. But the natural interpretation is that Dio published the pamphlet on dreams and omens in 196 or 197, and then began his narrative of the wars. The obvious occasion for him to have presented this to Septimius is at the time of the *Decennalia* of 202. The 'ten years spent collecting all the deeds of the Romans from the beginning down to the death of Severus' would then be the ten years from 202–11. The 'twelve years more' during which he wrote his *History* would be the years 212–23. There is of course no means of telling whether he composed at a uniform speed, or whether he began at the beginning and worked steadily forward. He might for example have found it easier to get Books 73–6, covering the years 180–211, out of the way first while they were still fresh in his mind. And he might have found it easier to write this part rapidly. He certainly made some revisions later. Millar's theory about the composition of the work differs considerably from this and is not here accepted. But he has shown convincingly that there is no warrant for the view that the famous Book 52 is directed at Severus Alexander or his advisers. Here Dio puts in the mouths of Agrippa and Maecenas a debate on the nature of the monarchy. Millar argues that this was composed in the reign of Caracalla, specifically for oral presentation before the Emperor at Nicomedia late in the year 214. This may well be true, but there is no means of proving it. It is just as likely that it was written in the reign of Elagabalus.[1]

[1] Dio 72.23.1–5 is the key passage. Millar's dating of the dream pamphlet to 193 and the *History of the Wars* to 197 seems quite arbitrary, cf. G. BOWERSOCK (1965) pp. 470ff., who points out the defects. The natural explanation of the statement in 23.5 – that when he began his *History* proper he 'took ten years collecting material on events down to the death of Severus' – is that the ten years were 202–211. Besides, it is difficult to see how Dio could have finished a history of the

In comparison with Dio, Herodian is a far lesser historian. His work survives complete (although it may have been unfinished) and covers the period from the death of Marcus Aurelius in 180 to the accession of Gordian III in 238. He describes his reasons for writing in his first chapter. He is recording the events of his own lifetime, because:

> If one were to compare this period with the period that began with Augustus, when the Roman Republic became a monarchy, we would not find, in that span of about two hundred years up to the reign of Marcus, such frequent changes of Emperor, the same varied fortunes of wars both civil and foreign, movements of people, and captures of cities, both in the Empire and in many barbarian lands. We would not find the earthquakes and pollutions of the air, or the incredible lives of usurpers and Emperors. . . . Since rule over the Roman Empire was held during these sixty years by more Emperors than would seem possible in so short a time, many things took place of a varied and remarkable kind.

In the second of his eight books he says that he intends to write an account of seventy, not sixty, years of imperial history, of which he has had personal experience. He may have changed his mind, encouraged by the success of his first book. In that case, however, he must have been an old man when he started, certainly over seventy. And he may well have died before completing the task – or have become too infirm to write any more. His claim to have lived through the period about which he writes is borne out by his assertion, seemingly genuine, that he was an eye-witness at Commodus's bizarre performances in the Colosseum, late in the year 192. His name and language point to origin

---

wars in time to present it to Septimius in the summer of 197, as Millar argues, let alone how he could have known enough about the dreams and omens to have had that pamphlet ready in June 193 (Millar, p. 29f.). There is no force in Millar's comment that Septimius would not have welcomed an account of the civil wars in 202. The work covered external as well as civil wars (πόλεμοι. . . . καὶ στάσεις μέγισται: 23.1). It is possible, as M. argues, that πόλεμοι refers to one war only (First Parthian, of 195). But on the interpretation adopted above the term would cover both Parthian wars – and Dio could not have had the work ready until 200 at earliest (cf. Bowersock, p. 471 – whose reference to the expedition into 'Mauretania' is presumably a slip for Mesopotamia). – Book 52: cf. Millar, pp. 102ff.

in the eastern half of the Empire. Not necessarily in Syria, however, as has frequently been stated. Much more likely is that he was, like Dio, a native of Bithynia, otherwise perhaps of Galatia or Cappadocia. Unlike Dio, he was not a senator. He had some employment in the imperial service, he reveals, but of a subordinate kind. He may have been a freedman.[1]

The worth of Herodian as an historian is a matter of dispute. E. Hohl, in a crushing analysis of Book 1, Book 2, 1–6, and Book 3, 11–12, showed more fully than ever before in how many details Herodian is inaccurate and unreliable. Herodian has been defended against this attack by F. Cassola, but the defence cannot be regarded as convincing. Time and again Herodian is simply wrong. Thus he carelessly states that a day or two elapsed between the murder of Pertinax and the accession of Didius Julianus. Cassius Dio is unequivocal: the elevation of Julianus was carried through by the evening of the same day – Julianus was able to inspect the dinner laid out in the Palace for Pertinax. Much more serious, he swallows the concocted official story about the murder of Plautianus, the all-powerful Praetorian Prefect. Most disturbing of all, he fails to distinguish between the first and second Parthian wars. He omits the first, of 195, and puts the second one after the Saecular Games of 204, instead of in 197–9. But he does have facts not preserved elsewhere – or rumours, gossip and the like, at least – such as details about the early life of Plautianus; and it would be foolish to neglect him.[2]

The third major literary source is the *Historia Augusta*. That curious work will no doubt continue to baffle its readers in perpetuity. But since the publication of Sir Ronald Syme's book *Ammianus and the Historia Augusta* in 1968, there ought to be considerably more agreement about its basic nature. The conclusions of Syme about the author of the *HA* are here accepted: that he was a mischievous fellow, writing in or about

---

[1] The quotation is from 1.1.4–5. – 'seventy years': 2.15.7. If he was an eyewitness of the games in late 192, – 1.15.4 – he must surely have been at least twelve years old then. – 'origin': cf. F. CASSOLA (1957a) pp. 220ff., G. ALFÖLDY, *Senat*, p. 113, n. 9 (also valuable on the date of the work). – 'employment': H. G. PFLAUM (1954). On Herodian cf. now especially G. ALFÖLDY, *Sturz* and the Loeb edition by C. R. Whittaker.

[2] Cf. E. HOHL (1954 and 1956 a, b); F. CASSOLA (1956a, 1957b).

the year 395, who wanted to mystify. To that end he adopted pretence. He produced a series of biographies of the Emperors from Hadrian to Carinus, including (for the sake of novelty, and to allow more scope for fiction) lives of pretenders and Caesars. To give the work more appeal, to make it more intriguing, he made out that it was a collection of biographies by six different authors writing about a hundred years before the actual time of composition.[1] (This spurious antiquity may have been deliberately enhanced by producing the work in an apparently mutilated form: as it stands, there is no Preface, and there is a lacuna in the second half. The lacuna, if deliberately created, would have excused the author from covering a particularly awkward period, the reigns of the persecutors Decius and Valerian. The author was a pagan and admired those Emperors. It might not have been politic to describe them in detail, in or about the year 395.)[2] To a large degree the date and character of the author of the *HA* do not matter here. The vital question is the worth of his sources, and how he used them; and to what extent he fabricated. The earlier *vitae* are often 'messy and heterogeneous: the compiler was hasty in execution (or supervision)'. But they contain good material.[3]

The *Severus* is really the last of these 'good lives', although the *Caracalla* and *Elagabalus*, particularly the former, have preserved some sound information in a garbled fashion. The author's patience with his source gave out in the course of the *Severus* (as it had done earlier, on occasion), and he finished it off with a chunk of Aurelius Victor and some fiction. As for the *vitae* of the 'usurpers' Niger and Albinus, and of Septimius's younger son Geta, they are almost wholly fiction. This was demonstrated long ago by J. Hasebroek (in 1916), and should not need restating. The trouble is, of course, that these 'minor lives' do contain some facts: the approximate dates and more or less correct nomenclature of their subjects, at least. It is tempting to try to rescue a few more gobbets, but the temptation must be sternly resisted, unless there is corroborative evidence. Here a natural difficulty arises. The corroborative evidence does not convince all scholars equally. Thus, in

[1] Sir R. SYME (1968a), *passim*, esp. pp. 176ff.
[2] For this hypothesis, cf. A. R. BIRLEY (1967a) p. 125f.
[3] Sir R. SYME (1968a) p. 211.

the *Albinus*, the Hadrumetine origin of the man: it is also mentioned in the *Severus*, by implication, and external evidence makes it plausible. In the same *vita* there is the story that Albinus had fought in Germany before going to Britain. That is *a priori* likely – a fair number of governors of Britain are known to have governed Lower Germany previously; and an inscription from Cologne may be restored to show Albinus in Germany at the right time and in a context suggestive of military activity. But not all are convinced.[1]

What was the source of the 'good' information? Sir Ronald Syme postulates an unknown biographer, who wrote Lives of the Emperors in the Suetonian manner, sober and factual. This source was evidently supplemented with doses from Marius Maximus, another biographer of the school of Suetonius. Maximus is cited about thirty times in the *HA*; and is one of the few authorities there named who actually existed – most of them are as fictitious as the six *scriptores* themselves. With some regret, Syme's theory and his *Ignotus* are not accepted here, and recourse is had once more to Marius Maximus as the main source. The arguments are complex and lengthy, and for this reason have been relegated to an appendix. In this context, Maximus is assumed to be the main source, and a few remarks about him are appropriate. There is little doubt that he is identical with the senator Marius Maximus, by his full names L. Marius Maximus Perpetuus Aurelianus. This man had a distinguished career, contemporary with that of Dio – though Maximus was a few years older, and played a much more prominent role. He commanded the Severan army at the siege of Byzantium, 193–5, and fought at the battle of Lugdunum in 197. Thereafter he governed three imperial provinces, was proconsul of both Africa and Asia (most exceptionally), Prefect of the City and *consul iterum ordinarius* in 223.[2]

---

[1] J. HASEBROEK (1916) pp. 13ff., accepted the Hadrumetineor igin. It was doubted by H. Dessau, reviewing H. in the *Wochenschrift für klassische Philologie* 35 (1918), cols. 391f., who is followed by e.g. *PIR*[2] C 1186 and T. D. BARNES (1967a) p. 87, n. 1. But cf. now G. ALFÖLDY (1967a) pp. 20ff., and A. R. BIRLEY (1969) p. 265f. Alföldy also shows (pp. 27ff.) that Albinus may have governed Lower Germany, offering a restoration of *CIL* XIII 8260 (p. 29). See also App. II.

[2] App. II.

Maximus was something of a scandalmonger, which gave him appeal
to the author of the *HA*. He was also extremely lengthy – *homo omnium
verbosissimus*, the author calls him at a later point. Ammianus Marcellinus records that he was a favourite author with the decadent aristocracy of late fourth-century Rome. Indeed, he says that they read
nothing but Maximus and Juvenal. This need not have detracted from
his worth as a supplier of bare facts. Many details preserved in the
Historia Augusta, about people and events of which Herodian is ignorant, and Dio's account is lost, surely come from the biographies by
Maximus. In the long run, it does not matter all that much if Maximus
is rejected as the main source of the hard facts in the *HA*. But close
analysis, or perhaps the eye of faith, does make a good many items in
the *HA* more meaningful if they are viewed as derived from Maximus.[1]

Mention of this lost work leads naturally to another lost source
mentioned by Dio, Herodian and the *Historia Augusta*, also by Aurelius
Victor: the autobiography of Septimius himself. This covered both his
'private and public life', in other words his life before and after his
accession. Of the first part, all that is known is that he made no mention
in it of his first marriage; and that he dwelt on the dreams and portents
that told him of his future grandeur. The second part certainly dealt
with the civil wars. Dio specifically notes that his own version of the
death of Albinus in 197 differs from that given by the Emperor. The
Augustan History may have known the autobiography only through
citation of it by Maximus. The mentions of the autobiography (some
of them, in the *HA*, perhaps bogus) scarcely go later than the end of the
civil wars. Septimius's main purpose in writing it may well have been
self-justification – the Augustan History notes that he made 'excuses
for his cruelty'. But it is not even known whether it was written in Latin
or Greek.[2]

The other literary sources require less detailed discussion. Of the
later historians Aurelius Victor, who wrote in 360, may be singled out.
He was himself an African and had an enormous admiration for

[1] App. II.
[2] The autobiography is cited or referred to by Dio 75.7.3, Herodian 2.9.4,
Victor, *de Caes*. 20.22 (whence *HA Sev.* 18.6), *HA Sev.* 3.2., *Nig.* 4.7, *Alb.* 7.1, 10.1.
See further below, p. 240.

Septimius. But as his account of the reign contains only some 700 words, its value is modest. Eutropius and the anonymous epitomator (pseudo-Victor) are even briefer. The latter has one useful tit-bit: a list of friends of Septimius, whom he enriched. The contemporary writers are far more important. Galen, who died in 199 or 200, has a few anecdotes about Septimius, Tertullian has interesting asides here and there, as well as throwing light on the social background of Roman Africa. Philostratus is extremely valuable. If nothing else, he is the only literary source that mentions Septimius's visit to Africa as Emperor. His biographies of the literary figures of the day, such as Aelius Antipater, who became *ab epistulis Graecis* of Septimius, are useful and entertaining.[1] As far as the legal sources are concerned, the monograph by W. Kunkel is a helpful and thorough examination of the jurists themselves. The interesting study by A. M. Honoré is somewhat too speculative. Here a caution must be entered. It has long been realised, and was reiterated forty years ago by C. E. Van Sickle, that the headings of imperial rescripts in the *Code* of Justinian are often totally inaccurate. To take a specific example, J. Kolendo has recently shown that the rescript generally considered to have been issued by Septimius from Viminacium on the Danube in March 202 (and thus to provide valuable information on his itinerary in that year, and its timing) cannot be dated to that time or place at all. As far as the content of the legal works is concerned, little work has been done from a strictly historical

---

[1] Victor: cf. generally C. G. STARR. Note the comments of Sir R. SYME (1968a) p. 201, n. 6, on *HA Sev.* 13.8 (*horum igitur tantorum ac tam inlustrium virorum interfector ab Afris ut deus habetur*): 'Perhaps the author was protesting against Victor's excessive estimate of a fellow-countryman – "*quo praeclarior in republica fuit nemo*" (20)'. For all its brevity, the section on Septimius is far longer than that allotted to any other Emperor in the *de Caesaribus*. See also p. 287f., below. – *Epitome de Caes.* 20.6 gives the friends: (Cornelius) Anullinus, Bassus (unidentifiable), (Fabius) Cilo and (Sextius) Lateranus. No clue, unfortunately, as to when these men became the friends of Septimius. Perhaps they were never more than *amici* in the technical sense (for which cf. J. CROOK [1955] pp. 21ff.). – Galen: *PIR²* G 24 gives the basic facts on his life; cf. also *RE* 7 (1912) 578ff., and see now G. W. BOWERSOCK (1969) pp. 59ff. – Tertullian: the literature is vast, cf. B. ALTANER, pp. 148ff. and add now the important article by T. D. BARNES (1969). – Philostratus: *PIR²* F 332; *RE* 20 (1941) 125ff. and see now Bowersock, pp. 1ff. and *passim*. – 'Visit to Africa': *v. soph.* 2.20.2, see below pp. 215ff. – Antipater: *ib.* 2.24 and below, esp. p. 207f.

point of view. No specialist in Roman law seems willing or competent to undertake a survey of imperial legislation in which the contribution of particular Emperors is analysed in its historical context, reign by reign. For Septimius, the twenty pages in Adolphe De Ceuleneer's elegant *Essai sur la vie et le règne de Septime-Sévère*, published in 1880, remains the only detailed investigation.[1]

The non-literary sources have greatly increased in volume since Platnauer and Hasebroek wrote their works on Septimius. In the field of epigraphic evidence, two areas may be singled out where there have been spectacular advances. Lepcis Magna, the birthplace of Septimius, has produced a whole series of inscriptions commemorating the imperial family, including the Emperor's parents, paternal grandfather, aunt, brother, sister and wives. The inscriptions of his grandfather L. Septimius Severus and brother P. Septimius Geta, in particular, provide welcome details about their careers. In addition, the epigraphy of Lepcis and to a lesser degree of its neighbours Oea and Sabratha illuminates the social life of Tripolitania and the Romanisation of its people to a remarkable extent. Most of these inscriptions are included in the *Inscriptions of Roman Tripolitania*, published in 1952 by J. M. Reynolds and J. B. Ward-Perkins. It is appropriate to single out the name of Julien Guey among those who have made good use of this material. One subsequent discovery must be mentioned here, the inscription from an Arch set up in 174 in honour of Marcus Aurelius. L. Septimius Severus, the future Emperor, is named on it as legate to the proconsul of Africa, C. Septimius Severus. Thus evidence from the *Historia Augusta* has been confirmed and elucidated. Besides this, the proconsul may be identified with a man whose career is known in full from another African inscription, where the name had been only partially preserved. The inscription was published by Mme Ginette Di Vita-Évrard in 1963. One can only express the hope that more epigraphic evidence will be made known in the future, that will throw further light on the Septimii of Lepcis. In the meantime new fragments of the *Acta* of the Septimian Saecular Games had been pub-

[1] On A. M. HONORÉ cf. pp. 238, n. 1 and 302, n. 1, below. – C. E. VAN SICKLE (1928b). – J. KOLENDO pp. 127ff. – A. DE CEULENEER, pp. 271–290 (containing a number of errors).

lished in 1931. G. B. Pighi included a revised text with full commentary in his work *De Ludis Saecularibus*, published in 1941.[1]

Among other individual inscriptions of particular interest for this study, the following may also be mentioned. A stone from Thaenae commemorating Aemilius Pudens, brother of the Praetorian Prefect and murderer of Commodus, Q. Aemilius Laetus, revealed his African origin. A stone from Augsburg, taken in conjunction with one previously known from Salonae in Dalmatia, has revealed the existence and career of a kinsman of Julia Domna, C. Julius Avitus Alexianus. A less important but still very interesting career is given on an inscription from Caesarea in Palestine: it shows that the cavalry commander Valerianus who struck the decisive blow at the battle of Issus in 194 was an equestrian officer named L. Valerius Valerianus. Finally, the inscription of the procurator T. Aius Sanctus has shown that the *ratio privata* was not, as the *Historia Augusta* alleged, the creation of Septimius Severus.[2]

Two major discoveries also dominate the papryological evidence. First and foremost, the *Feriale Duranum*, published definitely in 1959, in part V of the *Dura Europos Final Report* (but known for some twenty years before that from preliminary publications). Among the evidence here provided for the first time are the dates of Septimius's proclamation (9 April 193, rather than 13 April as previously thought) and of the capture of Ctesiphon (28 January 198), which was the occasion for the elevation of Septimius's elder son to the rank of Augustus. The second item is of a different kind. It is a collection of imperial responses, *Apokrimata*, on legal questions, made during the Emperor's stay in Egypt in 199–200. They were published in 1954 by W. L. Westermann and A. A. Schiller; and the latter, with H. C. Youtie, brought out an improved text in 1955.[3]

On the numismatic evidence comment can be brief. The coinage of

[1] 'Lepcis inscriptions': G. M. BERSANETTI (1942, 1946); S. AURIGEMMA (1950). Note J. GUEY (1950, 1951a, b, 1952, 1953, 1954). See further App. I.

[2] Laetus: *AE* 1949. 38. – Alexianus: H. G. PFLAUM (1962b), cf. App. I no. 17. – Valerianus: *AE* 1966. 495 (cf. Dio 74.7.4). – Sanctus: *CP* no. 179 *bis* (cf. H. NESSELHAUF [1964]).

[3] Cf. C. B. WELLES *et al.*, esp. pp. 197ff. The *Feriale* was first made available in the 1940 article by R. O. FINK *et al.*

the reign of Septimius now provides a far better tool for the historian than it did fifty years ago, thanks to the work above all of H. Mattingly, who published the fifth volume of the *Coins of the Roman Empire in the British Museum*, covering the period from Pertinax to Elagabalus, in 1950.[1]

From archaeological excavation, perhaps the most important single development concerns the British campaigns of Septimius. In 1961 R. E. Birley discovered that the Roman base at Carpow, on the south bank of the Firth of Tay, had been constructed early in the third century. It had previously been identified with the base *Horrea Classis*, known from Ptolemy and Ravennas, and it was assumed to have been a naval base for the first-century campaigns of Julius Agricola. The presence of this fortress well to the north of the Antonine Wall, some twenty-five acres in size and clearly intended to be permanent, places the expedition of 208–11 in a wholly new light. It had previously been assumed that it was punitive in nature, that 'it served two major ends, the repulse of the Maeatae and the establishment of a new frontier system based on Hadrian's Wall'. The evidence derived from excavation at Carpow continues to accumulate, and meanwhile air photography is providing an outline map of the progress of the campaign. There can be little doubt that Septimius intended to annexe a substantial portion, if not the whole, of Scotland. Here as elsewhere he was assuming the Trajanic role of *propagator imperii*.[2]

The study of historical reliefs has taken a notable step forward, both in Rome itself and in Africa. In 1967 a massive study of the Arch of Septimius Severus in the Roman Forum was published by Richard Brilliant, the fruits of thirty-five years of research by the American Academy in Rome. Meanwhile, the Arch of Septimius Severus at Lepcis Magna had come to light, and although the long-promised comprehensive study of its reliefs has not yet been published, preliminary studies have made the material known. One other item

---

[1] Strictly economic questions – such as the debasement of the coinage, on which see now J. GUEY (1962) – which mostly fall outside the scope of this biography, are handled thoroughly by T. PEKÁRY.

[2] Cf. R. E. BIRLEY (1962, 1963); A. R. BIRLEY (1967c); J. K. ST JOSEPH. See further below pp. 251ff., 259. The quotation is from F. MILLAR (1964) p. 148f., following K. A. STEER (1958).

deserves mention here, the remarkable painted portrait of Septimius, Julia and their sons, found in Egypt (with, inevitably, Geta savagely defaced). A study of this painting, the only imperial portrait of its kind, was published in 1936 by K. A. Neugebauer.[1]

The above survey has been confined to publications of source material. It is only right to add mention of various other works which have greatly eased the task of research. The second edition of the *Prosopographia Imperii Romani* was begun in 1933, under the editorship of Edmund Groag and Artur Stein. Their task has been inherited by Leiva Petersen, under whose guidance part IV, 3, appeared in 1966, containing names beginning with I and J. The work has thus reached the half-way mark. It has been indispensable to this inquiry. The same applies to two other works, *L'Albo senatorio* by Guido Barbieri, which appeared in 1952, and *Les carrières procuratoriennes équestres* by H.-G. Pflaum, which came out in 1961. Between them Barbieri and Pflaum provide a cross-section of the Roman governing class.[2]

In 1962 G. Walser and T. Pekáry published their useful bibliographical survey. It includes work on the period 193–284 that was published in the years 1939–1959. Work published before 1939 is in almost all cases listed in the bibliography of the *Cambridge Ancient History*, volume XII, which came out in that year. Walser and Pekáry do not cite two works which appeared in 1959, G. Charles-Picard's *La civilisation de l'Afrique romaine*, and M. Hammond's *The Antonine Monarchy*. Hammond presents a study of the constitutional aspects of the monarchy in the years 69–235, with an extensive bibliography. Charles-Picard's stimulating and evocative picture of Roman Africa is balanced by P. Romanelli's much longer *Storia delle province romane dell' Africa*, produced in the same year (this does find mention in the survey by Walser and Pekáry). In 1964 F. Grosso published his massive study, *La lotta politica al tempo di Commodo*. These three works are of great assistance in setting Septimius Severus in proper perspective: the

---

[1] Arch at Lepcis: cf. J. B. WARD-PERKINS (1948, 1951a, b); M. FLORIANI-SQUARCIAPINO; and see now A. M. McCANN, esp. pp. 74ff. (whose work on the iconography of the Emperor only became available to me after the completion of my manuscript).

[2] The various works on provincial Fasti also bring progress in this field (notably that by B. E. THOMASSON on the African provinces).

man from Roman Africa placed on the throne from which another African had struck down Commodus.[1]

In this biography, in contrast to earlier ones, more space is devoted to Septimius's life before his accession: nine and a half chapters deal with his background and career before his accession, seven and a half with his reign. As he became Emperor at the age of forty-eight and died at sixty-five, this emphasis can hardly be called disproportionate. Admittedly, much less is known of his life before 193; but this period is of great importance in arriving at a balanced assessment of him.

---

[1] No attempt has been made, either in this chapter or in the work as a whole, to provide a comprehensive bibliography of the Severan period.

II

PROLOGUE: AFRICA

Septimius Severus was born on 11 April 145, at Lepcis Magna on the North African coast, the son of P. Septimius Geta and Fulvia Pia. Lepcis Magna had had the status of a Roman colony for a generation, and was one of the most important towns in the rich Roman province of Africa. It lay on the easternmost fringe of the province, in the region or dioecese which took the name Tripolitania from Lepcis and its two western neighbours, Oea (modern Tripoli-Tarabalus) and Sabratha. The Empire was then at the height of its prosperity and power. The Emperor was Antoninus Pius. Pius gave his name to an era, 'the age of the Antonines', which has come to be synonymous with affluence and peace. He had succeeded Hadrian in 138. In the year 145 he himself was consul for the fourth time, with his nephew and adopted son, Marcus Aurelius, as his colleague. The year of Septimius's birth was thus known in Roman records as the year when Antoninus the Emperor for the fourth time, and Aurelius Caesar for the second time, were consuls.[1]

The son born to Geta and Fulvia Pia was given the names of his paternal grandfather, L. Septimius Severus. Just over fifty years later Septimius was to claim, by a legal fiction, that he was the son of Marcus Aurelius. As it happens, the Caesar's marriage, to his cousin Faustina, was taking place at almost the exact time when Septimius was born (not that such an awkward detail mattered). When this retrospective adoption was announced, in 195 or 196, a cynical senator congratulated

---

[1] Year of birth (145, not 146): J. GUEY (1956). – Lepcis: *IRT*, pp. 73ff. conveniently sets out the evidence for this spelling (against the less correct Leptis). – On the members of the family, see App. I. Consular date: *FC*, p. 41.

Septimius on 'finding a father'.[1] The implication was that his real
father Geta was a nobody. This was true enough in a sense. Geta was an
obscure provincial Roman, who never achieved any distinction in public life either at Lepcis or at Rome. But men of his family in the same
generation as himself were already Roman senators when the son of
Geta was born – P. Septimius Aper and C. Septimius Severus, both
well on the road to high office in the year 145. These two, probably
Geta's first cousins, were no doubt older than him. Perhaps Geta
lacked ambition. Maybe ill health prevented him from competing for
honours. It might be that the family's means did not extend sufficiently to send more than two young men into the Roman Senate (for
which the property qualification was 1,200,000 Sesterces). But that may
be doubted. Geta's sister Septimia Polla, who apparently died unmarried, was a very wealthy woman, and there is no reason to doubt
that Geta could have got the necessary financial backing. Whatever the
reason, Geta seems to have stayed all his life at Lepcis with his wife and
three children – he had another son, named after himself (probably the
elder of the two boys) and a daughter, Septimia Octavilla. He may have
been something of an eccentric. However obscure he may have been,
Marius Maximus found some details of his life and character to record.
But the Augustan History fails to transmit them.[2]

Life in Lepcis was provincial, but it was probably not always dull,
and Roman Africa had a brilliance of its own. It was beginning to play
an ever-increasing role in the fortunes of Rome. To understand who
Septimius Severus, Emperor of Rome from 193–211, was, it is worth
taking a brief look back at the development of civilisation in North
Africa.

Civilisation came to North Africa with the Semites. Traders from
Tyre and Sidon speaking a language that may be loosely described as a
kind of Hebrew (Phoenician or Punic), began exploring the western
Mediterranean at the end of the second millennium B.C. The Phoenicians had acquired expertise in seamanship and a penchant for trade

[1] Dio 76.9.4, cf. p. 190, below. – M. Aurelius and Faustina: A. R. BIRLEY
(1966a) p. 116.
[2] The relatives: App. I. – Property qualification: Suetonius, *D. Aug.* 41.1, cf.
A. H. M. JONES (1960), p. 29f. – Maximus: App. II.

over the preceding centuries, when Ugarit on the Syrian coast played an important part in the economic life of Egypt. At the time of great disturbances caused by the 'Peoples of the Sea' in about 1200 B.C., the Phoenicians were forced to look further afield. The North African coast possesses few natural harbours and easy landing-places that could serve as servicing-stations for voyages of trade and discovery. But the Phoenicians seized upon such suitable places as there were. Not quite the earliest of these bases, but ultimately the most important, was Carthage, *Kart Hadasht*, 'new city'. During the first half of the first millennium B.C. these Phoenician trading stations and supply depots gradually took on the character of towns. The process was accelerated and stimulated by the inexorable march of events in Asia. The rise of Assyria in the 8th century B.C. saw the mother-cities Tyre and Sidon crushed. Further colonists, this time refugees, came to North Africa. Carthage and her fellow Punic cities prospered.

They had to face rivalry from the Greeks. In about 600 B.C. Greeks from the coast of Asia Minor founded Massilia (Marseilles), but Carthage was by then strong enough to prevent further Greek expansion in that area. Most of Spain, Sardinia and Corsica became Carthaginian preserves – not to speak of the lands in the ocean, beyond the Pillars of Hercules (Straits of Gibraltar). Northern and central Italy were dominated by the Etruscans, allies of Carthage. And Carthage rapidly acquired the leading position among the western Phoenicians. Only in southern Italy (which was later called 'Great Greece', *magna Graecia*), eastern Sicily and Cyrenaica could the Greeks secure a firm foothold. Greek interest in North Africa had probably become intense as early as the beginning of the seventh century, but Cyrene was the only colony that they succeeded in planting there. In about 511 B.C. the Spartan adventurer Dorieus led settlers to a site at the mouth of the Cinyps River (Wadi el-Caam), a dozen miles east of Lepcis. The Carthaginian response was almost immediate. Three years later the would-be colonists were expelled and Lepcis (Punic *Lpqi*), which had been founded a century or so earlier, now became a bulwark against further Greek expansion. From then onwards the Greeks failed to penetrate west of Cyrenaica.

Carthage did not attempt to establish an extensive land empire in

North Africa. She and her satellites contended themselves with a basic minimum of agricultural land. The rest was left to the native peoples – the Libyans. The Libyans were the ancestors of the modern Berbers, whose language and physiognomy have seemingly survived three thousand years of domination by Phoenician, Roman, Vandal, Byzantine and Arab conquerors. Among the Libyans the most powerful group were the Numidians. But if Carthage did not annexe Numidian land, her cultural influence was far-reaching, stretching well beyond her self-appointed boundaries. And her indirect control of the native hinterland was firm. Above all, Carthage transformed the appearance of the land, particularly in what is now Tunisia. Africa was later to become 'the empire of Ceres', one of the principal granaries of the Mediterranean. The Punic settlers – less interested in cereal cultivation – introduced the vine and the olive. Tripolitania was to become one of the greatest olive oil producing areas of the ancient world.

Until the third century B.C. it was only the Greeks that challenged the Punic dominance of the western Mediterranean, and the Greeks failed to shake the hegemony of Carthage. But the gradual advance of Rome – with whom Carthage had had treaty-relations since the foundation of the Republic, at the end of the sixth century B.C. – was to lead to her downfall. The mercenary armies and fleets of Carthage lost the first long drawn out war (264–41 B.C.) to the citizen legions of Rome. Hannibal came within an ace of destroying Rome during the second war (218–201 B.C.) and his forces were in Italy for thirteen years, while Rome trembled. But Carthage was again defeated, when Rome took the war to Spain and then to Africa. Rome had invaded Africa during the first war (the expedition of Regulus in 256 B.C.), but that had been an ill-fated venture. This time there was no mistake. But even after Scipio's victory at Zama in 202 B.C. and the Roman-imposed terms that followed, no Roman annexation in Africa took place. Instead the power of Rome's principal ally, the Numidian king Masinissa, was increased at the expense of Carthage. During the half century in which this remarkable man ruled the Numidian kingdom, he greatly enlarged his boundaries and created a strong and unified state. What is more important, through the agency of Masinissa Carthaginian agricultural methods and Punic culture at all levels were introduced, bringing about the creation of a mixed Numido-Carthaginian or Libyphoenician civilisation over a large area of North Africa.

In 149 B.C. Roman fear and greed brought about the outbreak of the third and final war. Three years later Carthage was destroyed. The Roman general Scipio Aemilianus formally pronounced a curse over the levelled ruins, the site was ceremonially ploughed and salt was sown. It was forbidden to refound the city and her former territory constituted the Roman province of Africa.

The rich land of Tunisia attracted immigrants from Italy. In 122 B.C. the reformer C. Gracchus as tribune of the plebs attempted to plant a Roman colony at the site of Carthage, but his plans were abandoned on his death in 121 B.C., although a number of individual settlers remained on the lands assigned to them. Meanwhile the Numidian kingdom was approaching a crisis. In 112 B.C. the most powerful claimant to the contested throne, Jugurtha, found himself at war with Rome. After numerous humiliations and blunders by Roman commanders, the 'new man' C. Marius brought the war to an end in 105 B.C. The boundaries of the Roman province were still not greatly enlarged, but Marius gave land to a considerable number of his time-expired veterans in the northern part of the Numidian kingdom.

During the long reign of Masinissa, and under his successors, Lepcis had become subject to the authority of Numidia, although she retained considerable local autonomy. 'Only the language of the city has been affected by intermarriage with the Numidians', Sallust wrote sixty or seventy years later. 'The laws and customs are Sidonian [i.e. Punic] – they were able to retain them because of their great distance from the king's authority. There are considerable tracts of desert between them and the settled part of Numidia.' During the Numidian war, she had gone over to Rome. The predecessor of Marius, Q. Metellus, stationed four Cohorts there in response to an appeal for help. After the war Lepcis became a free city and retained this status until the time of Caesar. During the first half of the first century B.C. Roman business-men found their way to Lepcis. The first known example is a money-lender named T. Herennius, active in the 70s B.C. At the end of the civil wars the Republican forces regrouped in North Africa, after the death of Pompey. The redoubtable Cato led a force right across

Tripolitania under gruelling conditions, and stayed for a while at Lepcis. The city paid dearly for assistance rendered to Caesar's enemies. As a penalty an annual payment of three million pounds weight of olive oil was imposed. The city, together with the rest of the old Numidian kingdom, was incorporated into a second Roman province, Africa Nova.

Caesar took another, vital step. Carthage was, after all, refounded as a Roman colony, and Caesar settled veterans at a number of other places which likewise received colonial status. The triumph of Augustus, in the long civil wars that followed Caesar's murder, meant further changes in Roman Africa. The two provinces were amalgamated and administered by a proconsul, with one legion, the III Augusta. The western part of North Africa became the kingdom of Mauretania, under a king nominated by Rome – but not before a number of colonies of veteran soldiers had been established in the territory. In the African province likewise Augustus continued and completed Caesar's programme of colonisation. The Romanisation of North Africa was now irrevocably in train.[1]

[1] The foregoing pages have given only the barest sketch of the history of North Africa up to the time when Lepcis was finally incorporated within the Empire.

On the Phoenicians, cf. esp. the monograph by D. B. HARDEN. On Carthage, the works by G. CHARLES-PICARD (1956) and B. WARMINGTON are both useful. On Greek attempts at colonisation, note the interesting if speculative article by A. Graf Schenk v. STAUFFENBERG. On the Roman conquest, P. ROMANELLI is the most comprehensive. L. TEUTSCH emphasises the quantity of settlement before Caesar in his detailed analysis of the period from the Gracchi to Augustus. G. CHARLES-PICARD (1959a) is particularly valuable on economic questions, for which the collection of evidence by R. M. HAYWOOD (1938) is indispensable. Ancient literary references to Lepcis Magna are collected in *RE* 12 (1925) 2074f. and *IRT* pp. 73ff. A. DI VITA (1969) pp. 198ff. shows that Lepcis was already occupied at the end of the 7th century B.C. and therefore antedates Dorieus's arrival by about a century.

III

LEPCIS MAGNA

Lepcis can have had no option but to adapt herself to the new situation. But clearly there was no lack of enthusiasm. Whether from a desire to please its new masters, or from a genuine wish to adopt the Roman style, the Punic aristocracy played an active part in transforming Lepcis into a city of Roman type. Italian immigrants evidently began to arrive in Africa in the last decades of the first century B.C. Not only government-sponsored colonists, but men dispossessed in the upheavals created by the civil wars. *At nos sitientes ibimus Afros*, Virgil makes an Italian farmer, whose lands had been confiscated, say in his *Eclogues*, 'But we will go off to the thirsty Africans.' At Lepcis, one of these immigrant families was the Fulvii, the maternal ancestors of Septimius.[1] The Punic town lay right on the shore of the Mediterranean, on the west bank of its river (now the Wadi Lebdah). Like almost all rivers in this part of the world its bed is dry for most of the year. Then as now only a narrow coastal strip was really fertile. But this must have been intensively cultivated, and the territory belonging to Lepcis must have extended well beyond the immediate environs of the town. To the south-east the valley of the Wadi Sofeggin, whose northern tributaries drain the southern slopes of the Djebel, was densely settled in the period of the later empire. Settlement was already flourishing here in the first century A.D., and its beginnings belong to this time. The desolate marshland formed by the mouths of the Wadis Sofeggin, Zemzem and Bei el-Kebir effectively delimited Lepcitane territory on the east, or south-east. To the west the Djebel heights approach the sea some ten miles from Lepcis, and this may have marked the boundary with Oea (Tripoli) – an area where disputes were liable to break out.

[1] Virgil, *Eclogues* 1.64. – Fulvii: P. ROMANELLI (1958).

26

To the south-west of Lepcis the slopes of the Djebel, which runs in a north-east to south-west direction, were intensively cultivated. This area, enclosed on the north and west by the sea and the Djebel, on the south and east by the Cinyps river, makes an admirably self-contained and protected zone for agricultural development.[1]

There was indeed need of protection. The wild peoples of the Sahara oases far to the south were only too ready to make lightning raids on the rich coastal towns. Then they would disappear back into their seemingly impenetrable fastnesses, six hundred miles across mountain and desert. But in 21 B.C. the proconsul of Africa, P. Cornelius Balbus, achieved the remarkable feat of taking an army across the Black Mountain (Mons Ater, Djebel Soda) as far as Garama, the capital of the most renowned of these desert peoples, the Garamantes, whose name was to become synonymous with 'the ends of the earth'. Balbus's expedition had important results. The Garamantes, for one thing, abandoned their rocky fortress on Zinchecra and settled in the Wadi el-Agial below. Within a few decades this people far beyond the frontiers of the empire was constructing stone houses and tombs of Roman type, and using imported Roman pottery. This can only mean one thing: the Garamantes had had a treaty imposed by Balbus, by the terms of which, among other things, peaceful trade with the Roman province would be guaranteed. The objects of trade were many – ivory and gems, Negro slaves, ostrich feathers and the like, but perhaps most important of all, exotic animals. The jungles of West Africa had to provide the unfortunate wild beasts to sate the bloodthirsty appetites of the Roman arena. Lepcis, already wealthy from its olives, now had a secure new source of wealth – for there is little doubt that Lepcis, with Oea and Sabratha, was the chief beneficiary from the great expansion of trade which could now begin.[2]

At the very end of the first century B.C. Roman influence made

[1] In general, cf. D. E. L. HAYNES, esp. pp. 13ff., *IRT*, p. 3f. (and map, p. 277). – 'settlement . . . in the first century': cf the important study by A. DI VITA (1964), totally altering previous concepts. – 'disputes': see below, p. 31.

[2] Balbus: *PIR*[2] C 1331; B. E. THOMASSON, II, p. 11. – Garamantes: cf. now C. M. DANIELS. Note Virgil, *Ecl.* 8.44 (well before Balbus) and *Aen.* 6.794. – 'Transsaharan trade: cf. esp. the articles by S. AURIGEMMA (1940) and J. DESANGES.

itself felt in another, even more apparent, way. Before the Roman annexation the only building stone in use was the local sandstone, which crumbled easily and was unsuitable for any elaborate moulding or lettering. Unless covered with stucco its appearance was quite undistinguished. The earliest inscription from Lepcis belongs to 8 B.C. – and is the only one carved on this sandstone. The limestone quarries of Ras el-Hamman must have been opened soon afterwards, providing a magnificent building material, a high quality limestone similar to the travertine then in favour at Rome itself. This earliest inscription is in both Latin and Neo-Punic, the rather debased form of the Carthaginian language now spoken. It honours Augustus – 'the Emperor Caesar, Son of the Deified [Julius], Augustus, Consul Eleven Times, Hailed Imperator Fourteen Times, Holding Tribunician Power For The Fifteenth Time, Pontifex Maximus' – and the proconsul M. Licinius M.f. Crassus Frugi. The Latin text is inscribed on thirty-one blocks of sandstone, each half a metre square. Its main interest lies in the names of the Lepcitane notables, of which those of Iddibal, son of Aris, Muttun, son of Anno, and Annobal Tapapius Rufus, son of Himilcho, have survived. The stone recorded the priests (*flamines*) of Augustus Caesar, and the chief magistrates of the town, the *sufetes*. *Sufes* was the Punic name, the same as the Hebrew *shophet* which is translated Judge in the Old Testament; two *sufetes* were elected annually as joint mayors. The inscription was placed on the precinct wall of the market. Either the whole market, or the wall around it, was built at the expense of the last named, Annobal Tapapius Rufus, *flamen*, former *sufes*, and 'prefect of sacred affairs' (*praefectus sacrorum*), another Punic office. His first name, Annobal, is typically Punic – for it is simply Hannibal. The termination -bal recalls that these people were worshippers of the Ba'al of the Old Testament. Annobal, clearly a man of wealth and importance, had taken steps to Romanise his names. The Punic family name Tabahpī, was made to appear, in its transliterated form Tapapius, Latin in type, and he added the *cognomen* Rufus.[1]

Annobal Rufus's name appears on three other monumental stones,

[1] Building-materials: *IRT*, p. 82f. – 'earliest inscription': *IRT* 319. – *sufes*: *RE* 4A (1931), 643ff.

all of them lintels of the new grey limestone, from the town's new theatre. The three inscriptions, identically worded, all date some nine or ten years after the inscription from the market. Annobal is now dignified with additional titles: 'adorner of his country' (*ornator patriae*) and 'lover of harmony' (*amator concordiae*), Latin translations of titles traditionally bestowed on leading men in Punic cities. The first title was certainly deserved, for Annobal, as these stones record, 'had this made from his own money and dedicated it', although one cannot be sure whether he paid for the whole theatre or only a part. In the meantime the immigrant Fulvii, who call themselves 'the Fulvii of Lepcis', had not failed to show their loyalty to the ruler of the empire. In 3 B.C. they had set up statues to Augustus their 'preserver' and his grandson and adopted son, C. Caesar. The family of the Tabahpī, or Tapapii continued to play a leading role in public life, and several other inscriptions in Latin and neo-Punic record their benefactions for at least the next sixty years. The latest that can be dated belongs to 62, an inscription from the harbour area, honouring Nero. It records the construction of columns and other items under the supervision of Ithymbal Sabinus Tapapius, son of Aris. Thus two generations – sixty-nine years – after the first appearance of a Tapapius, some members of the family had still not acquired the highly prized Roman citizenship. But some of the Punic notables of Lepcis were rewarded in this way. For example the proconsul Q. Marcius Barea in the early forties A.D., at the beginning of the reign of Claudius. That is the logical explanation for the existence of numerous Marcii at Lepcis, several with the *praenomen* Quintus, perpetuating the memory of the magistrate who conferred the citizenship. One of the Tapapii may have been among the beneficiaries, Iddibal Tapapius son of Mago. Iddibal made a dedication to the deified members of the imperial family in 43, on which the name of the proconsul Barea figures prominently as dedicator. It would not be surprising if Iddibal paid for an expensive dedication to be carried out by Barea, precisely to ingratiate himself with the proconsul. Another Lepcitane who may have owed his Roman citizenship to the proconsul Marcius did not take his name. This was L. Annaeus Cornutus, later renowned as a Stoic and as the friend and teacher of the poets Persius and Lucan. Cornutus's *nomen* suggests that he was a client of Lucan or of Lucan's uncle Seneca, with whom the proconsul Marcius had links.[1]

The new Marcii were not the only Lepcitanes to benefit in this way. By the 70s the Punic names, the Annobals, Balsilechs, Balithos, the Bodmelqarts, Magos and Ithymbals, disappear from public records, to be replaced by Claudii and Flavii, Marcii, Paccii, Cornelii and Plautii, who had acquired citizenship from emperors or proconsuls. Certainly by 92 at the latest this was to become inevitable. An inscription of that year records details about Ti. Claudius Sestius, a second generation Roman, described by a whole string of traditional Punic titles translated into Latin (*amator patriae, amator civium, ornator patriae, amator concordiae*), as well as by the titles of the offices he had held. Sestius had paid for the erection of a massive altar in the *orchestra* of the theatre. He was given special honour 'because of his own and his ancestors' services', by the council and people of Lepcis, who are described for the first time as *ordo et populus*, the standard constitutional terms to describe the local government organs of Roman chartered towns, *municipia*. Two other inscriptions do indeed give the town the title of *municipium* before 92, one from 77 or 78, the other from 83, in which proconsuls and their legates are described as patrons of the *municipium*. The inscription of Claudius Sestius confirms that a transformation had indeed taken place at official level. It was not a case of the local authorities of a native African town calling their town a *municipium* because they felt themselves to be Romanised. This must have been an official act of the Emperor Vespasian. It is probable that the town was promoted from being a 'peregrine' or foreign community to a *municipium* of 'Latin' status. This would mean that those who held a magistracy would acquire full Roman citizenship, and the rest of the population would have an improved legal position. The chief magis-

---

[1] 'three other stones': *IRT* 321–3. – Fulvii: *IRT* 320, 328. – 'Ithymbal: *IRT* 341; cf. 273, 745 for other Tapapii (and 319, n. 8). – Barea and Iddibal: there are six QQ. Marcii at Lepcis, one C. Marcius (the proconsul was C.f.). Cf. A. R. BIRLEY (1969) p. 257f., following J. GUEY (1951b) p. 315. – Cornutus: *RE* 1 (1894), 2225f., *Supp.* 5 (1931) 995ff.; *PIR*[2] A 609. – L. Annaeus Seneca: *PIR*[2] A 617, etc. – M. Annaeus Lucanus: *PIR*[2] A 611, etc. – Barea was perhaps brother of the Stoic senator Barea Soranus, father-in-law of Titus and friend of Vespasian (before his accession): *PIR*[2] B 55.

trates continued to have the title *sufes*. But it was traditional practice for the original local titles of magistrates to be retained in such cases.[1]

From the time of Vespasian onwards all the leading citizens of Lepcis Magna have Roman names. The last non-Roman notable mentioned is on an inscription of the year 72, Iddibal, son of Balsillec, grandson of Annobal, great-grandson of Asmun – setting out three generations of his ancestry as if to emphasise that he at least was proud of his Punic inheritance, at a time when he and his peers were all destined to become Roman. He paid for the building and adornment of a Temple of Magna Mater in the Forum. Lepcis had certainly come to the attention of the Emperor at this time, as a result of events in 69, the year of the Four Emperors. Vespasian was engaged in his struggle with Vitellius and the whole Empire was in a state of upheaval. Lepcis's neighbour Oea took advantage of the situation. Valerius Festus, the legate of the single African legion III Augusta (who was *de facto* governor of Numidia, directly responsible to Rome and not to the proconsul of Africa) hesitated for a while before joining the winning Flavian party. Oea and Lepcis had been involved in a dispute. 'It had a trivial origin', Tacitus relates, 'in thefts of fruit and cattle by the peasants, but they were now trying to settle them in open warfare. Oea, being inferior in numbers, had called in the aid of the Garamantes, an invincible tribe, who were always a fertile source of damage to their neighbours. Thus the people of Leptis were in great straits. Their fields had been wasted far and wide, and they had fled in terror under the shelter of their walls.' Then Festus intervened. He followed up his suppression of the disturbance with a lightning punitive campaign to the far south which recalled that of Cornelius Balbus some ninety years

[1] Sestius: *IRT* 392. – *ordo et populus*: cf. H. U. INSTINSKY (1944a), writing without reference to Lepcis, from which evidence was not then available. – 'Two other inscriptions': *IRT* 342 (AD 77/8), 346 (AD 83). – *sufes*: *RE* 4A (1931), 643ff. – The change of status of Lepcis at this time is disputed. Cf. now A. R. BIRLEY *HAC*, pp. 6off., where reference is made to the views of the following scholars: J. GUEY (1951a), N. DEGRASSI, G. CHARLES-PICARD (1957), T. D. BARNES (1967a) (all of whom accept that the town became a *municipium* in the first century A.D.); and S. AURIGEMMA (1950) (against this view, followed by the editors of *IRT*, p. 80, without discussion). Note in this context the important paper by H. BRAUNERT (1966) illuminating the whole question of Latin status.

31 B.C.	*2 September:* Octavian, great-nephew of Julius Caesar, gains sole power after defeat of Antony at Actium.
27 B.C.	Octavian given name of AUGUSTUS.
23 B.C.	Augustus given *tribunicia potestas.*
4	Augustus adopts stepson Tiberius Claudius Nero, who becomes Tiberius Julius Caesar.
14	TIBERIUS succeeds to Augustus's position on latter's death.
37	GAIUS ('CALIGULA'), great-nephew of Tiberius, great-grandson of Augustus, succeeds Tiberius on latter's death.
41	Murder of Caligula. His uncle CLAUDIUS proclaimed emperor.
54	NERO, stepson of Claudius, nephew of Caligula, great-great-grandson of Augustus, succeeds Claudius on latter's death.
68	*6 June:* Suicide of Nero after revolts in western provinces. GALBA recognized as emperor.
69	*1–3 January:* VITELLIUS proclaimed emperor by Rhine armies.
	15 January: OTHO instigates murder of Galba and is proclaimed emperor at Rome.
	15 April: Vitellius' army defeats that of Otho in N. Italy.
	1–3 July: VESPASIAN proclaimed emperor by eastern armies.
	27–28 October: Defeat of Vitellius's forces in N. Italy.
	20 December: Vitellius killed at Rome.
79	Death of Vespasian, succeeded by elder son TITUS.
81	Death of Titus, succeeded by younger brother DOMITIAN.
96	*18 September:* Murder of Domitian at Rome. NERVA made emperor.
97	*October:* Nerva adopts Trajan as his son.
98	*28 January:* TRAJAN succeeds on death of Nerva.
117	HADRIAN, after ostensible death-bed adoption, succeeds his cousin Trajan.
136	*Spring or early summer:* Hadrian adopts L. Ceionius Commodus, who becomes L. Aelius Caesar.
138	*1 January:* Death of L. Aelius Caesar.
	25 February: Hadrian adopts T. Aurelius Antoninus, who becomes T. Aelius Hadrianus Antoninus and adopts Marcus and L. Commodus junior.
	10 July: ANTONINUS succeeds on Hadrian's death.
161	*7 March:* MARCUS succeeds on death of Antoninus (Pius), jointly with L. Commodus junior who becomes L. VERUS.
169	*January:* Death of L. Verus.
177	Marcus's only surviving son Commodus made joint emperor.
180	*17 March:* Death of Marcus, COMMODUS sole emperor.
192	*31 December:* Commodus murdered.
193	*1 January:* PERTINAX proclaimed emperor.
	28 March: Pertinax murdered, DIDIUS JULIANUS proclaimed emperor (Rome).
	9 April: SEPTIMIUS SEVERUS proclaimed emperor (Danube).
	1 June: Julianus killed at Rome.
197	*19 February:* Defeat of Septimius's last rival, at Lyons.
211	*4 February:* Death of Septimius at York.

previously. The Garamantes were battered into submission and gave no further trouble for over a century. Festus was decorated by the Emperor for his achievements and went on to a distinguished career.[1]

It would not be surprising if some enterprising Lepcitanes took advantage of the prominence into which events at first unwelcome had thrust their city. Valerius Festus may have been glad to plead the case for their advancement before the Emperor. In any case, Vespasian's actions elsewhere show that the grant of Latin rights to Lepcis Magna would have been fully in accordance with his policy of extending the citizenship – he gave Latin status to the whole of Spain. The mission of Festus and the overall policy of Vespasian thus provided promising prospects for favour to be granted to Lepcis. An occasion was offered when Vespasian began administrative and fiscal reforms in Africa, involving boundary changes and amendments to the regulations governing land-tenure. The proconsul Curtilius Mancia evidently supervised the arrangements in the latter category. Revision of boundaries and no doubt other measures were supervised by various special commissioners. One of these was the consular C. Rutilius Gallicus, whose presence in Africa is attested for the years 73 and 74. The people of Lepcis made a dedication in honour of Gallicus's wife Minicia Paetina at Turin, the commissioner's home. No doubt Gallicus himself was honoured likewise, although no inscription to him has survived. An excellent explanation for the honour done to Gallicus would be that he had supervised the promotion of Lepcis to the status of *municipium*.[2]

---

[1] Iddibal: *IRT* 300. – Festus: Tacitus, *Histories* 2.98.1, 4.49–50; D. 989; cf. B. E. THOMASSON, II, pp. 149ff. –. Garamantes: Pliny,*Nat.Hist.* 5.5, cf. C. M. DANIELS. The episode is handled by P. ROMANELLI (1959) pp. 285ff.

[2] Spain: cf. most recently H. BRAUNERT (1966). – MANCIA: cf. C. Saumagne in C. COURTOIS *et al.*, pp. 137ff. – Gallicus: cf. *RE* I A (1904) 1255ff. (by E. Groag), P. ROMANELLI (1959) pp. 295ff., R. SYME (1958) p. 638. Paetina: *CIL* V 6990. – The special importance of the Flavian Emperors' work in Africa (sometimes insufficiently emphasized) is underlined by T. KOTULA (1967) pp. 218ff. – Vespasian's interest in Tripolitania might conceivably have been first stimulated by his wife, who was, before their marriage, the mistress of a Roman knight from Sabratha (Suetonius, *D. Vesp.* 3.1: Statilius Capella). He had himself served as proconsul of Africa – *integerrime nec sine magna dignitate* – probably ca. AD 60/62 (B. E. THOMASSON, II, p. 42). Although turnips were thrown at him

After the acquisition of the new status, those who became full citizens by election to a magistracy would be enrolled in the Quirina tribe or voting district to which the Flavian imperial family belonged. But not all would take the names T. Flavius in honour of the imperial house. Some would adopt the names of proconsuls or other distinguished Romans, and special grants of full citizenship to worthy individuals probably continued to be made. For example, the name of the proconsul on the inscription of 77/8 already mentioned, C. Paccius Africanus, was probably perpetuated at Lepcis for one of these reasons. Septimius's first wife was a Paccia.[1]

If Festus's expedition had pacified the Garamantes, it also revived Roman interest in the Sahara. Probably in the late 70s a legate of III Augusta, Septimius Flaccus, took a force to their territory and went on further south 'for three months' journey, towards the Ethiopians'. The distance, or length, of his journey may be exaggerated, as it may be also in the case of 'Julius Maternus from Lepcis Magna', who went from Garama with the Garamantian king 'four months' journey to the south', reaching 'Agisymba, where the rhinoceroses congregate'. Ptolemy, who preserves this information, does not believe the details that he quotes about the journey. 'Ethiopians' can refer to any negroid peoples, and Agisymba cannot be identified. These details are perhaps not of great importance. The interesting thing is that Septimius Flaccus was at Lepcis – for Ptolemy specifically notes the distance between Lepcis and Garama based on Flaccus's experience. Lepcis was probably his base. The exact date of Flaccus's expedition is difficult to determine, but there are reasonable grounds for assigning it to c. 78–80. His destination suggests that the Roman government was interested in

---

in Hadrumetum (Suet., *ib.*, 4.3), this need have prejudiced him, if at all, only against Byzacena, and not against the province as a whole.

[1] Quirina: cf. *IRT*, p. 82, W. KUBITSCHEK, p. 150, M. HAMMOND (1940) p. 140f., T. D. BARNES (1967a) p. 88f. Cf. also A. R. BIRLEY (1969) p. 254f., *HAC* p. 64 (where the view that the Septimii might have belonged to the Pupinia, put forward by Barnes, is criticised). – There are eight Flavii at Lepcis whose names may derive from the first century: *IRT* 267, 432, 564 (and 568, 595), 638, 641, 700, 703–4. The others are either fourth-century or non-Lepcitanes. – Africanus: B. E. THOMASSON, II, p. 47f., cf. J. GUEY (1951b) p. 315, A. R. BIRLEY (1969) p. 258. – 'first wife': App. I.

making the transsaharan trade more secure. It may be no coincidence that Vespasian dedicated the Flavian Amphitheatre, or Colosseum, in 79. It was completed and opened by his son and successor Titus in June 80. Nine thousand wild beasts of all kinds were slaughtered for the gratification of the populace of Rome. The games lasted for a hundred days. It is legitimate to speculate that the authorities at Rome may have instigated Flaccus's expedition with a view to ensuring a supply of particularly exciting and rare wild beasts to fight in the new arena. The presence of a Roman of high rank named Septimius at Lepcis at this time may well have prompted one of the magistrates of the city, in the year 79 or thereabouts, to take the name Septimius when he acquired the citizenship. He may have already had the name Macer, which would now serve as his *cognomen*.[1]

It must be admitted that this reconstruction is almost entirely hypothetical. It might be that the ancestors of the Emperor Septimius Severus on his father's side, the Septimii, were Italian immigrants, as his mother's ancestors the Fulvii seem to have been. Be that as it may, very soon after the year 79 the Emperor's great-grandfather moved to Italy, taking his young son Severus with him. The main evidence for the family's presence in Italy at the end of the first century A.D. strongly suggests that the Septimii were by no means of Italian extraction. The motives for the first known Septimius's departure from Lepcis are not recorded. He bought an estate close to Rome, at Veii in southern Etruria. He was clearly a man of means, and was no doubt an *eques*

---

[1] Flaccus: Ptolemy 1.8.4. Cf. A. R. BIRLEY (1969), p. 255f., where it is argued that his command may be dated to this time and that his *nomen* may have been assumed by the Emperor's paternal ancestors. Some would deny the existence of *Septimius* Flaccus, identifying him with the epigraphically attested Cn. *Suellius* Flaccus, cf. P. ROMANELLI (1959), p. 204 and J. DESANGES, whose dating is consequently later in any case (as is that of B. E. THOMASSON, II, pp. 158ff., who, however, separates the two Flacci). The article of Desanges is valuable on the wild beast traffic. T. S. and P. MACKAY, p. 140f., have now published an inscription from Olba in Rough Cilicia, showing a Septimius as *legatus* in 75 or 76. If his post was that of governor (of Cilicia, reconstituted *c.* 72 according to D. MAGIE, p. 1440), identification with Flaccus would have to be ruled out. He might, however, have been a subordinate *legatus*. But at all events the inscription demonstrates unequivocally the existence of a senatorial Septimius at this time. – Colosseum: G. LUGLI, pp. 319ff., esp. p. 322. – Macer: App. I; cf. A. R. BIRLEY, *HAC*, p. 65, on *HA Sev.* 1.2.

Romanus, a knight. The source of the wealth can only be guessed at – it would be tempting to suggest that it was acquired from the expansion of transsaharan trade.[1]

The young Severus was taken to Italy when still a boy and grew up in southern Etruria. It seems that his education was completed by study with the great Quintilian, the leading teacher of the day. As he approached the age of twenty he seems to have had the chance of obtaining the *latus clavus*, the broad purple stripe on the toga which denoted senatorial rank and the right to seek entry to the Senate by holding the quaestorship at the age of twenty-four. But he was content with the 'narrow stripe' of equestrian rank to which his father's wealth entitled him and evidently made no effort to acquire ennoblement. He began to practise as a barrister, and wrote verses. He had friends in literary and senatorial circles, among them the poet Statius, author of the *Thebaid*. It is reasonable to suppose that his entrée into the circle of Statius may have been given him by the patronage of Rutilius Gallicus, the man perhaps responsible for the improvement in the status of Lepcis, who was no doubt one of several *patroni* of the *municipium*. Gallicus was one of the most influential senators of the reign of Domitian (81–96). He was consul for the second time, probably in 85, and Prefect of the City of Rome. He died in 92. Statius wrote a poem in honour of Gallicus, describing his career in flowery language – including a reference to his service in Africa:

[1] It is assumed in what follows, and throughout this work, that the grandfather of the Emperor, known from *IRT* 412 (quoted below, p. 39, n. 2) and 413, L. Septimius Severus, is most probably the same as the friend of the poet Statius, Septimius Severus of Lepcis. The identification was proposed by S. AURIGEMMA (1950), some of whose arguments were, however, erroneous. But it was challenged by J. GUEY (1951a), who is followed by G. DI VITA-ÉVRARD (1963). Likewise T. D. BARNES (1967a) dissociates the man on *IRT* 412–413 from the friend of Statius. But cf. A. R. BIRLEY, *HAC*, esp. pp. 63ff., 75ff., where the case for identifying the two is argued: the negative arguments against this are questionable (esp. that of Guey, that *iudices selecti* were not *equites*); the main positive evidence is that the future Emperor possessed property at Veii, as did the friend of Statius, cf. M. HAMMOND (1940), p. 143f. (who was naturally unaware at that time that the grandfather of Septimius the Emperor was called *Severus*, like the friend of Statius; the evidence of *HA Sev.* 1.2 naming the grandfather *Macer* was then accepted in the absence of evidence to the contrary). See further below, and App. I; also A. R. BIRLEY (1969), p. 253.

Libyci quid mira tributi
obsequia et missum media de pace triumphum
laudem et opes quantas nec qui mandaverat ausus
exspectare fuit?

In the summer of 95 Statius published the fourth in his series of occasional pieces, a book of nine poems addressed to his friends. The fifth of these is a 'lyric ode to Septimius Severus' in fifteen four-line stanzas. It should be noted at this point that one thing is almost guaranteed about Septimius Severus from the evidence of this ode: that he was extremely rich.[1] 'I salute the brave and eloquent Severus', the poet begins. There follows a description of Statius's country retreat near Albano, and a reference to the support Severus had given him when he competed in the literary festival there. The second half of the poem consists of a series of compliments to his friend. The theme is that no one would imagine that he had been born at Lepcis:

(29–30)
tene in remotis Syrtibus avia
Leptis creavit?

'Did your ancestral Leptis really bring you to life amid the far-distant Syrtes?' No, says Statius, 'who would not think that my charming Septimius had crawled in infancy on all the hills of Rome?':

[1] Quintilian: Statius in *Silvae* 4, *praef.*, describes him as a *condiscipulus* of Vitorius Marcellus, a friend and presumably pupil of Quintilian, cf. *RE* Supp. 9 (1962), 1744f. – '*latus clavus*': I take it that *Silvae* 4.5.41–2, 'content with the glory of the narrow purple' need only indicate that he had rejected an opportunity of entering the *vigintivirate*(on which, and the quaestorship, cf. pp. 69ff., 79ff., below), not, as e.g. T. D. BARNES (1967a), p. 88 assumes, that he had rejected the chance of the quaestorship. Hence he need not have been more than twenty at the time of this poem. – Gallicus: *Silvae* 1.4. cf. p. 33, n. 2, above. The quotation is from ll.84–87: 'Why should I praise the tribute, and marvellous obediences of Africa, and the spoils of triumph sent back from the midst of peace, and such riches as not even he who had given you your mandate had dared to expect? The date of *Silvae* 4 is given by the subject of 4.1, the seventeenth consulship of Domitian. – 'extremely rich': a certain opulence is guaranteed by the estates (not just at Veii). But the point is that a young provincial knight is unlikely to have been honoured with an Ode unless – as H. G. Pflaum has pointed out to me – he was a man of substance.

(33–4)
quis non in omni vertice Romuli
reptasse dulcem Septimium putet?

But, he goes on, after all, his father had brought him to Italy as a boy and he swam in Tuscan pools:

(39–40)
. . . adoptatusque Tuscis
gurgitibus puer innatasti.

Severus 'grew up among the sons of the Senate, content with the glory of the narrow purple' (41–2). Then come the really striking lines:

(45–6)
non sermo Poenus, non habitus tibi,
externa non mens; Italus, Italus!

'Your speech is not Punic, nor is your dress. Your mind is not that of a foreigner – you are Italian, Italian!' The poem concludes with a compliment to Severus's eloquence as a barrister, and his fondness for withdrawing to his father's home at Veii. Finally the poet suggests that his friend may be writing more verses before long.

The elaborate compliment paid to Septimius Severus would surely have had much less point if the Septimii were in fact of Italian extraction. Indeed, a member of a colonial family that had returned to Italy might well have been deeply offended to be told that he had not acquired – or had lost – certain 'native' habits or characteristics, and that he did not have a provincial accent. The poem is a pleasant illustration of the powerful magnetic attraction exerted by Roman culture on the native families in the more civilised parts of the western empire. And it shows the facility with which such native families could acquire all the qualities of Italian Romans. A contemporary of Septimius Severus, living in Rome at this time, was a young woman of British origin, Claudia Rufina. Rufina was praised by Statius's fellow-poet Martial in a manner strikingly similar to Statius's praise of Severus:

Claudia caeruleis cum sit Rufina Britannis
edita, quam Latiae pectora gentis habet!
quale decus formae! Romanam credere matres
Italides possunt, Atthides esse suam!

Martial may indeed have known Severus also, for he had a friend of that name who was a poet – but Severus was so common a *cognomen* that there can be no certainty.[1]

In September 96 Domitian was assassinated and a new – and very different – regime took over. The new Emperor Nerva, and Trajan his heir adopted in October 97, who succeeded to the throne in January 98, were generally welcomed. But the change of ruler must inevitably have meant a change in the circumstances of life in the capital. Poets like Martial and Statius, who had flattered Domitian with sickening adulation in their verses, no doubt found the change less than advantageous. Martial went home to Spain, ending many years of residence at Rome. Another poet, Silius Italicus, committed suicide with dignity. Statius is not heard of again.[2] The young Severus may have had to abandon thoughts of a career at the bar, or of any official post. He did at some stage obtain a minor position, being appointed to serve as a juryman on the panels that served the permanent *quaestiones* or law courts. As a knight Severus was a 'selected juryman', *iudex selectus*, and served in one of the first three out of the five *decuriae* or panels of jurors.[3]

---

[1] The quotation is from Martial 11.53: 'Though she was brought up among the sky-blue Britons, does not Claudia Rufina have the spirit of the Latin race! What graceful beauty! The Italian ladies can believe she is a Roman, the ladies of Athens that she is theirs!' – Severi in Martial include the poet invited to dinner by 11.57.

[2] On Nerva and Trajan see above all Sir R. SYME (1958), esp. pp. 1–44; and, on the death or withdrawal of poets, p. 88f.

[3] *IRT* 412: *avo d(omini) n(ostri) L. Septimio Severo, sufeti, praef(ecto) publice creato cum primum civitas Romana adacta est, du(u)mvir(o), fl(amini) p(er)p(etuo). in decuriis et inter selectos Romae iudicavit. Lepc(i)tani publ(ice)* (lines 1–5, here omitted, give the names and titles, for 202, of his grandson the Emperor). It is not really clear whether the *iudices selecti* served only in the first three of the five panels. The whole question is obscure and disputed, and some would reject the view here taken that a man who had been a *iudex selectus* was *ipso facto* a knight (for the arguments, cf. A. R. BIRLEY, *HAC*, esp. pp. 75ff.). It could be that Severus returned to Rome to become a *iudex* after 110, when he was *praefectus*, and then *duumvir* (see below, p. 42), although the order on *IRT* 412 need not imply this.

Whether or not he returned to Lepcis straight away after the changes at Rome, within a year or two a development took place at Lepcis that may have made his return necessary. For the new regime had allowed an unwelcome consequence to ensue from the removal of Domitian's iron control over provincial governors. Some of them now took the opportunity of practising graft on a large scale, with no fear of the consequences. The proconsul of Africa in 97–8, Marius Priscus, oppressed his province greedily. Lepcis Magna was directly affected. A member of its town council, Flavius Marcianus, had paid the enormous sum of 700,000 Sesterces to Priscus, in return for which the proconsul had inflicted various punishments on one of Marcianus's enemies, a Roman knight. He had been flogged, sentenced to hard labour in the mines, and finally executed in prison by strangulation. In another case which may have taken place at Lepcis also – it is mentioned in the same sentence by Pliny, who describes the affair – one Vitellius Honoratus had paid 300,000 Sesterces for a Roman knight to be exiled and seven of the man's friends to be put to death. If that had all taken place at Lepcis, there would have been clear reason for Septimius Severus to return to the place of his birth. His own friends or kinsmen may have been affected. Even if the Honoratus affair took place somewhere else in Africa, the wrongful execution of one of Lepcis's leading men, and the complete disgrace of another – Marcianus was a councillor – must have caused a terrific upheaval. Priscus had acted at Lepcis through the agency of his legate Hostilius Firminus, who had also taken money from Marcianus, though less than he had hoped for – 'it was proved from the account-book of Marcianus and from a speech that he had made in the Lepcis council that Firminus had helped Priscus with a particularly shameful service, and that he had bargained with Marcianus to get 200,000 Sesterces. He had in fact been given 10,000, which figured in the accounts under the heading of 'cosmetics' – a description that suited his dandified elegance well.

When Priscus's proconsulship ended in the summer of 98, action against him commenced. 'Many private individuals and one particular city', acting in a corporate capacity, preferred charges against him. That city was certainly Lepcis Magna. The case was prolonged. Priscus was at first accused of certain minor forms of extortion. He pleaded guilty and asked for damages to be assessed by a senatorial committee. Pliny and Tacitus were appointed counsel for the province, and revealed to the Senate that more serious offences were being passed over: Priscus was trying to escape trial for these by his plea of guilty to the first counts. An *inquisitio* or commission of enquiry was set up to summon witnesses from Africa, but in the meantime the lesser charges were proceeded with. Priscus was duly convicted on these, and deprived of his rank. Then, at least twelve months after the original accusation was laid (evidently in December 99), the trial on the criminal charges began. At the second session of the Senate devoted to the hearing, the Emperor Trajan presided as consul, in January 100. It was one of his first appearances in public at Rome since his accession two years earlier. (He had remained for more than twelve months with the armies in the north, after Nerva's death.) Pliny opened for the prosecution with a speech lasting nearly five hours. On the next day Salvius Liberalis, counsel for Priscus, replied for the defence. Then Tacitus made the second speech for the prosecution, a speech, says Pliny, that was 'eloquent, with all the solemnity that typifies his style of public speaking'. After this the defence had no alternative but to resort to a plea for lenience. On the third day Priscus was found guilty. But his punishment was not outstandingly severe – simply banishment from Rome and Italy and repayment of the bribe-money into the treasury. Marcianus was banished from Africa as well as from Rome and Italy. The legate Firminus had a comparatively minor penalty: loss of certain privileges – but not loss of his senatorial rank. Juvenal was to write some years later that Priscus's exile was by no means unpleasant. He had, after all, only lost the money that he had corruptly obtained in Africa. His own property was not touched, and he doubtless retired to his estates in the Spanish province of Baetica,[1] where, as Juvenal says,

---

[1] 'iron control': Suetonius, *Dom.* 8.2, where the contrast with what followed is explicit. – Priscus: Sir R. SYME (1958), p. 7of.; A. N. SHERWIN-WHITE, pp. 56ff., 160ff. The affair is described in Pliny *Ep.* 2.11. – Flavius Marcianus: the names demonstrate that he was of native, not immigrant, extraction. Regarded as a town-councillor in view of Pliny, *Ep.* 2.11.23, cf. *PIR*² F 313 and Sherwin-White, p. 169. (But Pliny's words would naturally mean that it was Firminus, not Marcianus, who addressed the *ordo*. Incidentally, Pliny's use of this term for the town-council of Lepcis would add weight to the view that it had become a *muni-*

he began 'drinking from the eighth hour of the day, while you, victorious province, lament'.[1]

Pliny and Tacitus were assigned to the case by the Senate (*adesse provincialibus iussi*). But it is legitimate to wonder whether the Lepcitane Septimius Severus may not have exerted some efforts to have these two men selected to act on behalf of his city. For it he was indeed taught by Quintilian, then Severus might claim Pliny as a fellow-pupil, though one some years older than himself. Lepcis did in any case send one of its sons into the Senate during the reign of Trajan. His name is unknown, but fragments of an inscription from Lepcis give details of his official career. The backing of a man of this position, together with efforts by Severus, would ensure that Lepcis's voice would be heard at a high level.[2]

Men from Roman Africa were now coming to the fore in increasing numbers, entering the Senate or gaining important procuratorial posts. As early as 80 a man from Cirta (modern Constantine in Algeria) was made consul, Q. Aurelius Pactumeius Fronto. It was a slow process at first, but as it gathered momentum there began to be as it were a geometric progression in the advancement of men from this region. They gave one another a helping hand.[3]

In 110 the importance of Lepcis was recognised when Trajan granted the town the status of *colonia*, the consummation of a century and a half of Romanisation. All the Lepcitani now became Roman citizens, and its chief magistrates now took the title of *duumvir*. L. Septimius Severus was one of the last pair of *sufetes* and one of the first two *duumviri*. As well as this, he held another, special post, that of 'publicly appointed prefect when Roman citizenship was first awarded' – that is, at the time when the town actually underwent the transformation from *municipium* to *colonia*. This indicates that the Emperor

---

cipium already – if Pliny could be trusted. But he does avoid technical terms, and this cannot be pressed.)

[1] Juvenal 1.49–59, cf. 8.119–120.

[2] Quintilian: Pliny, *Ep.* 2.14.9ff., 6.6.3, cf. p. 36f., above, – 'one of its sons': *IRT* 624 with J. M. REYNOLDS (1955), p. 131f.

[3] Pactumeius Fronto: *CIL* VIII 7057–8=*ILAlg* II 642, 644 (*cos. ex Afric[a p]rimo*); *ib.* 643. The African membership of the Senate is surveyed by A. PELLETIER, who, however, sticks rigidly to Africa *proconsularis*.

consented to serve as honorary first *duumvir* of the new colony, and that Severus, as the leading citizen, acted for him. The mass of the population was now incorporated into the Roman citizen-body. They were enrolled in the voting district of Trajan, the Papiria. The name of the town, which had perhaps been *municipium Flavium Lepcis Magna* for the past thirty-five or so years, now became *colonia Ulpia Traiana fidelis Lepcis Magna*. The people were divided into *curiae* or wards, also named after the imperial family.[1]

The Romanisation of Lepcis was now complete, outwardly at least. The process can be traced over a period of a hundred and twenty years. What is particularly striking is the enthusiasm for Roman culture on the part of the Punic notables and the ease with which natives and immigrants coalesced to form a new city. Punic culture did not completely disappear, and the Punic tongue was still spoken by families with Roman-sounding names. But Lepcis, economically powerful and now with the rank to match her wealth, was ready to send her sons to the highest positions in the empire.[2]

[1] 'status of *colonia*': S. AURIGEMMA (1950), J. GUEY (1951a), esp. p. 202, *IRT* p. 81, etc. and cf. p. 31, n. 1 above. – *curiae*: cf. now T. KOTULA (1968), esp. pp. 83ff. – On this kind of *praefectus* cf. *RE* 22 (1954), 1313ff., esp. 1318ff. (P. ROMANELLI [1959], p. 325, n. 4, has misunderstood J. Guey, whose interpretation of the relevant phrase in *IRT* 412 is excellent.)

[2] This coalescence of Italian and Punic elements in Tripolitania was analysed by L. H. THOMPSON in a paper read to the Libya in History Conference at Benghazi in 1968: I am grateful to Mr C. M. Daniels for this information. Septimius Severus himself, product of a union between the Septimii, a family of Punic origin (as here argued) and the Fulvii, of Italian settler stock, epitomises this process in his own person. – 'the Punic tongue': the latest example of a neo-Punic inscription at Lepcis is generally stated (e.g. still by F. MILLAR [1968], p. 130 and n. 50) to be no. 32, the neo-Punic version of *IRT* 318, from 92. But cf. J. GUEY (1953), pp. 351ff., esp. pp. 354ff., where the neo-Punic text of *IRT* 305 ('unpublished' when *IRT* appeared, cf. p. 13) is given. From this Guey argues that its date is probably later than 110. In general, on the use of neo-Punic cf. F. MILLAR (1968), who emphasizes, in particular, that it was this language (and not a Libyan dialect; note his warning, p. 128, against the use of the term 'Berber' for the non-Punic native language of Africa) which continued in use until the end of Roman rule in Africa, not least in Tripolitania, cf. esp. p. 132f. of his article. Cf. p. 49, below, on Septimius's fluency in 'Punic'.

IV

SCENES FROM PROVINCIAL LIFE

By the time that Lepcis became a colony, L. Septimius Severus, the leading man, or one of the leading men, of the town, was almost certainly married. The name of his wife, Septimius's paternal grandmother, is unknown. It may have been Octavia. One can only attempt to guess his age by looking at his son Geta. Geta's son, the future Emperor, born in 145, was probably not the eldest child, and Geta was probably not much younger than twenty-five at that time. So one may estimate that he was born not later than 120.[1]

During the years when Geta grew to manhood at Lepcis, the town continued to expand and develop. The inscriptions show that in the reign of Hadrian magnificent baths, of which substantial remains still survive, were constructed. An aqueduct built at the expense of one Q. Servilius Candidus brought in the water. This man is recorded on one inscription with the traditional Punic titles *amator patriae, amator civium, amator concordiae*. Private and official dedications alike, in honour of Hadrian and Antoninus Pius testify to the zeal of the Lepcitanes, in displaying their loyalty. One was a dedication to Venus by C. Claudius Septimius Aper. In the late 120s and early 130s Septimius's kinsmen, first P. Septimius Aper and then C. Septimius Severus, perhaps sons of Claudius Septimius Aper, acquired the *latus clavus* which Severus had rejected, and began senatorial careers. The two men are described as 'paternal uncles' of Septimius in the Augustan History (though they were more probably first cousins of his father Geta). Nothing is known of the career of Aper, except that he ultimately reached the consulship in 153. C. Septimius Severus's career is known in some detail. His first step on the ladder was the pre-

[1] Cf. App. I for details.

44

senatorial post of *IVvir viarum curandarum*: membership of the board of four that supervised the maintenance of the streets of Rome. He did not apparently see military service as tribune of a legion. But this was not exceptional. For although there were in theory some twenty-nine such commissions, and only twenty young men each year to fill them (the *vigintiviri*, of which the *IVviri* formed a part), in practice the number of places available was sharply reduced. Some tribunes served for more than one season, and some in more than one legion. But C. Septimius Severus went through the normal grades of the magistracies at Rome, presumably at the normal ages, being quaestor at twenty-four or twenty-five, tribune at twenty-six or twenty-seven and praetor at twenty-nine or thirty. He probably held the quaestorship shortly before his 'nephew' Septimius was born, *c.* 143.[1]

His career may have been helped by a powerful connection. One of the two Praetorian Prefects at the beginning of the reign of Antoninus Pius was a certain M. Petronius Mamertinus. One of this man's grandsons was named Petronius Sura Septimianus, suggesting that the Prefect's son or nephew may have married a Septimia.[2] But this marriage-connection, if it existed at all, probably did not take place till the late 150s. On the other hand, the families may have been linked already by the marriage of a Petronia to a Septimius, for a procurator of this period appears to have been called L. Septimius Petronianus. Be all this as it may, the Prefect Mamertinus could well have come from Africa. This alone would have helped men from the province to make their way at Rome. Africans were indeed beginning to be increasingly prominent at all levels in the imperial administration. One of the outstanding figures of the reign of Antoninus Pius was Q. Lollius Urbicus, third son of a local worthy in the Cirta region (northern Numidia). He had won his spurs in the Jewish war in Hadrian's reign, and was Pius's choice for the only major military undertaking of the twenty-three year reign. Urbicus went to Britain as governor at the

---

[1] Candidus: *IRT* 357–359; 275. – 'Private and official dedications': e.g. 362–3, 366, 368–9, 372–3, 375–6, 379. – 'Claudius Septimius Aper' and the kinsmen: App. I. *IRT* 316 is a dedication (of a statue of Cupid) to Venus Chalcidica, in honour of Antoninus Pius. – 'normal grades': cf. esp. p. 79f., below, and generally, chapters V–VI, and IX.

[2] App. I.

beginning of Pius's reign and after successful campaigning in Scotland supervised the construction of the new frontier system now known as the Antonine Wall, between the Forth and the Clyde. In 146 or soon after he was appointed Prefect of the City of Rome, the pinnacle of the senatorial career.[1] Apart from Urbicus, the most distinguished senator of African origin at this time was the jurist P. Salvius Julianus, who was made consul *ordinarius* in 148, a very special honour, as this year marked the nine hundredth anniversary of the foundation of Rome. Julianus's name is one of the most distinguished in the history of Roman jurisprudence. His family came from Hadrumetum, on the eastern coast of Tunisia. (There were links between Julianus's family and Italy. A kinswoman of Salvius Julianus, Aemilia Clara, married into a Milanese family. Her son, M. Didius Severus Julianus, half Italian and half African, was to cross the path of Septimius Severus of Lepcis Magna.)[2]

Africans were also prominent in court circles. The principal tutor of Aurelius Caesar was the Numidian orator M. Cornelius Fronto of Cirta, regarded by his contemporaries as the equal of Cicero (no doubt with some exaggeration). One of Marcus Aurelius's other tutors had also been from Africa, the *grammaticus* Tuticius Proculus from Sicca Veneria. A *grammaticus* from Carthage, Sulpicius Apollinaris, was one of the doyens of the teaching profession at Rome.[3] Besides these figures, another man from Africa may fairly be regarded as the most remarkable Latin writer of the age, Apuleius of Madauros, author of the *Metamorphoses*, or *Golden Ass*.[4]

An episode in Apuleius's life took place in Tripolitania in the late 150s, not, as chance would have it, at Lepcis Magna, but at neighbouring Oea and – the denouement – at the third town of the group, Sabratha. The affair is richly detailed by the pen of Apuleius himself. In the almost total absence of evidence for the early years of Septimius

---

[1] Cf. A. R. BIRLEY (1967a), p. 71f.

[2] W. KUNKEL, pp. 157ff.; *PIR*[2] D 77.

[3] Fronto: A. R. BIRLEY (1966a), esp. pp. 81ff. – Proculus: ID (1968b). Apollinaris: *RE* 4A (1930) 737ff. (and cf. p. 107, below).

[4] A brief resumé of the facts in *PIR*[2] A 958. Further references in later notes to this chapter. – Madauros: sometimes spelt Madaura, less correctly, cf. *RE* 14 (1928) 201.

himself, it is fruitful to turn to the case of Apuleius and the Sicinii of Oea. The light that it throws on social life in mid-second century Tripolitania may fairly be considered to illuminate the Lepcis in which Septimius passed his boyhood. Besides, there can be little doubt that the Septimii must have known of the affair and have taken a keen interest in it. Before the climax came in the *basilica* at Sabratha his family, even Septimius himself as a boy of eleven or twelve, may have listened to the astonishing sophist declaiming in public. Some of them may have gone to Sabratha assizes at the time of his trial and have heard the *tour de force* defence that he made before the proconsul – indeed, if the news of his prosecution got back there in time, one can conceive of some of the better educated men of Lepcis who took an interest in these things making a journey especially to attend the trial.

But this is to anticipate. An account must be given of the man and the circumstances which produced the oration he made in his own defence, the *Apologia*. He was born about the beginning of the reign of Hadrian, at Madauros on the borders of proconsular Africa and Numidia, the modern Mdaurouch in eastern Algeria. The town lies some fifty miles south of the port of Hippo Regius (Bone, or Annaba). Apuleius's father was one of the leading men in the town, an ancient Numidian settlement, subsequently, like Lepcis and its neighbours, thoroughly Romanised and made a *colonia*. His father had held all the local magistracies, and had even deputised as *duumvir* for one of the Emperors who held the post in an honorary capacity.[1] Apuleius and his brother were left a considerable estate by their father – two million Sesterces. Not quite enough, if divided equally, to qualify either for entry into the Senate, but making them comfortably off members of the equestrian order. At an early age Apuleius went to Carthage, some 150 miles from his home, to further his education. His affection for Carthage remained immense: 'Carthage is the revered teacher of our province,' he said years afterwards, 'Carthage is the divine muse of Africa, Carthage is the fountain of inspiration for the Roman world.'

---

[1] Apuleius, *Apologia* 24: '*in qua colonia patrem habui loco principis IIviralem*'. The true sense of this phrase seems not to have been noted previously. Cf. *RE* 22 (1954) 1318ff. for parallels. The grandfather of Septimius is seemingly another case cf. p. 42f., above.

From Carthage he went to Athens, the greatest university in the ancient world, and travelled further afield from there. Samos and Hierapolis in Phrygia are places he happens to mention that he had visited.[1] At Athens he drank in 'the imaginative draught of poetry, the clear draught of geometry, the sweet draught of music, the austerer draught of dialectic, and the nectar of all philosophy'. While at Athens he met a student several years younger than himself, Sicinius Pontianus of Oea. Apuleius befriended his young fellow-countryman, no doubt helping him with his studies, and generally with advice and support.[2]

From Athens Apuleius went to Rome, where he continued his studies and gained the entrée to the literary circles of the upper classes, including friends of the patrician senator Scipio Orfitus, as he later recalled. If, as is generally reckoned, the end of his famous *Metamorphoses* contains some autobiographical material, he went to Rome shortly after his initiation into the mysteries of Isis. On his arrival at the capital he became a fervent worshipper at the temple of the goddess on the Campus Martius, and was initiated further. His funds were by now becoming depleted and to support himself he began to practise as a rhetorician. He had thus found his vocation. When he returned to his native Africa his talents were greatly in demand.[3] In the absence of modern forms of entertainment, public lectures were immensely popular, and lecturers of talent became celebrated figures. One can only compare the success of lecture tours in nineteenth-century America.

But Apuleius still had an urge to travel, and in the winter of 156 began a journey by land to Alexandria, the greatest city of the Greek world. On his way he stayed at Oea, with his friend Appius Quintianus. He fell ill there, and his visit was prolonged. At this point he was visited by his old fellow-student from Athens, Sicinius Pontianus. Pontianus begged him to prolong his visit, and added that he himself would like to accompany Apuleius when he did resume his travels. He

[1] 'estate': *Apologia* 23. – Carthage: *Florida* 18, 35. The quotation is from *Flor.* 20, 41. – Athens: *Flor.* 18, 35 and 39; Apol. 72. – Samos: *Flor.* 15, 20. – Hierapolis: *de Mundo* 17.

[2] *Flor.* 20, 41; *Apol.* 72.

[3] Orfitus: *Flor.* 17, 31. – *Metamorphoses:* cf. now the interesting article by P. G. WALSH (on which see also p. 58f., n. 2, below).

urged that as Apuleius's illness would make it impossible to complete the journey that winter, he should wait for the following one. Clearly the intense heat of summer would make the journey out of the question other than during the winter months – and the sea journey was apparently avoided almost completely in antiquity. When Pontianus became very pressing Apuleius was able to persuade his hosts the Appii to let him stay with the Sicinii instead.

Pontianus's household consisted of his widowed mother Aemilia Pudentilla, and a younger brother Pudens – evidently a rather surly adolescent, who unlike Pontianus had had little opportunity or perhaps inclination for higher education. He was later alleged to speak virtually no Latin. His normal language was Punic, and he had been taught a little Greek by his mother. Even if this description of young Sicinius Pudens is somewhat exaggerated and prejudiced, it must surely indicate a state of affairs that was possible, even in a family of equestrian rank – with, perhaps, connections in the Senate. Pudens was only a few years older than Septimius from neighbouring Lepcis, who was said to have spoken fluent Punic.[1] Apuleius quickly made himself at home with the Sicinii, and the household settled down to a studious routine during his convalescence. As his health gradually improved, his friends persuaded him to give a public lecture. It took place in the town hall of Oea, the *basilica*, which was packed out for the occasion. The lecture was a rousing success – the audience shouted their approval with one voice (calls of *insigniter!*) and there were cries that Apuleius should stay at Oea and become a citizen of the town. When the audience had left, Pontianus put a proposition to Apuleius. 'This universal enthusiasm is a sign from heaven,' he said, and then revealed that he wanted Apuleius to marry his, Pontianus's, mother Pudentilla. 'You are the only friend I can rely on with complete trust and confidence.' He explained that his mother had many suitors. She was not a beautiful heiress, just a plain widow with children. But if Apuleius refused on this account, and wanted to reserve himself for a more attractive and wealthier match, he, Pontianus, would regard this attitude as

---

[1] On the characters involved, cf. e.g. the introduction to the edition by Butler and Owen (p. 59, n. 1, below), and now esp. J. GUEY (1954). – 'fluent Punic': *Epitome de Caes.* 20.8.

unworthy of a philsopher and a friend.[1] Pudentilla may not have been wealthy, but as Pontianus himself had pointed out, there were several men eager to marry her – and she had, in fact, an estate worth four million Sesterces.

After the death of her husband Sicinius Amicus some fourteen years previously her father-in-law, who had been made the guardian of the boys Pontianus and Pudens, was eager that she should marry another of his sons, Sicinius Clarus. Pudentilla was unwilling to marry her brother-in-law, but the old man threatened that if she married anyone else he would exclude his grandsons from their father's share of his property in his will. Pudentilla was thus more or less forced to comply, and became engaged to Clarus. However, she managed to put off the marriage, and it had still not taken place when the old man died, leaving Pontianus and Pudens as his heirs. No doubt as a result of the strain she was ill for some time, and was strongly urged to marry again for her health's sake before her elder son left home for good. He was by this time studying abroad. She refused to go through with the marriage to Clarus in spite of pressure from her late husband's other brother Aemilianus. But she was determined on a marriage of some kind, to protect herself, and she wrote to Pontianus, who by now had gone from Athens, to Rome, telling him so. He came back at once, in a hurry, determined to make sure that whoever was to be his stepfather, his own and his brother's inheritance would not be placed in jeopardy. It was at this juncture that Apuleius appeared at Oea.[2]

Apuleius had already spent a year or so with the Sicinii by the time that he became personally involved in the question of Pudentilla's remarriage. He had got to know her well. But his desire to continue his travels made him reluctant to tie himself down. However, once the thought entered his mind, he soon found – as he himself put it – that he was beginning to love Pudentilla. He agreed to become her husband. Pontianus had no difficulty in getting his mother to agree, and was all for arranging the ceremony at once. But Apuleius and Pudentilla persuaded him that they should not marry until Pontianus himself took a wife and his brother Pudens assumed the *toga* of manhood. Meanwhile

[1] *Apol.* 73.
[2] *Apol.* 68ff.

Pontianus was beginning the study of oratory under Apuleius's direction, and no doubt intended to go to Carthage to pursue this further. Apuleius continued to give public lectures, one of which was attended by the proconsul Lollianus Avitus, who was on a tour of duty in Tripolitania (during which he supervised improvements to the Theatre at Lepcis). Apuleius, who had probably met this eminent man when he had been at Rome, took the opportunity of recommending his future stepson to the proconsul. This would clearly be a useful advantage for Pontianus if he went to Carthage, where the proconsuls had their residence. Then came Pontianus's marriage and Pudens's entry into manly status, family events which were made public occasions by the high position of the Sicinii at Oea – which meant that a distribution of largesse was necessary. Pontianus married the daughter of one Herennius Rufinus, a man whose character Apuleius later presented in the blackest terms. At any rate, after his marriage Pontianus's attitude and behaviour towards Apuleius suddenly changed, and he now tried to prevent his mother from remarrying, evidently influenced by his father-in-law. Pontianus told his mother that Apuleius practised the black arts and had bewitched her into falling in love with him. Pudentilla wrote to him, attempting to calm him down:

> Since I determined to marry, for reasons that I explained to you, you yourself persuaded me to choose Apuleius as a husband in preference to all others, because you admired him and were eager that he should become a member of our family. But now that certain ill-disposed persons have accused us, and are persuading you against us, suddenly 'Apuleius is a magician', and I have been 'bewitched by him and love him'. Come to me then, while I am 'still in my senses'.

Pontianus and his wife, and Pudens, then returned to their mother's house, and stayed there for about two months.[1]

But then the marriage of Apuleius and Pudentilla finally took place, quietly, at her villa outside Oea. This course was chosen to escape the distribution of presents to the townspeople that had already been

---

[1] *Apol.* 74ff., esp. 82–3 and 87. – Theatre: *IRT* 533–5, cf. J. GUEY (1951b).

necessary, to the tune of 50,000 Sesterces, when Pontianus married.[1] At the same time the couple could avoid the round of dinner parties that were expected of newlyweds. But the ill feeling already generated was of course revived. It was felt by the rest of the family that Pontianus and Pudens would now lose their inheritance to the usurping stepfather. Apuleius persuaded Pudentilla to make over a substantial part of her late husband's property to her sons, in the shape of farms – to be valued at a low assessment – and from her personal property, lands, a large well-appointed house, a great quantity of wheat, barley, wine and oil, a large number of cattle, and four hundred slaves. This last item speaks more graphically than the others of the really substantial nature of the family's possessions. At the same time, urged by Apuleius, she gave them to understand that they had every prospect of inheriting the rest. Public opinion at Oea was won round by this gesture. Pontianus's father-in-law Rufinus was now criticised for setting son against mother, and Pontianus and Pudens came to ask for forgiveness. Besides this, Pontianus asked that Apuleius should explain the situation to Lollianus Avitus, for Apuleius had just written to the proconsul with an account of Pontianus's earlier behaviour, no doubt asking him to ignore the recommendation that he had made of the young man previously. Apuleius agreed, and gave Pontianus another letter to Avitus, to take to Carthage in person. Avitus was there awaiting the arrival of his successor, Claudius Maximus. This reconciliation must therefore have taken place in about May 158. Pontianus set off at once, and was favourably received. The proconsul congratulated him on mending his ways and gave him a reply to take back to Apuleius at Oea.[2]

But on his homeward journey Pontianus, who had been sending ahead letters written in the warmest tones to Apuleius, fell ill and died, evidently soon after his arrival at Oea. In his will he left everything to his mother and brother. The young widow, Rufinus's daughter, got nothing except some linen worth 800 Sesterces.[3] Herennius Rufinus

[1] *Apol.* 88, on which cf. T. KOTULA (1968), p. 118.

[2] *Apol.* 93–5. On the dates of Avitus's proconsulship, and of Apuleius's stay at Oea, cf. J. GUEY (1951b). On Avitus cf. also *PIR²* H 40. He was the patron of the father of the future Emperor Pertinax (p. 107, below).

[3] *Apol.* 96ff.

would clearly be incensed at the turn of events. His motives all along, quite obviously, had been to lay his hands on the estate of the Sicinii through the marriage connection. He now took steps to entice Pudens away from Apuleius, probably not a difficult task for there never seems to have been any affection between Apuleius and his younger stepson. Rufinus's daughter exerted her charms again, and Pudens left his mother's house a second time, moving to the house of his uncle Sicinius Aemilianus. Aemilianus must have been watching the turn of events with impotent rage. He was not the man to give in without a fight – some time previously he had contested the will of another member of his family (his own uncle), and the case had reached the court of the Prefect of Rome, Q. Lollius Urbicus. Urbicus had decided against him, on that occasion, and he had given an unfortunate exhibition of himself in the Prefect's presence – his violent insistence, in spite of the Prefect's verdict, that the will was a forgery, put him in danger of punishment for *calumnia*. Pudens, away from his mother's guidance, gave up going to school and spent his time drinking and going to the gladiatorial training establishment. Pudentilla fell ill again under the strain, and decided to make a new will disinheriting Pudens. But Apuleius dissuaded her.[1]

The change of proconsul in July 158 may have made Apuleius's enemies think they had a better chance than when Avitus, to whom Apuleius was known, was governing the province. Claudius Maximus, like his predecessor, came to Tripolitania and held assizes at Sabratha, probably in the autumn of 158. Apuleius attended the assizes himself, to appear in court on behalf of his wife in a case brought against her by the Granii brothers (about which no details are known: it was quite probably a dispute about the ownership of a piece of land, or something of that kind). Sicinius Aemilianus, brought forward by the Granii as a witness hostile to Apuleius, made a staggering assertion against him, accusing him of practising black magic to gain the hand of Pudentilla – and of murdering Pontianus. Apuleius challenged the accusation at once. His enemies realised that the proconsul viewed the charge with some suspicion, and decided to modify it. Four or five days later Apuleius was formally indicted on lesser charges: the principal

[1] *Apol.* 97–99. – Urbicus: *ib.* 2.

one was that he practised the black arts (which could be treated as a capital offence), and with it subsidiary charges that he was a dandy and a debauchee who had married an elderly woman simply to get her money. The charges were filed in the name of Sicinius Pudens, with his uncle Aemilianus merely listed as his 'representative'. An advocate, Tannonius Pudens, was engaged to present their case. Apuleius made his own defence, and the speech that he gave, no doubt considerably rewritten, survives as the *Apologia* – and of course, as the source of virtually all our information about the affair, makes it difficult not to judge the case from his viewpoint.[1]

Clearly Apuleius goes out of his way to blacken the characters of his opponents. It is more than likely that these people were not so bad as he paints them – and equally he himself may well have given genuine grounds for suspecting that he practised some kind of magic.[2] But one thing is certain. The speech is an authentic record from a trial that actually took place. It cannot be maintained, as some have been tempted to do, that it is another piece of fiction, in a more realistic vein, by the author of the fantastic *Golden Ass*. Apuleius may have been a novelist, among his other accomplishments, but he did not invent the characters in the trial at Sabratha. The names of most of the persons involved can be paralleled on contemporary inscriptions from Tripolitania.[3] The events described by Apuleius did indeed take place, even if his version is not necessarily the whole truth and nothing but the truth. For an account of provincial life 'with the lid off', the only rival to the *Apologia* is Cicero's *pro Cluentio*. Although Apuleius's enemies inevitably appear as relatively harmless in comparison with Cluentius's murderous persecutor Oppianicus, the fact that Apuleius's speech is the personal account of one side of the case gives it something extra that the *pro Cluentio*, for all Cicero's eloquence, lacks.

The speech cannot be summarised here, but it is impossible to resist the temptation to illustrate some of the details in it, for the vivid light

---

[1] *Apol.* 1. – Maximus: cf. A. R. BIRLEY (1966a), pp. 124ff.

[2] Cf. especially A. ABT. The arguments of L. HERRMANN that Apuleius was a crypto-Christian (and was attacked for this reason) are unconvincing: there would have been no point in concealing the attack, for one thing. See further p. 57f., below.

[3] Cf. esp. J. GUEY (1954).

that they cast on provincial life in Antonine Tripolitania. Among the documentary evidence produced by the prosecution, who had seized on every scrap or detail that could discredit Apuleius, were poems he had written, some of which were alleged to be obscene. Another was one to a certain Calpurnianus which had accompanied a special tooth-powder Apuleius had prepared at the latter's request – the much travelled sophist was clearly capable of turning his hand to many things. The prosecution naturally tried to put on this the connotation of mixing magic potions. At a later stage they produced the letter from Pudentilla to Pontianus, but quoted only the end of it, out of context: 'Apuleius is a magician and I have been bewitched by him and love him. Come to me then while I am still in my senses'. The accusation of black magic took various forms. Apuleius mocked his accusers – if he were really a magician, it was surely very reckless of them to attack him, for they would be putting themselves in danger of supernatural reprisals. He was said to have used a rare type of fish for magical purposes, to have hypnotised a young slave to make him prophesy in a trance, to have kept 'something mysterious' wrapped up in a linen cloth among the household goods at Pontianus's house, to have performed a nocturnal ceremony at someone else's house, and to have had a magic seal made. Apuleius answered the charges one by one, with evident relish. The fish were dissected for the purposes of scientific research. The slave was a sufferer from epilepsy. The objects covered with a cloth were connected with the Greek mystery-cult into which he had been initiated, and he appealed to fellow-initiates in court for confirmation of the necessity to remain silent about their nature. As for the 'nocturnal ceremonies', that was a pure invention, and the seal, allegedly of a skeleton, was in fact a statuette of Mercury, made for him quite openly by 'the craftsman Cornelius Saturninus, a man whose skill is famous among the townspeople and whose character is above reproach'.[1]

On the two latter charges Apuleius may well have been disingenuous. The 'nocturnal rites' were supposedly performed with his friend Appius Quintianus at the house of one Junius Crassus, which

---

[1] Cf. *Apol.* 6ff. (the poems). – The 'magic' charges are dealt with in 25–65: 29ff. (fish); 42ff. (slave boy); 53ff. (cloth); 57ff. (nocturnal rites); 61ff. (seal).

Quintianus was renting during Crassus's absence at Alexandria. Crassus did not appear in court and the prosecution produced his written testimony. Apuleius simply denies the charge and discredits the witness Crassus as a glutton and drunkard who had been bribed to invent the whole story. 'Why is Crassus not in court? I myself saw him here at Sabratha yesterday, Aemilianus, belching in your face ... I tell you that Crassus has long since been snoring in a drunken stupor, and has taken a second bath – or is now sweating out his drunkenness at the baths to be ready for a second binge after supper.' Or perhaps, he suggested, Aemilianus simply thought that the appearance of his witness, 'a young man with his face stripped of the beard and hair that ought to adorn it, his eyes heavy with wine, his eyelids swollen, his vacant grin, his slobbering lips, harsh voice, trembling hands, his breath reeking of the cookshop', would weaken the credibility of his sworn evidence. As for the seal, Apuleius sidesteps the charge, giving details of a statuette of Mercury, making it devastatingly obvious that it in no way resembles a skeleton and giving a detailed account of when and how it was made for him – but he does not really state unambiguously that his figure of Mercury is identical with the seal described by his accusers.[1]

After dealing with the accusations of magic he turns at last to the real issue, his marriage with Pudentilla. On specific questions he shows that the prosecution have concocted the evidence, for example in quoting only part of Pudentilla's letter (as already mentioned). Again, they had tried to prove that she was nearly sixty years old, whereas Apuleius demonstrated that she was twenty years younger than that. (As he himself was certainly over thirty the match would not then be at all unreasonable.) At this stage of the speech, having attacked the characters of Sicinius Aemilianus and his witness Junius Crassus already, he turned the full force of his invective on Herennius Rufinus, accusing him of being the prime mover in the conspiracy mounted against him. 'In his boyhood, before he became so hideously bald, he readily submitted to pederasts in every unspeakable way; as a young man he was a stage dancer ... except for his immorality he is said to have possessed none of the qualities of an actor.' Now that he is older,

[1] Cf. A. ABT, pp. 217 (291)ff., 222 (296)ff.

'his house is a home for pimps and the whole household is contaminated: his own character is disgusting, his wife is a prostitute, his sons are like their parents. . . . His wife was getting old and worn out and refused to go on supporting the whole family by her own actions' – so the daughter was then set to work, and seduced the affections of young Pontianus. This was good old-fashioned abuse.[1]

Apuleius's portrayal of Sicinius Aemilianus was couched in very different terms, obviously intended to be equally damaging, but bringing out aspects of the man's character and habits that have provoked an ingenious theory. He derides the man's show of austerity and his boorish disapproval of erotic verse. In a long passage he points out that Aemilianus has ample scope for criticising him, for he lives his life in the public gaze, whereas Aemilianus himself lives in obscurity, and hence 'you have the advantage of one who, while he himself is shrouded in darkness, surveys another who chances to have taken his stand in the full light of the day'. In the course of defending himself on the charge of the objects wrapped in the linen cloth, Apuleius contrasts his own religious piety with the total lack of interest in religion displayed by Aemilianus; who thinks it

a good joke to mock at things divine. For I learn from certain men of Oea who know him, that to this day he has never prayed to any god or frequented any temple. And if he happens to pass any shrine, he regards it as a crime to raise his hand to his lips in token of reverence. He has never given first fruits of crops or vines or flocks to any of the gods of the farmer, who feed him and clothe him; his farm holds no shrine, no holy place, nor grove. But why do I speak of groves or shrines? Those who have been on his property say they have never seen there one stone where an offering of oil has been made, one bough where wreaths have been hung.

The combination of an austere character with an unmistakable lack of traditional pagan piety might not in themselves be enough to convince one that Aemilianus was a secret Christian. But one little point suggests that he was, and that Apuleius knew it: in his description of Aemili-

---

[1] The marriage: 66ff. – Rufinus: 74ff.

anus's secluded way of life he uses the word *lucifugus* – 'shunning the light of day', the very expression used about the Christians in the *Octavius* of Minucius Felix, where they are described as a *latebrosa et lucifuga natio*. Besides this, the description in Minucius Felix of the Christians' refusal to pay their tribute to the shrines of the gods closely matches Apuleius's description of the behaviour of Aemilianus.[1]

Throughout his defence Apuleius played on his philosophical and literary expertise, in a manner calculated to win the respect and admiration of the proconsul. Claudius Maximus was one of the personal friends of the Caesar, Marcus Aurelius, and had a reputation as a philosopher. Apuleius claims Maximus as a fellow-authority on and admirer of Plato and Aristotle. He praises his patience in listening to his opponents' long-winded accusations, and his acuteness in cross-examination of their witnesses. Whatever Maximus's private opinions of the flamboyant orator, there seems little doubt that Apuleius's defence was successful.[2] Some time later he was chosen for the great

---

[1] 'Austerity', etc.: 10, cf. 66. – 'obscurity': 16. – lack of piety: 56. – *'lucifugus'*: *cum ipse humilitate abdita et lucifuga non sis mihi mutuo conspicuus (16)*. Cf. *Octavius* 8.4: *latebrosa et lucifuga natio, in publicum muta, in angulis garrula: templa, deos despuunt, rident sacra*, etc. Cf. *ib.* 10.2. The hypothesis here followed was put forward by E. GRISET (note however that that scholar erroneously describes Aemilianus as a native of Sabratha instead of Oea). It is unnecessary, with Griset, to re-date the *Octavius* to the 150s (rather than fifty or so years later). It is sufficient to recall that that work incorporates material from precisely this time, namely the anti-Christian writings of Cornelius Fronto (*Oct.* 9). Further than this one cannot really go: 'the origin of the African church is one of great "missing links" in Church History' (W. H. C. FREND, p. 361). But one thing should be noted, which might corroborate, very slightly, Griset's ingenious theory. L. Aemilius Frontinus, a senator from Oea (*IRT* 230) is plausibly regarded by J. GUEY (1954), pp. 115ff., as a kinsman of Aemilia Pudentilla. By the same token, Pudentilla herself was probably related to the Sicinii (before her first marriage), as the name Sicinius Aemilianus suggests. Now Frontinus is presumably the proconsul of Asia in the early 180s. That person is recorded by Eusebius (*H.E.* 5.18.9): a criminal named Alexander who came up for trial before him was released after 'falsely claiming the name of the Lord, having deceived the Christians there.' This suggests at least sympathy for Christianity in a representative of the Tripolitanian upper classes.

[2] *Apol.* 11, 25, 36, 38, 41, etc.; 35; 48. – It is not impossible that Maximus is the proconsul 'Tiberius' who, according to Tertullian (*Apologeticus* 9) suppressed the sacrifice of infants in the worship of Saturn (i.e. Ba'al Hammon): *infantes penes Africam Saturno immolabantur palam usque ad proconsulatum Tiberii, qui eosdem*

honour of serving as chairman of the provincial council with the title
'High priest of the province'. He is found at Carthage in the 160s,
highly honoured both by the people of that city and by the proconsuls.[1]

If any excuse were needed for introducing this account of Apuleius
at Oea and Sabratha into a biography of Septimius Severus, it need only
be stated once more that for the thirteen-year old Lepcitane boy the
trial at Sabratha must have represented one of the most striking events
of his youth. Connections between the three cities were close. It may
even be that the Granii brothers, whose lawsuit with Pudentilla provided the original opportunity for the attack on Apuleius, were men of
Lepcis.[2] Sicinius Pudens, that unprepossessing youth from Oea who
was Septimius Severus's near contemporary, may be the same as the
Pudens who half a century later composed a curious inscription in
honour of Septimius as Emperor, in gratitude for the advancement in
rank of his son, no doubt the same as the senator Q. Sicinius Clarus
Pontianus found governing the province of Thrace in the year 202.[3]
At all events, it would be curious indeed – though there is no means of

---

sacerdotes . . . crucibus exposuit, teste militia patriae nostrae. Claudius Maximus is,
as it happens, the only known proconsul of Africa (before Tertullian wrote) who
is likely to have had the *praenomen* Tiberius. G. CHARLES-PICARD (1954),
pp. 132ff., argues that the affair belongs precisely *'vers le milieu du IIe siècle'*. It is
just conceivable that Tertullian deliberately referred to the proconsul by his
praenomen, to avoid reminding his readers of Apuleius's *Apologia*, which the name
Claudius Maximus would have instantly evoked. Further, on the hypothesis that
Maximus is the same as the proconsul Tiberius, it could be argued that Apuleius's
opponents, knowing his active hostility to magical practices, may have hoped for an
especially sympathetic hearing at his tribunal. – P. G. WALSH, in an article
published in 1968 (but which unfortunately does not take Griset's hypothesis into
consideration) puts forward the interesting theory that the last part of the *Metamorphoses*, was an addition, from Apuleius's maturer years, to an originally light-
hearted romance; and that the strong religious (specifically Isiac) feelings there
shown might even have been intended as a deliberate counter to the growing
appeal of Christianity.

[1] Augustine, *Ep.* 138.19; *Florida* 9, 16, 17, 18, 20. – On the *Apologia* in general,
cf. in addition to A. ABT, the article by R. HELM, the edition by H. E. Butler and
A. S. Owen (1914), with introduction and notes, and the (slightly bowdlerised)
translation by H. E. Butler (1909).

[2] Cf. *IRT* 532, 642, 708–9 (Lepcis); and J. GUEY (1954), pp. 115ff.

[3] *IRT* 295, cf. J. GUEY (1952), pp. 25ff.; also *L'Albo* no. 479+Agg.

proof – if the Septimii, from whose ranks the lawyer friend of Statius had come, failed to take note of this *cause célèbre*, worthy indeed of the province of Africa, *nutricula causidicorum*. Septimius himself would have the chance of hearing Apuleius at Carthage within a few years, if he had not already done so when the great man was in Tripolitania – and Septimius was then to plead his own case in court also, although in an altogether less exciting and brilliant affair.[1]

It is time to return to the Septimii of Lepcis. By the 150s they had reached the heights of social eminence. Septimius's 'uncle' Aper was consul in 153. Meanwhile the other 'uncle' C. Septimius Severus commanded a legion in Syria, XVI Flavia Firma, and went on to govern the province of Lycia-Pamphylia. Between these two posts, or during his legionary command, he acquired some social distinction of no mean order, being co-opted into two priesthoods, the *sodales Hadrianales*, whose concern was the cult of the deified Hadrian, and the *quindecimviri sacris faciundis*. This latter body of men constituted, with the *pontifices*, augurs and *septemviri epulonum*, one of the four leading priesthoods of the Roman state, with the task of supervising consultation of the Sibylline books and, when occasion demanded, as it did only infrequently, of supervising Saecular Games. In spite of the legionary command, this Severus was probably not the most military of men, and certainly the Syrian army in the 150s was unwarlike in the extreme – when war broke out in 161 events were to demonstrate this. The soldiers stationed at Antioch, at least, used to spend more time lounging at tables in open-air cafés than with their units. The troopers had padded saddles. Gambling and heavy drinking were rife in the camps. The men of the XVIth at Samosata were probably not much better.[2]

Few details are recorded of the boyhood of Septimius Severus. It is said that his favourite game was 'judges', and that he himself would make his playmates act the part of lictors, carrying the bundles of rods and axes in front of him, while he took the role of the Roman magistrate. Of course his schooling is referred to – prowess in both Latin and

---

[1] Cf. p. 79, below. – Juvenal 7.148.
[2] Cf. App. 1. – Syrian army: A. R. BIRLEY (1966a), p. 173, citing Fronto *ad Verum Imp.* 2.1.19–20=Haines II 128ff., esp. 148ff.

Greek is mentioned in the Augustan History. Another late source speaks of his fluency in Punic. There is no real means of telling. One may accept the judgment of his contemporary Cassius Dio, who recalled that Septimius had been eager for more education than he actually got.[1] At the age of seventeen, in 162, he gave a speech, or declamation, in public, no doubt in his home town Lepcis. This marked the end of his formal schooling. His brother Geta had very probably already left Lepcis for the start of an official career. After serving as *decemvir stlitibus iudicandis*, one of the posts in the vigintivirate, he gained a commission as the senatorial tribune of the legion II Augusta in Britain. There was warfare in Britain at this time, and the governor, Sex. Calpurnius Agricola, very probably himself from Africa, may have been persuaded by some mutual acquaintance to give Geta the appointment.[2]

The Empire was now in a state of ferment. The old Emperor Antoninus Pius had died on 7 March 161, and his two adopted sons succeeded him jointly as M. Aurelius Antoninus and L. Aurelius Verus. The omens were good – and the birth of twins to the wife of M. Aurelius in August 161 seemed to confirm the augury. But in fact disaster threatened. The long Antonine peace was shattered on the eastern frontiers, the northern barbarians were threatening, and there was trouble in Britain. But these troubles may have seemed very remote to a young man with his way in the world to make. Soon after his formal speech at Lepcis, Septimius set out for Rome, 'to study'.[3]

It is appropriate to look back briefly at this moment, to assess the influence that his Lepcitane background must have had on him. In most respects he would be a typical representative of the provincial aristocracy, a member of one of the leading families in one of the principal

[1] 'Judges':*HA Sev.* 1.4, accepted by J. HASEBROEK (1921), p. 3f. – Education: *ib.*: *'Latinis Graecisque litteris . . . quibus eruditissimus fuit.'* *Epit. de Caes.* 20.8: *'Latinis litteris sufficienter instructus, Graecis sermonibus eruditus, Punica eloquentia promptior'.* Dio 76.16.1 (on which see below, p. 228f.).

[2] *HA Sev.* 1.5: *'octavo decimo anno publice declamavit'*, cf. J. HASEBROEK (1921), p. 4. – Geta: App. 1. – Agricola: A. R. BIRLEY (1967b), p. 73f.: perhaps a relative of Fronto's friend Calpurnius Julianus.

[3] Cf. A. R. BIRLEY (1966a), pp. 52ff. *HA Sev.* 15: *postea studiorum causa Romam venit.*

towns of a wealthy province. Lepcis Magna had long had the outward appearance of a thoroughly Roman city. It had had a theatre for more than a hundred and fifty years, an amphitheatre for more than a century. Now, in the very year that Septimius probably left for Rome (162), it acquired its own Circus, a large and imposing structure on the eastern side of the city, close to the shore. The ancestral Punic gods of course retained their place. Melqart and Shadrapa, the joint patrons of Lepcis, had become Hercules and Liber (or Bacchus). As Apuleius's speech would suggest, the Lepcitanes, like all Africans, were perhaps more openly superstitious than their counterparts in, say, Nemausus. The dazzling clarity of the North African night sky might well be expected to have inspired faith in astrology.[1] The streets of Lepcis were liberally adorned with phallic symbols. Not a sign of excessive sexual indulgence by the Lepcitanes. They were put there to ward off the evil eye. Nothing is known about Septimius's sex life as a youth. At the age of twenty-three he was to be accused of adultery. He was not to marry until he was thirty or thereabouts. It is not impossible that he had homosexual leanings, although the evidence is weak: Herodian alleges that Septimius was at one time in love with his kinsman Fulvius Plautianus. Certainly Plautianus later had an uncanny hold over Septimius. But it is only too easy to see why this particular story would have been invented.[2]

The muddled Antiochene chronicler John Malalas, writing four centuries later, says that Septimius was dark-skinned. There is not much chance of verifying this statement now (although one colour portrait has survived). But he also says that he had a long nose, which is definitely false. The later portraits show him with a short, slightly turned-up nose. His hair seems to have been naturally curly. Later he would grow a beard, as was still the fashion, not as long as some wore it. He was a small man, but powerful and energetic. The portraits sometimes give an idea of this energy: the eyes look

[1] In general, cf. D. E. L. HAYNES, pp. 71ff. – Amphitheatre and circus are now dated, cf. G. DI VITA-ÉVRARD (1965). – Melqart and Shadrapa: G. CHARLES-PICARD (1954), pp. 94ff., 127f.
[2] Phallic symbols: E. VERGARA CAFFARELLI, p. 111; G. CHARLES-PICARD (1959a), p. 285. – Adultery: see p. 79, below. – Plautianus: Herodian 3.10.6, cf. p. 235, below.

keen and searching. But sometimes also he appears brooding and abstracted.[1]

The Augustan History says that his voice was tuneful, but that 'he retained a trace of an African accent into old age'. The information may be invented. But it is at least plausible that he had an African accent. Occasional mentions in later writers provide some idea of what this accent was. The Africans dropped their aitches and mispronounced the letter L. They tended to lengthen short syllables at the beginning of words. Whether this was the product of Punic influence, and whether for the same reason they made a whistling noise over certain letters, is another matter. There is no real evidence. Septimius's sister Octavilla was later said, perhaps falsely, to have scarcely been able to speak Latin. But there is no doubt that Septimius himself, accent or not, was completely fluent. The African accent was a provincial Roman accent, not a foreign accent.[2]

[1] Malalas 12, p. 291. – 'Portrait': K. A. NEUGEBAUER (the skin appears suntanned). Cf. now A. M. McCANN for a full survey of the iconography.

[2] *HA Sev.* 18.9: '*canorus voce, sed Afrum quiddam usque ad senectutem sonans*', a much cited passage. – On the African accent, cf. P. MONCEAUX, pp. 185ff. – 'dropped aitches': Augustine, *Confess.* 1.18. – 'Letter L': Isidore, *Origines* 1.31.8; Pompeius Maurus, *Grammat. Lat.* (Keil), p. 286. – 'lengthening': Consentius, *Grammat. Lat.* (Keil), p. 392. – Octavilla:*HA Sev.* 15.7: '*vix Latine loquens*' (also much cited). Cf. p. 204, below. – Monceaux cites Jerome *Ep.* 103.5 for the view that Africans made a 'whistling' sound when they spoke Latin. But the *stridor Punicus* mentioned by Jerome could well mean Punic and not Latin with a Punic accent.

V

THE BROAD STRIPE

The Rome that the young Septimius came to in the early 160s must have been an exciting place, with an atmosphere of urgency. The long calm of Antoninus Pius's twenty-three years' rule had ended virtually at the moment when the dying Emperor breathed the watchword to the officer of the guard for the last time: 'Equanimity'. In his last moments Pius had spoken only of the foreign kings that angered him. His adopted sons had scarcely had time to grasp the reins of power before those foreign kings gave real cause for anger. They provoked a frontier incident on the Upper Euphrates. It was blown up into a major war by the rash response of the governor of Cappadocia, Sedatius Severianus. The governor found himself trapped with inadequate forces. A legion was wiped out, and Severianus committed suicide. The governor of Syria, Attidius Cornelianus, had the clear duty of preserving calm and maintaining Roman defences. But he was defeated by a Parthian force, and put to flight. The Syrian legions were all too obviously in a poor state of preparedness. C. Septimius Severus, who had commanded one of them a few years before, must have had a keen personal interest in the course of events. His brother Septimius Aper must also have been disturbed more than most by what had happened, for Sedatius Severianus had been his colleague in the consulship in the summer of 153. Severus had gone on from his own consulship a few years later to govern one of the German provinces. Here too there was trouble for Rome, and it may well be that he was directly on the receiving end of the assault, which was launched on the Upper German province.[1]

Marcus Aurelius had to take rapid action on a variety of fronts. His brother Lucius Verus was to go to the east. In late 162 he arrived in

[1] A. R. BIRLEY (1966a), pp. 149ff. – the kinsmen: App. 1.

Asia Minor after a somewhat leisurely journey. In the meanwhile one of the outstanding generals of the day, Statius Priscus, had been appointed to take over Cappadocia and the war in Armenia. He had only just been sent to govern Britain, where the situation was also disturbed, and he had to be replaced there. The man chosen was Calpurnius Agricola. At the same time one of Marcus's closest friends, Aufidius Victorinus, son-in-law of his former tutor Fronto, was made governor of Upper Germany, to cope with the German invasion. These changes at the highest level of command were only part of a whole series of transfers, promotions and new appointments that were being put through when Septimius arrived in Rome. A change of Emperor would in the normal course of events have brought some such measures in its train. But as Marcus had been sharing in some of Pius's power since as far back as the winter of 147, a real continuity in the administration would have been perfectly possible this time. As it turned out, the military crisis made a whole series of drastic changes necessary.[1]

Men from Africa soon came to the fore. Two compatriots of the orator Fronto are found playing an active role in the east. Geminius Marcianus of Cirta, commanding the legion X Gemina at Vindobona (Vienna) was directed to take reinforcements from the Danubian armies to the war. Antistius Adventus of Thibilis, already in the east in command of the legion VI Ferrata in Palestine, took over the Aquincum (Budapest) legion II Adiutrix when it arrived at the front. The new governor of Britain, Calpurnius Agricola, was probably also from Numidia. But the wars which were to occupy the entire reign of Marcus Aurelius saw men from virtually every province in the Empire, as well as Italians, some of lowly origin, taking a prominent role. Statius Priscus, who won the first Roman victories in the east, and Pontius Laelianus, who seems to have acted as chief of staff to Lucius Verus at the beginning of the war, were both natives of Italy. Avidius Cassius, who won the final victories in the east, was a native of Syria, likewise Claudius Pompeianus, who played a leading role in the northern wars. A general who played a distinguished role on both the

---

[1] A. R. BIRLEY (1966a), pp. 165ff. – Priscus and Agricola: A. R. BIRLEY (1967b), p. 73f. – Victorinus: G. ALFÖLDY, *Reichsbeamte*, pp. 38ff. – 'winter of 147': *Inscriptiones Italiae* XIII.1, p. 207.

Euphrates and the Danube, Claudius Fronto, came from proconsular Asia. Two men from western provinces prominent in high commands were Martius Verus and Julius Verus, from Gaul and Dalmatia respectively. One of the Praetorian Prefects, Macrinius Vindex, and his son who held high positions as a senator, were from the north-west, from Cologne in Lower Germany, or possibly from Colchester in Britain. Valerius Maximianus, who had a meteoric military career, was Pannonian.[1]

But when the imperial dynasty was itself provincial in origin, and so firmly entrenched, this was in no way surprising. Trajan and Hadrian sprang from colonial families that had been settled in Spain for hundreds of years. Trajan's wife Plotina came from Nemausus (Nîmes) in Gaul, the home of Antoninus Pius's ancestors. Marcus himself, nephew by marriage of Pius, and thus linked with the Gallic provincial aristocracy, was from another Spanish colonial family, although his grandfather had married into the most blue-blooded Italian nobility. Leading men from North Africa, as has been seen, had begun to rise to prominence even before Trajan's accession, and Trajan and Hadrian played a large part in promoting the wealthy men from the Greek-speaking provinces also to positions to power and influence. The long and peaceful reign of Pius had allowed the rise of the provincials to proceed gently and unobtrusively, if with little encouragement from Pius himself. When it ended, and the Antonine peace suddenly broke up, it was entirely natural that men from all over the Empire should be selected to take a leading part in the defence. Some of these outstanding provincials were of Italian immigrant descent. Others, such as Avidius Cassius and Claudius Pompeianus, were descendants of men who had received the Roman franchise from Emperors or governors.[2]

---

[1] Marcianus: cf. now *PIR*[2] J 344, A. R. BIRLEY (1968b), p. 220 and n. 23. – Adventus: ID., p. 219f. (and *PIR*[2] A 754). – Laelianus: *RE* 22 (1953) 39. Cf. G. ALFÖLDY (1967), p. 28, who argues that he was from Baeterrae in Narbonensis. – Cassius: *PIR*[2] A 1402. – Pompeianus: *PIR*[2] C 973. – Fronto: *PIR*[2] C 874. – Martius Verus: G. ALFÖLDY, *Senat*, p. 147, citing *CIL* XIII 5690, 186 and 2503. – Julius Verus: *PIR*[2] J. 618. – Vindex: *CP* nos. 161, 188+*add*. – Maximianus: *CP* no. 181 *bis*+*add*.

[2] Cf. above all Sir R. SYME (1958), esp. 585ff., 598ff. Note his comment,

Thus it would be entirely mistaken to view the arrival of the young Septimius at Rome, seeking senatorial rank early in the reign of Marcus, as anything but entirely normal. On the contrary, with two close kinsmen who had already served as consul, and an elder brother already started on a senatorial career, it would have been strange if he himself had opted out. The broad purple stripe of senatorial rank, which, according to Statius, his grandfather could have had for the asking, was granted him by Marcus at the request of C. Septimius Severus.[1]

But Septimius gained thereby no guarantee of an outstanding career. The new Emperor had only one criterion in making appointments, merit. There is no sign that Septimius ever really made his mark at the beginning of his career. He could not of course enter the Senate, as quaestor, until he had passed his twenty-fourth birthday, which would be in April 169. But one might have expected that he would obtain a commission as tribune with a legion. At latest by the summer of 164, when he reached his twentieth year, he may have hoped for such a post. He may perhaps, with the support of his kinsmen, have canvassed for a tribunate by letter or through intermediaries. But C. Septimius Severus cannot have been in a position to exert much influence. Although it is not absolutely certain when he had governed his German province, he was clearly not judged a success, for no further military commands were assigned to him. He might of course have been ill, or unwilling. But a man who had commanded a Syrian legion and the two-legion army of one of the Germanies should have been a suitable person to play an active part in the wars. It could well be that he had been the immediate predecessor of Victorinus in Upper Germany and that he had been dismissed for incompetence. It may be noted that he himself had not served as military tribune in his youth, and one may

---

p. 168: 'In the estimate of their personality as men and emperors, zealous speculation has run riot with the supposed influences of race and blood, of soil and landscape. . . . It is all vanity. The things that matter are education and national spirit, wealth and energy and rank.' (The reference is to the dynasty created by Trajan and Hadrian.)

[1] *HA Sev.* 1.5, cf. A. R. BIRLEY, *HAC*, p. 670f.

suspect that his talents were in no way adapted for military command in war.[1]

However this may be, Septimius 'omitted the military tribunate', in the laconic phrase of the Augustan History, derived ultimately perhaps from his autobiography. His brother Geta did obtain a tribunate. He went to the legion II Augusta in Britain. The legion was based at Isca (Caerleon), but in the 160s, when Geta was there, it will undoubtedly have operated for much of the time in the north of the province. It seems likelier, although there is no real proof either way, that Geta was the elder of the two brothers. In that case, it would be reasonable to assume that he was in Britain with Calpurnius Agricola. This is the first, admittedly very tenuous, link that can be established between the Septimii and men from the western region of proconsular Africa, Numidia. Geta's military service in Britain is important in two other ways for his brother's future. There is a strong possibility that he became acquainted with Helvius Pertinax in that province, for the latter served in two posts there in the 160s. Geta's experience in Britain can hardly fail to have made an impact on him, and when he next saw his brother he must have given him some account of the province. It is important to recognise that Calpurnius Agricola's governorship was a time of considerable military activity. But this activity was entirely devoted to strengthening and refurbishing Hadrian's Wall and its hinterland. Any hopes of reoccupying southern Scotland after its abandonment in the mid-150s had been emphatically given up: *tunc necessaria gloriosis praeposita*. Not all the men on the spot may have accepted or approved the necessity. Events in Britain in the 160s have a bearing on Septimius's own campaigns there forty years later.[2]

---

[1] 'Twenty-fourth birthday': Sir R. SYME (1958), p. 652; J. MORRIS (1964), p. 317. – Military tribunate: see p. 69 and n. 1, below. – C. Septimius Severus: App. 1.

[2] *HA Sev.* 2.2: *'omisso tribunatu militari'*. These words are restored by conjecture, but there can be no doubt about them. The statement conflicts with Eutropius 8.8 and Victor *de Caes* 20.28, 30 (whence *HA Carac.* 8.3, *Get.* 2.4). On this problem cf. App. 1, note to no. 29. – Geta: App. 1, no. 30. – Pertinax: p. 109f., below. – Agricola: J. P. GILLAM (1953), cf. E. BIRLEY (1961), p. 249f. The quotation is from Velleius Paterculus 2.110 (referring to 6). See also p. 245 and n. 2, below.

Septimius's omission of a tribunate may have been his own choice. But even if he tried unsuccessfully for a tribunate, this is not surprising. Although there were more legions, each with one vacancy, than the twenty candidates who might seek a commission every year, other factors complicated the picture. Some young men with inclination or aptitude, or with influential relatives or patrons, served for more than one season and sometimes in more than one legion. Such cases must have been especially frequent when there was warfare on several fronts. The young *tribunus laticlavius* had little real responsibility in practice (although in theory he was second in command of the legion). But in time of war too frequent changes of personnel must have been unwelcome to those in command. And, after all, when the fighting was fierce, the death of a general might make it necessary for the tribune to assume *de facto* his latent powers as deputy-legate.[1]

Geta had gone to Britain after the normal mandatory year in the vigintivirate at Rome. In his case, as one of the *decemviri stlitibus iudicandis*, who as their name indicates formed exactly half of the twenty young men thus designated as potential senators each year. No sign from this that he was singled out as either an especially promising or an especially weak aspirant for high office or command. The Augustan History biographer does not record any post in the vigintivirate at all for Septimius. This silence, combined with a confused story elsewhere about his early career, has led to the view that he did not occupy any such post. This assumption is unjustified. One may be confident that soon after his arrival in Rome in 162 or 163, Septimius did spend a year as a *vigintivir*, either as *decemvir* like his brother, with duties in the courts, or in one of the other three groups. He may have been a *triumvir capitalis* or a *quattuorvir viarum curandarum*. But he will hardly have been a *triumvir monetalis*, to judge from his background and later career. This function, involving its three holders in some titular authority over the workings of the mint, was reserved in the first instance for patricians. Other vacancies went to plebeians with powerful patrons and obvious potential for future high command. It is

---

[1] On the tribunate cf. above all E. BIRLEY (1953b), p. 200. – '*de facto*': a contemporary example is D. 8834a (cf. *RE* 1A [1914], 1125); a later one is D. 1188 (cf. G. ALFÖLDY [1967], pp. 61ff.).

perhaps not very likely either that he became a *quattuorvir*, with the task of supervising the streets of the capital, although C. Septimius Severus had held this post in his youth. The *quattuorviri* tended, like the plebeian *monetales*, to be young men marked out as future generals. It is after all statistically most likely that he was *decemvir* like his brother and it is really pointless to speculate further. But one cannot exclude the possibility that he began his career as a *triumvir capitalis*. This board of three had the unattractive task of presiding over executions, among other duties. Analysis of the careers of men who began their public life in this post shows that only a handful ever attained distinction – and these exceptions can be explained by the working of special circumstances. Indeed, the conclusion is inescapable that the *triumviri capitales* in any given year were generally those future Senators deemed least likely to succeed. This aspect of the post cannot have failed to escape notice. A *capitalis* was very likely regarded as a dud. Had Septimius been one, he would doubtless have passed discreetly over that inauspicious opening to his career in his autobiography. And the author of the Augustan History did not find any other evidence to supply the gap in his knowledge.[1]

164 seems the most likely year for Septimius to have served as a *vigintivir*. His formal duties must inevitably have brought him into touch with the leading men in Rome to some limited degree. But even the granting to him of the *latus clavus* on his arrival at Rome in 162 would already have placed him on the threshold of public life. The *laticlavii* from the time of Augustus had been encouraged to attend sessions of the Senate, to gain experience. In his early years Septimius must have forged contacts with some of the men who would later play an important part in the fateful year 193. It is reasonable to guess that during this period in Rome he may first have met two men from Spain, Cornelius Anullinus and Fabius Cilo. Anullinus, ten years or more his senior, was from Iliberris (Granada) and Cilo, a year or two younger than Septimius, came from Iluro in the same region. Anullinus must have become praetor in 163 or soon after. Septimius may also have met

---

[1] The vigintivirate was mandatory, cf. J. MORRIS (1965), p. 24, citing Tacitus, *Annals* 3.29. On different types of XXviri: E. BIRLEY (1953b), pp. 201ff. On their token duties: *RE* 8A (1958) 2570ff.

his near contemporary Clodius Albinus from Hadrumetum in pro-
consular Africa, and Pescennius Niger, an Italian of equestrian family.
Much senior to Septimius and with connections at the palace was
Didius Julianus, a man of Milanese family, whose mother came from
Hadrumetum and was a close relation of the great jurist Salvius
Julianus.[1]

Consideration of what senators and men of influence the young
Septimius may have met can only be speculative at best. But it is
valuable to bear in mind the men that he could have come to know at
this time. The letters of the younger Pliny show how Pliny himself in
his youth relied on his links with the great men of the day, and then, as
he climbed higher in the ladder of office, exerted his influence to
further the careers of his protégés at all levels. Such was the normal
duty of a Roman senator. In the case of Septimius the direct evidence
is lacking. The Pliny of the Antonine age, Cornelius Fronto, was still
alive and flourishing when Septimius came to Rome. Some of his
correspondence with his friends – and with his imperial pupils – has
been preserved, and this must be glanced at presently for the light it
throws on Rome in the 160s.[2]

But first, mention must be made of the only information which has
been preserved about Septimius's life at this time – the omens which
gave him hopes of future greatness. In his autobiography he recorded
numerous curious episodes and dreams which at various stages in his
life led him to hope that he would become emperor. Some were even
depicted in works of art after events had seemed to prove their accuracy.
The Augustan History has several anecdotes, some of which – perhaps
all – derive from Septimius's own account. Cassius Dio likewise
includes a number in his History. Dio was to show himself to be, like
Septimius, a fervent believer in the veracity of omens and signs of all
kinds that could foretell future events. Soon after Septimius's accession he wrote his first historical work, an account 'of the dreams and
omens that caused Severus to hope for the imperial power'. It is all too

---

[1] Anullinus and Cilo: App. iii. – Albinus: G. ALFÖLDY (1968). – Niger: *RE*
19 (1937) 1086ff. – Julianus: H. G. PFLAUM (1966), pp. 6off.

[2] Pliny: cf. Sir R. SYME (1958), pp. 75ff. – 'careers of protégés': cf. e.g. *Ep.*
1.14, 1.24, 2.13, 3.2, 4.4, 4.15, etc.; and some fifteen of those in Bk. 10. – Fronto:
cf. esp. H. G. PFLAUM (1964).

easy to suppose that the omens in question were only seen to be significant when what they foretold had already been fulfilled. It is more instructive to reflect that Septimius was only one of numerous senators who convinced themselves with varying degrees of fervour that supernatural powers were showing them signs of future eminence. The age was highly superstitious. Even the Emperor Marcus, with his lofty rationalising Stoic beliefs, was to show that he was not altogether free from this kind of faith in the power of the irrational. Belief in and practice of astrology was on the increase and Septimius was a prominent addict. But it was not new for men of his class to be so affected – had not Hadrian been a devotee? It had already misled many as well as giving dramatic evidence of its validity to a few. In other times its practice was feared and suppressed by the authorities. In the reign of Marcus a man could indulge his belief in omens and consult an astrologer about his future without exciting tyrannical reprisals.[1]

At the moment when Septimius first set foot in Rome, his host at the house where he was to stay happened to be reading the life of the Emperor Hadrian – and he will have been reading aloud as was then the custom. The young man may have decided in advance that he would take as an omen the first words that he heard spoken in the city of Rome. It is easy to guess at some particular phrase that he may have heard that could have given him special hope. But it must be conceded that the Augustan History biographer would have found it easy and perhaps amusing to invent this particular story, to embellish his work. This note of caution must apply to all the omens that he supplies which are otherwise unattested. With stories of this kind it does not perhaps matter too much one way or the other. But it would be unwise to neglect those that are authenticated by Cassius Dio. Their historical importance is small – they merely add a little colour. But they do exemplify a salient feature of Septimius's character, his extreme superstition. The biographer gives a group of four other such omens, only two of which are found in Dio. The first, if authentic, would neatly

---

[1] Dio 72.23.1 – On Septimius's superstition: F. H. CRAMER, pp. 208ff.
– Marcus: generally rational to a degree, but note the influence of Alexander of Abonuteichus and the Arnouphis affair (A. R. BIRLEY [1966a], pp. 223f., 237ff.).
– Hadrian: cf. e.g. *HA Had.* 16.7 (and 2.4), and, generally, Cramer, pp. 162ff.

illustrate how the young *laticlavius* was being prepared for public life. He was invited to dine at the palace, and came incorrectly dressed, wearing the *pallium* or Greek cloak instead of the formal toga. To remedy his mistake one of the Emperor's togas was given him. This may simply be a literary invention, designed to introduce the next omen, which Dio also records. The same night, after the banquet (Dio does not have this detail), Septimius had a dream, in which he was sucking the teats of a she-wolf, like Romulus. Dio sets this dream at the time 'when he was enrolled into the Senate'. The context of the story in the Augustan History would place it earlier, and it may be that Dio's phrase should be understood as referring to the award to the *latus clavus*. The third omen, also found in Dio, is not specifically assigned to this same occasion in the Augustan History, although it might well have occurred at the same banquet. One of the Emperor's servants inadvertently offered the imperial chair to Septimius, who promptly sat down on it, 'not knowing that this was not permitted'. The Augustan History rounds off the account with the story that 'once when he was asleep in a stable a snake wound itself round his head. The members of the household were alarmed and shouted, and the creature went away without harming him'.[1]

However ill-informed about Septimius's life in these years we may be it is fair to assume that he had already displayed in these early years something of the characteristics or traits of personality that impressed Dio and Herodian later. Dio describes him as small but physically powerful, a man of few words but with an active and original mind. Herodian speaks of him as a born administrator, a man of great energy who was used to living under rough conditions and was capable of hard physical effort, quick to understand a problem and take action on it immediately. The Augustan History's character-sketch, including plausible details about his tastes in food and his African accent, betrays itself by the allegation that he was 'huge' in stature. Dio, who saw him many times, will hardly have distorted the truth to say the opposite of this. Thus the story that he had an African accent may

---

[1] *HA Sev.* 16. – 'Reading aloud': cf. Augustine *Confessions* 6.3.3 (his surprise that Ambrose read silently). – 'four other omens': *HA Sev.* 1.7–10; Dio 74.3.1 and 3.

arouse suspicion. It may be a guess by the biographer. But in that case it is a reasonable and informed guess. After all, Septimius's grand-father – who had been brought up in Italy – had been complimented by Statius for *not* having an accent. Provincial accents naturally existed in the Roman Empire and some provincials had been embarassed by this at Rome. Hadrian, as quaestor in 101, was laughed at in the Senate for 'his somewhat rustic pronunciation' – clearly a Spanish accent. He took steps to remedy the situation by intense application to eloquence in Latin. Two generations later much had changed. For one thing, a new style of oratory prevailed. Hadrian suffered his embarassment the year after Pliny and Tacitus, recognised leaders of the Roman bar, had prosecuted the proconsul Marius Priscus. Now the 'new style' (*elocutio novella*) of Cornelius Fronto was the vogue. A prominent feature of that style was the use of words which the classical writers and orators from Cicero to Pliny rejected as old-fashioned and demotic – or provincial. The Roman provinces, it may be argued, had preserved the old ways of speech and vocabulary. At Rome, the upper classes affected a more stilted, consciously literary style, setting themselves on a plane above the urban *plebs* and the peasantry. In the provinces the gentry had no such pretensions. When provincials began to dominate the cultural and political life of the capital, their preferences prevailed. The 'unaffected' style that Fronto favoured was, in his own view, truer and less artificial than that of Cicero. To an unprejudiced observer Fronto's obsession with the *mot juste* gives him the very opposite of an unselfconscious, natural style. The important thing, however, was that to be provincial must now, in the 160s, have become almost the mode. How much this affected attitudes to pronunciation one can only speculate. But it is difficult to imagine that a provincial accent would have provoked much mirth by the time Septimius entered the Senate.[1]

---

[1] Dio 76.16.1; Herodian 2.9.2; *HA Sev.* 19.7-10. – On his alleged tastes in food (and his 'native vegetable'), cf. Sir R. SYME (1968a), p. 201: 'It is invention' is his conclusion. – Statius, *Silvae* 4.5.45, cf. p. 38, above. – Priscus: p. 40f., above. – Hadrian: *HA Had.* 3.1. – *elocutio novella*: Fronto, *de eloquentia* 4.1=Haines II 80, cf. e.g. *CAH* XII, pp. 513ff. Note esp. Fronto *de eloq.* 3.8=Haines II 80: *ego immo volgaribus et obsoletis (sc. verbis utor)*; also *Epist. Graecae* 1.5=Haines I 136, where he jokingly calls himself 'a Libyan of the nomad Libyans'. For recent literature on Fronto (and A. Gellius) cf. *Lustrum* 10 (1965) pp. 213ff.

Septimius's grandfather had had literary learnings. He himself 'received less education that he would have liked'. But it is not unreasonable to wonder whether he may have gained entry to the literary *salon* of Cornelius Fronto. Certainly there is no sign that he ever had philosophical leanings. One would not expect him to have joined the Emperor and his admirers at the lectures of Sextus of Chaeronea. He is unlikely to have attended dissections performed by the young doctor from Pergamum, Galen, which attracted an audience of scientifically minded senators. But the chance of hearing the great Fronto converse or discourse may well have attracted him. Fronto's way of life in the 160s may not have resembled the halcyon days of twenty years before, when enthusiasts for learning would call on the great man simply to hear the flow of conversation and repartee. The times were no doubt long since gone by when a man going through the entrance hall of the palace could listen in as Fronto and his friends discussed the various Latin words for dwarf. Marcus Aurelius had given up this sort of thing more than fifteen years before. Lucius Verus was away in the east.[1]

Fronto continued to correspond with the Emperors, sending off a flow of comfort and advice to Marcus, weighed down by his responsibilities, and to Lucius, clearly in danger of neglecting his in favour of high – or low – living. Fronto's other favoured pupil was now his son-in-law. While Victorinus and Gratia were away in Germany, Fronto and the elder Gratia looked after their young grandsons Fronto and Victorinus. A letter probably written in 162 or 163, soon after Victorinus went to Germany, conveys a picture of the old orator blissfully happy responding to the elder boy's constant *da!* ('give') by supplying him with 'pieces of paper and writing tablets – things that I want him to ask me for'. (If Septimius called on the great man he no doubt met these boys. Some thirty-five years later, while he himself was in the east as Emperor, M. Aufidius Fronto and C. Aufidius Victorinus served in turn as consuls, in 199 and 200.) It is equally likely that

---

[1] Sextus: Philostratus, *v.soph.* 2.1.9. – Galen: e.g. Flavius Boethus (refs. in *PIR*² F 229), M. Vettulenus Civica Barbarus, Sergius Paullus, Cn. Claudius Severus (Galen 14.613, 629 K.). Cf. now G. W. BOWERSOCK (1969), pp. 59ff. – 'dwarf': A. Gellius, *Noctes Atticae* 19.13; cf. A. R. BIRLEY (1966a), pp. 82ff.

Fronto favoured his visitors with an account of his ever-present ailments, lumbago and so forth.[1]

But Fronto was still active enough to take an interest in other matters besides his health, his family and his imperial ex-pupils. His young compatriot Arrius Antoninus of Cirta, serving in northern Italy as one of the newly instituted *iuridici*, was flooded with firmly worded appeals, in the form of avuncular advice, to look after the interests of various of Fronto's clients in that region. One Caelius Optatus received a letter in which Fronto warmly, though in terms long conventional, recommended another friend, Sardius Saturninus, whose sons 'are constantly in my quarters'. One of these sons was recommended by Fronto to the influential Petronius Mamertinus, son or nephew of Pius's Praetorian Prefect of that name. This man had a link with a family of Septimii, perhaps the one from Lepcis. This is the nearest one can get to any hint that Septimius may have had access to a member of Fronto's circle. Be this as it may, Emperor Septimius showed especial favour to men from Numidia, Fronto's home. It is not unlikely that he first formed connections with men from Numidia in Rome rather than in Africa.[2]

It was customary for young *laticlavii* who aspired to enter the Senate to practise advocacy in the Roman courts at an early age. Pliny, for example, appeared in the Centumviral Court as junior counsel at the age of eighteen. There is every reason to believe that Septimius would have done likewise. The whole of his education will have been directed towards perfecting his ability as a public speaker. (The only direct evidence comes in a phrase of Aurelius Victor.) But at least he was competent enough, at the age of twenty-three, to plead a case (his own) before a magistrate. Fronto was the doyen of the Roman bar, and

---

[1] 'comfort': e.g. Fronton, *de feriis Als.* 3=Haines II, 4ff.; *de bello Parthico*=Haines II 20ff., etc. – Lucius: note *ad Verum Imp.* 2.6=Haines II 84f. (esp. 86: *temperes et reparcas et modificeris desideriis omnibus* etc.); *HA Verus* 7.10, Lucian *Imagines* and *pro Imaginibus* (on Panthea); *HA Verus* 4.6ff., 6.1–5, etc. (cf. A. R. BIRLEY [1966a], pp. 172ff. – '*da!*': *ad amicos* 1.12=Haines II 172. – ca. 'AD 199 and 200': *PIR*[2] A 1385, 1394, cf. p. 210f., below.

[2] Arrius Antoninus: *ad amicos* 2.6–8=Haines II 174ff. – Optatus: *ad amicos* 1.9=Haines II 240. – Mamertinus: *ad amicos* 1.10=Haines II 242 (cf. App. 1). See generally H. G. PFLAUM (1964). – Numidia: cf. G. ALFÖLDY, *Senat*, esp. p. 126.

it is quite possible that Septimius, like the sons of Sardius Saturninus, sat at his feet.[1]

In 165 Fronto was beginning to be active in a new role, as an historian. He was preparing a history of the Parthian war, which was being brought to a successful conclusion in that year with a Roman invasion of Mesopotamia. The war ended in the following year. Lucius Verus returned as a conquering hero and in October 166, with Marcus, celebrated a triumph. Septimius is unlikely to have missed the occasion, the first of its kind for nearly fifty years. The troops that had gone east to reinforce the eastern armies went back to their bases on the Rhine and Danube. The victory in the east had apparently been sweeping. Roman generals crossed the Tigris into Media in 166, and in the previous year the twin Parthian capitals of Seleuceia and Ctesiphon had been sacked. There was no doubt talk at Rome of reviving Trajan's policy of annexing Mesopotamia. Hadrian had rejected this, and Trajan's new eastern provinces had been hastily abandoned on his death in 117. Hadrian's whole policy of peaceful retrenchment was now being seriously questioned and some no doubt favoured a revival of Trajanic aims and methods in the east. But whatever may have been said or hoped by Lucius Verus and his staff or by circles in Rome, Marcus Aurelius can scarcely have considered adding to Roman responsibilities in that quarter. The campaigns of Calpurnius Agricola in Britain and of Victorinus in Germany would be sufficient to illustrate that serious problems elsewhere demanded attention. But these provinces were not the most crucial. The real threat to the Empire's security lay directly to the north of Rome itself, beyond the upper Danube. Pressure had been building up among the peoples of Bohemia, Moravia and Slovakia. The governors of the frontier provinces had instructions to refrain from military action until the eastern war was

---

[1] Pliny, *Ep.* 5.8.8, cf. 1.18.3. – *Epitome de Caes*, 20.28: *primo litteris, dehinc imbutus foro.* – Septimius had after all gone to Rome *studiorum causa* (*HA Sev.* 1.5). This would mean primarily the study of oratory. If he had been a *contubernalis* of Fronto, like e.g. Sardius Saturninus's sons, that fact ought to have been recorded in the sources. But, without suggesting that he enjoyed that degree of intimacy with the great man, it is legitimate to speculate that he did his best to learn something from Fronto at this time. Cf. also below p. 240f., on his subsequent literary abilities.

over. In the meantime two new legions were being recruited in Italy under the supervision of two of Lucius's generals, returned from the east before the war there was over. In 166 or 167 the first wave of barbarian invaders broke through into Pannonia. Much worse was to come.[1]

The festivities associated with the triumph gave a façade of public rejoicing. But trouble soon followed. The soldiers returning from the east, who included praetorian guardsmen, brought plague with them. Within a few months Rome became a thoroughly unhealthy place to live in. Thousands died, and the upper classes suffered with the rest. Senators and other men of wealth no doubt retired to their country estates. Even senators of moderate means, such as Pliny the younger had been, possessed a variety of landed property in different parts of the peninsula. Senators of provincial extraction were in any case required to have at least a proportion of their wealth invested in Italian iand – Trajan had set the minimum at one third, Marcus reduced it to a quarter. Septimius must have had a place to go to, or else his property qualification for entering the Senate would have been invalid. Later on, except for an apartment in Rome, his only property was 'a single farm at Veii', clearly part of his grandfather's estate. But Southern Etruria, however pleasant a place to withdraw to in normal times, was uncomfortably close to Rome. What is more, Lucius Verus had a pleasure villa outside Rome on the *via Clodia*, which must have brought sources of potential infection even closer to the country house of Septimius.[2]

It must have been an obvious decision to leave Italy and return for a time to Africa. Entry into the Senate would still be assured, in due course. Septimius still had to wait until he entered his twenty-fifth year, on 11 April 169, or rather for the quaestorian elections in January of that year. In the meantime Africa was a much healthier place to be. Besides, his brother Geta had probably left Rome again already, to be quaestor to the proconsul of Crete and Cyrenaica. Septimius may have gone home to Lepcis, and from there across the barren tract that inter-

[1] Cf. A. R. BIRLEY (1966a), pp. 191ff., 201f.; ID *Seventh Congress*.

[2] Triumph and plague: A. R. BIRLEY (1966a), pp. 198ff., 202ff. – 'Italian land': Pliny, *Ep.* 6.19.4, *HA M.Ant.* 11.8. – 'Veii': cf. M. HAMMOND (1940), pp. 142ff., emending *HA Sev.* 4.5 to *unum fundum Veientem*, followed by A. R. BIRLEY, *HAC*, p. 63f. – 'pleasure villa': *HA Verus* 8.8–9.

vened, to Cyrene, to visit Geta. But after Rome Lepcis may well have seemed a dull backwater. One may suspect that Septimius gravitated to Carthage in the year 167. There he could – for example – have heard the great Apuleius at last, if he had not already done so.[1]

His activities in Africa are revealed explicitly by one episode only, in the Augustan History. He was a wild young man, the biographer records, hinting that he got into a lot of trouble. One instance is given. A jealous husband evidently suspected Septimius of seducing his wife, for he was prosecuted for adultery. He dispensed with counsel and pleaded his defence in person. The judge in the trial was either the proconsul Salvius Julianus, or his legate, Didius Julianus. The author of the Augustan History (misled by Aurelius Victor) found it too difficult a task to distinguish between these two men. However this may be, Septimius was found not guilty. If it were the proconsul himself who presided over the case and acquitted him, one might well be prepared to believe Septimius innocent of adultery. If it were Didius, one would not be quite so sure. There is no means of telling where the case came up – or where the lady in the case lived. It might have been at Carthage, perhaps even at Lepcis. The Augustan History does not even put the case in Africa, and some have suspected the story as a fiction. But now that Salvius Julianus is attested as proconsul for the period 1 July 168 to 30 June 169, with Didius as his legate, there is no longer any reason to doubt it.[2]

If there was any basis for the prosecution, it might be fair to construe any misbehaviour of Septimius as a last fling before attention to his future at Rome became necessary. By January 169 at latest, one should expect that he was back at the capital, endeavouring to secure election as quaestor. The evidence suggests that the original minimum age of thirty had been modified early on in the Empire to twenty-five. Hadrian, if not his predecessors, had then allowed a further reduction of one year: a man in his twenty-fifth year could count as qualified. Election was now in practice the affair of the Senate, and to be elected

[1] 'twenty-fifth year': cf. p. 80, n. 1, below. – Geta: App. 1, no. 20. – *HA Sev.* 2.1–2 does not state that he returned to Africa, but that is plausible. Cf. A. R. BIRLEY, *HAC*, p. 68.

[2] *HA Sev.* 2.1–2. Cf. A. R. BIRLEY, *HAC*, p. 68; H. G. PFLAUM (1966), p. 6off.

quaestor meant being co-opted into the Senate. Up till the end of the first century A.D. some genuine competition for the tribunate and praetorship may have continued. But there is no trace at any stage during the principate of competition for the quaestorship. Once a man had gained the *latus clavus* and had been *vigintivir*, it must have been automatic to proceed to the next stage. After all, there were twenty quaestorships each year, one for each of the *vigintiviri*. But the *vigintiviri* would mostly be eighteen or nineteen years old, and would wait five or six years before becoming quaestors. A number of Septimius's fellow-*vigintiviri* may have been eliminated by war or plague. The same thing applies to his immediate predecessors. All things considered, it is highly unlikely that Septimius had any need to wait a year. It is probable that he was elected in 169, and took office on 5 December that year, for twelve months. Thus Septimius entered the Senate, joining the venerable assembly, now well over six hundred strong, which constituted the *élite* of an Empire containing some sixty million people. He was *vir clarissimus*, the 'Right Honourable'.[1]

[1] 'minimum age': 'twenty quaestors': cf. Sir R. SYME (1958), p. 652, J. MORRIS (1964), p. 317. – 'competition': cf. A. N. SHERWIN-WHITE, p. 119f. – '5 December': cf. e.g. *RE* 14 (1928) 415. – 'Elections': cf. A. N. SHERWIN-WHITE, pp. 23–27, 179ff., 260, 292. But that scholar seems to be mistaken over the assignment of duties: there were ten proconsular provinces at this time – Africa, Asia, Achaia, Baetica, Bithynia-Pontus – for which Lycia-Pamphylia was substituted in the early 160s, cf. A. R. BIRLEY (1966a), p. 190f. – Crete-Cyrene, Cyprus, Macedonia, Narbonensis and Sicily. Each had only one quaestor, so far as is known, which means that ten, not twelve, out of the annually elected twenty, served outside Rome. There were two *quaestores Augusti* (perhaps four when there were two Emperors?) and two *quaestores urbani*; a further six must have been assigned to the consuls. – 'six hundred strong': J. MORRIS (1965) would put it at 600; cf. also G. Barbieri in *L'Albo*, pp. 415f. (who shows that the number had certainly reached 900 by the earliest third century). – 'sixty million': any figure is based on informed guesswork, at best; cf. the useful discussion by G. CHARLES-PICARD (1959a), pp. 45ff. (with special reference to Africa). – *vir clarissimus*: cf. A. N. SHERWIN-WHITE, p. 637.

VI

INTO THE EMPEROR'S SERVICE

At the beginning of each year lots were cast in the Senate for the proconsulships of the ten provinces still administered in the Republican style. Ten of the twenty quaestors would be at the time assigned to these provinces. Their duties would not begin until they left the city in the spring – at latest before 13 April – to go to their province, where their year of office would begin on 1 July. The other ten quaestors would serve in Rome. The Augustan History does not specify where Septimius served. From its silence one may assume that it was at Rome. Equally, since nothing is said about it, one may assume that he was not one of the Emperor's two personal quaestors, and that he was not elected as the Emperor's candidate. He may have been one of the two urban quaestors, whose residual duties, after the supervision of the state treasury had been taken away, were light. Otherwise he will have been assigned duties by the consuls. Only the two *ordinarii* and one suffect of 170 are known for certain. The *ordinarii* were Erucius Clarus and Gavius Cornelius Cethegus, the suffect Hoenius Severus. The latter was an Italian patrician, as was Cethegus, a pupil of Fronto. Fronto rated Cethegus's eloquence highly in a letter to his pupil's father. The satirist Lucian says the man was a fool. But the family was influential. The other consul, Erucius Clarus, was the son of a friend of Pliny who had eventually become Prefect of Rome, with a second consulship in 146. His own son was to be consul in the fateful year 193. The family had estates in Africa.[1]

[1] The title of this chapter recalls, intentionally, the paper by E. BIRLEY (1953b), 'Senators in the Emperors' service'; Septimius's career falls into the third of the three types, or groups, there defined (p. 198f.). – 'ten provinces': see p. 80, n. 1, above. – 'lots': there is no clear evidence for the time of year for this pro-

A major change in affairs of state had taken place during Septimius's absence from Rome. In the spring of 168 the Emperors had left for the northern wars. They had inspected the Danubian front and returned to winter at Aquileia. Life in winter quarters on the Adriatic had irked Lucius Verus. His war in the east had been conducted from far pleasanter bases – Daphne on the Orontes and Laodicea on Sea. The presence of his dedicated elder colleague and adopted brother demanded from him an attention to duty that he found difficult to maintain. In midwinter the spread of plague among the troops had provided a welcome excuse for the Emperors to withdraw to more salubrious quarters. They began the return to Rome, but within a few days Lucius died from a stroke. He had barely passed his thirty-ninth birthday. Septimius may have been back in Rome in time to witness the funeral and deification.[1]

The enforced return to Rome thus delayed Marcus's plans even more than he can have anticipated. He took the opportunity of raising funds for his projected campaign with a striking symbolic act, the auction of precious gems, clothing and furnishings from the palace. The sale went on for two months in the Forum of Trajan. A pressing concern for the Emperor was what he should do about his widowed daughter Lucilla. She was a high-spirited and headstrong young woman, not lacking in physical charms. Some young senators of noble birth may have considered themselves eligible to be the second husband of a princess and stepfather to an Emperor's child. But it was surely recognised that Marcus Aurelius took no particular note of a man's origin, whether in appointing men to high office or in choosing husbands for his daughters. The eldest was married to a man from proconsular Asia, Claudius Severus. Lucilla's two youngest sisters were perhaps already betrothed. One was to marry Burrus, son of the rising Numidian general Antistius Adventus, the other, Sura Mamertinus. The latter was possibly a kinsman, if a very distant one, of Septimius. It would doubtless be quite absurd to suggest that Septimius himself

---

cedure. – '13 April': M. HAMMOND (1959), p. 298 and n. 69. – 'Candidates': *id*., p. 246 and nn. – Consuls of 170: *FC*, p. 48, cf. *PIR*[2] E 95 (Clarus; also 94, 96–7 and G. ALFÖLDY, *Senat*, p. 143f.); G 98 (Cethegus); H 189 (Severus).

[1] Cf. A. R. BIRLEY (1966a), pp. 211ff., 217ff.

had any hopes – even in his dreams – of gaining the hand of Lucilla. But the choice of her husband is something that he must have watched with considerable interest. In the event almost everyone must have been surprised, not least Lucilla herself and her mother. The Emperor married his daughter to a Syrian of equestrian background, Claudius Pompeianus. Indirectly this match was to affect the fortunes of Septimius. Pompeianus soon became the principal military adviser of his father-in-law, and was able to advance the career of his protégé Helvius Pertinax.[1]

In October the Emperor returned to the northern front. Soon after entering office as quaestor Septimius will have felt personally the effect of one of Marcus's measures. The Emperor had conscripted gladiators into the army, thereby creating difficulties for those who had to put on public games. One of the few independent duties left to the quaestors in Rome was the putting on of games shortly after their election. Septimius may have been able to use his connections at Lepcis to ensure a supply of suitably exotic and ferocious wild beasts. But if the games put on by the quaestors during Septimius's term of office were inadequate, the urban *plebs* and senators alike soon had far more serious matters to worry about. In the spring of 170 the Emperor launched his long-delayed offensive across the Danube. Its intention evidently was to prepare the way for the annexation of the Transdanubian lands. It was a disastrous failure. Roman losses were enormous. In the ensuing chaos a flood of northerners descended into the Empire. The inhabitants of the capital must have been thunderstruck by the news of the Roman defeat, on a scale not suffered since the disaster to Varus and his legions in 9. But that had taken place well beyond the Rhine, and the victorious Germans had failed to cross that river. This time the enemies of Rome were much closer to the heart of the Empire. One group swept into Greece, while two German tribes, outflanking the Emperor's battered forces, broke into Italy itself. It was fortunate for Rome that Aquileia, the great trading-city at the head of the Adriatic, acted as a magnet for the invaders. They could easily have pressed on southwards, crossed the Pó and gone on to Ariminum

---

[1] 'Funds', 'Lucilla': A. R. BIRLEY (1966a), pp. 218ff. – 'Sons-in-law': H. G. PFLAUM (1961) (on Mamertinus: App. 1) – Pertinax: pp. 108ff., below.

(Rimini) and Fanum Fortunae (Fano), the road-head of the *via Flaminia* that led straight across the Apennines to Rome.[1] Septimius, who was himself to lead an invading army by this route twenty-three years later, will have been impressed at this time by the defencelessness of Rome. A force coming down on the city from Pannonia would find little in its path to oppose it. Through the efforts of Pompeianus and Pertinax in particular, Italy was cleared of the first foreign invaders since Hannibal. The situation was gradually restored in this and the following year, and the Emperor was able to resume his offensive in 172. But many lives had been lost, not least among the officers. Many special measures were necessary. Septimius's brother Geta may have made a modest contribution to the security of Rome and Italy at this critical time. When land communications between Rome and the Danube were blocked or threatened, it was essential to maintain the sea-routes across the Adriatic, and the few Italian ports south of Ravenna were especially important. At about this time – the exact year cannot be fixed – Geta was made *curator* of Ancona. The appointment came after he had been aedile and was probably still under thirty. The *curatores* of towns in Italy and the provinces were normally concerned with the auditing of the municipalities' finances. This alone may well have been a vital matter when supplies were passing from Ancona across to Salonae (Split) in Dalmatia. As *curator* of Ancona in 170 or soon after Geta may, however, have had added responsibilities.[2]

Although Septimius himself did not participate in any of the major actions of the 170s, his career was naturally affected by the difficulties of the time. He was too junior to be given any high responsibility, but there were gaps to be filled at all levels. At some stage in 170 or early 171 it became clear that there would not be enough quaestors to serve in the provinces in the latter year. Septimius was asked, or perhaps ordered, to serve a second term. He was assigned to the province of

---

[1] 'Games': M. HAMMOND (1959), p. 296 and n. 54. – 'Gladiators': *HA M.Ant.* 21.8 (cf. p. 94f., below). – 'Offensive': A. R. BIRLEY, *Seventh Congress.* – Invasion of Italy: A. R. BIRLEY (1968b), arguing that it took place in 170.

[2] Geta: A. R. BIRLEY (1966a), pp. 228ff.; G. M. BERSANETTI (1942), esp. pp. 112ff.; A. R. BIRLEY (1969), pp. 261ff.; and App. 1, no. 30. – *curatores*: M. HAMMOND (1959), p. 446 and nn.

Baetica. It seems possible that the proconsul under whom he was to serve may have been Cornelius Anullinus. In 193 this man would emerge as a major supporter of Septimius in the struggle for the Empire. It may be that the two were already acquainted. If the lot were operated strictly, the assignment of quaestors would be a matter of choice. But not infrequently personal choice was permitted. It is at least worth bearing in mind that Septimius's second term as quaestor was the result of a request by Anullinus, asking for him by name.[1]

Septimius will have been obliged to leave Rome for southern Spain before 13 April, in accordance with a regulation established by Claudius. Several routes would have been open to him. But evidently before his departure he learned of his father's death and he went instead to Lepcis to settle the affairs of the family. While he was still in Africa events prevented him from taking up his Spanish appointment. Moorish tribesmen took ship and invaded the peninsula. It was only twenty years since their rebellion in Mauretania had been suppressed and the defences of western North Africa extensively reorganised. Now they were after a richer prize, and they could hardly have chosen a more favourable moment to attack. There was only one legion in the entire peninsula, and it was stationed hundreds of miles from Baetica, at Leon in the Asturias. The single legion in Africa could not be safely transferred, especially as it was already weakened by lending troops to the Danubian armies.[2] And the northern armies themselves could hardly be called upon at this time. Marcus Aurelius again turned to his old friend Aufidius Victorinus. The province of Baetica was temporarily taken out of the Senate's control and joined to Tarraconensis, under Victorinus's overall authority. Cornelius Anullinus was made commander

[1] On the double quaestorship, cf. A. R. BIRLEY, *HAC*, p. 69 and n. 47, where parallels are adduced. – Anullinus: App. III. – It is of course conceivable that the text of *HA Sev.* 2.3, which appears to indicate the double quaestorship, is at fault. This was suggested long ago by A. DE CEULENEER, p. 17 and n. 4: '*le passage ne me parait comprehensible qu'en supposant le* post quaesturam *intercalé par un copiste* (note: *On a alors une phrase assez simple:* quaesturam diligenter egit omisso tribunatu militari, sorte Baeticam accepit. *Ce second membre de phrase complète le premier*'). But on the whole, given the historical context, it seems preferable to accept the statement in *HA Sev.* 2.3 as it stands.

[2] '13 April': Dio 60.17.3. – 'father's death' . . . 'invaded': *HA Sev.* 2.3–4 – 'rebellion': A. R. BIRLEY (1966a) p. 114. – 'legion . . . weakened': D.2747, cf. *CP* no. 198.

of the legion, VII Gemina, which was presumably sent down to Baetica from Leon. Victorinus's modest forces were strengthened by the despatch of a special force under the procurator Julius Julianus. Julianus had just completed clearing up operations with this unit in the Balkans.[1]

When the Senate was obliged by the dictates of military or economic necessity to hand over a province to the Emperor – for only the elastic imperial administration could deal with an emergency situation and provide the military means of solving it – care was always taken to avoid upsetting the system permanently. The normal solution was for the Emperor to surrender one of his own minor provinces to the Senate. The province selected to compensate the Senate for Baetica was the island of Sardinia, the only possible choice. It would not have done to unbalance the ratio of senatorial and imperial provinces in the west still further in favour of the latter. Septimius thus spent the best part of twelve months in Sardinia. Nothing is recorded about his stay there. If he was already as energetic and ambitious as he later showed himself to be, he must have wondered whether he would ever achieve greatness. Service in Sardinia can scarcely be said ever to have led that way before. One aspect of the island may have some slight interest for him. Sardinia in antiquity bore the stamp of Africa rather than of Italy. The Punic influence was still strong.[2]

The *leges annales* which still regulated the old Republican magistracies apparently laid down that a *biennium* must elapse between each office. The 'two years' interval was interpreted liberally to mean anything over twelve months. But Septimius can have had little prospect of securing election as aedile or tribune of the *plebs*, the next obligatory stage in the *cursus honorum*, until the elections of January 173. This would have allowed him, as tribune, to take office on 10 December 174 (or 1 January 175 if he had become aedile). Of course, at all times – and particularly at times of crisis – the rules could be adjusted to accelerate

---

[1] VII Gemina, Victorinus: G. ALFÖLDY, *Reichsbeamte*, pp. 40, 123. Note that many years later (199) Anullinus held a second consulship with a son of Victorinus as his colleague: *FC* 56. – Julianus: *CP* no. 180.

[2] 'ratio'. cf. p. 80, n. 1, above. – Sardinia: cf. *Sardegna Romana* (1936), esp. I, pp. 69ff.

the careers of promising men. The procedure followed was that of *adlectio*. The Emperor, in his censorial capacity, could enroll a man into a higher grade, allowing him to dispense with at least a year's service if not more. Thus Septimius's contemporary, Julius Pompilius Piso – who had served in two legions as military tribune – after the quaestorship was adlected *inter tribunicios* and after his praetorship went on to important military commands. Clearly men who were needed on active service could not be held back by the formalities of the ancient city magistracies. Indeed, there were now senators who had been given their rank of *vir clarissimus* and ex-praetor at the front, and would not enter the *curia* in Rome for ten years – men like Helvius Pertinax. There is no sign in the Augustan History or elsewhere that Septimius Severus was at any stage deemed sufficiently vital to the state to be allowed special privileges of this kind.[1]

In the meantime employment of another kind was offered. C. Septimius Severus, by 173 a fairly senior consular – particularly when plague and war had thinned the ranks of the Senate – was chosen by lot to be proconsul of Africa. He selected Septimius as one of his three *legati pro praetore*. Septimius will have proceeded to Carthage at the end of June. It seems to have become normal at this period for the three legates to be assigned to three regions of the province. One would remain in Carthage, deputizing for the proconsul in his absence and assisting him when he was there. The others would have their duties in the western and eastern parts of the province, the one in Hippo Regius, the other supervising Byzacena and Tripolitania, with Hadrumetum and Lepcis Magna as his two chief centres of activity. The proconsul himself retained the overall responsibility and could tour the whole province during his year of office. C. Septimius Severus must have devoted some personal attention to the western sector of proconsular Africa, that part of Numidia which still remained under his authority – rather than coming under the control of the legate of III Augusta. He is attested as patron of Thubursicu Numidarum, where the people

---

[1] *leges annales*, etc.: J. MORRIS (1964), ID. (1965), p. 29; M. HAMMOND (1959), p. 247f. – Piso: *PIR*² J 477. He was evidently a Greek from Ephesus: *AE* 1967, 482. – '10 December': *RE* 14 (1928), 415. – Pertinax: pp. 112ff., below. – 'plague and war': *HA M.Ant.* 13.5, 22.7.

erected a statue to him. Part of the base, on which his full senatorial career was set out, has been preserved. This link between Septimius's kinsman and Numidia was probably of importance for Septimius's own future.

The presence of C. Septimius Severus is also recorded at Lepcis Magna, his home, at the opposite end of the province. His name appears, together with that of Septimius his legate, on the inscription from an Arch dedicated in 174 in honour of Marcus Aurelius. Since this is the earliest record of Septimius's name – and a recent discovery – it may be set out in full here:

> *Imp(eratori) Caes(ari) M. Aurelio Antonino Aug(usto) Arm(eniaco)*
> *Med(ico) Par(thico) Ger(manico) P(ontifici) M(aximo) tr(ibuniciae)*
> *pot(estatis) XXVIII imp(eratori) co(n)s(uli) p(atri) p(atriae), arcus*
> *ex HS CXX m(   ) n(   ) ab Avilio Casto in eum et statuas*
> *legatis, praeter HS (   ) quae de publico adiecta sunt, dedicatus*
> *C. Septimio Severo proco(n)s(ule), L. Septimio Severo leg(ato) pr(o)*
> *pr(aetore)*

'To the Emperor Caesar Marcus Aurelius Antoninus Augustus, Armeniacus, Medicus, Parthicus, Germanicus, Pontifex Maximus, in his twenty-eighth term of tribunician power [A.D. 174], hailed *imperator*, consul, father of his country, the Arch is dedicated, paid for from the 120,000 Sesterces left in his will, for it and for the statues, by Avilius Castus, with the addition of the sum of [left blank] Sesterces which have been added from public funds, Gaius Septimius Severus being proconsul, Lucius Septimius Severus being propraetorian legate.'

This inscription provides yet another example of the wealth, and love of ostentatious public benefaction, of the notables of Lepcis. C. Avilius Castus was already on record as a leading man of Lepcis. When 'in response to universal demand the Council decreed that a two-horse chariot should be set up' in honour of his son, Castus, 'satisfied with the honour' thus shown, had paid for the work with his own money.[1]

---

[1] C. Septimius Severus: App. 1. – 'legates': B. E. THOMASSON, I, pp. 58ff. – 'regions' (dioceses): *ib.*, pp. 67ff. The details are disputed, the evidence being

The proconsul himself may not have presided at the dedication of the Arch. But the stone surely shows unequivocally that Septimius returned to his native city, endowed with official authority and retinue, *mandatu proconsulis*. It provides good reason for accepting as authentic the story contained in the Augustan History. When Septimius – perhaps on his first arrival at Lepcis – preceded by lictors bearing the *fasces* which denoted his authority, was embraced by an old acquaintance, he had the man flogged. The demonstration was followed up by an announcement by the legate's herald: no plebeian was to embrace a legate of the Roman people in this undignified way again.

The arrogant and hot-tempered streak that this episode reveals is borne out on future occasions. His arrogance may have been encouraged by something else that happened during this spell of duty in Africa. In 'a certain African town', not specified by the Augustan History, he consulted a *mathematicus* or astrologer. When the details of his birth had been revealed and the astrologer had computed the result, the man was incredulous. He had seen a great future (*ingentia*) ahead, which he evidently found incompatible with the young man he saw in front of him. 'Give me your real horoscope, not someone else's,' he told Septimius. Septimius swore that it was indeed his own, and was then told 'everything that afterwards came to pass'. Cassius Dio records that Septimius later concealed the full details of his birth. It would not do for it to be widely known what was in store for him.[1]

---

incomplete. On the whole I incline to the view of S. Gsell (cited by T., p. 75) in *ILAlg.* I, p. ix, but it may well be that, as T. argues, pp. 75ff., following E. Albertini, the diocesan boundaries were not rigidly fixed at this time. – Thubursicu Numidarum: *ILAlg.* I 1283, cf. G. DI VITA-ÉVRARD (1963), pp. 410ff. (It is right at this point to note that in his unpublished London Ph.D. dissertation Dr J. Morris had already identified the man in this inscription, previously regarded as -*rius Severus*, instead of [*C. Septi*]*mius Severus*, with Septimius's consular kinsman, many years before the discovery of the Lepcis inscription.) Mme. Di Vita-Évrard argues convincingly, pp. 398ff., that the proconsular year was 173–174 (rather than 174–175). – Castus: *IRT* 633.

[1] Flogging:*HA Sev.* 2.6. – Astrologer: *ib.* 2.8. Cf. Dio 76.11.1. J. GUEY (1956) uses this description of the horoscope for his brilliant demonstration that Septimius was born in 145 (when the astral conjunctions could indeed be construed as promising *ingentia* – which they could not for the same day in 146). See further A. R. BIRLEY, *HAC*, p. 65f. The observations of F. H. CRAMER, p. 209 are instructive.

By the end of his term as legate, Septimius had entered his thirtieth year and was still unmarried. It is probable that he took the opportunity during his return to Lepcis of finding himself a wife. The girl he chose was called Paccia Marciana. Her names reveal that she was ultimately of Punic or Libyan, rather than Italian origin: her ancestors had clearly derived citizenship from the first-century proconsuls Marcius Barea and Paccius Africanus. Her family was possibly linked distantly with that of Septimius's mother, the Fulvii. But a leading provincial family such as the Septimii, or the Fulvii, would inevitably have some marriage links with most of the other upper-class families in their own town. Nothing is known for certain of any of Paccia's relatives.[1]

If Septimius had first entered the Senate in December 169, as has been suggested, he would certainly now be ready and eager to set his foot on the next rung of the ladder. It seems that he had now attracted the attention of the Emperor (or his advisers – Marcus Aurelius was still far from Rome, at the front). He was chosen tribune of the *plebs*, with the distinction of being one of the Emperor's *candidati*. His year of office began on 10 December, presumably in the year 174. Paccia Marciana, if she did not accompany him back from Africa in the summer, must have followed soon after. The marriage took place during, or immediately after his term of office. Nothing whatever is known of this marriage, which lasted for some ten years until Paccia's death. There were almost certainly no children – or none that survived infancy – unless credit is given to a particularly suspect story in the Augustan History. According to this version, Septimius had two daughters, who were old enough to be married in 193. They would therefore have been born in the years 176–180. There is no other record of any daughters of Septimius. He himself was silent about his first marriage in his autobiography, although he later had statues erected in memory of Paccia.[2]

[1] Marciana: App. 1. – It is just possible that *IRT* 555, a fragmentary *cursus* inscription from Lepcis, was set up in Septimius's honour at this time, cf. A. R. BIRLEY, *HAC*, p. 70f.

[2] *HA Sev.* 3.1: *tribunatum plebis Marco imperatore decernente promeruit eumque severissime exertissimeque egit.* Cf. A. R. BIRLEY, *HAC*, p. 70f. (*contra* J. HASE-BROEK (1921), p. 8). *ib.* 3.2: *uxorem tunc Marcia(na)m duxit, de qua tacuit in historia vitae privatae.* Cf. A. R. BIRLEY, *HAC*, p. 71f. – 'no children': *HA Sev.*

The tribunate was in a sense even more obsolete than the other Republican magistracies preserved under the imperial regime. Their once powerful position as initiators of legislation in the assembly of the *plebs*, and their right of veto, had quickly lapsed. After all, the Emperors possessed the tribunician power themselves. But their most ancient duty and right, to protect fellow citizens from injustice, will have remained, in theory at least. In practice this involved watching to see that other magistrates, especially the praetors, did not endanger the rights of Roman citizens. Some judicial functions may have been passed to them. But, as has been pointed out, when Pliny was tribune of the *plebs* he refused to practise at the bar during his term of office, so that the ancient dignity of his office should not be sullied. His sanctimonious reference to the course that he followed shows only too clearly that others rarely did this – and the implication is that tribunes did not normally find their duties an obstacle to their private activities.[1]

However this may be, Septimius is stated to have performed his duties 'with great rigour and energy'. And there may indeed have been the occasion, during the year 175, for the tribunes to take some part in preserving calm and public order. In April that year, following a false report that Marcus Aurelius was dead, the governor of Syria, Avidius Cassius, proclaimed himself Emperor. Once he had taken this step, he could not go back on it, even though it was soon confirmed that Marcus was alive – and prepared to spare his life. Cassius, one of the heroes of the Parthian war, had been endowed for several years with special overall authority over a large part of the eastern Empire. He had support from the Prefect of Egypt and elsewhere. But Martius Verus, the governor of Cappadocia, remained loyal to Marcus. The rebellion was over by June. Cassius was murdered by one of his own officers. But there had been panic at Rome, and the Emperor was obliged to send

---

8.1 is the only mention of the daughters (and their marriage to 'Probus' and 'Aetius'). Almost certainly a spurious piece of information, cf. J. HASEBROEK (1921), p. 49, with references to earlier discussions. Cf. also G. M. BERSANETTI (1946), p. 37, n. 2.

[1] Tribunate: cf. Pliny, *Ep.* 1.23 (and A. N. SHERWIN-WHITE, p. 139f.); M. HAMMOND (1959), p. 294f. and nn.

detachments from the northern legions to protect the city. Most of the Praetorian Guard will have been at the front, and the forces available in the capital were minimal. The heir to the throne, Marcus's only surviving son, Commodus Caesar, was at Rome. A boy of thirteen, he was still under the guidance of tutors. The Emperor summoned him to the front, and he was invested with the *toga virilis* in July. Before his departure the young prince performed his first public act, distributing largesse to the people.[1]

These events must have made a deep impression on Septimius. He will have heard lively discussion of the upheaval in the east. There was gossip impugning the reputation of the Empress Faustina – that she had written secretly to Cassius, encouraging him to make his coup, in the belief that Marcus was dying. Senators whose homes were in the east must have felt particular anxiety – and some, whether eastern or not, may have received messages from the pretender beseeching support. Cassius may have had many supporters among the Senate. Septimius probably had no personal links with any of them. But he must have realised that Cassius's rising had more behind it than a piece of opportunism by an ambitious general. There was unquestionably a fierce struggle in progress among the Emperor's advisers concerning his war policy. Marcus Aurelius was determined to annexe the territories of his principal enemies beyond the Danube. The eastern provinces will not have viewed this war with enthusiasm. It may not be fanciful to detect among Cassius's supporters elements that wanted a return to a purely Hadrianic policy. For all his philhellenism Marcus was behaving in the manner of a Trajan, waging an all-out war of conquest. But in contrast to Trajan's Dacian wars, the northern campaigns of Marcus were bringing no profit to anyone, least of all – it could have been argued – the wealthy eastern provinces.[2]

There was something else for senators to gossip about in 175. Helvius Pertinax, the freedman's son and ex-schoolmaster, was made consul, with Didius Julianus as his colleague. The appointment was not completely unprecedented, but it caused a good deal of ill-feeling.

[1] *HA Sev.* 3.1. – Cassius: A. R. BIRLEY (1966a), pp. 252ff.
[2] Faustina: A. R. BIRLEY (1966a), p. 253, etc. – 'war policy': A. R. BIRLEY, *Seventh Congress.*

Soon after this Pertinax, who went to the east with the Emperor in the summer, returned to the Danube as governor of Lower Moesia. Septimius Geta was made legate of the legion I Italica, not long after this, and probably served under the command of Pertinax. Shortly before taking up his command he had been co-opted into one of the ancient priesthoods, the *fetiales*, whose task it was to make solemn declaration of war. The college of the *fetiales* did not rank with the *pontifices, augures, quindecimviri* and *septemviri* as one of the major priesthoods. But it had great prestige. Aufidius Victorinus was a fellow-member. It is not known whether Septimius obtained a priest-hood of any kind, but his kinsman C. Septimius Severus was both a *quindecimvir* and a *sodalis Hadrianalis* and is likely to have made efforts to have Septimius co-opted into one or other of these colleges.[1]

Septimius probably remained in Rome during 176, awaiting the next stage in his career, the praetorship. He was designated praetor for 177 at the beginning of the year. But he did not achieve the honour of being *candidatus* of the Emperor again. The Emperor returned to Italy in the autumn. He had been away for seven years. On 27 November Commodus was granted *imperium* and celebrated a joint triumph with his father on 23 December. On 1 January he was consul and was given the tribunician power, soon followed by the title of Augustus. There were thus once more two Emperors, the younger being only fifteen years old. If it was not stated publicly – which it may well have been – Marcus Aurelius's intention was plain. From this time onwards his own death would no longer place the succession in jeopardy. When he died, Commodus would need no further powers – all he lacked was the priestly dignity of being *pontifex maximus*. There can be no doubt that Septimius was deeply influenced by this act, which he witnessed at close quarters as a magistrate of the Roman People. For he was to follow this precedent to the letter, in a more extreme form, with his own son.[2]

Some of the eighteen praetors each year had additional titles and specific duties – the praetor *urbanus, peregrinus, hastarius*, and so on.

---

[1] Pertinax: pp. 113ff., below. – Geta: App. 1, no. 30. – Victorinus: G. AL-FÖLDY, *Reichsbeamte*, pp. 38ff. – C. Septimius Severus: App. 1.

[2] *HA Sev.* 3.3. – Commodus: A. R. BIRLEY (1966a), p. 269f.

The remainder presided over the permanent courts manned by the *iudices*. The Augustan History does not specify any particular praetorship in Septimius's case (although this may be on account of the author's ignorance or lack of interest). He may well have presided at one of the courts where his grandfather had served as a simple juryman. The praetors had to work relatively hard – certainly in comparison with the tribunes – for the courts were in session for well over half the year. Marcus Aurelius had increased the number of days when legal proceedings could be carried on to two hundred and thirty. Presumably November and December were still vacation periods, so for the other ten months of 177 Septimius will have been kept busy. And he will have needed to take his duties seriously, for there is evidence that Marcus supervised the praetors with especial care.[1]

All the praetors were liable to heavy expenses, for they were expected to put on games, as were the quaestors. If this had been unusually expensive when Septimius was quaestor, it must have become even more so now. All over the Empire those whose holding of office obliged them to put on public spectacles were finding the task increasingly difficult. The supply of gladiators had become increasingly limited. In the course of 177 the matter was raised in the Senate, and as a result a decree was passed to reduce the price of gladiators. Septimius did not put on games during his praetorship – it may be that the economic position prevented it. But it may be that he was sent off to his next post – his first in the Emperor's service – before his year of office was up. This would have obliged him to miss the games, which he gave in absence, according to the biographer. The post that he received was in Spain, in the province of Hispania Tarraconensis. No details are given by the biographer, but it is practically certain that he was *legatus iuridicus*, or deputy head of the civilian administration, with special responsibility for Asturia and Callaecia. There is evidence that the Moors were again causing trouble in Spain at this period, and it is not impossible that Baetica had reverted to imperial control again (if indeed it had yet been transferred back to the Senate). The governor and the legionary legate no doubt had military duties at this time. In

[1] Praetors: M. HAMMOND (1959), pp. 292ff. and nn. – 'special care': *HA M.Ant.* 24.2, cf. 12.3–4.

that case Septimius's role as *iuridicus* will have been of especial importance.[1]

The Augustan History has nothing more to record about his stay in Spain, except for two dreams, one of which certainly belongs later. In the other dream he was told to restore the Temple of Augustus at Tarraco. If there was any basis for this subconscious command, one must assume that Hadrian's restoration of the temple fifty years before had not lasted long. His term as *iuridicus* would not normally have lasted for more than three years at the most. By the beginning of 180 he will have been hoping for promotion. It was to come in the shape of a legionary command in Syria. But, perhaps before Septimius had obtained this appointment, Marcus Aurelius died on 17 March 180, at Vienna on the Danube. The fateful sole reign of Commodus had begun.[2]

The philosopher Emperor had ruled nineteen years and ten days. The Empire had been through a considerable ordeal – almost continuous warfare against external enemies, rebellion, plague. And yet, as Ammianus Marcellinus was to put it in the fourth century, 'after calamitous losses things were restored anew . . . with unanimous ardour highest and lowest hastened, as if to a calm and peaceful haven, to an honourable death in the service of the republic'. Out of the whole Empire, almost the only part that had not been directly affected was Septimius's homeland, proconsular Africa, already the richest part of the west, and now still further at an advantage. Septimius himself can hardly be said to have contributed much. But he and other senators will have noted the incredible devotion to duty by the Emperor. Marcus Aurelius spent more than half his reign away from Rome, with the armies. Septimius was to follow this example as Emperor. Another and telling example was Marcus's unequivocal rejection of the notion that the Antonine dynasty was based on the 'adoptive principle'. Indeed, he may hardly have recognised the existence of any such prin-

[1] 'gladiators': cf. J. H. OLIVER for text and commentary. – 'games': M. HAMMOND (1959), p. 293 and n. 29. – Spain: *HA Sev.* 3.4, cf. esp. G. AL-FÖLDY, *Reichsbeamte*, p. 88f. But he prefers 146 as the year of Septimius's birth. – Moors: *CP* no. 221+*add.*

[2] Dreams: *HA Sev.* 4.4 (temple) and 5 (see p. 124, below). – Death of M. Aurelius: A. R. BIRLEY (1966a), pp. 286ff.

ciple. The rebellion of Cassius may have forced his hand a little, obliging him to accelerate the promotion of his son to a share in his powers. But he had no scruples in associating a fifteen year old boy with himself as Emperor. This must have made a deep impression on Septimius.[1]

[1] Amm. Marc. 31.5.14.

VII

A CAESAR BORN TO THE PURPLE

No one had had any experience of an Emperor like Commodus, a Caesar born to the purple. The seventeenth Emperor of Rome, he was the first who had been born during the reign of his father. What is more, by the series of adoptions begun by Nerva, and continued by Trajan, Hadrian and Pius, the dynasty to which he belonged had now produced a sixth Emperor (one more than the Julio-Claudians). Commodus could call himself 'son of the deified Marcus', but by virtue of those adoptions he could and did style himself 'great-great-great-grandson' (*adnepos*) of Nerva as well. Not for nothing was he called 'most nobly born of all Emperors'.[1]

It was indeed to that ill-starred family that men will have turned their minds in 180. Since the accession of Nero in 54, there had been no Emperor as young as this. Commodus was only eighteen when Marcus died, just two years older than Nero had been when he gained the throne. The omens now appeared more favourable. Commodus succeeded a father who had been almost universally popular, and who had been revered by the Senate. The suspicion that Marcus had been poisoned by Commodus (as Claudius had been by – or for – Nero), if

[1] *nobilissimus*: D. 397, cf. Herodian 1.5.5–6. – On Commodus see above all the massive study by F. GROSSO (1964). Dissent from that scholar may be possible in matters of detail, but his work contributes enormously to our understanding of the latter second century A.D. – In the view of Dio (71.36.4) the accession of Commodus marked the descent from a kingdom of gold to a kingdom of rust and iron. The comment is famous, cf. F. MILLAR (1964), p. 122f., who observes that 'it implicitly satirizes elements in Commodus's imperial propaganda'; and, more important, that it sums up the attitude of the upper classes – who, in spite of the serious military and economic position under M. Aurelius, had at least been 'treated with courtesy and tact' by the Emperor. The relatively peaceful reign of Commodus saw that courtesy and tact disappear completely.

present as early as this, will not have been widespread.[1]

Commodus may have been a lonely figure. His mother had died when he was fourteen. His twin brother had died when he was only four, and a younger brother four years after that. There were five sisters, all but one considerably older than Commodus. Lucilla, the second eldest, who had been the wife of Lucius Verus, was an Augusta. She was twelve years older than Commodus, and detested her husband Ti. Claudius, Pompeianus, who had been Marcus's principal military adviser, and was old enough to be Commodus's – and Lucilla's – father. He was with Commodus on the Danube. Other senior advisers from the imperial family were there too: Bruttius Praesens, the Emperor's father-in-law, and Vitrasius Pollio, husband of a cousin of Marcus. One of Marcus's best friends, Aufidius Victorinus, was ruling the City of Rome as Prefect. These and their like were the foundations of Marcus's hope that his son's reign would continue along the lines of his own.[2]

The new Emperor needed no further powers. There was merely the need to adjust his name and titles. But in spite of an apparent continuity in the administration, it is fair to suppose that there was a rush of applications for jobs, at all levels. Those who had connections at the court will have sought to use them. It is just at this time that Septimius Severus received his next post, the command of the legion IV Scythica in Syria. Some of the new appointments made by Commodus may have been set in motion already by Marcus before his death. Others may have been made on the advice of Pompeianus and the other senior men.

[1] Nero: *PIR*[2] D 129 (born December 37, succeeded Claudius October 54). – Poisoning: Dio (71.33.42) believed it.

[2] Mother: *PIR*[2] A 716. – 'twin': A 1512. – 'younger brother': A 698. – 'sisters': cf. esp. H. G. PFLAUM (1961) (but on the youngest, Vibia Aurelia Sabina, cf. A. R. BIRLEY [1966a], p. 321, n. 1). Herodian 1.8.3 calls Lucilla the eldest, which has led to the view that her older sister Faustina was dead by 180. But as Herodian is inaccurate on the number of sons (he says 'two' were born to Marcus in 1.2.1, but cf. Birley, p. 321), there is no reason to take him literally here. It would have been natural for a writer like him to assume that Lucilla, an Augusta, was the eldest. – Pompeianus: *PIR*[2] C 973, cf. Pflaum. – Praesens: *PIR*[2] B 165. – Pollio: D. 1112. – Victorinus: G. ALFÖLDY, *Reichsbeamte*, pp. 38ff. – 'Marcus' hope': cf. F. GROSSO (1964), pp. 95ff. (possibly valuing too highly the factual content in Herodian's speeches, 1.4–5).

But Commodus will already have found other voices more persuasive than that of his elderly and plebeian brother-in-law.[1]

In the *Meditations*, which Marcus Aurelius had been writing during his last campaigns, he had thanked the gods that he found good teachers for his children. Only three are named in the Augustan History, and only one of these is more than a name. This was Aius Sanctus, Commodus's tutor in oratory. Sanctus had combined his instruction of the prince with a career in the imperial service. In March 180 he had been for several years in Egypt, as Prefect. His teaching duties had clearly ended. Marcus Aurelius had himself studied oratory with Fronto – and other tutors – until his twenty-sixth year. Besides, he was an ardent and industrious student of philosophy from his boyhood until his death. No philosophy teachers at all are recorded for Commodus. One is driven to the melancholy conclusion that Marcus may have overreacted against his own upbringing. Faced, as Emperor, with nothing but continuous warfare, he may have decided that he had been over-educated – and in the wrong fields – for his role. For the last two and a half years of his life he had Commodus with him at the front. Among other motives he must have wished his son to acquire military experience at first hand. Other instruction may have continued. But it certainly ceased for good when Marcus died. Commodus had no 'higher education'.[2]

There was another difference. Marcus had not entered the imperial family until the age of sixteen, after a boyhood closely supervised by a host of relatives. Commodus, born a Prince, probably did not see his father at all – or only briefly – from the age of eight to the age of thirteen. Marcus was away on campaign. He was by nature 'lacking in evil qualities', Cassius Dio was convinced. As his near contemporary, Dio had ample opportunity to form a judgment. The Augustan History biographer seems almost to be going out of his way to contradict Dio. His report may derive from another contemporary, Marius Maximus, the neo-Suetonius of the third century. Maximus, a little older than

---

[1] 'IV Scythica': *HA Sev.* 4.4, cf. P. THOMSEN and A. R. BIRLEY, *HAC*, p. 72.
[2] *Meditations* 1.17.19. – 'teachers . . . named': *HA Comm.* 1.6 – Sanctus: *CP* no. 178 bis. – 'twenty-sixth year': A. R. BIRLEY (1966a), pp. 118ff.

Dio, was serving in the northern armies at the end of Marcus's reign. The verdict of the Augustan History is savage in its condemnation: 'From early boyhood cowardly, dishonourable, cruel, lustful, defiled in mouth and debauched.' A sarcastic aside is added, that he had some talent for pottery, dancing, singing and whistling – 'qualities unsuited for the imperial station'. And an instance is given, very probably apocryphal, to illustrate the streak of cruelty, an episode from Commodus's boyhood.[1]

Herodian avoids speculation about Commodus's character – perhaps wisely, since he himself was probably an infant in 180. But nevertheless he gives a report of the emperor's outward appearance at that time: 'He was in the prime of youth and he was most attractive to look at because of his well-proportioned body and the manly beauty of his face. His eyes had a commanding look and flashed like fire. His hair was naturally blond and curly. When he walked in the sunlight it shone like fire (so that some thought he sprinkled it with gold dust before coming out) while others regarded it as a sign of divinity, saying that a heavenly light shone out above his head. And the first down was just beginning to appear on his cheeks.' Later, the flashing eyes were dulled (by drink) – and the shining locks were no longer naturally shiny. Commodus did at this later time resort to gold dust. But one may assume that at his accession he was a handsome and attractive youth.[2]

His parents had been first cousins. Children of such unions sometimes tend towards extremes. Clearly, the sober and philosophical inclinations of his father were totally lacking. But the most prominent member of his parents' family, their grandfather Annius Verus, was noted for his devotion to games-playing (he was an expert amateur ball-player). Marcus had been brought up in his house, and there were various temptations there of a sexual kind (which he managed to avoid). He refers to this in the *Meditations*, where he also notes that he did not become a partisan of any of the gladiatorial teams. It may be guessed that he was reacting against a dominant passion of his grandfather's household. Old Verus's daughter, Commodus's grandmother

---

[1] 'sixteen': A. R. BIRLEY (1966a), pp. 53ff. – 'eight to thirteen': i.e. 169–175. – Dio 72.1.1; *HA Comm.* 1.7ff. – Maximus: App. II.
[2] Herodian 1.7.5

Faustina I, had a reputation of levity in her behaviour. But there is no need to look for the influence of heredity. Marcus Aurelius was not a particularly typical product of his age. His co-emperor Verus, with his love of the stage and the arena, was a closer reflection of prevalent fashions and sentiments. Commodus, who was only seven when Verus died, may nonetheless have wanted to ape the man whose names – Lucius Aurelius Commodus – he bore. At any rate, there is no need to believe the stories raked up later, that Marcus was not his real father. It seemed natural that the man he became must have been the son of a gladiator and it seemed incredible that Marcus could have fathered a son like Commodus – hence the gossip that he was illegitimate.[1]

For a few months after his accession Commodus remained with the armies on the Danube. Then the exhortations of Pompeianus and the other *amici* proved insufficient. Peace was made with Rome's northern enemies. Commodus returned to a rapturous welcome at Rome. He was lazy. This was perhaps his chief characteristic. Not simple physical indolence – for he was to show himself a superb athlete. But mentally lazy. The courtiers knew how to play on his weaknesses – those among them, that is, who were themselves unmilitary, and eager to return to the centre of the empire. Chief among these was his chamberlain (*a cubiculo*), Saoterus, a Bithynian. Cassius Dio, also a Bithynian, seems to have regarded this man without hostility. He is mentioned merely *en passant* in what survives of the *History*. Herodian knew nothing about the man. But the Augustan History, true to form, has a detail – which the scandal-mongering Maximus will not have failed to record – that when Commodus celebrated the triumph for the German wars on 22 October 180, 'Saoterus, his *subactor*, was placed in the chariot behind him. Often Commodus turned his head round and publicly kissed him. He did the same in the *orchestra* as well.' Saoterus's function on this occasion was to hold the golden crown above the head of the *triumphator*. But the word *subactor* has a double meaning. Marius Maximus, and many others, were disgusted. Saoterus soon acquired paramount influence over Commodus. No Roman Emperor had let

[1] 'games-playing': A. R. BIRLEY (1966a), p. 32f. – 'temptations': *Med.* 1.17.2, 7. – 'teams': *ib.* 1.5. – Faustina I: *HA Pius* 3.7. – Verus: *HA Verus, passim* –'illegitimate': *HA M.Ant.* 19.1–11.

favourites of this kind exercise such power since the dark days of Nero. To those who had served Antoninus Pius and Marcus Aurelius, it must have been sickening. For the members of the imperial family, it must have been equally unnerving. Yet given the quite exceptional dynastic claims of Commodus and the charismatic nature of his position, any action would be difficult. Five years earlier, Avidius Cassius had not hesitated to claim the throne on a false report of Marcus's death. The immediate collapse of his rebellion, and his murder following the news that Marcus was after all alive, will have served as a warning to impatient and ambitious army commanders. And things were now different. In 175 Commodus was still a boy. Now he was recognised as Emperor. Any rival would need vast prestige to gain acceptance. Marcus had chosen husbands for his daughters with the apparent deliberate intention of preventing counter-claims from that quarter. Only one of Commodus's six brothers-in-law, the obvious source of a rival to his throne, could be described as an aristocrat.[1]

In spite of these difficulties, there was an attempted coup less than two years after Commodus's return to Rome. With the benefit of hindsight it is possible to view the entire twelve and a half years of his reign as a long drawn-out battle for survival by an Emperor who was nonetheless, for much of the time, seemingly unaware of the danger. A succession of favourites held the real power like Grand Viziers, and Commodus devoted himself to pleasure. Meanwhile, with the exception of a few unambitious and devotedly loyal men like Claudius Pompeianus, the most prominent among the ruling classes plotted incessantly and manoeuvred for his inevitable removal.[2]

The first attempt was made by Lucilla, the former Empress. Not with her husband's connivance, however. But two of the other brothers-in-law were to be executed for conspiracy later in the reign. In a second conspiracy, uncovered immediately after that of Lucilla, the military men can be seen to have had a bid ready – and a cousin of Commodus,

[1] Cf. F. GROSSO (1964), pp. 99ff. – Saoterus: *ib.*, pp. 113ff. – 'six brothers-in-law': the husbands of his sisters, cf. H. G. PFLAUM (1961) (and pp. 82f., 98, above), and the brother of his wife (L. Bruttius Quintius Crispinus: *PIR*[2] B 170). – 'an aristocrat': M. Peducaeus Plautius Quintillus, cf. A. R. BIRLEY (1966a), p. 321f.: he was a nephew of L. Verus).
[2] Cf. for this view of the reign the article by F. CASSOLA (1965).

perhaps intended to be used as a pawn, was implicated. There were signs of unrest in different parts of the Empire throughout the reign. The British army, for example, twice attempted to force the throne on nervous and reluctant generals.[1]

The hatred that Commodus brought on himself because of Saoterus gave a group centred round Lucilla its cue in 182. Her motive is alleged to have been jealousy at the loss of her privileges in favour of the new Empress Crispina. It may be only Herodian's naivety that led him to believe that the loss of the front seat at the theatre caused her to act. But it could be that her resentment was used by others. Two men are named. One was her lover Ummidius Quadratus, adopted son of Marcus's nephew and by birth stepson of Commodus's eldest sister. The other was Lucilla's prospective son-in-law, Quintianus, a nephew of her husband Pompeianus. He too was said to be Lucilla's lover. These two men, closely connected to the dynasty by marriage, were predictable claimants to Commodus's throne.

But they bungled the job. As Commodus entered the hunting-theatre Quintianus, his trusted boon companion, appeared in the narrow passageway. He held out his weapon, proclaiming rhetorically: 'This dagger the Senate sends you!' The little speech gave the Emperor's bodyguards time to seize the assassin before he could act on it. *Fatuus* was the opinion that the Augustan History has of Quintianus, no doubt echoing Marius Maximus, who may have been a derisive onlooker. Quintianus and Quadratus were executed, along with others. Lucilla was exiled to Capri at first. Later she too was killed. Her husband Pompeianus withdrew from public life, pleading the excuse of failing eyesight. He had not been involved, but others had been, including one of the two praetorian prefects, Tarutienus Paternus. For the time being he escaped undetected. And perhaps in the confusion that followed the attempt, he and his colleague Tigidius Perennis had Saoterus murdered by the secret police.[2]

Commodus took the loss of his favourite badly. The ambitious

---

[1] 'two . . . brothers-in-law': Burrus and Mamertinus, cf. pp. 126, 132 – 'British army': pp. 120, 125 below.

[2] Cf. F. GROSSO (1964), pp. 145ff. Herodian 1.8.3–8; *HA Comm.* 4.1–5; Dio 72.4.4–5. – Paternus: for the *nomen* and *praenomen* (P.) cf. E. BIRLEY (1968), p. 44.

Perennis took his chance. He instigated the dismissal of his more distinguished colleague, who was 'kicked upstairs' by the award of senatorial rank. A few days later evidence was produced implicating Paternus in another conspiracy, and he was executed. This second conspiracy was potentially much more serious. Paternus's alleged involvement with the Lucilla affair suggests that he may have been trying to use her group to remove Commodus, leaving the throne vacant for his own candidate. This was Salvius Julianus, whose son was betrothed to Paternus's daughter. Julianus, son of the great jurist, was commanding an army at the time the plot was detected, perhaps that of Upper Germany. Dio asserts that the charge was false. But it is plausible. Salvius's kinsman Didius Julianus, then governing Lower Germany, was dismissed and summoned to Rome. He cleared himself with difficulty, and was ordered to withdraw to his native Milan. Apart from Paternus and Salvius Julianus, two of the consuls of 182, two ex-consuls, the *ab epistulis* Vitruvius Secundus, and Vitrasia Faustina, were also put to death. The involvement of the *ab epistulis* is a clear hint that Paternus had been attempting to use the imperial secretariat to contact the provincial armies.[1]

More heads were to roll. The Quintilii brothers, who had shared the consulship over thirty years before, were executed. Quintilius Condianus, son of one of them, was then in Syria. He was hunted down and killed. The pursuit of Condianus was a dramatic affair. Pertinax the governor of Syria, and Septimius Severus as one of the three legionary legates, will have had to take a leading role in this distasteful task. Condianus did not submit tamely, as so many had in the past to the assassins of a tyrannical Emperor. Dio, who was at this time in the neighbouring province of Cilicia, which his father was governing, gives a detailed account. Condianus feigned death, by drinking the blood of a hare, falling purposely from his horse and vomiting the blood out, after which he was carried in as if dead. While he made his escape, a dead ram was cremated in his coffin. The story got out and he was

---

[1] Cf. F. GROSSO (1964), pp. 153ff. *HA Comm.* 4.1.7–10; 3.2; Dio 72.5.1–2; *HA Did. Jul.* 1.9.–2.2 and Dio 73.11.2, cf. Grosso, p. 162 and n. 5. The province where Salvius Julianus was commanding an army is not known for certain, cf. Grosso, p. 156, n. 7 (p. 157).

hunted everywhere. Many suspects who resembled him were executed and their heads sent to Rome. His eventual fate was never discovered.

Witnessing what was happening both in Rome and Syria and else-where, Septimius cannot have felt secure. Before the end of 182 the blow fell. Pertinax was dismissed from his Syrian command. At the same time, or soon after, Septimius himself was sacked.[1]

---

[1] Condianus: Dio 72.6.1 – 7.2, cf. *HA Comm.* 4.9, F. GROSSO (1964), p. 158f. Dio records (6.4–5) that (some eleven years later) a man appeared before Pertinax, then Emperor, claiming to be Condianus. The impostor was exposed by his ignorance of matters Greek.

VIII

THE GREAT MARSHAL

Septimius's journey to Syria must have affected him in many ways. It was, for one thing, probably his first experience of the Greek-speaking part of the Empire. One cannot of course exclude that he had been to neighbouring Cyrenaica from Lepcis, during his boyhood, or even to Alexandria. But travelling through Greece and the great cities of Asia, at this time at the peak of their prosperity, must have been an absorbing experience for anyone with an interest in antiquity – which Septimius certainly possessed. Perhaps more than this though, it may have been a curiously moving experience for a man from Punic Africa to visit the heartland of Phoenician civilisation, to see Tyre and Sidon, the mother cities of Carthage. Septimius will have found that the predominant language was Aramaic, a Semitic tongue closely related to the Punic that he and his fellow-Africans still used. Greek was the language of the state and of culture. Aramaic was the language of the people.[1]

The most immediately significant experience for Septimius in Syria would be that he would serve under the command of the governor Pertinax. This contact was a fateful one for Septimius's entire future. P. Helvius Pertinax was one of the most remarkable figures of that or any age of Roman history. Born in north-west Italy, at Alba Pompeia in Liguria, he was the son of a freedman. That a man whose father had been a slave had even reached the eminence of the consulship had, some years earlier, attracted considerable surprise and comment, not all of it favourable. His future was to be even more remarkable.[2]

---

[1] 'interest in antiquity': cf. *HA Sev.* 4.7, 17.4, and pp. 205ff., below. – Aramaic: cf. e.g. *CAH* XI p. 622f.

[2] There is now an extensive literature on Pertinax. The *vita* in the *HA* supplies the basic outline (1.1–4.4, in particular, on his career before accession). The

Yet his astonishing career in the imperial service had not begun until he was thirty-four, almost precisely the age of Septimius himself when he went to serve under Pertinax. The great marshal's father, Helvius Successus, like other freedmen – the example that springs to mind is the father of the poet Horace[1] – had determined to advance his son's career by giving him a good education. He was sent to Rome to study with the celebrated *grammaticus*, Sulpicius Apollinaris of Carthage. Entry to Apollinaris's classes was perhaps secured through the mediation of Successus's patron, the well-connected senator Lollianus Avitus, on whose estates the Helvii lived. When his tuition from Apollinaris ended, Pertinax became a teacher himself. In the conservative atmosphere of the reign of Pius, a man of his antecedents had little prospects of any dramatic rise to success. Pertinax must have been a schoolmaster for at least ten years. Finally, in 160 he became discontented with his low income and decided on a very different kind of career. He asked his father's patron to get him a commission as a centurion. This would have assured him a steady job with reasonable pay and prospects for the rest of his working life. There had even been men, such as the great Marcius Turbo forty years before, who had risen to be Praetorian Prefect from such beginnings.[2] Pertinax had left his application for a

---

authenticity of much of this was impugned unjustifiably by R. WERNER, whose arguments were refuted by G. BARBIERI (1936), cf. also *PIR*[2] H 73 and *CP* no. 179. The accuracy of the *vita* has been confirmed by the *cursus*-inscription set up *c.* 169, from Brühl near Cologne, published by H. G. KOLBE in 1962. F. CASSOLA (1966) has published a short monograph on the career of Pertinax up to 180, and an article (1965) on his career under Commodus, which will be referred to as appropriate. Pertinax was born on 1 August 126, at Alba Pompeia. (In this chapter, information from the *vita Pertinacis* or Cassius Dio, to which references are readily available in *PIR*[2] H 73, is not given in every instance in the notes.) There is no particular reason why Pertinax's father need be considered to have spent all his life in Liguria, cf. A. R. BIRLEY (1969), p. 271f.

[1] Horace: cf. *PIR*[2] H 198.

[2] Apollinaris:*HA Pert.* 1.4. – Avitus:*HA Pert.* 1.5, cf. *PIR*[2] H 40. This is the same Avitus that was involved in the affairs of Apuleius. – 'conservative': cf. esp. E. BIRLEY (1953b), p. 208 and J. MORRIS (1965a), p. 29, where 'Servilianus' should be corrected to 'Severianus'. – 'ten years': F. CASSOLA (1966), p. 8 argues that he was a teacher for a short time only. – 'get him a commission': for discussion of the ways of gaining commissions in the Roman army, cf. esp. E. BIRLEY (1953a), pp. 141ff., ID. (1963), also H. G. PFLAUM (1950), pp. 195ff. – Turbo: *CP* no. 94.

commission rather too late to hope for this. However, Lollianus Avitus, for all his prestige, seems to have failed to acquire a centurionate for Pertinax. Perhaps he did not try very hard. Or possibly something made Pertinax change his mind. At any rate, he accepted instead an ostensibly more attractive post, as prefect of a cohort in Syria. This was the first grade of the equestrian *militiae*. Pertinax must therefore have acquired the rank of Roman knight at this time, with – in his case – the award of the *equus publicus*. Perhaps Avitus, or some other patron, supplied the funds necessary to give him the property-qualification of 400,000 Sesterces. He certainly did not get the money from his father.[1] But the point is that as prefect of an infantry battalion five hundred strong, of non-citizen soldiers, Pertinax had acquired only a short-service commission, with no fixed length of tenure. When he was replaced, there would be no guarantee of further employment.[2] The details of his beginnings in the imperial service are therefore tantalisingly incomplete.

A clue is provided by Cassius Dio, who appears to state that Pertinax began his army career through the mediation of another patron, whom he had met in the course of his teaching. This was Claudius Pompeianus, a native of Antioch in Syria. Pertinax might even have given lessons in Latin to this Greek-speaking senator. Pompeianus may have made the acquaintance of the governor of Syria while revisiting his home. Attidius Cornelianus, the governor under whom Pertinax was to serve, had been in Syria since 157. Pertinax's first meeting with Cornelianus was inauspicious. No doubt in his eagerness to take up his duties, he made use of the government posting-service to get to Antioch, without having the official pass (*diploma*) that was required. As a punishment the governor refused him any transport to get to his

---

[1] 'failed to acquire': for this interpretation cf. E. BIRLEY (1953a), p. 137, ID. (1957), p. 181, also *PIR²* H 73, followed by H. G. KOLBE, p. 411. No centurionate is recorded on the Brühl *cursus*. F. CASSOLA (1966), p. 8f. assumes that he must have held a centurion's commission. – 'prefect of a cohort': *HA Pert.* 1.6. – *equus publicus*: this information is supplied by the Brühl *cursus*, cf. Kolbe, pp. 410ff. In my view the *equus publicus* was not automatically awarded to all *equites Romani*, cf. A. R. BIRLEY, *HAC*, pp. 75ff. – '400,000 Sesterces': cf. e.g. M. HAMMOND (1959), p. 129 and n. 14. – 'money from his father': cf. *HA Pert.* 9.7 (*minimum patrimonium*, etc.).

[2] Cf. E. BIRLEY (1953a), pp. 133ff., esp. p. 145.

unit. Pertinax had to walk. This suggests, incidentally, that even if Pertinax, as a Roman knight, had now acquired some modest wealth, his means would not extend to equipping himself with his own horse.[1]

Unfortunately for Rome, the rigidity of Attidius Cornelianus over the *cursus publicus* regulations was not mitigated by military capacity. The following year the Parthian war broke out. In 162, after the defeat of Severianus in Cappadocia, Cornelianus attempted to restore the situation. He was ignominiously defeated. The Syrian army had been in a slack and undisciplined condition. Before long the balance was redressed. The expeditionary force under L. Verus came to Syria before the end of the year, and in 163 a great victory was won by Statius Priscus in Armenia. Pertinax had the opportunity to show his talents, showing a capacity for 'hard work'. Perhaps the new governor Cn. Julius Verus sent in a favourable report on him to the *ab epistulis*. Pertinax was promoted to the second grade of the equestrian officer's career. It may seem surprising that from Syria he was sent to distant Britain. But the Roman government never hesitated to transfer men from one end of the empire to the other, when the need arose. There was indeed a need in Britain for experienced men. The governor Calpurnius Agricola had probably asked Rome for battle-trained men – or perhaps specifically for men of high intelligence and maturity. It could even be that Julius Verus, himself a former governor of Britain, was asked directly to recommend an officer that he judged would be suitable for service in Britain.[2]

Pertinax became one of the five equestrian tribunes of the legion VI Victrix at York. These officers were not normally employed in direct command over troops. Their duties were mainly administrative. An ex-schoolmaster with several years of military service behind him, and one who had probably seen some fighting, will have been an invaluable

---

[1] Dio 73.3.1, cf. F. CASSOLA (1966), p. 13f., who rightly sees the importance of the statement that Pertinax's *teaching* had brought him into contact with Pompeianus. See further on this passage p. 112f., below. – *cursus publicus*: cf. e.g. A. N. SHERWIN-WHITE, p. 627f., etc.

[2] Cornelianus:*HA Pert.* 1.6 (not named, but cf. J. MORRIS [1965a], p. 29). – 'Parthian war': cf. pp. 64ff., above. – Julius Verus: *PIR*[2] J 618. – *ab epistulis*: cf. esp. E. BIRLEY (1953a), p. 142f., ID (1963), p. 21f. – 'Promoted':*HA Pert.* 2.1. – Agricola: p. 68, above.

staff officer. Calpurnius Agricola was engaged on an extensive re-organisation of the British frontier in the face of hostility both in the Scottish Lowlands and in the Pennines. The decision taken in principle by Julius Verus five years earlier, to abandon Scotland, was now carried into effect thoroughly. Hadrian's Wall was reoccupied in strength and became the frontier line once more. Pertinax's duties may have taken him away from York, close to the frontier. Legionary detachments were now being stationed at Corbridge on Tyne, which was becoming an almost unique military town, rather than a normal fort. There was only one place in the Empire at all like it, Dura-Europos in Syria, on the Euphrates. Pertinax may soon have gone to the Wall itself. He was given another unit, either the I or II Tungrians, a part-mounted infantry battalion, one thousand strong. If it was the I Tungrians, his base will probably have been Housesteads, in the central sector of the Wall. During his service in Britain it is just possible that Pertinax made the acquaintance of Septimius's brother Geta, who served as senatorial tribune with the legion II Augusta there in the 160s.[1]

Before the Parthian war ended preparations were in hand for the inevitable war on the Danube frontier. It was therefore an indication that Pertinax continued to show promise that his next appointment was to command a unit in that region. He was given the command of a cavalry regiment in Moesia. As *praefectus alae* he had now reached the third *militia*. His friend and patron Pompeianus was also serving on the Danube, in the much more exalted position of governor of Lower Pannonia, with his headquarters at Aquincum (Budapest). It may be coincidence, but Pertinax appears for the first time in the historical record in this province, adjacent to Upper Moesia. An altar has been found at Sirmium (Sremska Mitrovica) on the Save, dedicated to 'Jupiter Best and Greatest and Mars the Protector' by 'P. Helvius

---

[1] 'equestrian tribunes': E. BIRLEY (1953a), pp. 143ff. – Corbridge: I. A. RICHMOND (1943); also E. BIRLEY (1959). – Dura: cf. e.g. M. ROSTOVT-ZEFF (1938). – 'another unit': *HA Pert.* 2.1, *ac retentus*, was so interpreted by E. BIRLEY (1957), p. 18, and cf. *PIR*[2] H 73 (p. 64), whose opinion has been confirmed by the Brühl inscription, cf. H. G. KOLBE, p. 413f. – Geta: p. 68, above, and App. 1, no. 30. – On the dating of these posts, cf. A. R. BIRLEY (1968b), p. 223f.

Pertinax, prefect'. Sirmium was soon to become an important military headquarters. It was also on Pertinax's route from Britain to Moesia. But one may suspect that Pertinax's presence at Sirmium was brought about by Pompeianus, and that his unit was transferred to reinforce the Lower Pannonian garrison. In this post Pertinax will have been close to the first ominous outbreak of war, when Upper Pannonia was invaded by a force of six thousand Germans. The officer who repulsed them, Macrinius Avitus, was a little senior to Pertinax and, like him, had come to the Danube from the VIth legion in Britain.[1]

Pertinax had now reached a turning point in his new career. In normal conditions he might well have been obliged to retire from the service. There was only one further promotion open to him as an equestrian officer, the fourth *militia*. But the number of appointments available was so small as to make it out of the reach of most. The further alternative was to jump into the procuratorial service. No doubt with the backing of Pompeianus, Pertinax was appointed procurator of the *alimenta* system for the district of the *via Aemilia* in northern Italy. Although it was on the lowest rung of the ladder, with a salary of 60,000 Sesterces a year, the area had key significance at this time. It was almost certainly the year 168, precisely when the Emperors established their base at Aquileia. Pertinax was soon promoted again, his salary increasing to 100,000 Sesterces with the appointment as prefect of the German fleet. This appointment cannot have lasted long, perhaps less than a year, for Pertinax was then given a special procuratorship in Dacia, with a salary of 200,000 Sesterces. Thus within three years at the most he had climbed through all the grades of the procuratorial hierarchy. Within the 200,000 or ducenary category there were, it is true, variations of prestige, and he still had some way to go before reaching the topmost rung of the ladder. But the promotion he had achieved in the space of three years is very striking. The people of Cologne, where the German fleet was based, erected a statue to him when the news of his promotion came through.[2]

[1] 'third *militia*': *HA Pert.* 2.1, cf. H. G. KOLBE, p. 414f. – 'altar': D. 407, cf. F. CASSOLA (1966), pp. 8–10. – In spite of the arguments of Kolbe, it remains possible that Pertinax commanded a milliary *ala* in Moesia, cf. A. R. BIRLEY (1968b), p. 223f. and n. 49. – Avitus: *CP* no. 188+add.

[2] 'retire': cf. E. BIRLEY (1953a), p. 145. – 'fourth *militia*': cf. esp. E. BIRLEY

His new appointment was in a zone that lay in the thick of the action. In 170 Italy was invaded while Marcus Aurelius was trying unsuccessfully to launch a Roman offensive across the Danube. Roman losses were heavy, and they included one of the leading generals, M. Claudius Fronto, who was killed in battle. It is impossible to establish precisely where Pertinax was at the moment of the invasion. But at about this time his career took a backward turn. He was dismissed from his Dacian post, and not given any further appointment. This is all the more surprising in that his patron Pompeianus had now reached a new pinnacle of influence, having married the widowed Lucilla. One may surmise that the removal of Pertinax may have been engineered by enemies of Pompeianus, too weak to attack the Emperor's son-in-law in person. But Pompeianus soon needed Pertinax's assistance. He was entrusted with the task of clearing the invaders out of Italy, and selected Pertinax as his aide. Pertinax performed well, and was rewarded with promotion to the Senate. There was a desperate need for senators with military talent, and after a short period he was given the rank of ex-praetor and the command of a legion, the Pannonian I Adiutrix. Marcus had been informed of his dismissal in Dacia, and wanted 'to compensate for the wrong done him'. With this legion he completed the rout of the invaders by clearing the provinces of Raetia and Noricum. Soon after came a mysterious episode, the Rain Miracle. The long-delayed Roman offensive had at last begun. A Roman force operating in enemy territory was surrounded, exhausted from the heat and with no drinking water. A sudden cloudburst revived them and stunned the enemy, who were further disarrayed by hail and thunderbolts. The Roman victory which followed was commemorated on the coinage and in the sixteenth scene of the Aurelian Column. The followers of various religions claimed that their prayers had brought about the rain. Most versions of the story speak of the Emperor's presence – and some credit him with the prayers that brought the rain. But one source states that Pertinax was in command of the troops saved by the miraculous storm. Circumstantial evidence suggests that this is correct and that Pertinax

---

(1966), pp. 55ff. – 'alimenta': cf. esp. *CP* no. 179 (also A. R. BIRLEY [1968b], p. 223, n. 49). – Aquileia: A. R. BIRLEY (1968b). – For the other items, H. G. KOLBE, pp. 415ff., F. CASSOLA (1966), pp. 11ff.

was there as legate of the legion I Adiutrix in 172. The prestige Pertinax gained among the troops must have been immense.[1]

Pertinax probably went from his legionary command to govern the province of Upper Moesia, before being appointed consul in 175, with, as his colleague, Didius Julianus. The conjunction later seemed to have been fateful. Julianus's connections would have ensured him the consulship as his rightful due. Pertinax's tenure of the *fasces* (*in absentia*) provoked some to quote Euripides: 'Things of this kind wretched war brings to pass.' The Emperor, as if to answer critics, made a speech recommending Pertinax as consul, with 'a eulogy of him', and an account 'of everything that he had done or suffered'. Marcus frequently praised Pertinax both before the troops and to the troops, and 'publicly expressed regret that he was a senator and could not be made Praetorian Prefect'. In April 175 there was the rising in the east, when Avidius Cassius proclaimed himself Emperor, but was subsequently killed by one of his own officers. For the second time in the reign the east was in turmoil. Cassius was a Syrian, and had won considerable support. Marcus went to the east, and Pertinax was among the *comites* who accompanied him, though his second visit to Syria was brief. He returned to the Danube, governing successively Lower Moesia and Dacia and both provinces have left traces of his activity as governor, which cannot be accurately dated. But before the death of Marcus in 180 Pertinax was appointed governor of Syria.[2]

[1] '170' etc.: A. R. BIRLEY (1968b). – 'dismissed': *HA Pert.* 2.4, cf. F. CASSOLA (1966), pp. 14ff., etc. – 'Pompeianus needed Pertinax' etc.: *HA Pert.* 2.4–5, Dio 71.3.2–4, cf. Cassola, pp. 15ff., 30f., Birley pp. 215f., 221ff. – 'promotion', etc.: *HA Pert.* 2.5–6, cf. Cassola, pp. 15ff. – 'Rain miracle': cf. A. R. BIRLEY (1966a), esp. p. 326 (hesitant there about the date), Cassola, pp. 32ff. (But I do not follow Cassola's view [pp. 31ff.] that Pertinax was *praepositus vexillationibus* at this time. M. Valerius Maximianus, whose career [AE 1956, 124] he cites as a parallel, does not support his case: once he became a senator, Maximianus commanded vexillations in his capacity as legionary legate.) Cassola also devotes a lengthy discussion, pp. 17–28, to *adlectio*. Unfortunately he fails to distinguish clearly between *adlecti* (such as Pertinax and Maximianus) and *lato clavo exornati* (such as Septimius and his brother Geta). The latter category was a normal and continuous feature, not deserving special comment. But increase in numbers of *adlecti* in the strict sense is very marked in the reign of M. Aurelius.

[2] 'Upper Moesia': this is argued by A. R. BIRLEY (1963) expanding an idea of E. BIRLEY (1957), pp. 10, 18. F. CASSOLA (1966), p. 40, who was evidently

The significance of this appointment is manifest. In the year before his death Marcus had sensed that he had not long to live. He wanted to ensure the succession, and above all to ensure that Commodus continued to rely on Claudius Pompeianus. By placing a protégé of Pompeianus in this key province he could secure both the allegiance of the east and the maintenance of Pompeianus's influence after his death.

As governor of Syria, Pertinax had now, at the age of fifty-three, reached the summit of the senatorial career. In normal circumstances he would have looked forward to an honourable retirement, with the option of serving for a year as proconsul of Asia or Africa some fifteen years after his consulship, perhaps a second consulship might be hoped for, or even the Prefecture of the City of Rome.[1] But the retirement that was forced upon him only two years after the death of Marcus must have seemed a cruel anti-climax.

---

unaware of the paper by A. R. Birley, denies the possibility that Pertinax governed Upper Moesia before his consulship. – consulship: cf. *PIR*[2] H 73. – Euripides, *Suppliants*, *l.* 119, quoted in Dio 71.22.1. – 'speech': *HA Pert.* 2.10. I presume that his consulship entitled him to the honorific title of *comes*, by now seemingly reserved for consulars (cf. the list of epigraphically recorded *comites* assembled by H. G. PFLAUM [1962b], p. 90f.). – 'Danube': *HA Pert.* 2.10. I see no reason to take this, with Cassola, p. 39f., as a special command *ad Danuvii tutelam*. It seems preferable to regard the phrase as introducing the mention of the Moesian and Dacian commands. – 'Syria': *HA Pert.* 2.11–3.1, cf. Cassola, p. 41.

[1] Cf. esp. F. CASSOLA (1965), pp. 451ff. – 'Asia or Africa': cf. B. E. THOMASSON, I, pp. 14ff., esp. p. 30f.

IX

JULIA DOMNA

As legate of IV Scythica Septimius held the most prestigious of the three Syrian legionary commands. XVI Flavia, which his kinsman Severus had commanded, was at Samosata on the Euphrates. III Gallica was at Raphaneae in the southern part of the province. Where IV Scythica was stationed is unknown. But it was somewhere near Antioch, for whenever someone had to deputise for the governor, it was the legate of the Fourth who filled the role. Besides, it has been noticed that well-connected young men served IV Scythica as *tribunus laticlavius* with unusual frequency. Tribunes from an influential background would presumably have been able to pick which of the three legions to serve in, and proximity to Antioch would affect their choice. One of those who served in this post while Septimius commanded the legion may have been L. Marius Perpetuus, younger brother of the future general and biographer of the Caesars, Marius Maximus – if so, Perpetuus probably got his commission from Pertinax. The Augustan History states that Septimius was stationed 'near *Massilia*'. A simple emendation of the text produces the reading *circa Massiam*. Massias, or Massyas, was the name given to the plain that stretches from Chalcis, south-east of Antioch and south of Beroea (Aleppo), down to Epiphania (Hama). Somewhere in this flat land, broken only by the depression of the Orontes river on the west, and merging on the east into the pre-desert, Septimius served as commander of six thousand legionaries.[1]

[1] For the legions: cf. E. Ritterling in *RE*' 12 (1925), 1525f., 1560ff., 1765f. – 'kinsman Severus': App. I. – 'it has been noticed': *RE* 12, 1560. – Perpetuus: App. II. – 'near *Massilia*' etc.: cf. P. THOMSEN, but note the reservations of A. R. BIRLEY (1969) p. 261 n. 85. Thomsen identifies *Massyas* with a particular site,

He was certainly at Antioch from time to time, and had some official duties there. It may even be that he was acting governor for a short time, after Pertinax's dismissal. However this may be, the uninhibited Antiochenes made fun of him on some occasion, according to the Augustan History. No details or reasons are given. But Septimius remembered the slight. Apart from official business, one event which he is likely to have gone to Antioch to see is the Antiochene Olympics. They were held every four years for forty-five days, starting in the month of August. Marcus Aurelius had abolished all public spectacles at Antioch as a punishment for the people's support of the rebel Cassius. Commodus was petitioned to allow the games to be held again, and granted the request. No doubt Claudius Pompeianus still had some influence at the opening of his reign – a man named Pompeianus, perhaps a member of his family, was Secretary of the re-organised games held in summer 181. The teeming population of this city needed placating with public entertainment, as Lucius Verus had found – to his own satisfaction – twenty years previously. At this time Antioch may have had as many as half a million inhabitants, making it the largest city in the east after Alexandria.[1]

There was much here for Septimius to see and reflect upon. He will have come across Parthians and others from beyond the frontier. The Euphrates, which marked the boundaries of the Empire, lies only one hundred miles in a direct line from Antioch. Septimius can hardly have failed to note the vulnerability of the Syrian frontier and of the Syrian capital. As legate of IV Scythica he guarded the central sector of the province's defences, protecting Antioch.

From his base in northern Syria it would not be a long journey to

---

the modern Masyaf. But this is much too far away from Antioch (and rather too near to Raphaneae, although there are cases of legions placed fairly close together, e.g. X Gemina at Vindobona and XIV Gemina at Carnuntum). It is preferable to take *Massyas* in a wider sense, cf. e.g. *RE* 14 (1930), 2165f., where it is regarded as the name of 'a valley in Central Syria'.

[1] 'official duties there . . . made fun of':*HA Sev.* 9.4: *Antiochensibus iratior fuit, quod et administrantem se in oriente inriserant*, cf. Herodian 2.10.8. 'Olympics . . . Secretary of the games': cf. G. DOWNEY, pp. 230ff. – Lucius Verus: Fronto, *Princ.Hist.* 17=Haines, II 216,*HA Verus* 4.6, 6.1, etc. – 'half a million': Downey, p. 582f.

Tyre and Sidon. It is hard to believe that Septimius did not take the chance of going down there. At any rate, he did travel some way south. Cassius Dio reports that he consulted the oracle of Zeus Belos, that is, the local Ba'al, at Apamea. This city lies on the Orontes, about half way between Antioch and Emesa. The god's reply to his inquiry was a quotation from Homer:

> Eyes and head like Zeus who delights in the thunder,
> Like Ares his waist, his chest like Poseidon.

Whether Septimius instantly believed that the oracle in some way predicted a royal future for him when it quoted this description of Agamemnon, is not recorded. But he noted the words carefully.[1]

At some time during his stay in Syria he surely visited Emesa. The city may have seemed a dark and perhaps sinister place, for it was built of volcanic basalt. Since he visited the Temple of Ba'al at Apamea, it would have been understandable if he went to the much more famous Temple at Emesa. The people of that city revered a huge black stone, conical in shape. Perhaps it was a piece of the local basalt, but the Phoenicians claimed it had come down from Zeus – so it may have been a meteorite – and that it was an unworked image of the sun. The shrine was rich and widely renowned. 'All the neighbouring princes and rulers sent generous and expensive gifts there every year', according to Herodian. The priesthood was held by a family descended from the former native dynasty, that had ended a century earlier when the principality of Emesa and Arethusa was incorporated in the province of Syria. The family had long borne the Roman *gentilicium* Julius, a clear indication that they had received the citizenship before the reign of Claudius. The priest of Elagabalus, or Heliogabalus, as Greeks and Romans rendered the god's name, was an impressive figure. He was clad in 'barbaric' costume with long-sleeved gold-embroidered purple

[1] 'come across Parthians' etc.: cf. G. DOWNEY, pp. 232f., 254ff. (talking of Persians, perhaps imprecisely in the first instance, on the Syriarch Artabanios, mentioned by Malalas 285.17–19, cf. Downey, p. 232, n. 151). Cf. also F. GROSSO (1964), pp. 570 ff., with useful bibliography. – 'oracle': Dio 78.8.6, cf. Homer, *Iliad* 2.478–9. Dio adds that S. got a less favourable oracle when he was Emperor, cf. p. 204, below.

tunic reaching to his feet, gold and purple trousers, and a jewelled diadem on his head. At the time of Septimius's stay in Syria the priest was Julius Bassianus, whose Latin-sounding *cognomen* was a Romanised form of the Phoenician priestly title *basus*. He was well connected. He had two daughters, of whom the elder was married to a senator, Julius Avitus Alexianus. The younger was still unmarried. Her horoscope apparently foretold that she would marry a king. Presumably for that reason she had been named Domna, which is the same as the Aramaic name Martha, and means 'wife of a lord or king'. Septimius will have noted this with interest.[1]

Septimius's dismissal from his legionary command is not described in explicit terms. Nor indeed is the removal of Pertinax from the governorship. But the nature of Pertinax's replacement, and its date, is made clear by the Augustan History's statement that after his return to Rome and his attendance – for the first time – in the Senate-house, 'he was immediately ordered by Perennis to withdraw' to the family-property in Liguria. This 'exile' lasted for three years, and was ended by the fall of Perennis in 185. Hence Pertinax's dismissal clearly belongs to the immediate aftermath of the conspiracy of Lucilla. As a protégé of Lucilla's husband – even though Pompeianus had not been involved – he would be suspect. In the case of Septimius no such clue is given. He may have stayed on for a while after Pertinax's departure – at least, for long enough to make the acquaintance of the new governor, Domitius Dexter. He may also have overlapped with Fabius Cilo, who served as legate of XVI Flavia in the early 180s. All possible close contacts of Septimius with senators and other men of influence must be closely watched for at this stage in his career.[2]

The Augustan History does not state outright either that Septimius was dismissed or that he was told to withdraw from public life. But when his next move is observed in the context of the events of 182 there

[1] Herodian 5.3.4–7. It may be of course that the opulence of the temple and its priests only became exceptional after 193 (the description is Herodian's prelude to the coup of Elagabalus, 218). – 'a family': cf. App. I for details (nos. 10–18, 37–38). Note that Julius Avitus may not have become a senator until 193 or later – 'horoscope': cf. p. 123, below and App. I, no. 12.

[2] 'Pertinax' replacement', etc.: *HA Pert.* 3.1–3, cf. e.g. F. GROSSO (1964), pp. 145, 162f., F. CASSOLA (1965), p. 455. – Dexter and Cilo: App. III.

seems little reason to doubt it. He went to Athens 'to study, and for religious purposes, and to see the monuments and antiquities'. Tourism was by now something of a vogue. Less than twenty years before Pausanias had published his guide to ancient Greece, to cater for this very taste. There is no need to speculate what a tourist would have wished to see at Athens in the 180s – the Parthenon and the other monuments of the Acropolis, the Temple of Olympian Zeus completed by Hadrian, and the rest. Septimius had probably heard about Athens since his boyhood. One only has to recall that Sicinius Pontianus of Oea had studied there. A number of Lepcitanes had probably done likewise.[1]

The religious motives – *sacrorum causa* – are less clear, and are not specified. One may suspect a desire to be initiated into the Mysteries of Eleusis. Thus he could emulate the example of four Emperors – Hadrian, L. Verus, and most recently Marcus Aurelius and Commodus in 176. One can equally do no more than speculate about his studies, by reflecting which of the well-known teachers were living and working at Athens at this time. The great Herodes Atticus would be dead. One of the greatest of his pupils, Adrian of Tyre, was probably by now professor of Rhetoric at Rome. Septimius may have heard another pupil of Herodes, Chrestus of Byzantium. The holder of the chair of Rhetoric at Athens was now Julius Pollux, a pupil of Adrian. A man of mediocre talent, his main claim to fame was as author of an *Onomasticon* and as the composer of the wedding hymn for Commodus's marriage some years before. One teacher that Septimius may have met and liked at this time was Aelius Antipater of Hierapolis in Phrygia, his exact contemporary. At any rate, Antipater was later to be closely associated with Septimius as Emperor. There may have been others whose lectures Septimius attended at this time. Apollonius, a native of Athens, who held the archonship and was hierophant of the goddess Demeter at Eleusis, was one who may have impressed him.[2]

[1] 'withdraw from public life . . . Athens', etc.: *HA Sev.* 3.7, cf. F. GROSSO (1964), p. 163 and n. 3, A. R. BIRLEY, *HAC*, p. 72. – Pontianus: cf. p. 48., above.
[2] 'Four Emperors': A. R. BIRLEY (1966a), pp. 168, 266f. – 'Well-known teachers': the information derives from Philostratus *v.soph.* Cf. 2.1 (Herodes, cf. *PIR*² C 802); 2.10 (Adrian, cf. *PIR*² H 4); 2.11 (Chrestus); 2.12 (Pollus, cf. *PIR*² J 474, F.

At best these activities can only have palliated the boredom and frustration that so ambitious a man must have felt. The news from Rome in 183 and 184 will have occupied his attention, but it must have been hard for him to discern from it what the future was to bring. Commodus inaugurated the year 183 as consul, for the fourth time, with Victorinus, still City Prefect, as his colleague. But the reins of government were firmly in the hand of the Prefect of the Guard, Tigidius Perennis. The Emperor took a new title, Pius, and victories in the north won him fifth and sixth salutations as Imperator. Meanwhile fighting was going on in Britain, following the disaster there at the opening of the reign. The governor was Ulpius Marcellus, who ruthlessly suppressed the north Britons, and seems to have restored the abandoned Antonine Wall as the frontier, winning Commodus a seventh salutation and the title Britannicus. But his harsh character, vividly illustrated by Cassius Dio, caused trouble with the legions. There was an attempted coup, when the troops tried to invest a legionary legate named Priscus with the purple. He wisely refused. But Perennis took reprisals. The legates of the British legions were all dismissed and their duties assumed by equestrian officers. This was a severe and unprecedented blow against the system of cooperation between Senate and Emperor. No senator can have viewed the reduction of posts in the *cursus* with equanimity.[1]

GROSSO [1964], pp. 121 ff.); 2.24 (Antipater, cf. *PIR*² A 137, *CP* no. 230; also p. 207f., below); 2.19 (Apollonius). Cf. now G. W. BOWERSOCK (1969).

[1] 'consul': *FC* p. 51. – Victorinus: G. ALFÖLDY, *Reichsbeamte*, pp. 38ff. – Perennis: cf. the article by G. M. BERSANETTI (1957); further, F. GROSSO (1964), esp. pp. 164ff. (but I do not accept Grosso's argument, pp. 139ff., that Perennis was first appointed Praetorian Prefect by Commodus.) – 'Pius . . . Imperator': Grosso, pp. 145ff. dates the assumption of 'Pius' to between 10 December 182 and 3 January 183, cf. 163f.; also 615f., 518f. (on Imp. V and VI). – Marcellus: A. R. BIRLEY (1967b), pp. 76 and 81f. (also p. 246, below). Described by Dio 72.8.2–6. Discussed at length by Grosso, pp. 176ff., 445ff., who also devotes much space to the mysterious affair of the legionary legates. Valuable though Grosso's analysis is, I do not find it entirely satisfactory. For further discussion see now A. R. BIRLEY (1971). Here I must mention only that I do not accept his arguments (esp. pp. 11ff.) for dating the Priscus affair to 186. Grosso is followed by F. CASSOLA (1965), p. 460. F. MILLAR (1964), p. 129f. unfortunately does not deal with Priscus in his account of the death of Perennis. The relevant passages on the legionary legates are *HA Comm.* 6.2 and Dio 72.9.2.

Perennis's hostility to the Senate was far-reaching, if the Augustan History may be believed. Apparently many senators were put to death. Yet at the same time Perennis's own sons advanced rapidly to the heights of the senatorial *cursus*. One of them was given the principal credit for victories on the Danube. The prominence thus achieved by his family gave plausibility to the rumour that Perennis was plotting to place his own son on the throne. At the Capitoline Games on 15 October 184 a dramatic episode took place. Commodus had just taken his seat. Everyone was waiting for the performance to begin, when a man dressed in the ragged clothes of a Cynic philosopher ran out, silenced the crowd, and public addressed the Emperor: 'This is no time to celebrate festivals. . . . The sword of Perennis is at your throat. . . . His sons are winning the allegiance of the armies of Illyricum.' Perennis had the man put to death at once. The affair had obviously been arranged by his enemies – and he had many. A significant feature of this abortive attack on Perennis was the pointed reference to the Pannonian legions which he was alleged to have as his chief support. This is an unambiguous indication that men knew the support of that army to be vital for any attempt on the throne. Since the beginning of the second century it had been the army of the Danube, rather than of the Rhine, which was predominant.

The confused conditions that prevailed in the western half of the Empire finally provided the opportunity to overthrow Perennis in the following year. The impression of confusion is heightened by the fact that the death of Perennis is described in totally different terms by Dio and Herodian, although each of these writers was alive at the time and may even have been in Rome. But Herodian's version is clearly inferior. He attributes the fall of Perennis to the arrival at Rome of soldiers from Pannonia who revealed his secret plans. Dio has another story. The soldiers who came to Rome were fifteen hundred men from the army of Britain – and Commodus actually allowed them to carry out Perennis's execution themselves. His account – which is of course preserved only in abbreviated version – assigns the inspiration for this act to the legionary legates, or rather ex-legates. It is hard to understand why or how a contingent of troops from Britain should have turned up outside Rome. Dio gives no clue that it was anything other than a deliberate sending of a deputation. This may be doubted. It is probable that a force from the British army was already operating on the continent for another purpose, the suppression of brigandage. The end of the Marcomannic wars had left bands of runaway slaves and deserters roaming through Gaul, Spain and Italy. An inscription that may belong to this period shows that troops from Britain fought in Armorica under an equestrian officer. The former legionary legates may somehow have been able to exert influence on these men. The soldiers of the army in Britain were already mutinous and discontented. The ex-legates had a grievance. There was a powerful ally in the palace, the freedman Cleander, who may have urged Commodus to believe the accusations against Perennis.[1]

The death of the Prefect brought about many changes. Ulpius Marcellus was recalled from Britain, was tried and narrowly escaped with his life. There were other trials also. The place of Perennis as real master of the Empire was now taken by Cleander. Brought to Rome from Phrygia as a slave, to be a pack-carrier, he had become an imperial freedman and succeeded Saoterus as chamberlain. Now that Perennis was gone, Cleander bestowed and sold entry to the Senate, army commands, governorships, procuratorships. The great Aufidius Victorinus, renowned for his incorruptibility, preferred not to remain and watch. He committed suicide. But others had less scruples, especially those whom the domination of Perennis had thrust to the side. Pertinax was brought back and appointed governor of Britain, with the mandate of eliminating the spirit of mutiny in the army there. Septimius too was recalled, and received his first governorship, being appointed legate of Gallia Lugdunensis.

In this province he had no military force under his command, with

---

[1] 'hostility . . . Danube': *HA Comm.* 5.1–6.2. – 'Capitoline Games': I find F. GROSSO's (1964) solution, p. 173f., of the chronological problems in Herodian's narrative (1.9.2–5) convincing. E. HOHL (1954), p. 16f. dismisses the episode – only recorded by Herodian – as the product of that author's imagination. This is too extreme. – 'confusion': the point is well made by F. MILLAR (1964), p. 129. – 'brigandage . . . Armorica': cf. *CP* no. 196, where Pflaum argues the case, starting with the inscription D. 2770+add. Grosso, pp. 176ff. is dubious. Cf. Herodian 1.9.7, Dio 72.9.2–3, *HA Comm.* 6.2 – Cleander: Dio 72.9.3, cf. Grosso, pp. 189f.

the exception of the Urban Cohort at Lugdunum, five hundred strong. But he had a large province, stretching from its capital on the Rhône, which was also the meeting-place of the annual assembly of the three Gallic provinces, to the Atlantic and Channel coasts. His duties were those of any Roman governor: to keep the province quiet and peaceful, and to act as its Chief Justice. There may have been particular difficulties at this time, on account of the widespread and increasingly dangerous activities of the deserters. In 186 there was serious trouble in the southern part of the adjacent province of Upper Germany. In 187 one of the deserters' leaders, Maternus, is said to have been daring enough to try to assassinate Commodus at Rome itself.[1]

Soon after Septimius's arrival at Lyons, his wife died. He did not intend to remain a widower. But this time his burning belief in the power of the supernatural, and his own ambition, led him to make a careful choice of bride. 'He made inquiries about the horoscopes of potential brides, and since he had heard that there was a woman in Syria whose horoscope predicted that she would be married to a king, he sought her as his wife – that was Julia, of course – and through the mediation of friends he gained her hand.' Although this is not explicit in the Augustan History's account, he had surely learned Julia's horoscope while he was in Syria.

[1] Marcellus: Dio 72.8.6. F. GROSSO (1964), pp. 183ff., who rightly emphasizes the importance of this neglected passage, fails in my view to prove his dating of the recall and trial of Marcellus to late 184. – Cleander: cf. esp. *CP* no. 180 *bis*+ *mant.add.* (p. 1007f.). – Victorinus: Dio 72.11.1–4, cf. Grosso, p. 214f. – Pertinax: 3.5–6, 8–9; Dio 72.9.2, 73.4.1, cf. F. CASSOLA (1965). – Septimius: *HA Sev.* 3.8. – 'Urban Cohort': cf. *RE* Supp. 10 (1962), 1129f. – 'duties': cf. *Digest* 1.18.1ff., esp. 13. – 'deserters': E. HOHL (1954), pp. 17ff. does not believe in the existence of Maternus, recorded only by Herodian 1.10. However, he is willing to admit the occurrence of a *bellum desertorum* of some kind, mentioned *en passant* by *HA Comm.* 16.2, cf. *Pesc.Nig.* 3.4. Grosso, p. 235f. dates the Maternus affair to 187. But he goes much too far in elaborating what are in my view clearly bogus pieces of evidence in *HA Pesc.Nig.* and *Clod Alb.* to build up a picture of the deserters' war in the III Galliae. He also uses the Rottweil tablets, esp. pp. 436ff. They appear to record the suppression of disturbances in Upper Germany in 186. Cf. H. G. PELAUM (1963), p. 230f. for an improved text, further, G. ALFÖLDY (1967), pp. 44ff. Grosso, pp. 490ff. discusses the *expeditio Germanica tertia* (*HA Comm.*, 12.8 shows clearly, however, that it never took place; the inscription D. 1574, if it does refer to this, need only prove that some preparations had been made for the expedition before it was cancelled).

It must have been early in the year 187, if not before, that Septimius wrote to Syria. The marriage took place in the summer of that year. Julia was a striking, indeed beautiful woman, to judge from her later portraits, with fine and sensitive features. As Gibbon put it, she 'deserved all that the stars could promise her. She possessed . . . the attractions of beauty, and united to a lively imagination a firmness of mind, and strength of judgement, seldom bestowed on her sex.' She and Septimius would no doubt have had three languages in common, Greek, Latin and Aramaic – for it can hardly be doubted that the Punic-speaking Septimius would have been able to master the language of Phoenicia. Julia was a woman of culture, but it is doubtful whether her fluency in Latin was outstanding. It is likely that they spoke to each other in Greek, at first. Soon, no doubt, Julia would have acquired proficiency in Latin – apart from a year in the polyglot island of Sicily, she was not to return to a Greek *milieu* for six years.[1]

Some time after his proposal of marriage had been accepted, Septimius had a dream: the Empress Faustina, dead these eleven years, was preparing the bridal chamber for him and Julia, in the Temple of Venus, near the Palace at Rome. He had other dreams at Lugdunum, to one of which he attached a deep meaning. In one, water seemed to gush from his hand. In another, the Roman Empire itself, personified, approached him and saluted. Most impressively of all, someone took him up to a high mountain, from which he could see Rome and all the world. 'As he gazed down on all the land and all the sea, he laid his hands on them as one might on an instrument capable of playing all modes, and they all sang together.' This is Cassius Dio's version. The Augustan History, which has more or less the same story (though it places the dream at the time he was in Spain), has the variant that 'the provinces sang together to the accompaniment of the lyre and flute'.[2]

Julia soon conceived. Their first child, a son, was born on 4 April 188. He was given the *cognomen* Bassianus after his mother's father, the high priest of Ba'al. His *praenomen* is not recorded, but it was probably that of his father, Lucius. The child is said to have had a Christian

[1] *HA Sev.* 3.9, cf. A. R. BIRLEY, *HAC* pp. 72f. and App. 1.
[2] D. Faustina: Dio 74.3.1. – Lugdunum dreams: *ib.* 2–3, *HA Sev.* 3.5, cf. J. HASEBROEK (1921), p. 9f.

wet-nurse. If the statement – in Tertullian – is true, two comments are in place. First, there was certainly a strong Christian community at Lugdunum. It had been severely attacked just over ten years before, when numbers had been martyred, but there is no suggestion that it had been wiped out. On the contrary, it is not unlikely that the martyrdoms had strengthened it. Second, of the ten named martyrs of 177, six had Greek names (and the Greek origin of two is explicitly mentioned by Eusebius). A Christian nurse at Lugdunum is likely to have been an immigrant Greek, perhaps even from Syria, and this will have commended her to Julia.[1]

Probably at the end of this year Septimius's governorship in Gaul ended and he returned to Rome, where his name went into the ballot for a proconsulship in the New Year. He received Sicily. Julia was pregnant again, and early in 189 a second son was born. He was named after Septimius's father and brother: P. Septimius Geta. In midsummer the family went to Sicily. It is not impossible that Septimius's brother was his predecessor as proconsul. His career also may have suffered a setback while Perennis was in power. It is impossible to tell at what pace his rise in the *cursus* proceeded, but its stages were closely parallel to that of Septimius: a legionary command (in Lower Moesia), a provincial governorship (Lusitania) and a proconsulship.[2]

While Septimius had been in Gaul the pace had quickened in the murderous politics of Commodus's reign. In Britain Pertinax had been almost lynched by his own men when a legion broke into open mutiny. This may have been when he refused to let the British army set him up as Emperor – 'for they wanted to set up any one (other than Commodus) as Emperor, preferably Pertinax himself'. While in Britain Pertinax took a surprising step. He wrote to Commodus, informing him that the Emperor's brother-in-law Antistius Burrus was seeking

[1] Bassianus: App. I. The nickname Caracalla which he was given after his father's death is avoided in this work except in chapter 17. – 'wet nurse':-Tertullian, *ad Scap*. 4.6. – 'martyrdoms': Eusebius *HE* 5.1. There is some debate about the background, cf. J. H. OLIVER, W. H. C. FREND, pp. 1ff., A. R. BIRLEY (1966a), pp. 275ff. for the theory (which is that of Oliver), criticised by T. D BARNES (1968a), p. 518f. (this article and another – 1968b – it should be noted, have placed the study of the persecutions in a wholly new light).

[2] 'returned to Rome . . . Sicily': *HA Sev*. 4.2, cf. A. R. BIRLEY, *HAC* p. 73. – Geta: App. I, no. 31. – 'brother': App. I, no. 30.

the throne, in association with his fellow-Numidian Arrius Antoninus. Antoninus must have been well known to Pertinax, and Burrus's father, Antistius Adventus, had served with distinction as a general in both Parthian and Marcomannic wars. It is fair to suppose that Pertinax had some evidence for his allegation. It may be, for example, that the two men had approached him, by letter or through an intermediary, wanting the support of the three disaffected British legions and their commander-in-chief. It may therefore have been an act of self-preservation to unmask the plans of Burrus – who, it may well be, might have seemed to Pertinax incapable of the task, not *capax imperii*. There may have been another motive. Burrus is said to have been 'denouncing and reporting to Commodus' everything that was being done – by the freedman Cleander. As Pertinax himself had regained his influence thanks to Cleander, he may have been persuaded by the freedman to act against a man whose outspokenness threatened to end his power. The death of Burrus, which apparently involved the fortunes of many others, probably occurred in 187. Soon after this, Pertinax asked to be relieved of his command: 'The legions,' he said, 'were hostile to him because of his strict discipline.' He returned to Rome, and was given the relatively undemanding civilian post of supervising the *alimenta* system.[1]

He had become something of a hero on account of his success in quelling the mutiny. 'When a horse called Pertinax won a horse-race – it was raced by the Green faction and was favoured by Commodus – its partisans raised a great shout: "It is Pertinax!" The others, their opponents – in disgust at Commodus – added a prayer, shouting out: "If only it was!", referring to the man, not the horse.' By now Cleander was beginning to feel more confident. Early in 188 he disposed of the Praetorian Prefect Atilius Aebutianus, the latest of the numerous successors to Perennis's command over the Guard. He now obtained direct personal authority over the praetorians, not as normal Prefect

[1] Pertinax in Britain, etc.:*HA Pert.* 3.5–10,*HA Comm.* 6.10–12, 8.4; Dio 72.9.2, 73.4.1. The whole Burrus and Antoninus business is hideously complicated. Cf. F. GROSSO (1964), esp. pp. 253ff. and F. CASSOLA (1965), pp. 464ff. Death of Burrus: *HA Comm.* 6.11. In spite of *HA Pert.* 3.7, there is no necessity to believe that the deaths of Burrus and Antoninus (next note) happened at the same time. – *alimenta*: cf. F. CASSOLA (1965), pp. 460ff.

but as 'Bearer of the Dagger', *a pugione*, with two colleagues as Prefects. After reaching this position Cleander had no compunction in arranging the death of Arrius Antoninus.[1]

In the summer of 188 Pertinax went to Africa as proconsul. His term of office is alleged to have been stormy with rioting at Carthage provoked by prophecies from the priests of Juno Caelestis – the Punic goddess Tanit. A year later in Sicily Septimius was also involved with the supernatural. But in his case he was responsible himself. 'He was accused of consulting seers or astrologers about the imperial position.' There is no reason to doubt the accuracy of this report in the Augustan History. After ten years with an Emperor like Commodus on the throne, the atmosphere of intrigue and uncertainty must have been intense. When he returned to Rome in the summer of 190, he had to face an investigation – the charge could be construed as treason. The case was taken by the Prefects of the Guard, and he was exonerated – his accuser being crucified.[2]

While he had been away some dramatic changes had taken place. Pertinax had become Prefect of the City on his return from Africa. The year 190 was the year of the twenty-five consuls. Commodus, holding office for the sixth time, opened the year with Petronius Sura Septimianus as his colleague (brother of the Emperor's brother-in-law Mamertinus). Commodus obviously resigned the *fasces* after a matter

---

[1] The horse: Dio 73.4.1–2 (this was while he was still in Britain. See p. 140 below, for the re-appearance of the horse), discussed by F. GROSSO (1964), p. 453f. – Aebutianus: Grosso, pp. 239ff. throws new light on the dating of this man's Prefecture. – Cleander: cf. *CP* no. 180 *bis, mant.add.*, discussing esp. *AE* 1961, 280. I follow Pflaum's interpretation here in spite of Grosso's criticism, pp. 262ff. – Arrius Antoninus: *HA Comm.* 7.1. This places his death shortly before Cleander's own (see p. 129, n. 1).

[2] Africa: *HA Pert.* 4.2 there is much dispute over the date, cf. mostly recently F. CASSOLA (1965), pp. 462ff. G. CHARLES-PICARD (1959b) has a fascinating analysis of *HA Pert.* 4.2 (where he reads *canum*, interpreted as priests of the goddess), and seeks to show that Pertinax deliberately provoked a grain shortage: somewhat too macchiavellian, even for the reign of Commodus, cf. F. GROSSO (1964), pp. 624ff. And the date Picard adopts, 189–190, raises problems, cf. Cassola, *l.c.* C. R. WHITTAKER, p. 353 suggests that partisans of Burrus and Antoninus fomented trouble against Pertinax. While in Africa Pertinax had occasion to pass sentence on Septimius's kinsman Plautianus, so it would appear: cf. App. 1. – Sicily: *HA Sev.* 4.3, cf. J. HASEBROEK (1921), p. 14f.

of days. His successor will have served as suffect consul with Sura Septimianus for the rest of January, and a new pair of suffects must have taken office at the beginning of each of the remaining eleven months of the year. It was a scandalous climax to Cleander's selling of offices. Septimius was one of the twenty-five consuls, who, Dio specifically states, were 'appointed by Cleander'. But before Septimius's year of office in Sicily ended in midsummer 190, Cleander had fallen. The death of Arrius Antoninus had made him intensely unpopular with the volatile *plebs*. In addition, he had made himself at least one highly dangerous enemy, Papirius Dionysius. This man, after a distinguished equestrian career begun under Marcus, had been serving as Prefect of the *annona*. He was then appointed Prefect of Egypt, a normal promotion for a man of his status. But he may not even have reached Egypt, or, if he did, his promotion was rapidly cancelled, and he was recalled to be Prefect of the grain-supply. Such retrogradation was highly unusual at Rome. But back in his old position he was well placed to hurt Cleander. He deliberately created a corn-shortage, a sure way to arouse unpopularity in the capital against any Roman government.[1]

Rumours swiftly blamed Cleander for the situation. Herodian, who was in Rome shortly after this, if not during the crisis, simply repeats them as if they were true: 'Cleander, by buying up most of the grain supply and putting it in storage, hoped to get control of the people and the army – if he first made them short of necessities and then relieved their wants by lavish free distributions. The Romans however hated the man and blamed him for all their troubles.'

Significantly the discontent broke out during a performance in the Circus Maximus. This vast sports stadium was capable of seating at least two hundred thousand spectators. It was a standing source of

[1] Pertinax: *HA Pert.* 4.2–4, cf. F. CASSOLA (1965), p. 464. – 190: Dio 72.12.4, *HA Sev.* 4.4, cf. A. R. BIRLEY, *HAC* p. 74. – Sura Septimianus: App. I. – Dionysius: *CP* no. 181. F. GROSSO (1964), pp. 290ff., discusses the Dionysius affair at great length. However, his attempt to tie the chronology down firmly is invalidated by J. Rea's new reading of P. Harris 71.26, lines 6–9 (cf. O. W. REINMUTH, pp. 102ff. However, Reinmuth is mistaken in asserting that Dionysius was not Prefect of Egypt at all; this is proved by *IGR* I 135). The affair is handled at length by C. R. WHITTAKER. Some of his conclusions are invalid, but his attempt to place the affair in its context as one of many popular disturbances from the period 180–235 is valuable.

128

danger if the mob got out of hand. As Prefect of the *annona*, with his offices a few yards from the Tiber end of the Circus, Dionysius may have been the official who controlled the seating for the shows. It would then have been easy for him to arrange for the favourable positioning of his agents.

> As the horses were about to start the seventh lap, a crowd of children ran into the Circus led by a tall maiden of grim appearance – who, afterwards, because of what happened, people thought must have been a goddess. The children shouted out in unison, long and bitterly. The people took up the chant, and then began to shout out every conceivable insult. Finally the mob jumped down from their seats and went to look for the Emperor, calling out many blessings on him and many curses against Cleander.

Commodus was at this moment at the Villa he had confiscated from the Quintilii, a few miles out of Rome along the *via Appia*. Cleander sent a few soldiers against the mob, but it was undeterred, especially, Dio records, 'because it was encouraged by the strength' of some other 'troops'. Who were these troops? Dio's abbreviated account gives no clue. But in disturbances at the theatre and on other such occasions, the official whose duty it was to keep order was the City Prefect with the fifteen hundred men of the Urban Cohorts.

Pertinax was thus allowing the troops under his command to fight the Guard. For fighting did in fact break out between the praetorian cavalry – or possibly it was the *equites singulares*, Horse Guards – and the Urban Cohorts, the latter entering the conflict on the side of the crowd when the cavalry began to ride them down. Commodus sent for Cleander, in panic, and had him beheaded.[1]

---

[1] Dio 72.13 is more reliable than Herodian 1.9.2–5 on this remarkable affair. The now extensive literature is discussed by F. CASSOLA (1965), pp. 464ff., referring esp. to E. HOHL (1954), C. R. WHITTAKER and F. GROSSO (1964). *HA Comm.* 7.1–2 attributes the fall of Cleander to a wave of unpopularity caused by the execution of Arrius Antoninus. (This, even if inaccurate, at least suggests that the latter event was not long before 190.) – 'controlled . . . seating': cf. D.5049. – 'duty to keep order': cf. Grosso, p. 298f. and *RE* Supp. 10 (1962), 1132f. (against other views). – Cassola, following Whittaker, prefers to believe that Pertinax was a supporter of Cleander, and that the successful attack on the latter was aimed in part against him.

Pertinax's change of front vis-à-vis Cleander is not difficult to explain. For one thing, he had had the chance to observe the man at close quarters. Besides this, both Dionysius and another key figure, Julius Julianus, who were keenly interested in getting rid of Cleander, were men whom Pertinax is likely to have known well and trusted. It seems that Julianus was serving as Prefect of the Guard, with one Regillus, under Cleander. When Cleander was killed, they acquired substantive control – if only briefly. Julianus's career had begun many years before as prefect of a cohort in Syria at precisely the time when Pertinax himself was there in that rank. He too, like Pertinax, had commanded vexillations in the Marcomannic wars. Dionysius, although not primarily a military man, had had an administrative post during the second Marcomannic war at the end of Marcus's reign. Pertinax could have felt solidarity with men of this kind.[1]

Julianus's fellow-Prefect Regillus was soon removed. By 15 July 190 Julianus was sole Prefect. Since Septimius on his return from Sicily was acquitted by 'the Prefects of the Guard', the investigation perhaps took place between 1 July and 15 July. On the other hand he may have been summoned home before his full year was up at the end of June. Again, Julianus may have been given another colleague after the fall of Regillus. One Motilenus is mentioned as having been Prefect after the death of Cleander. Cleander's fate was not allowed to disturb the arrangements for the consulship – too many were involved. Septimius duly held office, with the otherwise unknown Apuleius Rufinus as his colleague. After his month's tenure of office, no appointment was immediately forthcoming. A period of waiting in the background was in any case desirable, for a new blood bath was about to begin. Septimius was 'without employment for about a year after his consulship'.[2]

---

[1] 'change of front': this is all very speculative. – Julianus: *CP* no. 180. Cf. also L. L. HOWE, p. 67f. and E. BIRLEY (1968), p. 45f. on Regillus (*HA Comm.* 7.4).

[2] F. GROSSO (1964), esp. p. 271f., rightly points out that *CIL* XIV 4378 shows Julianus to have been sole Prefect in early July 190. His speculation about Julianus's position prior to that is unfortunately too dependent on the older reading of P. Harris 71 (cf. p. 128, n. 1, above). – Motilenus: cf. E. BIRLEY (1968), p. 46f. (*HA Comm.* 9.2), cf. Grosso, p. 324f. – Apuleius Rufinus:*HA Sev.* 4.4, cf. p. 128, n. 1, above. – 'without employment': *HA, ib.*

X

THE CONSPIRATORS

The fall of Cleander had inevitable repercussions among the ruling classes. Pertinax's position was safe – and the imperial mint issued coins commending the conduct of his Urban Cohorts. But Julius Julianus did not long enjoy his position at the pinnacle of the equestrian order, the reward for more than thirty years' service. The veteran general was embraced in public and called 'Father' by Commodus. But he had to submit to indignities at the Emperor's hands. Being pushed into a swimming-pool by Commodus, when clad in the formal toga and in the presence of his own staff, could be laughed off, perhaps. But it was another matter when the Prefect of the Guard was made to dance naked before the Emperor's concubines, clashing cymbals and making grimaces. The charade did not last long. Julianus was murdered.[1]

Other executions followed. One of these must have been noted with anxiety or at least particular interest by Septimius and Julia. A prominent Emesene, who may well have been a kinsman of Julia, was the victim, one Julius Alexander. The motive for this murder as given by Dio sounds surprising but may well be plausible: it was because 'he had brought down a lion with his javelin, from horseback'. The Emperor who prided himself on his gladiatorial skill could not endure competition. Commodus's mania for the arena was soon to become further intensified. The Augustan History states that Alexander was executed for rebellion. That may well have been the official version, justified by the man's behaviour when he learned that the assassins had

---

[1] 'coins': *BMC* IV p. clxv, followed by F. GROSSO (1964), p. 299f. – Julianus: Dio 72.14.1, *HA Comm.* 11.2–3, 7.4. Grosso, p. 321, dates his death to early 191. It could have been in late 190.

arrived at Emesa. He somehow contrived to kill both them and his enemies in the city, and set off for the Euphrates, hoping for asylum with Parthia. 'And he would have escaped,' says Dio, 'if he had not taken a boy-favourite with him, for he was an excellent horseman himself. But he could not bear to abandon the boy, who was exhausted. So when he began to be overtaken, he killed both the boy and himself.'[1]

This was only the beginning of the bloody purge. The Augustan History gives the names of fifteen senators, at least twelve of whom were ex-consuls, who were put to death in the last two and a half years of the reign. They included Sulpicius Crassus, proconsul of Asia, Commodus's brother-in-law Mamertinus and the latter's brother Septimianus. Another victim was a woman of noble birth, first cousin of Marcus Aurelius, Annia Fundania Faustina. Her daughter Vitrasia had been murdered after the conspiracies of 182 and she herself was living in Achaia at the time, no doubt in deliberately chosen retirement. As for the fifteen senators, the Augustan History notes with all of them that they were killed *cum suis*, 'together with their kin'. And the biographer adds, after recording the death of Annia: *et alios infinitos*. It may be an exaggeration that 'innumerable others were put to death'. But there can be no doubt that many more than the fifteen senators and one noblewoman lost their lives. The panic that was thereby created must have been accentuated by the recurrence of plague, the greatest outbreak that Dio – who was too young at the time to remember the great plague of 166–167 – ever experienced: 'two thousand people often died at Rome in a single day'. He added a curious story. 'Also at this time, many others, not only in the City but throughout most of the Empire, died at the hands of criminals who smeared deadly drugs on tiny needles and were hired to infect people with them.' Whatever the facts behind this peculiar anecdote, it reveals a great deal about the climate of the time.[2]

[1] Alexander: Dio 72.14.1–3, *HA Comm.* 8.3; cf *PIR*² J 134, F. GROSSO (1964), pp. 322ff.

[2] 'Purge': *HA Comm.* 7.5–8, cf. F. GROSSO (1964), pp. 357 ff., who dates its beginning in accordance with his date for the death of Julianus, cf. p. 131, n. 1, above. – 'plague': Dio 72.14.3–4, cf. F. MILLAR (1964), p. 131, Grosso, pp. 250ff. (who dates the outbreak to 188/189, preferring Herodian's implied date 1.12.1–2 to that suggested by Dio's order of events).

The death of Cleander had left a power vacuum, which Julius Julianus had not filled. In 191 unmistakable signs appeared that Commodus himself, now aged twenty-nine, was at last asserting his own authority. Coins of the late 190 had proclaimed a new 'Golden Age of Commodus'. Now, in 191, Commodus changed his names. Abandoning Marcus and Antoninus, that he had inherited on his feather's death, he reverted to his original names, Lucius Aelius Aurelius Commodus. There can be no doubt that he was finally sloughing off any allegiance, even token, to the memory of Marcus. If there was any positive indication in the change, it could be that it showed merely that Commodus was now going to be 'his own man'. Or perhaps it was intended as deference to the memory of Lucius Verus, after whom he had been named originally. The coinage now began to identify Commodus with Hercules, and his devotion to oriental cults was intensified – those of Isis and Serapis, and Mithras, in particular.[1]

Meanwhile a new Praetorian Prefect had been appointed. This was Aemilius Laetus, a man from Thaenae in Africa. His previous career is unknown. It may be that he owed his appointment to the freedman Eclectus, Cleander's successor as chamberlain. Eclectus had started in the service of Lucius Verus, after whose death he joined the household of Ummidius Quadratus. After the latter's execution in 182 he entered the imperial household again, together with Marcia, the freedwoman who was Quadratus's mistress. She became the mistress of Commodus, and after the death of Cleander acquired immense influence over him. Laetus, Eclectus and Marcia between them now had the task of controlling Commodus, if this should be possible.[2]

Laetus is the first certainly known African to have commanded the Guard. It was yet one more sign of the continually increasing advance of men from this part of the Empire. It is worth recording here that the Christian leader at Rome at this time was an African, Pope Victor. As

---

[1] Coins: *BMC* IV, pp. clxvi, clxxvii, clxxxi–ii. Cf. F. GROSSO (1964), p. 319. – Names: cf. esp. Grosso, p. 319f., etc. – 'Hercules . . oriental cults': Grosso, pp. 331ff.

[2] Laetus: *AE* 1949. 38, supplying his *origo*. Cf. A. R. BIRLEY (1969), p. 252f. – Eclectus: *PIR*² E 3, cf. F. GROSSO (1964) p. 168, n. 6, etc. – Marcia: Grosso p. 168, n. 3, etc. She was supposedly a friend of the Christians, cf. W. H. C. FREND, pp. 318ff., Grosso p. 674f., etc.

the first Latin-speaking Bishop of Rome Victor was to play a key role in the development of the Church. This is another example of the dominant influence that men from Africa were now exerting at all levels of society. It is no surprise to read in the Augustan History that Commodus planned a visit to Africa, probably early in 191. This project was abandoned – it was only a pretext to get an extra grant of money voted, the biographer alleges. This is unlikely. Commodus could easily have laid his hands on whatever funds he needed. There may have been another motive, but one can only speculate. Perhaps, after the murders of Burrus and Antoninus, it was thought necessary to restore his popularity in Africa. After all, that province supplied two thirds of Rome's corn.[1]

Laetus soon began to exercise his power. His brother Pudens, a former legionary centurion, was attached to the Emperor's personal bodyguard. In the summer of 191 Laetus put through a surprising appointment. Septimius was made governor of Upper Pannonia on his recommendation. With its three legions, this province could be of vital importance. No large army lay nearer to Italy. Yet Septimius was an unlikely man to choose. Few men were given command of so large an army unless they had first had some experience of post-consular provincial government or, in the case of Upper Pannonia, unless they had governed the Lower province immediately before their consulship. Septimius had done neither, and his previous military experience was strictly limited to his legionary command in Syria. He had never served on Rhine or Danube. The Roman imperial governments clearly did not permit specialisation, and it was rare for a man to serve two terms in the same province. But this avoidance of specialisation was not carried to extremes. Service somewhere on the northern frontiers was generally

---

[1] Victor: cf. G. LA PIANA pp. 222ff. Note his apt comments, p. 224: 'The fact that in the year 193, when Septimius Severus, born of an equestrian family in Roman Africa, was recognised as emperor, the Christian community of Rome was also governed by a bishop who was a native of the same Roman Africa, is highly suggestive. Needless to say, there is no direct link, but they bear witness to the importance then acquired by the African element in the life of the capital, and both facts affected more than is commonly recognised the future destinies of empire and of church.' – 'Commodus planned', etc.: *HA Comm.* 9.1, cf. F. GROSSO (1964) pp. 344f., 626, etc. – 'two thirds . . . corn': R. M. HAYWOOD (1938) pp. 42ff.

a prerequisite for a governor of one of the major provinces there.[1]

Septimius may not have been made aware at first of the reasons for his selection. But his star was in the ascendant – and no doubt his credit rating improved also. Up to this moment his property in Italy had consisted of a small house in Rome and the farm at Veii. Shortly before his departure for his province he purchased elaborate gardens, *horti*, in the city.

At the same time or a little later, his brother Geta was also appointed governor of a Danubian province, Lower Moesia, with two legions. When Clodius Albinus of Hadrumetum was made governor of Britain the result was that men from Africa controlled eight of the northern legions. It may be that some, if not all, of the other northern provinces were placed in the hands of men from Africa too, or at least in the hands of men whom Laetus and Pertinax could trust. The governor of Dacia, appointed at latest in 192, was one Q. Aurelius Polus Terentianus. Study of his nomenclature suggests, although it cannot prove, that he was a native of Africa. In any case, he had almost certainly served under Pertinax in Britain a few years before; and as a *fetialis* he was a fellow-member of the same priestly college as Septimius Geta. Another *fetialis*, incidentally, was sent to Lower Moesia to command one of the legions. This was L. Marius Maximus Perpetuus Aurelianus, the future biographer of the Caesars, whose younger brother had perhaps served under Pertinax and Septimius in Syria.[2]

Legionary legates were appointed directly by the Emperor (or in his name). At a lower level, provincial governors had wide powers of patronage. The influence wielded by Septimius, Geta, Albinus and Polus Terentianus would be felt in many areas. They had the right to give commissions to officers up to and including the rank of *tribunus laticlavius*. Septimius alone could offer positions to three *tribuni laticlavii* and fifteen *angusticlavii*, and had in his army seven auxiliary cohorts and five *alae* of cavalry (one of them an elite milliary *ala*), in

[1] Pudens: *AE* 1949. 38, cf. A. R. BIRLEY (1969) p. 252f. – 'Upper Pannonia': *HA Sev.* 4.4, cf. A. R. Birley p. 261; also E. BIRLEY (1953b) p. 211, ID. (1957) p. 10.

[2] Property: *HA Sev.* 4.5, cf. pp. 36ff., above. – Geta: App. I, no. 30. – Albinus: G. ALFÖLDY (1968), A. R. BIRLEY (1969) p. 265f. – Terentianus; App. III. – Maximus: App. II.

command of which he could place his own nominees. One of the *tribuni laticlavii* that he appointed seems to have been a kinsman, Julius Septimius Castinus.[1]

In 191 Commodus decided to hold the consulship for the seventh time, for 192. Pertinax was chosen as his colleague – Commodus was, the Augustan History says, pleased with the sixty-five-year-old Prefect of the City. No reason is given for his satisfaction. Pertinax is said to have performed his duties as Prefect 'with extreme gentleness and consideration'. Unfortunately the text of the Augustan History is defective at this point, making it unclear whether this had anything to do with Commodus's feelings about him. However this may be, either in 191, or soon after Commodus and Pertinax inaugurated the year 192, Pertinax was approached by Laetus and Marcia to participate in a conspiracy to murder the Emperor. He accepted. Without doubt he was already Laetus's choice as successor to Commodus.[2]

There had been many attempts against Commodus's life. The entire reign is a story of miscarried conspiracies. This time careful steps were taken to ensure success. The packing of the major northern provinces with safe men has already been described. Egypt was always of crucial importance. In the second half of 192 the Prefect Larcius Memor, who had been in office for less than two years, was replaced by one Mantennius Sabinus. No explicit connection has been recorded between Sabinus and the conspirators. But it may be more than a coincidence that his wife came from Praeneste, where Pertinax's father-in-law Flavius Sulpicianus had estates. It is reasonable to guess that Pertinax and Sabinus were on terms of more than nodding acquaintance. As important as Egypt was Syria. Events in Parthia had

---

[1] On appointments, cf. E. BIRLEY (1953a) pp. 141ff., ID. (1957) p. 4. – The governors' right to appoint cavalry officers is not so certain. For the garrison of Upper Pannonia see the convenient list given by J. FITZ (1962) p. 37; further A. Mócsy in *RE* Supp. 9 (1962) 617ff. – E. BIRLEY (1963) p. 29 and n. 5, on *CIL* XIII 6646, notes that by an unusual promotion an *aquilifer* of the Upper Pannonian legion I Adiutrix was made centurion in the Upper German legion VIII Augusta: 'transfers such as [this] . . . may well have contributed to the readiness of the legions in the two Germanies to support the cause of Septimius . . . in AD 193.' – Castinus: App. III.

[2] 'Pertinax . . . chosen': *HA Pert.* 4,3-4, cf. A. R. BIRLEY (1969) esp. pp. 250ff. – 'already Laetus's choice': *ib.*

created a delicate situation there. The Parthian king Vologaeses III had been either challenged or was about to be deposed after reigning for over forty years. Laetus and Pertinax may have been unable to control the selection of the governor of Syria. The post went to Pescennius Niger. Dio says that he was given the job precisely because of his mediocrity. This may have made him seem harmless. In a suspect passage, the Augustan History alleges that he owed the appointment to an athlete with whom Commodus trained, Narcissus. The two consular proconsulships, Asia and Africa, were given to Asellius Aemilianus and Cornelius Anullinus. Aemilianus was a kinsman of Clodius Albinus, hence perhaps of African origin. He had also been Niger's immediate predecessor as governor of Syria. It may have been thought that he could exert some influence over the Syrian legions if need should arise. Anullinus, a Spaniard, may have been a friend of Septimius Severus.[1]

Towards the end of the year 192 Commodus's pathological inclinations became even more extreme. He now identified himself completely with Hercules. As the Roman Hercules the Emperor wished to become the divine founder of Rome, and the city was renamed *colonia Commodiana*. All the months of the year were likewise changed and were now to bear his own extravagant nomenclature – which had now conveniently expanded to make up the exact number required: Amazonius Invictus Pius Felix Lucius Aelius Aurelius Commodus Augustus Hercules Romanus Exsuperatorius. Places and institutions of all kinds throughout the Empire were now to exchange their own names for that of Commodus.[2]

---

[1] Egypt, Sabinus: A. R. BIRLEY (1969) p. 268f. – Vologaeses: cf. N. C. DEBEVOISE p. 255; and *RE* Supp. 9 (1962) 1851. A new king began minting coins in AD 191: Debevoise regards him as a rival to the old king, whereas in *RE* he is taken to be a co-ruler. He was to reign as Vologaeses IV. – Niger: Dio 74.6.1, *HA Pesc. Nig.* 1.5. Dio records (72.8.1) that he and Albinus performed well in a Dacian war, probably in AD 183 (F. GROSSO [1964] pp. 517ff.). Nothing else is certain. C. R. WHITTAKER p. 352 n. 29 assumes that he is the Niger who was Praetorian Prefect for six hours (*HA Comm.* 6.6, cf. E. BIRLEY [1968] p. 45) – perhaps because he is too ready to accept the fabricated career in *HA Pesc. Nig.*? – Aemilianus: A. R. BIRLEY (1969) p. 270. and pp. 172 and n. 2,175 and n. 1, below. – Anullinus: App. III, and p. 84f, above.

[2] Cf. F. GROSSO (1964) pp. 360ff., esp. 365ff., 369ff. The best account is

Marius Maximus, the source for the more reliable parts of the Augustan History, was already serving on the Danube in 192. He thus did not witness these bizarre events to their final conclusion. This may be why there is no trace or mention in the Augustan History of an event at Rome in that year which deeply impressed both Dio and Herodian, who saw it. 'A fire that began at night in some house leaped into the Temple of Peace and spread to the Egyptian and Arabian warehouses. From there the flames were carried up into the Palace and consumed very extensive portions of it, so that nearly all the state records were destroyed.' Dio took it as an omen. This in particular – the destruction of the archives – made it clear to Dio that the calamity portended by this fire would not be confined to the city but would extend over the entire world. The great doctor Galen had particular cause for regret. Many of his writings were housed in the Palace libraries and were destroyed by the blaze. Herodian, like Dio, described the fire in dramatic terms, regarding it as a portent of impending disaster. The fire was preceded by a slight earthquake, and the Temple of Peace, which he calls 'the largest and most beautiful building in the city', was according to him totally destroyed – 'and some conjectured that the destruction of the Temple of Peace was a prophecy of war'. He also records that the fire destroyed the Temple of Vesta and exposed the sacred Palladium to public view for the first time since its legendary journey from Troy to Italy. The Vestal Virgins hurriedly carried the statue along the Sacred Way into the Palace.[1]

Herodian and Dio both give detailed eye-witness accounts of Commodus's last public display in the arena. Probably at the Plebeian Games, which lasted fourteen days in November – unless it was at new, specially founded games – people came to Rome from all over Italy and the neighbouring provinces to see the Emperor shoot down deer, roe-buck, lions and leopards. On one occasion he shot down a hundred lions with a hundred javelins. On another he shot off the heads of ostriches with crescent-headed arrows – and the birds continued to run around.

---

supplied by Dio 72.15.1ff. Note also *HA Comm.* 8.5–9, 11.8 – 12.9 (on which cf. H. NESSELHAUF [1966]), etc.; Herodian 1.14.8–9.

[1] Maximus: App. 2. – Fire: Dio 72.24.1–3; Galen 2.216K, 13.362K; Herodian 1.14.1–6. For discussion and dating cf. F. GROSSO (1964) pp. 361ff.

These performances won him some admiration for his marksmanship, Herodian says. Dio gives even more details, adding that he killed a hundred bears on the first day, 'shooting down at them from the railing of the balustrade':

> For the whole amphitheatre had been divided up by means of two intersecting cross-walls, which supported the gallery that ran its entire length. The animals, divided into two groups, could thus be speared more easily from any point, at short range. In the middle of the 'contest' he became tired. He took some chilled sweet wine in a club-shaped cup from a woman, and drank it in one gulp. At this both we and the people all shouted out straightaway the words so familiar at drinking-sessions: 'Long life!'

Dio hastens to defend himself against anyone who might think that he was 'sullying the dignity of history' by recording details of this kind. These were the events that dominated life in the capital, and he was there to see them.[1]

In the mornings the Emperor shot down wild beasts. In the afternoons he fought as a gladiator – fighting with shield in right hand and sword in left, 'Indeed he took great pride in the fact that he was left-handed.' 'Standing beside him as he fought,' Dio continues, 'were Aemilius Laetus the Prefect and Eclectus the chamberlain. When he had fought his bout – and, of course, won – he would then kiss them just as he was, through the visor of his helmet.' Whenever Commodus himself was fighting, the senators and knights were obliged to watch. 'Only Claudius Pompeianus the elder never appeared, but sent his sons, and did not come himself, preferring death rather than see the Emperor, the son of Marcus, do such things.' The rest of the senators were obliged not only to attend but to join in chorused chants of admiration: 'You are Lord and you are first and most fortunate of all men! You are victorious, you will be victorious! From everlasting you are victorious, Amazonian!' The common people, according to Herodian, himself

---

[1] Herodian 1.15.1–6; Dio 72.20.1, 72.18.1–4. – 'Plebeian Games': cf. A. R. BIRLEY (1969) p. 248 and n. 5.

clearly a fascinated onlooker, flocked in large numbers to these games. They may have done so on the first day. But Dio notes that many did not come and others left after a brief look. For one thing, a rumour had got about that Commodus intended to pursue his self-identification with Hercules to the extent of shooting some of the spectators, who were thus to play the role of the Stymphalian birds. Dio and his fellow-senators were made to feel the danger themselves: 'Having killed an ostrich and cut off its head, he came up to where we were sitting, holding the head in his left hand and raising his bloody sword in his right. He said nothing, but he wagged his head with a grin, showing that he would treat us likewise.'

Dio's reaction may be described as verging on the hysterical: 'Many of us would have been killed on the spot, for laughing at him – for it was laughter rather than the fear that took hold of us – if I had not chewed some laurel leaves that I took from my garland, and persuaded the others sitting next to me to do the same. By moving our jaws steadily we could thus conceal that fact that we were laughing.'

It was at the time of these games that Commodus displayed the old champion racehorse from the Green stable, now put out to grass in the country. The horse was shown to the people at the last race of the year in the Circus Maximus, its hooves gilded, and a gilded skin on its back. A great shout went up: 'It is Pertinax!' On the last day of the games, when he was about to begin his bout as a gladiator, Commodus handed his club to the like-named Urban Prefect. Whether these things seemed as significant at the time as Cassius Dio suggests is another matter. But if Cassius Dio was superstitious, the urban *plebs* as a whole will not have been less so, and superstitions could be worked on. It is legitimate to suspect that the episode of Pertinax the racehorse may have been engineered.

According to Dio, Commodus's behaviour began to worry Laetus and Eclectus, and they tried to restrain him. Commodus replied with threats. Terrified, they formed a plot against him to preserve their own lives. It seems, still following the version of Dio, that Commodus intended to kill both the new consuls on New Year's Day 193, and to take their place as sole consul, garbed in the costume of a gladiator. 'Let no one doubt this statement,' he concludes, giving as corroboration for the story the fact that Commodus cut off the head of the hundred-foot high statue of the Sun god that stood outside the Colosseum and replaced it with his own portrait (adding a club and a bronze lion at its foot to give the composite figure the appearance of the new Roman Hercules). After taking Marcia into their confidence, Laetus and Eclectus chose New Year's Eve to carry out the murder, while the people were celebrating the holiday. (The court was at this time in the Vectilian House on the Caelian Hill; Commodus said he could not sleep in the Palace.) Marcia administered poison. Commodus however vomited and did not succumb. He suspected what had been done and began to look threatening. The athlete Narcissus was then sent in to strangle him in his bath.[1]

This then is the assassination, these the actors and their motives, as presented by Cassius Dio. Herodian gives basically the same picture, but in a more elaborate fashion, with a few extra details (although one must remember that Dio's version is only preserved as abbreviated by John Xiphilinus). The decision was sparked off, Herodian says, by Commodus's sudden revelation on New Year's Eve of his plans for the following day. Marcia pleaded with him to change his mind, but he summoned Laetus and Eclectus, giving them orders to prepare the ceremonies. He then took his midday siesta, after first writing down on a tablet – made of linden-wood, Herodian is careful to note – the names of those who were to be put to death that night. The names of Marcia, Laetus and Eclectus headed the list, followed by those of a large number of leading senators. By chance a boy favourite picked up the tablet as a toy while the Emperor slept, Marcia found it, and passed it to Eclectus, who showed it to Laetus. They quickly arranged for Marcia to give Commodus a poisoned cup of wine when he returned from his bath. He fell asleep, but awoke vomiting. Then Narcissus (in this version a young nobleman, not an athlete) was sent in to finish him off.

Even more markedly than Dio, indeed quite unequivocally, Herodian indicates that the decision to murder Commodus was taken suddenly, only a few hours before it was carried out. Neither Dio nor

---

[1] Dio 72.19.1 – 21.2; Herodian 1.15.1; Dio 73.4.3–4 (the horse and the club); 72.22.1–6 (the murder and its cause). – Vectilian House: *HA Comm.* 16.3.

Herodian suggests that Pertinax, who was straight away offered the throne, had any inkling in advance of what was happening.[1] The Augustan History, or its source Marius Maximus, knew better. Pertinax was involved in the conspiracy, which had its origin some while before, and was consummated when the moment was ripe.[2]

How many of the men set in positions of power by Laetus and Pertinax had been warned of what was to take place is an open question. The fact remains that the conspirators had chosen their time supremely well – during a festival, when even the praetorians were to a large extent unarmed and unprepared for action. It becomes tempting to suspect that in some of the excesses perpetrated by Commodus in the last weeks of his life he was egged on, not restrained, by Laetus and Eclectus. One may well wonder about the poisoned needles rumour – and about the fire. It would have been a daring scheme deliberately to encourage an autocrat who was already demented to indulge his megalomania further, with the purpose of increasing the fear and hatred with which he was regarded. But it might have been worth attempting, and it would have made the news of his murder, when achieved, very much more palatable to those who might otherwise have reacted with suspicion or sorrow. The only hint that the conspirators had anything of this kind in train is provided by the Augustan History. According to that work, Commodus's 'insane wish that Rome should be named the "Colony of Commodus" was put into his head while listening to the blandishments of Marcia'. One could of course say that the conspirators merely took the easier course, acquiescing in, or even encouraging the behaviour of their insane master. But it is just as reasonable to conclude that they had been waiting for many months for the moment when they could kill him. After the murder, they naturally took care to put out a detailed story to explain their actions in a manner that would palliate the crime. It is hard to believe that Dio was deceived. His devotion to the memory of Pertinax must have obliged him to pass over the latter's participation in silence. But his urgent

---

[1] Herodian 1.16–17. – 'inkling in advance': cf. A. R. BIRLEY (1969) esp. p. 249f.

[2] Cf. A. R. BIRLEY (1969) pp. 250ff.

insistence that no one should disbelieve the story of the plot to kill the consuls surely betrays him.[1]

It was probably already dark when Commodus was murdered. Laetus and Eclectus at once sent word to Pertinax. He had to make sure that it was not a trick, and sent his most trusted companion to see the body. When this man had confirmed the truth of the report, Pertinax left for the camp of the Guards, in secret. His arrival caused some alarm at first, but Laetus and his agents allayed the troops' fears. Pertinax made a speech, claiming that Commodus had died a natural death and that Laetus and Eclectus had thrust the imperial power on him. He promised to give them a donative of twelve thousand Sesterces per man. The end of his speech upset them: ' "There are many disturbing features about the present situation, fellow-soldiers, but with your help the rest of them will be put right again".' What was intended, probably, as no more than a vague and generalised reassurance seemed to the men like a veiled threat. 'He was a mediocre orator', the Augustan History records, adding that he was 'smooth [*blandus*] rather than good-natured, and was never regarded as a straightforward man [*simplex*]'. The response was neither immediate nor unanimous. But when a few, no doubt primed by Laetus, finally shouted out the acclamation, the rest followed. He was now *imperator*. It was not yet midnight.[2]

---

[1] 'blandishments of Marcia': *HA Comm.* 8.6.

[2] 'already dark': cf. E. HOHL (1956a) p. 4. – 'sent word': this is Dio's version (73.1.1). The *HA Pert.* 4.5 does not have this, merely stating that: *Commodo autem interempto Laetus praef. praet. et Eclectus cubicularius ad eum venerunt, ut eum confirmarent, atque in castra duxerunt.* There is no conflict, however: the *HA* has merely omitted a stage. – 'in secret' . . . 'troops' fears': Dio 73.1.2. – 'Commodus . . . thrust on him': *HA Pert.* 4.6–7. – 'donative . . . veiled threat': Dio 73.1.2–3. – 'mediocre . . . smooth': *HA Pert.* 12.1. – 'response . . . rest followed': *HA Pert.* 4.7, cf. Dio 73.1.2. – 'not yet midnight': this is clear from *HA Pert.* 4.8, which gives the *dies imperii* as *pr. kal. Jan.*, i.e. 31 December. C. W. J. ELIOT p. 77 n. 9 refuses to accept this, for no good reason (he simply prefers Dio and Herodian, 'the two best authorities'). The Kalends of January started at midnight (cf. Plutarch, *Quaest. Rom.* 84). E. HOHL (1956a) has shown that Herodian is grossly inaccurate on these events. His account (2.1.1 – 2.2.10) is therefore largely ignored here and in what follows.

XI

THE YEAR 193

Pertinax went straight from the praetorian camp to the Senate house. It was still pitch dark and a mist was rising rapidly from the low ground around the Circus Maximus. He ordered the doors of the *curia* to be opened, but the janitor could not be found. Pertinax walked over to the Temple of Concord close by, and sat waiting while arrangements were made. Claudius Pompeianus then arrived to see him, lamenting the fate of Commodus. The old man had not been seen at Rome by Cassius Dio for at least the past ten years. He had been living in retirement. Had he been forewarned and asked to come to Rome to lend moral support to his former protégé? It is impossible to believe that news of the murder of Commodus could have reached his estate at Terracina sixty miles away in time for him to get to Rome before the night ended. His appearance on the scene so soon after Commodus's death is yet another indication that the story told by Herodian – and implied in the surviving excerpts from Cassius Dio – is a piece of propaganda. Pertinax urged Pompeianus to take the throne. Pompeianus could see that Pertinax was already invested with the *imperium* by the soldiers, and refused. The offer was no doubt a purely formal gesture.[1]

---

[1] 'mist': *HA Comm.* 16.2. – 'dark . . . fate of Commodus', 'Pertinax urged . . . refused': *HA Pert.* 4.9–10. Dio 73.1.4 also says that it was still dark. – 'not seen at Rome': Dio 73.3.2. The surviving extracts and epitomes of Dio fail to mention that Pompeianus was in Rome before dawn on 1 January 193 or that Pertinax offered him the throne. Pompeianus had been absent formerly alleging bad eyesight and old age as excuses. During the brief reign of Pertinax his eyesight, and health generally, recovered. After that, his ill-health returned. Cf. Dio 73.3.2–3. – Terracina: cf. *HA Did. Jul.* 8.3 (he was back on this estate during the reign of Didius Julianus). – Herodian omits the offer to Pompeianus but alleges that Pertinax invited (M.' Acilius) Glabrio (cos. II ord. 186) to accept it, at the meeting

I. AERIAL VIEW OF LEPCIS MAGNA

Key:

1. Arch of Severus
2. Hadrianic baths
3. Arch of Trajan
4. Market
5. Theatre
6. Forum vetus
7. Colonnaded street

8. Severan forum
9. Severan basilica
10. Wadi Lebdah dam
11. Amphitheatre and Circus
12. Oea Gate
13. Arch of Marcus Aurelius
14. Hunting baths

2a Nicaea (Iznik), home of the historian Cassius Dio: remains of the theatre. The poplars to the right mark the edge of the lake along which the battle was fought in A.D. 194.

2b Carnuntum, where Septimius had his headquarters as governor of Upper Pannonia, and where he was proclaimed Emperor on April 9, A.D. 193. In the middleground lies the course of the Danube, marked by the tree-line, with the hills in the background showing enemy territory. In the foreground is part of the amphitheatre.

2c The palace of the governor at Carnuntum. The Danube runs from left to right beyond the trees.

3 Commodus (*BMC Rom. Medals* no. 12); Niger (*BMC* Sev. no.
302); Pertinax (*BMC* Pert. no. 37); Albinus (*BMC* Sev. no. 284);
Severus (A.D. 193: *BMC* Sev. no. 4)

Five emperors or would-be Emperors. Of those involved in the
events of A.D. 193 only Didius Julianus is omitted here. The coin
of Albinus was struck after his break with Septimius: for a coin of
Albinus as Caesar, see plate 4a.

(a)　　　　　　　　　　(b)

4a Gold coin of Clodius Albinus as Caesar (*BMC Sev.* no. 103), struck while he was still in alliance with Septimius.

4b The reverse shows the native deity of Albinus's home, Hadrumetum: Saeculum Frugiferum, Ba'al Hammon.

4c Two Parthian kings: Vologaeses IV (l.) and his successor Artabanus (r.) and the reverses.

(c)

The *curia* was now opened and the consuls and magistrates with the
other senators entered. It was still night. Pertinax did his best to greet
them, although there was such a jostling throng that it was difficult for
anyone to approach him. In an off-hand way he announced to them
that he had been chosen Emperor by the soldiers, but 'I do not want the
office and I shall resign it today, because of my age and poor health and
the distressing situation'. His health was excellent, except for slight
lameness; and he was a little overweight. The stated unwillingness to
serve was another formal gesture. He was unanimously acclaimed as
Emperor. The consuls – Clarus and Falco – made speeches in his
honour. Then a remarkable scene took place. The senators poured out
a savage chanted litany of execration against the fallen tyrant. Marius
Maximus gave the acclamations in full, and they are reproduced by the
Augustan History. The recurring theme came with the words *unco
trahatur*, 'let him be dragged with the hook'. 'Put it to the vote! We all
call for him to be dragged with the hook.' Pertinax intervened to inform
them that Commodus had already been buried. At his orders, the
procurator of the imperial estate, Livius Larensis, who had been
guarding it, had handed the body over to the consul designate, Fabius
Cilo. No doubt in his capacity as *sodalis Hadrianalis*, Cilo had it placed
in the Mausoleum of Hadrian, the Castel Sant' Angelo. In due course
a purely factual tombstone was placed there, giving Commodus his full
names and titles, with his ancestry back to Nerva, and styling him as he
had preferred to be known in his last two years, L. Aelius Aurelius
Commodus, instead of M. Aurelius Commodus Antoninus. It will have
cost no effort to deprive him of the names Marcus Antoninus, that he
had rejected and had so little deserved. But the extravagant titles of the
last months, Hercules Romanus, Amazonius, and the rest, were left
out, as were Pius and Felix.[1]

---

of the Senate (2.3.3–4). In Dio (73.3.3) Glabrio is said to have been honoured,
together with Pompeianus, by being given a seat on the same bench as Pertinax in
the Senate. E. HOHL (1956a) pp. 11ff. argues that the story was inserted into one
excerpt of Dio by someone who knew Herodian's version; and that the whole story
is invented. It might be safer to conclude that Dio's story (the facts, that is, not
necessarily Dio's words) was known to Herodian, who embroidered it (and perhaps
confused Glabrio with Pompeianus).

[1] 'The *curia* . . . speeches in his honour': *HA Pert.* 4.11 – 5.1; Dio 73.1.4 – 2.1.

Pertinax's report caused an outcry: 'Let the buried murderer be dug up and dragged by the hook!' One of the *pontifices*, Cingius Severus, gave it as his opinion, speaking as *pontifex* on behalf of the college, that Commodus had been wrongfully buried. The office of *pontifex maximus* was of course momentarily vacant, and Cingius was no doubt senior *pontifex*. At least, he added, his statues must be overthrown and his name should be erased from all public and private records – and the names of the month should return to what they were before. The motion was evidently accepted. Renewed shouting broke out. Dio comments that 'all the shouts that they had been accustomed to chant in rhythmic fashion, in the theatres, to flatter Commodus, were repeated with certain changes that now made them sound ridiculous'. Pertinax finally spoke again. He expressed his thanks to the senate, and also, especially, to Laetus. At the mention of Laetus the consul Falco interjected: 'We can tell from this what sort of Emperor you will be – the fact that we can see Laetus and Marcia, the instruments of Commodus's crimes, behind you.' Pertinax made a gently sarcastic reply. 'You are a young man, consul, and you do not know the necessity of obedience. They obeyed Commodus against their will, and as soon as they had an opportunity they showed what they had always been wanting.'[1]

The customary titles and powers were voted. Exceptionally, the title *pater patriae*, Father of his Country, which by tradition previous Emperors had not accepted until a decent interval had elapsed, was granted as well. Pertinax revived in his official style, the title of *princeps senatus*. He then went to the Capitol to pay his vows to the gods. Meanwhile the Senate voted his wife Flavia Titiana the title of Augusta, and that of Caesar for his son. These titles Pertinax rejected on their behalf.

Pertinax's physical condition is described by *HA Pert.* 12.1. Dio 73.1.5 mentions his slight limp. Marius Maximus quoted a lengthy letter of Pertinax which demonstrated his *horror imperii* (*HA Pert.* 15.8). – 'savage litany': *HA Comm.* 18–19 contains a full text (cf. App. II). The role of Larensis and Cilo is described *ib.* 20.1–2. Larensis (*CP* no. 194) is the host in Athenaeus's *Deipnosophistae*. For Cilo cf. App. III. – tombstone: D. 401.

[1] Outcry: *HA Comm.* 20.2–5, cf. Dio 73.2.1–3. – 'expressed thanks ... "been wanting"': *HA Pert.* 5.1–3, cf. A. R. BIRLEY (1969) p. 250f. Cf. E. HOHL (1956a) p. 7f.

Finally he entered the Palace. When the tribune of the guard asked for the watchword, he replied '*militemus*', 'let us be soldiers'. This did nothing to allay the nervousness that the praetorians had already begun to feel when he spoke to them in the camp. He had chosen it without thinking – it was the same watchword that he had given in all his commands. On the first day he entertained the magistrates and leading men at a banquet.[1]

The following day, 2 January, the statues of Commodus were overthrown. And Pertinax gave the same watchword, 'let us be soldiers'. The soldiers reacted unfavourably. In any case, they disliked the prospect of service under a sixty-six year old Emperor. On 3 January the annual oath of loyalty had to be taken. During the ceremony some of the praetorians attempted to stage a coup, and dragged a senator named Triarius Maternus into the camp. Maternus fled, naked, came to Pertinax in the palace, and then left the city. No action was taken against him.[2]

The lesson was not lost on Pertinax. He ratified the concessions that Commodus had made to the troops and the veterans, no doubt on 7 January, the normal day when time-expired men serving in the capital received their discharge. At the same time he introduced a whole series of proposals in the Senate. Treason trials were abolished, the exiles were restored, and the good name of those who had been unjustly executed was restored. The imperial finances had been seriously depleted by Commodus: the imperial treasury was virtually empty. The donative to the troops, coupled with a bounty to the *plebs*, made matters worse. An obvious way to raise some funds rapidly lay ready to hand: an auction of Commodus's luxury goods, including the extravagant costumes in which he had performed his extraordinary charades, and the imperial carriages. These were 'the very latest masterpieces of the art': some had seats that could be moved round into the shade or the breeze, others were equipped with mileometers and clocks, and others still were designed 'for the indulgence of his vices',

---

[1] Dio 73.5.1, *HA Pert.* 5.4–6.2, cf. 6.9.

[2] *HA Pert.* 6.3–5. On Maternus cf. G. ALFÖLDY, *Reichsbeamte* p. 87f. If the same as the *cos.ord.* 185 he may once have been in favour with Perennis, and may have been known as an enemy of Pertinax.

as the Augustan History enigmatically puts it. The imperial household included large numbers of concubines, buffoons and other non-essential personnel. These too were sold, bringing in immense sums. Some of them, the Augustan History adds maliciously, found their way back to minister to the old man's pleasure.[1]

Steps were also taken to regulate the Senate itself. The proper grades of seniority had been upset by the countless adlections, from which Commodus's favourites, especially Cleander, had derived so much profit. Pertinax laid down that those who had served as praetor should take precedence over those who had been adlected. Ironically, he had himself been adlected *inter praetorios* by Marcus Aurelius, over twenty years before. This move caused a lot of ill-feeling, the Augustan History reports, a statement clearly derived from Marius Maximus. Maximus was one of the senators affected by the change. This may be one of the reasons for the less than wholeheartedly favourable verdict on Pertinax that the Augustan History reproduces. During January Pertinax will have made the arrangements for the next year's magistrates. Cassius Dio was among those named: he was designated praetor.[2]

One of the first steps taken after the new Emperor had been installed in power must have been to inform the provincial governors of what had taken place. Some of them may not have been surprised. But when the news came through many of them were suspicious that it was a trick, a test of their loyalty by Commodus, and imprisoned the couriers. The season of the year did not facilitate rapid transmission of messages. But even so, in 69 the news of the revolt of the Rhine on 1 January, sent by the procurator at Trier, had reached Rome in less than nine days. There is no reason to believe that the news of Pertinax's accession took any longer than this to get to the Rhine and Danube armies. The news may have taken longer to reach overseas provinces. In 68 the freedman Icelus had reached Galba at Tarraco with

[1] 'concessions': *HA Pert.* 6.6. – '7 January': cf. C. B. WELLES p. 197 (on col. i, line 7 of the *Feriale Duranum*). – 'proposals, etc.': *HA Pert.* 6.7-8, cf. Dio 73.5.2-3; *HA Pert.* 7.3-9.10, cf. Dio 73.5.4-5. – 'old man's pleasure': The Teubner text reads *Severum* in *HA Pert.* 7.9, but the MSS. have *senem* = Pertinax, which makes excellent sense. He was no paragon and the *HA vita* is not a eulogy.

[2] 'adlections': *HA Pert.* 6.10, cf. App. II. – 'Dio . . . praetor': Dio 73.12.2.

the news of Nero's death after only seven days' journey from Italy. But that was in the summer. Nonetheless, this time the news reached Novius Rufus, the governor of Hispania Tarraconensis, by the beginning of February at latest. A decision that he made settling a dispute was issued under the new emperor's authority on 11 February. In Egypt the news was not issued until 6 March. Mantennius Sabinus may not have received word until shortly before making the announcement, for winter navigation from Italy to Alexandria was not easy. But one may suspect that he had waited some time until the news could be confirmed. When his proclamation was issued, the wife and son of Pertinax were given the titles which Pertinax had rejected. It will be remembered that the wife of the Prefect of Egypt was a neighbour of the wife of Pertinax. Feminine influence may perhaps be inferred.[1]

The caution which the governors displayed is not surprising. It may be explained simply in terms of their fear of Commodus. But there was a specific incentive: it had been Commondus's practice to keep the children of provincial governors at Rome as guarantees of fidelity.[2]

Septimius reacted to the news characteristically. After making sacrifice and administering the oath of allegiance to the new Emperor, he returned to his quarters in the evening, fell asleep and dreamed a portentous dream. In this dream he saw a large and noble horse carrying Pertinax along the central portion of the Sacred Way. But when the horse reached the *comitia* at the far end of the Forum, it unseated Pertinax and threw him to the ground. While Septimius stood there, the horse slipped under him, took him up and carried him on its back. Then it stopped, in the middle of the Forum, lifting him up high so that he was seen and cheered by all. This dream, according to Herodian, was the climax of the long series of supernatural signs that

---

[1] 'a trick': Dio 73.2.5–6. – AD 69: cf. e.g. Tacitus, *Histories* 1.12ff. – Icelus: Suetonius, *Galba* 22. – Novius Rufus: *CIL* II 4125, cf. G. ALFÖLDY, *Reichsbeamte* p. 42f. – Egypt: the papyrus (BGU 646 = Wilcken *Chestomathie* 490) is translated in the Loeb *Select Papyri* no. 222. – Titiana: *PIR*[2] F 444. Pertinax junior: H 74. Titiana is named Augusta on the coins of Alexandria also. Otherwise only on a Gallic milestone. Similarly with the son (Caesar on three Arabian milestones as well). Cf. A. R. BIRLEY (1969) p. 269f.

[2] Herodian 3.2.3–4 (a victim of the practice was the proconsul of Asia, Asellius Aemilianus, cf. p. 163, below).

had fed his burning ambition. It finally confirmed him in the belief that he would get everything that he hoped for.[1]

Meanwhile, he was already a key figure. Pertinax 'did not remove any of those whom Commodus had put in charge of affairs'. He said that he was waiting for the anniversary of the founding of the city, 21 April. Considering that most of those holding office had probably been appointed with the approval, if not by the direct nomination, of Laetus and Pertinax himself, this is not surprising. But there were vacancies to fill. The obvious one was the City Prefecture, which he had held himself. He appointed his father-in-law Flavius Sulpicianus. The only other recorded promotion that he made was done as a favour to Septimius. A man whom he himself, when proconsul of Africa, had condemned for corrupt practices, was given some unspecified post. The man's name is given in an extract from Cassius Dio as 'Fluvius'. This will be one of the Fulvii, Septimius's mother's family, almost certainly its best known member, Fulvius Plautianus, a man of equestrian rank. According to Herodian, he had in fact been condemned for certain offences prior to 193, which favours the identification with 'Fluvius'. Plautianus was soon to enter on the stage at Rome, and it would be plausible to suppose that it was he that was now given some post by Pertinax, either at Rome, or in Septimius's province.[2]

Pertinax's relations with Aemilius Laetus soon began to deteriorate. At the beginning, Laetus was full of praise for the new emperor. It was no doubt with pride and pleasure that he despatched couriers to overtake a barbarian delegation, on its way back home with a subsidy in gold that Commodus had handed over. The gold was demanded back. The envoys were to tell their people that Pertinax was now ruler. Laetus knew that the name of Pertinax carried some weight beyond the Danube. As governor of the principal military province on the Danube, Septimius had no doubt been responsible both for the original passage of the envoys to Rome and for their return.[3]

[1] Herodian 3.9.5–6. Cf. H. BLOCH.

[2] *HA Pert.* 12.8, a significant passage, cf. A. R. BIRLEY (1969) p. 251. – Sulpicianus: cf. esp. H. G. PFLAUM (1966) pp. 59ff.; also Birley p. 266. – Plautianus: App. I, where the excerpt from Dio, and other evidence, is discussed, with particular reference to F. GROSSO (1968).

[3] Dio 73.6.1–3.

A new foreign policy was implied by this episode. At home a vital matter was the safeguarding and improvement of the corn supply. If this should fail, the urban *plebs*, which had shown in 190 that it was still a force to be reckoned with, might get out of hand again. In early March Pertinax visited Ostia to inspect the arrangements at the port. In his absence a second attempt was made to stage a coup, again by the praetorians. This time their candidate was the consul Falco. The attempt fizzled out. Falco was declared a public enemy by the Senate, but Pertinax asked that he should be pardoned. 'May it never happen that any senator should be put to death, even for just cause, while I am Emperor,' he said, jumping to his feet. At the same meeting of the Senate he spoke bitterly of the soldiers' ingratitude, claiming that he had given them as much as Marcus and Lucius at their accession, in spite of having far smaller funds available. This was not quite the truth. Pertinax's donative was not all that large. There were many soldiers and freedmen present in the *curia* and they reacted unfavourably to the exaggerated claim. Pertinax had long had a reputation for meanness. Now he was trying to cover it up.[1]

The Falco affair is mysterious. Cassius Dio asserts that Laetus and the Praetorians were behind it, and selected Falco. One may have leave to doubt this, especially when Falco's bitter attack on the Prefect at the Senate's meeting on 1 January is recalled. However, it is possible that Laetus engineered the coup, with the deliberate intention of suppressing it, for purposes of his own. The Augustan History is of some help, although the text is fragmentary in parts: the biographer reports that, according to many people, Falco did not know that he was being put forward as a candidate for the throne. In other words he was framed and show trials followed. A number of soldiers were executed, even if Falco himself was spared. Laetus had this done, but it was – of course – carried out in the name of Pertinax, whose unpopularity with the soldiers increased sharply. Laetus's own relations with Pertinax are said to have deteriorated – the Emperor found fault with him because of 'the foolish advice he had given'. But even if this statement is true,

---

[1] *HA Pert.* 10.1–7; Dio 73.8.1–5. Cf. E. HOHL (1956a) p. 16. It is worth noting that Falco was married to a kinswoman of Avidius Cassius (great-niece). Cf. *PIR*² C, Stemma, p. 166.

this is not sufficient basis for accepting that Laetus was the moving spirit behind the third and final attempt to remove Pertinax, which followed soon after. For, as will be seen, Laetus's role in this was that of a helpless bystander, and he did not profit in any way.[1]

The successful coup came on 28 March. Pertinax had planned a visit to the Athenaeum for a poetry recital, but changed his mind and sent his escort back to the barracks. The rest of the guard was there that day. A disturbance broke out – what specifically started it is not recorded. Pertinax apparently had time to send Sulpicianus his father-in-law to the camp, and to summon a special meeting of the Senate. But while he was returning to the Palace some two or three hundred men were on their way there with drawn swords. They arrived just as Pertinax was inspecting the Palace slaves in the portico. The Augustan History states that the troops were urged on by the attendants, who hated Pertinax. The Emperor, informed of their entry by his wife, sent Laetus to meet them. But the Prefect covered up his head and went to his own house. The Emperor then went out to confront the troops in person. The men were overawed at first when he spoke to them, at length and in a serious tone, and sheathed their swords. Then one of them, a Tungrian named Tausius, shouting out, 'This sword the soldiers have sent you!', fell upon him. He covered his head with his toga, with a prayer to Jupiter the Avenger, and was struck down. Only Eclectus defended him, and even managed to wound two of the assailants before being killed. The soldiers cut off the Emperor's head and stuck it on a spear. That was the end of the reign of Pertinax. It had lasted eighty-seven days.[2]

Unlike the conspiracy against Commodus, on this occasion no successor was ready. This alone is a major consideration in exculpating Laetus of guilt for the murder of Pertinax. He may perhaps bear some negative responsibility for his refusal to make any resistance. But no doubt he knew the temper of the troops well enough. The fact that he did not produce a new candidate for the throne, and that he did not participate in the scenes that followed, shows that he was not the

[1] Cf. A. R. BIRLEY (1969) esp. p. 252 n. 12.

[2] *HA Pert.* 10.8–11.13; Dio 73.9.1–10.3 Herodian's account is inadequate, cf. E. HOHL (1956a) esp. pp. 17ff.

moving spirit this time. The coup can only be explained as an act of mutiny by the troops. There was nothing unprecedented about this. Only eight years previously Perennis had fallen victim to a band of mutinous troops from the British army. Subsequent events in Dio's lifetime were to prove, as his own account of them reveals, that the possibility of such outbreaks was constantly increasing. By the mid-third century no Emperor was to be safe from his own troops for more than a few years at the most.[1]

When Sulpicianus heard the news he at once began a move to have himself declared Emperor. In his capacity as City Prefect he commanded the Urban Cohorts, and may have hoped for their support. Convincing promises might have won over the praetorians as well. It would seem that the group that had actually struck down Pertinax belonged to the Horse Guards, the *equites singulares*; but all the City troops will have been wary of accepting as their new Emperor the father-in-law of one who had just been murdered. Two tribunes of the Guard clearly recognised the difficulty and went out to look for an alternative candidate. They waited outside the Senate-house, and there they found their man. Didius Julianus, with his son-in-law Cornelius Repentinus (whose father had been Prefect of the Guard thirty years before), came to attend the meeting of the Senate that Pertinax had summoned. But the doors of the *curia* were closed. The tribunes urged him to seize the throne. He pointed out that another man was already in possession, but they overrode his objections and took him to the camp. Sulpicianus's followers refused to let him through the gates.[2]

Then ensued one of the most sordid episodes in the history of Rome. Two rival candidates made rival bids for the throne, as if at an auction. Eventually Julianus got up on the wall. He warned the men not to

[1] Cf. A. R. BIRLEY (1969) p. 273: it was later asserted that Clodius Albinus was the guiding spirit behind the overthrow of Pertinax, cf. p. 185 below. If there was a conspiracy, Laetus was surely not its leader. It is possible to view Pertinax as a kind of Neguib. But who was the Nasser in 193? Hardly Laetus. When the stakes were so high, it is, admittedly, hard to believe that one or more persons of high rank were not involved. But it was not necessarily so.

[2] The affair is best analysed by E. HOHL (1956a) pp. 19ff. – Repentinus: cf. now G. ALFÖLDY, *Reichsbeamte*, pp. 143ff. – 'Two tribunes': E. BIRLEY (1968), p. 48f.

choose an Emperor who would avenge the death of Pertinax and gave written promises that he would restore the good name of Commodus. Finally, when Sulpicianus reached the figure of 20,000 Sesterces per man, Julianus raised his bid by 5,000, shouting it out in a loud voice and holding up his fingers as well to indicate the amount. This won him the throne.[1]

Towards evening he came to the Forum to meet the Senate in the *curia*. He had appointed two new Prefects of the Guard. Laetus's career was at an end. Julianus was escorted by a vast number of Guards, carrying their standards as if prepared for battle. The senators were nervous, not least Cassius Dio, who had successfully prosecuted Julianus in court on several occasions. Julianus told the Senate that the throne was vacant, and claimed that he himself was the best qualified to fill it. The claim was not as boastful or empty as Cassius Dio makes it sound. He was possibly the senior consular living, with the sole exception of Claudius Pompeianus. He had had a long career in the imperial service, having commanded a legion and governed four imperial provinces. He was well-connected. During the reign of Commodus he had been in trouble several times – almost a guarantee of acceptability to the Senate. (On the last occasion he had been protected by Laetus.) Pertinax had respected him also. The two men's careers had indeed been closely parallel since the year 175, when they had been colleagues in the consulship. Shortly before his death Pertinax had been guest of honour at the betrothal ceremony of Julianus's daughter. Pertinax had told the girl's fiancé, who was also her cousin, to respect his uncle, adding that Julianus was 'my colleague and successor' – not only had Pertinax and Julianus shared the *fasces* but Julianus had succeeded Pertinax as proconsul of Africa in 190. Pertinax's remark seemed like an omen, in retrospect. A comment by Julianus at this meeting of the Senate was viewed in a similar light later on. When the consul designate formally proposed the motion 'That Didius Julianus be declared Emperor', Julianus said, 'Add Severus as well'. His full names were M. Didius Severus Julianus.[2]

[1] Cf. previous note.
[2] Cf. in general E. HOHL (1956a) esp. pp. 23ff. For the career of Didius

Julianus had no fears about either the British or Danubian armies. He had connections through his mother with Hadrumetum, the home of the governor of Britain Clodius Albinus, and the same African links may have served to inspire his confidence in the reaction of Septimius and other northern commanders to his accession. But whatever his relations had been with the governor of Syria, he soon had cause to fear him. On 29 March the *plebs* shouted insults at him as he went to the Senate-house and even threw stones at him. Dio records that 'they all began shouting, as if by preconcerted plan, calling him a thief and a parricide'. At first Julianus took it coolly and promised them money. But this failed to pacify them and he had to use force. A mob then poured into the Circus Maximus, where they spent that night, and the following day. There they chanted out slogans, calling on Pescennius Niger and the Syrian army to come to their support.[1]

Julianus's prospects of success were slim from the start. He could rely only on the praetorians, to whom he had paid a donative even higher than he had promised. But the Guards had not succeeded in imposing an Emperor of their choice for more than a century and a half, since the accession of Claudius. With the death of Nero 'the secret of the empire was made public: that an Emperor could be made elsewhere than at Rome'. The provincial armies had learned this lesson in 68–69 and again in 97. Besides, the Praetorian Guard had done no fighting since the Marcomannic wars ended in 180.[2]

The news of the attempted coups of Maternus and Falco will have prepared Septimius and his fellow-governors for rapid action. It is not hard to believe that a contingency plan had already been concerted by 28 March, if indeed Laetus had not made arrangements with Septimius and others in 192 as to action they should take if something were to go wrong on 31 December. The news of Pertinax's murder had to be

---

Julianus, cf. esp. H. G. PFLAUM (1966) pp. 6ff. – 'betrothal ceremony': *HA Pert.* 14.4–5, *Did.Jul.* 2.3. – 'comment by Julianus': *HA Did. Jul.* 7.1–2.

[1] 'No fears': *HA Did. Jul.* 5.1. – 'Hadrumetum: cf. A. R. BIRLEY (1969) p. 266. – '29 March': Dio 73.13.2–5. He sent a man to assassinate Niger: *HA Did. Jul.* 5.1. The theory of E. MANNI, that Niger had already proclaimed himself Emperor before the death of Pertinax – in other words, had rebelled against Pertinax – was shown to be groundless by G. M. BERSANETTI (1949).

[2] 'even higher than he had promised': *HA Did.Jul.* 3.2.

FRISII
CHAUCI
LANGOBARDI
CHERUSCI
SEMNONES
R. Oder

GERMANIA
INFERIOR
R. Rhine
XXX ULPIA
Cologne
Bonn
I MINERVIA
CHATTI
R. Elbe
R. Morava

Trier
Mainz
XXII PRIMIGENIA
R. Main
MARCOMANNI

BELGICA
Strasbourg
VIII AUGUSTA
Regensburg
III ITALICA
Vindobona
(Vienna)

GERMANIA
SUPERIOR
R. Danube
Augsburg
II ITALICA
X GEMINA
Carnuntum
XIV GEMINA

Besançon
RAETIA
NORICUM
Savaria
PANNONIA
SUPERIOR

Gt. St. Bernard
Brenner
Julian Alps
Poetovio
R. Drav

Milan
Aquileia
R. Save

Verona
DALM

R. Po

Via Aemilia
Ravenna

Ariminum
Ancona
Salonae

Interamna

Rome

Map 1   THE MAR•

Miles

50   0   50   100   150   200

over 9000 ft.

3000-9000 ft.

600-3000 ft.

R. Vistula

BURI

COTINI

DI

Váh

Kron

Brigetio
I ADIUTRIX

Aquincum
(Budapest)
II ADIUTRIX

R. Tisza

JAZYGES

C a r p a t h i a n s

COSTOBOCI

R. Dniester

R. Seret

R. Prut

POROLISSENSIS

Potaissa
V MACEDONICA

TRES

Apulum
XIII GEMINA

APULENSIS

Sarmizegetusa

Mursa

DACIAE

Transylvanian Alps

R. Olt

Sirmium

Singidunum
IV FLAVIA

Viminacium
VII CLAUDIA

MALVENSIS

R. Danube

Tropaeum
Traiani

XI CLAUDIA

MOESIA

Naissus

SUPERIOR

I ITALICA

MOESIA INFERIOR

Serdica
(Sofia)

Philippopolis

T H R A C I A

Adrianopolis

MACEDONIA

Byzantium

ROME

taken some 735 miles from Rome to Carnuntum – if Septimius was still at the Pannonian capital. He might well have moved to the south-western borders of his province to await developments, when the news of the Falco coup reached him. He had allies in Rome. Fulvius Plautianus may have been one. His brother-in-law, husband of his sister Octavilla, may have been at Rome and there were also various kinsmen of his wife. Fabius Cilo, who had perhaps by now held his consulship, if he was not still in office, will have been another friend. Someone must have rushed the news to him.[1] He may have known the fate of Pertinax by the evening of 1 April. It would take little time to ensure the support of the legates of the three legions in his province and the governors of Raetia, Noricum and Lower Pannonia. The governor of Lower Pannonia, C. Valerius Pudens, later to receive high office from Septimius, must have given him unstinted support at this time. He could rely on Geta in Lower Moesia. But he will have sent messages to the two German provinces, and to Dacia and Upper Moesia as well. It is impossible to tell how long it would have taken him to receive replies from all these provinces. But by 9 April, the twelfth day after the murder of Pertinax, he felt secure enough to act. The Carnuntum legion XIV Gemina, and no doubt some other troops, were summoned, and he was saluted as Emperor. The Augustan History states that he tried to resist – *repugnans*. This was the conventional display of reluctance. He had no intention of refusing. Septimius depicted himself to the troops as the avenger of Pertinax. One of his three Upper Pannonian legions, I Adiutrix, had been commanded by Pertinax twenty years before. Some of the men still in the legion would have served under Pertinax. The same applied even more strongly to the six legions in the Moesias and Dacia. Septimius therefore emphasised his

[1] A.v.DOMASZEWSKI (1898) argued that Septimius Severus was all along Laetus's candidate for the throne, and that Pertinax was an emergency stop-gap choice. No one now seems to accept this theory. – '735 miles': for a useful examination of the distance involved cf. C. W. J. ELIOT. (But his estimate of the time involved is far too high in view of the parallels cited above p. 148f.) – 'south-western borders': as it happens, one late source says that he was proclaimed Emperor at *Savaria* (*Epit. de Caes.* 19.2). Perhaps a simple mistake, due to the place's later importance. *Savaria* led to confusion with Niger's province *Syria* in Victor *de Caes.* 19.4 and Zonaras 12.7. – The kinsmen: App. I. – Cilo: App. III (he may have been in Umbria).

attachment to the murdered Emperor by adding his name to his new official, if still only usurped style: Imperator Caesar L. Septimius Severus Pertinax Augustus. He will have refrained from laying claim to the tribunician power, which could only be conferred in Rome. There is one other thing for which Septimius may have waited before he acted on 9 April: news that his sons were safe. At any rate, one of his first actions on deciding to bid for the throne was to send a secret message for them to be brought to him. Fabius Cilo may have been the man who ensured their safety.

Preparations for the march on Rome would already have begun before the proclamation. But there would still be much to do. A particular concern was the attitude of Clodius Albinus. Since Albinus was from Hadrumetum, the home of Julianus's mother, he could not be regarded as reliable. With his three legions and the enormous number of auxiliary regiments in Britain, he could clearly pose a serious threat to Septimius's western flank. He could cross to the continent with a sizable army in a matter of months, and could well undermine the loyalty of the Rhine armies, as a former governor of Lower Germany. Septimius therefore sent emissaries offering Albinus the title of Caesar, which carried with it the prospect of succession to the throne, if anything should happen to Septimius. Since Septimius's elder son, Bassianus, was barely five years old, the move could fairly be regarded as a genuine offer, which it would be worth Albinus's while to accept. Albinus now styled himself D. Clodius Septimius Albinus Caesar, and he remained in Britain.[1]

Before Septimius began his march, news may have reached him that

---

[1] Pudens: App. III. – Geta: App. I, no. 30. – The *dies imperii* is given by the *Feriale Duranum* col. ii, line 3: cf. C. B. WELLES p. 199. – *repugnans*: HA *Sev.* 5.1. – 'avenger of Pertinax': *ib.* 5.5, cf. Herodian 2.10.1–9, etc. – Cilo: App. III. – Albinus: cf. esp. G. ALFÖLDY (1968). – 'emissaries': Dio 73.15.1–2 makes it clear that this was done before Septimius reached Rome, indeed his words suggest that it was before he left Pannonia. Cf. Herodian 2.15.1–5. HA *Sev.* 6.9–10, *Nig* 4.7 and *Alb.* 3.2–6, are contaminated. *Alb.* 10.3 is clear and sensible, but there is no chronological detail. Cf. App. II (p. 325). The emissary is named as Heraclitus in *Sev.* 6.10, cf. App. III under *Aurelius Heraclitus*. C. E. VAN SICKLE (1928a) has a sensible review of what Albinus' new status was (very limited). Before 1 June, when Septimius got the tribunician power himself, he could hardly have given it to Albinus. But he never did give it to him.

Pescennius Niger had proclaimed himself Emperor at Antioch, and that the east, together with Egypt, had gone over to him. Niger thus had a force of ten legions at his disposal, against Septimius's sixteen from the Rhine and Danube armies, as well as, in theory, the three from Britain. In the meantime Septimius's agents will have been soliciting support from Novius Rufus, the governor of Hither Spain, who had one legion, and from the legate of the Numidian legion, Naevius Quadratianus. It was forthcoming in both cases. The news of Niger's move cannot have come as a surprise, for the report of the murder of Pertinax must have been followed almost at once by the news of the riots in favour of Niger by the Roman *plebs*. But Septimius's prime concern was to seize Rome. The east could wait. But a force was sent from Geta's Lower Moesian army down into Thrace.[1]

Inscriptions provide details about two men who played a vital if subordinate role in the *expeditio urbica*, as the march was styled. One was M. Rossius Vitulus, a former equestrian officer who had served in both Germany and Pannonia. He was appointed quartermaster-general (*praepositus annonae*) with the task of ensuring the army's food supplies. He was probably a native of Trieste, and hence would have direct personal knowledge of the territory through which the march was to go. The other was L. Valerius Valerianus, also an equestrian officer, possibly of Pannonian origin, who was given command over the cavalry. The advance guard was led by one Julius Laetus, who had undoubtedly been serving in one of the northern provinces, either as a legionary legate in Upper Pannonia, or perhaps as governor of either Raetia or Noricum.[2]

---

[1] Niger's proclamation, etc.: cf. *RE* (1937) 1088 – Novius Rufus: G. ALFÖLDY *Reichsbeamte*, p. 42f. – Quadratianus: App. III. – 'down into Thrace': Dio 73.15.2, Herodian 2.14.6, *Ha Sev.* 8.12.

[2] Vitulus: *CP* no. 224, where it is argued that he had served in Pannonia as an equestrian officer continuously for fifteen years up to AD 193 resided in Africa. Far more likely that he was a native of only five towns enrolled in Vitulus' tribe (Pupinia, cf. W. KUBITSCHEK p. 271) and that he had retired some time before. – Valerianus: *AE* 1966. 495. The cavalry were *peregrini*, i.e. evidently from beyond the frontier. Marcus Aurelius had been prepared to use barbarians in a civil war (cf. *AE* 1956, 124). Although the names are very common, as the editors of *AE* point out, there is a good chance that he was one of the Poetovio Valerii, on whom cf. G. ALFÖLDY (1963). I regard it as likely that he was procurator of

While Septimius and Niger were seizing control of most of the Empire, Julianus blithely had coins issued proclaiming himself ruler of the world, *rector orbis*, and asserting the unity of the armies, *concordia militaris*. Septimius was declared a public enemy by the Senate, at his request (as Niger no doubt was also), when the news of the revolt got back to Rome. The soldiers in his army were offered an amnesty if they withdrew their support of Septimius before a certain date. One Valerius Catullinus was designated Septimius's successor. Envoys of consular rank were selected to take Julianus's appeal to the northern armies. They included Vespronius Candidus, a former governor of Dacia, under whom both Albinus and Niger had served early in the reign of Commodus. A more practical step was the assignment of a former officer in the secret police (*frumentarii*), M. Aquilius Felix, to the task of assassinating Septimius. The murder of senators had been this man's speciality.[1]

According to Herodian, Septimius and his army appeared on the borders of Italy before it was known that he had been proclaimed. This may be doubted. But Julianus totally failed to block the Alpine passes. The best he could manage was to send one of the Praetorian Prefects, Tullius Crispinus, to take command of the Ravenna fleet and lead some resistance with it. But Septimius, proceeding via Emona (Ljubljana) and Aquileia, met no resistance in taking Ravenna, and Crispinus fled.

Meanwhile Julianus was attempting to construct fortifications at Rome. The city became an armed camp. Even elephants designed for performance at the games were conscripted for military use. But, according to Dio, who watched the proceedings, Julianus's preparations were futile and ineffective: 'At times we were overcome with laughter.' The praetorians were loth to undertake the kind of military engineering at which the legions were so skilled, and some of them

---

Cyprus *after* his posts in the Civil Wars. The inscription is certainly very confused in its order anyway. Cf. now J. FITZ (1969) p. 129, who reasonably suggests that he was living at home in Pannonia in April 193. – Julius Laetus: *HA Did. Jul.* 8.1 and cf. App. III.

[1] 'Coins': *BMC* V pp. 11f., 14ff. – 'Public enemy . . . amnesty': Dio 73.16.1, *HA Sev.* 5.5, etc. – Catullinus and Candidus: *HA Did. Jul.* 5.6–7, cf. G. ALFÖLDY, *Senat* p. 152f. *L'Albo* no. 520. – Felix: *HA Did. Jul.* 5.8, etc., cf. *CP* no. 225.

hired substitutes to do the work for them. The marines summoned from the Misenum fleet could not drill properly. And the elephants could not be trained to carry towers and threw their drivers. At this stage, Julianus had Laetus and Marcia murdered – he reckoned that Laetus was going to support Septimius.[1]

Meanwhile Septimius was continuing to move at speed. The senatorial envoys went over to him, not before the unpopular Vespronius Candidus had nearly been lynched by the troops. The news that a senatorial deputation was on its way had at first caused Septimius some anxiety, but as it turned out he managed, by bribing them, to induce the envoys to address the troops in his favour and then to desert to him. Likewise Aquilius Felix adroitly changed sides. Julianus now began to panic. He proposed to the Senate that the priests, Vestal Virgins and senators should go out to meet the advancing army in the attitude of suppliants. It was a sign that his authority was already negligible that his motion was rejected after a speech by Plautius Quintillus, a son-in-law of Marcus Aurelius. After contemplating a mass purge of the Senate, and then abandoning the idea, he finally had a decree passed making Septimius joint ruler with himself. He sent Tullius Crispinus to announce this move to Septimius, and meanwhile nominated a third Prefect of the Guard, Veturius Macrinus, who he knew had already been appointed to this post by Septimius. Crispinus was intercepted by the Septimian advance guard under Julius Laetus, whose recommendation to put him to death was authorised by Septimius. Julianus filled his place by the appointment of Flavius Juvenalis, whom he no doubt knew to be, like Veturius Macrinus, acceptable to Septimius. Septimius's agents were now active in Rome itself, posting placards which announced his programme.[2]

[1] Herodian 2.11.3. – Ravenna, Crispinus: *HA Did. Jul.* 6.3–4; Dio 73.17.1. – 'fortifications . . . elephants': *ib.* 5.9: Dio 73.16.1–3. – Laetus and Marcia: *HA Did. Jul.* 6.2: Dio 73.16.5.

[2] Candidus: Dio 73.17.1 (*Exc. Val.* 336). – Felix: *CP* no. 225, H. NESSELHAUF (1963) pp. 74ff. – For the rest, cf. *HA Sev.* 5.6–9, *Did. Jul.* 6.3 and 6.5–8.2, Dio 73.17. 1–3. – Macrinus and Juvenalis: App. III. It is suggested by one of the editors of the *Feriale Duranum* that the acclamation commemorated on 21 May may have been the recognition of Septimius as Emperor by the senatorial envoys. But the other suggestion made is more plausible (p. 178 n. 1, below). Cf. C. B. WELLES, p. 208f., for discussion of col. ii, l. 10 of the *Feriale*. – F. GROSSO (1968) argues

Julianus had now reached the end of the road. He again summoned the Senate and demanded advice, but no one would commit himself. As a final despairing gesture he appealed to Claudius Pompeianus to share the rule with him, but Pompeianus revived the excuses that had kept him out of public life in Commodus's reign, old age and weak eyesight. The praetorians had now received a direct order from Septimius, ordering them to keep the murderers of Pertinax under arrest. The order was obeyed, and the fact was announced to the consul Silius Messala. He summoned a meeting of the Senate in the Athenaeum. Julianus was condemned to death, Septimius was proclaimed emperor, and Pertinax was deified. Julianus was killed by a common soldier in the Palace, deserted by all except his son-in-law Repentinus and the Prefect Flavius Genialis. He had borne the title of Emperor for sixty-six days. It was 1 June. Septimius was at Interamna, just over fifty miles north of Rome. Seven and a half weeks had elapsed since his proclamation and he had won Rome without a battle. The march must have been exhausting. Surrounded day and night by a picked bodyguard of six hundred men, who did not once take off their breastplates, and sharing their hardships himself, he had delayed at no city in his path except to address a few words to the people and make sacrifice.[1]

Messengers from Pescennius Niger were now beginning to appear, bearing proclamations to the people and letters to the Senate. Septimius had them intercepted, and at the same time he sent Plautianus to search for and seize Niger's children. The children of Asellius Aemilianus were also taken into custody. Reports indicated that the proconsul of Asia, after some hesitation, had thrown in his lot with Niger.[2]

Immediately after the meeting of the Senate a deputation of one hundred senators went to greet Septimius, who remained encamped at Interamna 'as though moving through enemy territory'. When they

---

from Dio 73.15–4 that Julianus made Plautianus a high official at this time, to conciliate Septimius: cf. App. I.

[1] *HA Did. Jul.* 8.2–8, *Sev.* 5.9–10, Dio 73.17.3–5. The date is given by Dio 73.17.5. 'Interamna: *HA Sev.* 6.2. Herodian 2.11.1ff. gives a breathless description of Septimius' rapidity. Dio 73.15.3 has the vivid detail.

[2] 'Messengers . . . children': *HA Sev.* 6.7–8, 10. – Aemilianus: Herodian 3.2.3, cf. A. R. BIRLEY (1969) p. 270.

arrived they were searched for concealed weapons and he remained armed in their presence, with armed guards standing round. The next day the entire palace staff – slaves and freedmen – appeared. They may have brought a supply of ready cash with them, for Septimius now presented each member of the senatorial delegation with seven hundred and twenty gold pieces. (The reason for making the figure seven hundred and twenty, rather than a round number, may perhaps lie in the depreciation of the silver currency – it may well have been possible to exchange seven hundred and twenty aurei for twenty-five thousand denarii, nominally worth one thousand aurei.) Those who wished were invited to remain in his entourage for the final stages of his journey.[1]

Septimius's next and most pressing concern was the treatment of the Praetorian Guard. First he formally reappointed Flavius Juvenalis to the position of Prefect. It is worth noting that the only record of a man bearing these names is of a centurion in the Numidian legion III Augusta in the year 162. It would have made an appropriate choice for Septimius to have put an African who had risen through the centurionate in command of the Guard. The other Prefect, Veturius Macrinus, cannot have been a young man either. He had served as Prefect of Egypt for two years at the beginning of the reign of Commodus, but he had received no further promotion, and he had therefore been out of the service for ten years.[2]

Meanwhile Septimius issued secret instructions to the tribunes and centurions of the Guard. To the troops he issued a proclamation: they were ordered to put on parade uniform, leave their weapons in the camp, take the oath of allegiance and assemble to greet him outside the city. The language of the proclamation conveyed the implication that the carrying out of these orders would ensure their continuance in service. The officers of the guard ensured that the orders were obeyed. Septimius mounted the tribunal for what was expected to be a speech

[1] Interamna: *HA Sev.* 6.1–4. Cf. J. HASEBROEK (1921) p. 38 on the 720 *aurei*. (The passage may however be an intrusive invention.)

[2] Juvenalis: *HA Sev.* 6.5; App. III. – Macrinus: App. III. He may have been sacked by Perennis in 183, and failed to regain his position. (Note that his rapid promotion in 180–1 would be explicable if in 180 – *AE* 1953.79 – he was governing both Mauretanias simultaneously, not just Tingitana as Pflaum assumes, *CP* no. 179 *bis*.)

of welcome. But a detachment of his own men was already on its way to the *castra praetoria*, where they seized the armoury and manned the entrances. As the praetorians waited for the Emperor to speak, the Danubian soldiers surrounded the parade ground. Then Septimius began. He attacked them bitterly for their treachery to Pertinax, telling them that even if they had not actually murdered him, their failure to kill the assassins made them responsible for his murder. He formally discharged them from the service, and ordered them to remove themselves beyond the hundredth milestone from the City on pain of death. They were told to take off their uniforms and their ceremonial daggers, inlaid with silver and gold. Most complied, those that hesitated had their belts and uniforms ripped off. The mounted men were told to let their horses go. One horse refused to leave his rider, but kept following and neighing. The man killed the horse and then himself; 'And,' says Dio, 'it seemed to those that watched that the horse too was glad to die.'[1]

This was the end of the old *élite* corps of the Roman army. The five thousand praetorians, nearly all Italians and from provincial families of Italian stock, had had a disproportionate influence on the course of events for over two hundred years. Service in the Guard was regarded with envy by the legionaries. The pay was much higher, conditions were more favourable and the length of service was shorter. Septimius will have begun almost at once, during June, to form his new Guard, twice the size of the old one and manned by soldiers who had served in the northern legions. In partial compensation for the exclusion of Italians from the Guard, he also increased the size of the urban cohorts and the *vigiles*.[2]

There had been panic at Rome among the civilian population, as well as among the guilty praetorians, as Septimius approached. The reaction was partially justified. Septimius himself, after advancing as far as the gates uniformed and on horseback, dismounted and changed

---

[1] This famous scene has been much discussed. *HA Sev.* 6.11 is very brief. Dio 74.1.1–2; 2.3–6 and Herodian 2.13.1–12 provide details. – 'Secret instructions': Marcius Rustius Rufinus (App. 3) was probably one of the co-operative officers of the Guard. He soon went on to various key military and administrative posts.

[2] E. BIRLEY, *Ep. Stud.* 8, p. 64f., based mainly on M. Durry, *Les cohortes prétoriennes* (1939).

into civilian dress. But the entire expeditionary force, both infantry and cavalry, escorted him fully armed. Dio's account of the entry, 'the most brilliant spectacle of any that I have seen', fails to give a fully objective impression. It was written only a few years after the event, as part of the history of the civil wars that he presented to Septimius, and later incorporated, with some changes, into his complete work. He describes how the whole city was decked with garlands of flowers and with laurel branches and shone with the light of torches and burning incense. (Tertullian implies that only the Christians failed to participate. Dio, if he knew or cared, in accordance with his practice does not mention them.) This much of Dio's account is no doubt factual. But when he goes on to add that the white-robed citizens were radiant-faced as they uttered shouts of good omen, one may suspect that his language is disingenuous. When he says that the soldiers 'stood out conspicuously in their armour as they moved about like participants in some holiday procession', it is clear that tact has triumphed over accuracy. One must turn to the Augustan History for a truer impression. Septimius went first to the Capitol to make sacrifice. Then to the Palace, preceded by his legionaries trailing the standards of the disbanded Praetorian Guard, a sign of his bloodless victory. The soldiers were quartered all over the City, in temples and porticoes and even in the shrines on the Palatine. Septimius's entry inspired 'hatred and fear', the biographer concludes, for the soldiers seized goods without paying for them and threatened to lay the city waste.[1]

The following day Septimius came to the *curia*, once more escorted by an armed guard. In a speech he justified his seizure of power, claiming that his coup had been made in self-defence: Julianus had sent men 'notorious for assassinating generals to murder him'. Most will have

[1] 'Panic': Herodian 2.12.1–2. – 'Dio's account': 74.1.3–5. – Tertullian: *Apol.* 35.4. Cf. F. MILLAR (1964) pp. 139f.; 179. – The *HA :Sev.* 7.1–3. Cf. Herodian 2.14.1–2, who emphasises the remarkable fact that the capture of Rome was bloodless. *armatus* in *Sev.* 7.1 is probably inaccurate, cf. M. Fluss in *RE* 2A (1923) 1954. The date of the entry into the City is argued to be 9 June by Fluss, *l.c.* and J. HASEBROEK (1921) p. 40, with reference to *CIL* III 11082, VI 224. But cf. R. O. FINK pp. 140, 167ff: that day was the festival of the Vestalia and need have no bearing on Septimius' entry, which can only be dated approximately – it must surely have been very soon after 1 June.

known that Julianus took this step only after Septimius's march had begun. Still, he was under no necessity to be particularly apologetic about his actions: for, as he told them, he had come to avenge Pertinax – whom the Senate had clearly preferred to Julianus. But to make it clear that no purge was to begin, he asked that a decree of the Senate should be passed, 'that the Emperor shall not be permitted to put a senator to death without consulting the Senate'. One Julius Solon, who had bought his senatorial rank from Cleander, had the honour of introducing the formal motion. While the session was in progress the soldiers began to create a disturbance outside, demanding that the Senate grant them a bounty. The sum that they named was 10,000 Sesterces a man, 2,500 denarii – the equivalent of at least six, perhaps eight years' pay per man. They claimed as a precedent the grant of this sum to Octavian's soldiers in 43 B.C. It is remarkable that the soldiers should have had knowledge of an event two hundred and thirty-five years before their own time: some of them were perhaps better educated than Dio gave them credit for. But no doubt this colossal donative had become part of legionary folklore. Septimius was eventually able to pacify them with a tenth of what they asked, and then sent them away. It cannot have been easy to raise funds at this time, after two Emperors had given out donatives. One may wonder whether steps were taken to recover any of the money that Julianus had lavished on the praetorians – a total of at least a hundred and fifty million Sesterces. It was probably to pay the donative to his troops that a special issue of coins was struck. They bear the names of all the Rhine, Danube and Dacian legions, with the single exception of the Vienna legion X Gemina. That unit had no doubt been left behind in its entirety to safeguard the Pannonian frontier.[1]

Septimius's next public act was to order the state funeral and deification of Pertinax. At his request, the Senate formally bestowed the name Pertinax on him. Cassius Dio's elaborate description of the

[1] 'The following day . . .': Herodian 2.14.3–4; *HA Sev.* 7.4, 5.8. – decree of the Senate: *ib.* 7.5; Dio 74.2.1–2, cf. A. R. BIRLEY (1962). – 'disturbance': *HA Sev.* 7.5–7; Dio 46.46.7, cf. the interesting comments of G. R. WATSON pp. 113, 198, who suggests that some of the men may have known about Octavian's donative from reading the works of Appian (*BC* 3.94). – 'Special issue': cf. H. Mattingly in *BMC* V, pp. lxxxiif., xcvii, 21ff., 118; J. FITZ (1962) pp. 38f., 89f.

ceremonies in honour of Pertinax has been preserved by Xiphilinus. A wooden platform was built in the Forum near the Rostra and on it a shrine surrounded by ivory and gold columns. A funeral bier, likewise made of ivory and gold, was placed within it, on which lay a wax effigy of Pertinax in triumphal dress. The Emperor, with the senators and their wives, approached in mourning dress. Then the busts of famous Romans were carried past the bier, followed by male choirs singing a funeral lament, symbolic bronze representations of the provinces, followed by the city guilds. More portrait busts were then carried past, this time of famous men from all nations. The troops rode and marched past and finally funeral gifts were laid before the bier. Then Septimius mounted the Rostra and delivered the customary eulogy, to shouts of approval from the senators. When it was over the bier was taken down from the platform by the priests and magistrates – including those designated to take office the following year, of whom Dio was one. They handed the bier to pall-bearers selected from the equestrian order, who proceeded with it to the Campus Martius, followed by the senators, 'some of us beating our breast and others playing a dirge on the flute'. Septimius came last of all. A three-storey funeral pyre had been built, surmounted by a gilded chariot that Pertinax had once driven. The offerings and the bier were placed in it, Septimius and the relatives of Pertinax kissed the effigy, and then withdrew to a safe distance. Magistrates, *equites* and soldiers paraded round the pyre and then the consuls fired it. When it began to blaze, an eagle flew out and upwards, symbolising that Pertinax had been deified. The worship of the new god was to be supervised by the *sodales* appointed for the cult of the Antonine Emperors, and Pertinax's son was made *flamen Helvianus*.[1]

The ceremony was an important gesture, which would give some credence to his claimed intention of modelling his administration on that of Pertinax – and that of Pertinax's own exemplar, Marcus Aurelius. Now there were more practical matters to attend to, first and foremost the preparation for the campaign against Niger. Septimius refused for the time being to make any public reference to his rival. But one of the first acts before he reached Rome must have been to

[1] Dio 74.4.1 – 5.5; cf. *HA Pert.* 15.1–5; *Sev.* 7.8–9.

despatch his friend Fabius Cilo to take command of a force at Perinthus, in Thrace. Cilo was to prevent Niger's troops advancing any further into Thrace.[1]

The mint began striking coins in the names of Septimius and of Albinus. The first issues stressed the generosity of the Emperor, presumably indicating that he had issued a *congiarium* to the *plebs*, and the fertility of the age, as well as, inevitably, the loyalty of the legions. The *saeculum frugiferum* had already been advertised on the coinage of Pertinax. Its reappearance now is interesting. It was also the Latin name of an African deity, Ba'al Hammon. The god was worshipped in many parts of North Africa, but it was the patron deity of Hadrumetum, the home of Albinus. The Caesar's own coins stress the 'divine foresight' by which Septimius provided against future eventualities with his choice of successor. The first coins struck for Julia Domna celebrate the goddess Venus, both Venus Victrix who had won Caesar his Civil War victories, and Venus Genetrix, the divine ancestress of the original Julian family.[2]

Meanwhile Septimius and Albinus were designated to hold the consulship jointly for the year 194. Septimius had little time for dealing with civilian matters. He left Rome less than thirty days after his triumphant entry. He did find time on 27 June to give an adjudication on a point of law. It is preserved as the first of over a hundred and fifty rescripts from him included in the Code of Justinian. Interpretation of the law was to be one of the key features of his reign. In the capital itself, particularly in the Emperor's absence, the Prefect of the City played a preeminent role in the administration of justice. Immediately after his arrival he had appointed a friend of his named Bassus to the office. Just before the expedition departed Bassus gave up the Prefecture, after holding it for less than a month. It may be that Septimius wished to take Bassus to the east with him, or it could be that he had been intended as a stop-gap only, until more permanent arrangements

---

[1] 'claimed intention': esp. Herodian 2.3; cf. A. R. BIRLEY (1969) p. 273, ID., *Seventh Congress.* – 'refused . . . reference': *HA Sev.* 8.6. – Cilo: App. III.

[2] 'first issues': *BMC* V pp. 20ff., 117ff. – *saeculum frugiferum : ib.* pp. 2 (Pertinax), 20, 119 (Septimius), 38, 134ff. (Albinus), cf. below p. 177 and n. 1. – Venus: *ib.* pp. 27f. Julia of course became Augusta, perhaps from 1 June. Cf. *PIR*[2] J 663. The name Domna is often omitted from coins and inscriptions.

could be made. At any rate, the man whom Septimius left as City Prefect was C. Domitius Dexter, once the successor of Pertinax as governor of Syria, and hence perhaps Septimius's own former commanding officer there for a short time. Undoubtedly the City Prefect would have an exceptional importance during the absence of a newly created Emperor. The same applies even more strongly to the commanders of the Praetorian Guard – for some of the Guard at least would be left in Rome, with one of the Praetorian Prefects. But no certain information is available.[1] All that can be said is that the sources give scarcely no hint of trouble for Septimius in the city of Rome during his absence, in spite of the popular support that there had been for the rival that he was going to meet.

There were of course other men besides the City Prefect left behind to watch his interests. The ex-centurion Aquilius Felix was one. He was placed in simultaneous control of three important bureaux, public works, Crown property (*patrimonium*) and the private property of the Antonine family (*ratio privata*). This would be a strategic role; and he could use it as a cloak for other activities. The same may apply to Sex. Varius Marcellus, nephew of Julia by marriage – a native of Apamea in Syria, he was married to her niece Julia Soaemias. Marcellus was soon to hold the post of procurator of the water supply, which may also have been a purely nominal appointment, allowing him to watch the Emperor's interests in Rome. Steps were also taken to put new men into the Senate. One Ti. Claudius Claudianus, an African from Rusicade in Numidia, was made praetor. He had perhaps been serving as procurator or equestrian officer in one of the northern provinces. He was soon to take up a legionary command in Dacia. Another man put into the Senate at this time, it would seem, was Claudius Gallus, perhaps a kinsman of Claudianus. He too was soon to

[1] 'designated': explicit only in *HA Alb.* 6.8, but obvious enough. – 'little time': the information in *HA Sev.* 8.1–2 (on the alleged sons-in-law) is rightly rejected as invented by J. HASEBROEK (1921) p. 54. The statements in *HA Sev.* 7.9 and 8.3, that he paid off his friends' debts, and proscribed and executed the friends of Julianus, may have some truth behind them. But 8.4–5 (especially on the *res frumentaria*) looks intrusive, perhaps false also. – '27 June': *Cod. Just.* 3.28.1. – 'Prefect of the City': cf. generally G. VITUCCI. – Bassus: *HA Sev.* 8.8, otherwise unknown: perhaps the friend 'enriched' by Septimius (*Epit. de Caes*,) 20.6). Cf. *L'Albo* no. 88, also 525 (Vibius Bassus). – Dexter: App. III.

have an important position. A third African who must have had a responsible post at this time is L. Alfenus Senecio from Cuicul in Numidia, perhaps another of Septimius's new senators.[1]

But the prime consideration at this time must have been the raising of new troops. It is even possible that Septimius had already taken the decision to create three new legions, although it is difficult to believe that he could have formed them before his departure. It could be that the official pretext for these military preparations was an expedition against the Parthians. At any rate, the new legions were to be called the *legiones* I, II and III Parthicae. But it is probable that the Augustan History is accurate when it states that Septimius officially set out 'to set affairs in the east in order' (*ad conponendum orientis statum*). This non-committal terminology will have deceived no one. News from the east was still of course being suppressed in Italy. Septimius had a trump card, for he had gained custody of the children of all those who held official positions in the eastern provinces, except those of Niger. Plautianus was still pursuing them, and Septimius may have hoped that when they fell into his hands he could use them as a bargaining counter to make Niger given in without a fight. In the meantime he sent troops to Africa. Apparently he feared that Niger would advance through Egypt and Cyrenaica and seize the province. This would completely cut off the grain supply from Rome. It would also have caused Septimius's home town of Lepcis Magna to fall into his rival's hands. The move was possibly taken on the advice of the proconsul Anullinus, who may even have returned from his province in time to join the expedition before its departure. But Septimius's anxiety may have been palliated to some extent by the hope that the prefect Mantennius Sabinus would try to swing Egypt out of Niger's camp at the first opportunity.[2]

[1] Felix: *CP* no. 228; H. NESSELHAUF (1964) pp. 74ff. – Marcellus: App. 1. – Claudianus, Gallus, Senecio: App. III. – F. GROSSO (1968), esp. pp. 14ff., shows convincingly that Plautianus had become Prefect of the *vigiles* by the spring of 195: see further App. I.

[2] 'New legions': cf. E. BIRLEY, *Ep. Stud.* and ID.(1963), p. 24f., suggesting I and III were formed in Numidia; J. C. MANN (1963), p. 486. – 'officially set out': *HA Sev*, 8.6. – 'children': Herodian 3.2.5. Niger's children were evidently still at large, to judge from *HA Sev*. 8.12. – Africa: *ib*. 8.7. – Anullinus, Sabinus: App. III.

XII

THE WAR AGAINST NIGER

The expedition left Rome by the *via Flaminia*, the route by which Septimius had arrived only a month before. He soon ran into difficulties. At Saxa Rubra, less than ten miles north of the city, the troops mutinied over the choice of camp site. But this trouble was evidently overcome without difficulty – perhaps with a rapid distribution of the new coins struck in the legions' honour. The quartermaster on the 'city expedition' (*expeditio urbica*), Rossius Vitulus, now had charge of the 'war-chest for the expedition' (*arca expeditionalis*), proof, if proof were needed, that Septimius was continuing to cement the loyalty of his troops by disbursements of money.[1]

Septimius's departure from Rome by the northern route indicates that he travelled east by land. It might have been too risky to cross from Brundisium to Dyrrachium and follow the *via Egnatia*, when Niger's forces were still in Europe. Indeed, Niger, who had apparently made Byzantium his headquarters, inflicted heavy casualties on Fabius Cilo's defending force, in an attempt to seize Perinthus. This battle induced Niger to advertise a victory on his coinage. The success made him grow conceited, and his followers called him a new Alexander, Dio records. The realisation that Niger had every intention of fighting for the Empire prompted Septimius to take the step that he had so far avoided. The Senate was asked to declare Niger and Asellius Aemilianus public enemies. Septimius was particularly angered at Aemilianus's actions. He may have hoped the man would change sides. Instead, Aemilianus was playing a leading role in command of Niger's army.[2]

---

[1] Saxa Rubra: *HA Sev.* 8.10. – Vitulus: *CP* no. 224 and cf. p. 160, above.

[2] 'Niger . . . seize Perinthus', 'Byzantium': Dio 74.6.3, *HA Sev.* 8.12–13, Herodian 3.1.5 – 2.1. – Cilo: App. III. – coins: *BMC* V p. 73f. – 'new Alexander':

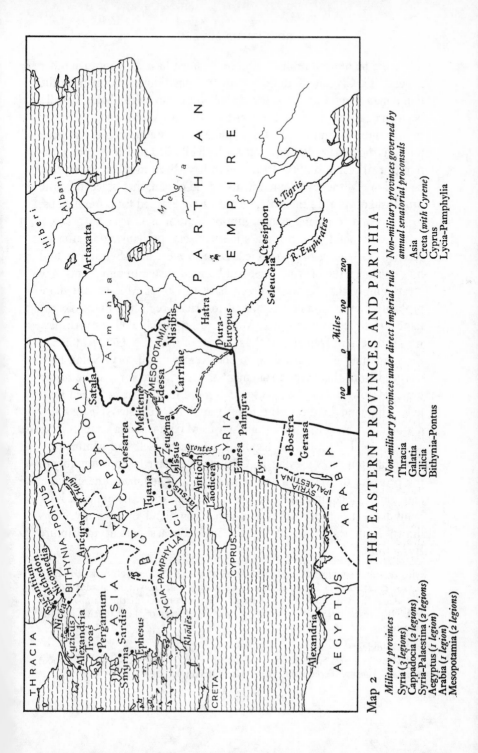

Map 2

THE EASTERN PROVINCES AND PARTHIA

Non-military provinces under direct Imperial rule

Thracia
Galatia
Cilicia
Bithynia-Pontus

Non-military provinces governed by annual senatorial proconsuls

Asia
Creta (*with Cyrene*)
Cyprus
Lycia-Pamphylia

Military provinces

Syria (*3 legions*)
Cappadocia (*2 legions*)
Syria-Palaestina (*2 legions*)
Aegyptus (*1 legion*)
Arabia (*1 legion*)
Mesopotamia (*2 legions*)

Before he himself reached Thrace, he must have sent ahead another general, Ti. Claudius Candidus, with an expeditionary force from the Pannonian army. Candidus, perhaps of Numidian origin, had originally been an equestrian officer at the end of Marcus Aurelius's reign. Early in the reign of Commodus, after holding a procuratorship, he had been put into the Senate. But as a senator he had failed to achieve any position of real responsibility. It may even have been in the year 193 that he held one of the few appointments he did obtain, that of legate to the proconsul of Asia. In that case, he must have escaped from Aemilianus, to be given a command against him by Septimius.[1]

At some point in Septimius's journey east, probably soon after he reached Naissus, his brother Geta came to meet him. Septimius 'told him to govern the province that had been entrusted to him'. This may mean simply that he was ordered back to Lower Moesia, but more probably Geta was now transferred to Dacia, replacing Polus Terentianus. His successor in Lower Moesia was probably Pollienus Auspex, who had been in Dalmatia at the moment of the coup. Geta had hoped for something else, according to the Augustan History. Some have deduced from this cryptic statement that he hoped for a share in the imperial power. This may be so. It is more likely that he hoped for a field command in the forthcoming war. The Augustan History undoubtedly derives the story from Marius Maximus, Geta's subordinate as legate of I Italica – the legion that Geta himself had commanded more than ten years previously. Geta may not have taken favourably to the prospect of Maximus and others like him acquiring the glamour and glory of commanding troops in battle, while he remained far behind the front. Maximus was given command of an army corps drawn from the Moesian legions, and the assignment to capture Byzantium.[2]

Dio, 74.6.2a. – 'public enemies': *HA Sev.* 8.13. On Aemilianus cf. A. R. BIRLEY (1969) p. 270f. – G. M. BERSANETTI (1938) has shown the inadequacy of Herodian's heavily rhetorical account of Niger's conduct in this campaign. D. MAGIE (1950) pp. 669ff., 1538ff. has a useful survey of the campaign and the evidence.

[1] Candidus: App. III.
[2] Geta: *HA Sev.* 8.10, cf. App. 1; also App. II, p. 313 and A. R. BIRLEY (1969) p. 262. – Auspex, Terentianus: App. III. – Maximus: App. II.

Niger had done his best to defend the coast of Asia Minor, the command being in the hands of Aemilianus. But as he watched first Marius Maximus's army settling down to besiege him in Byzantium and then Septimius himself arrive to make his headquarters at Perinthus, less than fifty miles away, he clearly began to lose his confidence. Added to this was the fact that Septimius would by then have had Niger's children brought to Perinthus. He therefore made an offer to Septimius, that they should share the empire. This was rejected out of hand. Septimius was prepared to spare Niger's life if he submitted and went into exile – but he refused to pardon Aemilianus.[1]

In the autumn Claudius Candidus took the Pannonian army across the Hellespont or the Sea of Marmara. On the mainland opposite the island of Cyzicus he defeated Aemilianus, who fled to Cyzicus, no doubt trying to reach Niger at Byzantium. But soon after leaving Cyzicus he was captured and executed by Candidus. His army fled eastwards, out of the province of Asia into Bithynia. Candidus pursued on both land and sea. In traditional fashion two great Bithynian cities reacted oppositely. Nicomedia responded to the Septimian victory by an immediate change of side, sending offers of support. Candidus sent his troops ahead there, outflanking the enemy. True to form Nicomedia's ancient enemy Nicaea gave a welcome to Niger's army. Niger himself now managed to make his way from Byzantium to Nicaea to take personal command of his forces.[2]

Candidus led his troops against Nicaea from the north. The battle took place in the narrow passes west of the city, leading past Lake Ascania to Cius. Cassius Dio has a fairly detailed account of the struggle. As a native of Nicaea, he was able to hear the accounts of eyewitnesses. Candidus had stationed his troops on the high ground and at

[1] 'Niger ... in Byzantium': among modern writers only M. PLATNAUER (p. 85f.) explicitly states that Niger was at Byzantium in person – which seems clear enough in Dio 74.6.3; cf. Herodian 3.2.1. – Aemilianus: Herodian 3.2.2ff.; Dio 74.6.1. – Perinthus: Dio 74.6.3, cf. *RE* 2A (1923) 1956f. – children: *HA Sev.* 8.11 (Septimius treated them with equal honour to his own children). On Plautianus cf. App. 1. – 'an offer': *HA Sev.* 8.14–15.

[2] Cyzicus: *HA Sev.* 8.16 (confused); Dio 76.6.4; Herodian 3.2.1–9 (9 deals with Nicomedia: Fabius Cilo was perhaps made *curator* of Nicomedia *pro tem.*, cf. App. III). – Niger at Nicaea: Herodian 73.2.10; Dio 74.6.6.

first they had the advantage, although the fighting was confused. Some of the enemy were shooting arrows from boats on the lake. Then Niger himself appeared and the Septimians began to give way. At this point Candidus displayed outstanding qualities of leadership: 'He seized hold of the standard-bearers and forced them to turn round to face the enemy, rebuking his men for taking flight.' This saved the day, and Niger's forces only escaped complete destruction through the onset of darkness. The battle must have taken place in December, or early January at the latest, for news of Septimius's victory reached Rome by 31 January. And by 13 February Egypt had gone over to him. Niger's army retreated rapidly, and Niger himself hurried on ahead to Antioch.[1]

Septimius now took possession of Asia as well as Bithynia. Fabius Cilo was made governor of the latter province. Claudius Candidus took at least part of his victorious Pannonian army into the province of Asia, where he pursued 'public enemies of the Roman people on both land and sea'. Claudius Xenophon, formerly procurator in Moesia and Dacia, and sub-prefect of the *annona*, was made procurator of Asia. Although there were no executions of prominent figures, except of Aemilianus, there will have been large scale confiscations and other penalties imposed on the cities that had supported Niger with misguided enthusiasm.[2]

The two victories had caused his army to acclaim him as *imperator*. He was able to add first Imp. II and then Imp. III to his titles, which, from the opening of 194, now included *pater patriae*. Unlike Pertinax, he had allowed at least a token interval to elapse before he accepted this distinction. The mint of Rome hastened to strike new coins following each victory. After the battle near Cyzicus, as well as 'the Emperor's victory' and the 'spirit of the Roman people', the ancestral gods of Lepcis Magna, the *di auspices* – Hercules and Father Liber – make their

---

[1] The battle is described by Dio 74.6.4–6. – 'reached Rome': he was already IMP. III on 31 Jan. (*CIL* XVI 134). Cf. D. MAGIE p. 1539, *BMC* V p. lxxxvii, etc. – Egypt: *BGU* I 326 II, cf. Magie p. 1538f.; A. R. BIRLEY (1969) p. 269. – 'Niger hurried on . . .': Herodian 3.2.10.

[2] Cilo, Candidus: App. III. – Xenophon: *CP* no. 222. – 'no executions . . . enthusiasm': *HA Sev.* 9.3 (apparently contradicted by 9.6 – but that refers to the aftermath of Issus).

5a The Euphrates from the Wall of Dura-Europos.

5b The *praetorium* (commander's house) at Dura. The files of the
XXth Cohort of Palymyrenes at Dura have provided invaluable
information on the history of the Roman army and the Empire as
a whole (cf. esp. C. B. Welles).

6   The Berlin Tondo, found in Egypt, painted on wood. (See K. A. Neugebauer).

7 Septimius, flanked by his two sons, shown in a triumphal chariot on the Arch at Lepcis Magna.

8 Julia Domna looking towards her husband and sons on frieze D of the Arch
   at Lepcis Magna. See also plates 9 and 10 for the central and right-hand
   scenes from this portion of the frieze.

first appearance on the Roman coinage. The victory at Nicaea-Cius produced reverses of Mars the pacifier and Peace herself, and the figure of Septimius is shown clasping hands with Jupiter. Eternal Rome is figured on the bronze coinage, another issue of which shows Africa, with elephant-skin headdress and a lion at her feet, and corn-ears in her bosom. The exceptional prominence given to the province on the coinage was no doubt caused in part by its importance in supplying Rome with cereals. But in this and the following year the coinage of Albinus repeatedly shows the African deity *saeculum frugiferum*. On one particularly fine *aureus* the god is represented seated with sphinxes on either side of his throne, and wearing a fez-like headdress. The figure closely resembles a Punic relief found in the shrine of Ba'al Hammon at Hadrumetum. This emphasis, combined with Septimius's coinage honouring the *di auspices*, leaves no doubt that Septimius believed it was important to advertise the African background of himself and his chief ally.[1]

Cornelius Anullinus now took over as commander-in-chief of the expeditionary army and began advancing through into Galatia and Cappadocia. Septimius remained at Perinthus, where the sixth birthday of his son Bassianus was celebrated on 4 April. Niger was making frantic preparations. He fortified the passes of the Taurus and raised further troops. But his support was dwindling. The defection of Egypt was followed by that of Arabia, whose governor, P. Aelius Severianus Maximus, was a native of Perinthus. One of the two legions in Palestine, VI Ferrata, may have followed suit. Certain individual cities also threw off their allegiance and proclaimed their support for Septimius. Two of these, Laodicea and Tyre, were severely punished by Niger. One might expect to find that Emesa had early supported the husband of Julia Domna. Proof is lacking, but there is a strong possibility that this city came out openly for Septimius as early as 193 and issued coins in his name.[2]

---

[1] IMP. II and III: cf. p. 176 n. 1. – *pater patriae*: *BMC* V p. lxxxvii, and *ib.* pp. lxxxviiff., xcviiff. on the coins. – *saeculum frugiferum*: *ib.* p. lxxxixf., cf. A. R. BIRLEY (1969) p. 265f.

[2] Anullinus: App. 3. Dio 74.7.1–8 names him as commander at Issus. – A 'birthday': cf. *RE* 2A (1923) 1956f. (rather doubtful, as only recorded in Jordanes *Getica* 84). – Niger: Herodian 3.2.10 – 3.2. – Severianus Maximus: App. III. – VI

Only Herodian records a battle at one of the passes fortified by Niger. His account appears to indicate that the Septimians forced the pass during the winter or spring, for he speaks of a fall of snow. The decisive battle was to come near Issus, where Alexander had defeated Darius more than five hundred years before. Niger came out to meet the enemy as they moved down into the Gulf of Alexandretta. Both Dio and Herodian have detailed accounts of the battle. Dio's must certainly be preferred, for he gives a convincing account of the manner in which the victory was gained. Anullinus's men were helped by a heavy thunderstorm and rain from behind them driving at the faces of the enemy. But the decisive factor was Anullinus's move in sending Valerius Valerianus round with the cavalry to take Niger's army in the rear. As it turned out, they were already retreating, their morale lowered by the thunderstorm, when Valerianus appeared and they were trapped. According to Dio they suffered losses amounting to twenty thousand. Niger fled to Antioch. Anullinus followed and soon after captured the city. Niger apparently intended to flee to the Parthians, but he was caught on the outskirts of the city and killed. His head was cut off and sent to Septimius, who sent the head to the army besieging Byzantium, to induce that city to surrender. But it had no effect. The defeat and death of Niger can hardly have been much later than the end of April.[1]

Ferrata acquired the title *constans*: *RE* 12 (1925) 1593. – Laodicea, Tyre: Herodian 3.3.3–5. – Emesa: *BMC* V pp. cxviiff.

[1] 'Only Herodian': 3.3.1–2 describes a minor clash at a pass in Cappadocia, 3.3.6–8 an apparently major encounter at a pass in the Taurus. This second clash took place after a storm when rain fell mingled with snow, which suggests a date in spring, cf. D. MAGIE p. 1539f. (Unfortunately, the whole thing may be pure rhetoric.) – Issus: Dio 74.7.1–8; Herodian 3.4.1–5. – Valerianus: the man named in Dio is clearly identical with L. Valerius Valerianus *praepositus vexillationum peregrinarum*, cf. *AE* 1966.495 (no reference to Dio). J. FITZ (1969) p. 132 n. 2 rejects the identification. *HA Sev.* 9.1 repeats an error found elsewhere, that Niger was defeated and killed at Cyzicus: cf. App. II. On the place: Dio 74.8.2 speaks of flight to the Euphrates, Herodian 3.4.6 says he was caught in the outskirts of Antioch. The date: cf. Magie p. 1540. It is possible that the final submission of the Syrian army is commemorated in the *Feriale Duranum* (col. ii, b. 10) cf. C. B. WELLES, p. 208f. In that case, Issus could be dated more or less exactly, to 21 May 194 or a little earlier.

Pescennius Niger must remain a shadowy figure. On his proclamation as emperor he had assumed the additional name Justus, as if to announce the main theme of his rule. But he had little chance to put it into effect. Whether he would have succeeded is another matter. Cassius Dio notes that he was of equestrian origin. In a fragment of Dio's account of the reign of Commodus there is a mention of his winning military renown, together with Albinus, in a war against the Dacians in the early 180s. But Dio says that he was appointed governor of Syria because of his negative qualities – 'he was remarkable for nothing, good or bad'. In other words, a grey figure who could be safely appointed to the key province of Syria during the confused last period of Commodus's reign – especially as the Parthian Empire was racked by civil war in 191. His coins portray him with long, narrow head, rather thick lips and a tense expression. The legends and reverse types represent him as the favourite of numerous gods. Herodian sneers at his vanity – and the anecdote about the 'new Alexander' recorded by Dio, already quoted, might seem to confirm this. The author of the Augustan History, in a frank prelude to his biography of Niger, noted that it was an unusual and difficult task to record the lives of those 'who through the victories of others remained pretenders to the throne only'. This did not deter him from concocting a curious farrago that passes for a factual biography, based on the thin substratum of fact – the tale of Niger's 'presumption, the battle in which he was overcome, and the punishment that he suffered' – that he found in his source's account of Septimius Severus.[1]

Septimius now proceeded into Asia, following in the wake of his successful army. In honour of the battle of Issus he took a fourth acclamation as Imperator. He still refrained from exacting vengeance against the senators who had supported Niger. It would have been foolish to do so, when disaffected senators had a potential rallying point in the person of Clodius Albinus. Dio records how one Cassius Clemens defended his behaviour: ' "I did not know either you or

[1] On Niger cf. *RE* 19 (1937) 1086ff. Cf. also G. ALFÖLDY, *Senat*, p. 149. – Parthian Empire: cf. N. C. DEBEVOISE p. 255. – Coins: *BMC* V pp. cviiff. (too inclined to believe *HA Pesc. Nig.*). Cf. Dio 72.8.1, 73.13.5, 14.3, 15.1, 74.6.1–2, Herodian 2.7.3 – 9.1, 2.14.6, 3.1.1–7, 43.4.1–7, *HA Pesc. Nig.* 1.2 (cf. App. II on this *vita*).

SEPTIMIUS SEVERUS

Niger," he said, "but since I was surrounded by his followers I had to look to the moment, not to fight against you but to depose Julianus." '
Septimius 'admired his frankness', and allowed him to retain half his property. Presumably the other prominent men, including most of the eastern governors and legionary legates, lost everything. One of the senators affected was a certain Flavius Athenagoras. Septimius later returned a million Sesterces out of his confiscated property to the man's daughter as a dowry.[1]

An important step was to replace these men with his own nominees. The names of some of Septimius's new governors are recorded. Q. Venidius Rufus, a kinsman of Marius Maximus, who had been commanding the Bonn legion I Minervia, was made governor of Cilicia. Syria was treated drastically – it was divided into two. Syria Coele, northern or 'hollow' Syria, with the legions IV Scythica and XVI Flavia, remained consular. Syria Phoenice, with III Gallica, was now governed by the legate of that legion. The capital of the new province was Tyre, mother-city of Carthage and the western Phoenicians. Tyre was also given the *ius Italicum*, exempting its citizens from the tribute paid by provincials. The first governor appointed was Ti. Manilius Fuscus, who had been legate of the Dacian legion XIII Gemina. Rewards and punishments were now distributed to other cities which had taken a positive stance for either side during the war. Antioch was severely punished. Septimius now had the opportunity to get his own back on the people who had made fun of him when he was a legionary legate. The city was entirely deprived of its civic status and relegated to a parish of its rival Laodicea, which replaced it as capital of Syria Coele and also acquired the *ius Italicum*. Similar measures were taken with other cities.[2]

[1] Imperator IV: cf. *BMC* V p. lxxxff., xcixff., etc. – Clemens: Dio 74.9.1–4. – Athenagoras: *Digest* 22.1.6. Perhaps identical with *PIR²* C 429, *Carminius Athenagoras*, certainly a member of that family from Attuda in Phrygia. Cf. *L'Albo* nos. 113–115, 222, 733, 1031. – T. D. BARNES (1968c) esp. p. 594 plausibly argues that the future Emperor Gordian I (an easterner, from Galatia or Cappodocia, cf. A. R. BIRLEY [1966c]) may have been among those expelled from the Senate at this time for supporting the losing side.

[2] Rufus, Fuscus: App. III. – 'Rewards and punishments': cf. G. DOWNEY pp. 239ff.; D. MAGIE, p. 1540. – In the meantime, if not earlier, Plautianus was sent back to Rome to be Prefect of the *vigiles*: cf. App. 1.

180

An anecdote included in the biography of the obscure third-century poet Oppian may belong to Septimius's journey through Asia Minor in this year. When the Emperor came to the city of Anazarbus, some forty miles north of Issus, the entire populace came out to greet him – with the exception of the poet's father the 'philosopher' Agesilaus. He evidently despised such displays of empty pomp and ceremony. But Septimius was angry, and banished him to the island of Melita off the Dalmatian coast. His hot temper and vindictiveness remained dominant characteristics – Agesilaus stayed in exile until after the Emperor's death.[1]

No steps were taken to degrade or punish the army that had fought for Niger. But it should be noted that an ex-centurion in the secret police, P. Vibius Marianus, was made chief centurion of the legion III Gallica. No doubt a man of his background could carry out any necessary restoration of discipline. A fair number of Niger's troops had indeed taken refuge beyond the Euphrates, and various of the rulers in northern Mesopotamia had shown active support to Niger. Besides this, Septimius had some justification for taking action beyond the frontier. Apparently the city of Nisibis, although far beyond the Euphrates and only some fifty-odd miles from the Tigris, was in some sense dependent on Rome – it may even have had a token Roman garrison. When it was attacked by three peoples that had given aid to Niger – the Osrhoeni, Adiabeni and Scenite Arabs – Septimius took his opportunity. He rejected the claims of an embassy, that the attack on Nisibis had been made in his interest, against 'soldiers that had favoured Niger's cause'. Early in the spring of 195 he mounted an invasion of Mesopotamia. Cassius Dio, the only one of the three main sources who gives any details, is scornful: it was done 'out of a desire for glory' – the same motive that he had imputed to Trajan. Considerations of this kind may have entered into the decision. It would have been politic to gain some success over a foreign enemy after more than a year of civil war. Besides, with Byzantium still unconquered, it may have seemed premature to return to the west. A campaign was opportune: it would allow legions that had taken opposing sides at three battles to fight together against a common enemy, and, besides,

[1] Cf. *PIR*² A 457.

the Parthian Empire was now weak. Added to all these considerations one may fairly suppose that Septimius had already formed a serious, long-term design to extend the eastern frontier. His own experience fifteen years earlier as legate of IV Scythica, and Julia Domna's personal knowledge of the situation in Syria, may have led him to believe that the Euphrates was seriously defective as a line of defence.[1]

Presumably crossing the Euphrates at Zeugma, his first act was to depose the Osrhoenian king Abgarus. He then proceeded to Nisibis, where he established his headquarters. Julia accompanied him, and on 14 April her presence by his side was officially recognised by the grant to her of the title *mater castrorum*, 'Mother of the Camp'. Early in the campaign Septimius assumed new titles, Arabicus and Adiabenicus. Surprisingly, the new titles appear on the coinage before any addition to the number of his acclamations. Hence one can only suppose that some great achievement early in the campaign is commemorated thereby – an achievement won before any serious fighting had taken place. The answer must be that the Arabs and Adiabeni had offered submission soon after Septimius entered Mesopotamia. It is interesting to note that the titles in their fullest form are Parthicus Arabicus, Parthicus Adiabenicus, emphasising that the peoples who had surrendered were vassals of the Parthians. Apparently, Septimius rejected the title of Parthicus on its own to avoid giving offence to the Parthian king. In any case, there was no fighting with the Parthians themselves. In the course of the year 195 three victories were won, which brought successively the titles Imperator V, VI and VII. The coins display two captives, seated back to back, on round shields, wearing pointed hats and with their hands bound. If the Arabs and Adiabeni did offer submission early in the campaign, they soon caused more trouble – other-

---

[1] Marianus: *CP* no. 273 + add. – 'refuge': Herodian 3.4.7 actually says 'beyond the Tigris'. He goes on (8–9) to state that they materially aided the 'barbarians' i.e. Parthians (?or Persians) by teaching them 'the use and manufacture of weapons'. – 'various of the rulers': Herodian 3.1.1–3, 3.9.1 speaks of Barsemius, King of Hatra. – Nisibis: Dio 75.1.2–3, discussed by D. MAGIE p. 1541. – 'desire for glory': Dio 75.1.1, cf. 68 on Trajan. Further criticism in 75.3.2–3. Cf. F. MILLAR (1964) pp. 141, 208; also A. R. BIRLEY, *Seventh Congress*, on Dio's attitude to expansion of the Empire – Dio was unwilling to accept that his hero M. Aurelius had been an expansionist. – 'His own experience . . .': cf. p. 115f., above.

wise there would hardly have been three further battles. The victories were probably hard won. The Senate decreed a triumph to him. But this he rejected – in case it should appear that he was celebrating a triumph for his victories in the civil war. A triumphal arch was, however, accepted.[1]

The desert conditions caused severe hardship among his troops, and such water as was available was at first rejected by the troops until Septimius called for a cup and drained it. He will have been familiar with desert wells from his boyhood in Tripolitania. Dio's account, from which this anecdote comes, is too fragmentary to be really informative. He does however give the names of five of Septimius's generals. The first move out of Nisibis was made by three army corps, commanded by Claudius Candidus, Lateranus and Laetus. It is surprising to find the name of Lateranus among them. This man, T. Sextius Lateranus, was a member of an Italian patrician family. But he was not the only man of his kind with Septimius. Lollianus Gentianus, son of Pertinax's patron, was serving as *comes* of the Emperor. Laetus is probably the same as the Julius Laetus who had led the advance guard in the march on Rome. After the completion of their mission, 'laying waste the

---

[1] Abgarus: *PIR*[2] A 8 (since C. Julius Pacatianus – App. III – was made procurator of Osrhoëne in 195 it seems more logical to follow the interpretation of *PIR*[2] than that of D. MAGIE, p. 1543f. There is no proof that the *legiones Parthicae* were not formed until 197, but even if they were not, it would not affect the issue). – Nisibis: Dio 75.2.3. – 14 April: *PIR*[2] J 663 (p. 314). See the important discussion by H. U. INSTINSKY (1942) pp. 200–211 on *mater castrorum*. (In spite of the arguments of H. W. BENARIO [1958b], I see no reason to doubt the view best expressed by Instinsky pp. 204ff. that the other titles – *mater senatus et patriae* – were not assumed until 211-212. Benario's use of *CIL* VI 3401 = XIV 2255 = D. 2398 is inconclusive: the stone may well have been re-cut several times.) Instinsky emphasises pp. 201ff. that Julia Domna was hereby inheriting the role of Faustina II. He aptly cites the important observations of A. ALFÖLDI (1934) p. 69: Julia's statue was now placed in the *sacella* of military units; this was direct imitation of Marcus's action with Faustina, not a result of Julia's 'orientalising' influence. – Arabicus, Adiabenicus:' *HA Sev.* 9.9–11. Cf. *BMC* V pp. 33, 35 (no. 86) for the titles with Imp. III. Other salutations (V-VII): cf. *ib.* pp. lxxxviiiff. (but Mattingly allots Imp. V, for no good reason, to the war against Niger. This is a suitable opportunity to refer to the question of the tribunician day. I follow M. HAMMOND [1959] pp. 73, 96 with references to earlier studies, against Mattingly, *BMC* V pp. lxxviiiff., in the view that the *trib.pot.* was still renewed annually on 10 December). – 'triumph etc': *HA Sev.* 9.10. – 'Arch': cf. R. BRILLIANT p. 92f., also Instinsky p. 217.

barbarians' land and capturing their towns', a second sweep was made, with the three corps commanded this time by Cornelius Anullinus, Laetus and a certain Probus, otherwise unknown. Herodian's account is unfortunately worthless, as he has confused this campaign with the later eastern war; and the Augustan History reports it in one sentence. The only other light on the campaign comes from a Syriac source, the Msiha Zkha, which indicates that Vologaeses of Parthia had fomented revolt or aggression by the Osrhoeni and Adiabeni against Rome, but that he himself was distracted from active participation by the need to crush a rebellion in Persis and Media. His absence may have been decisive. Septimius proceeded to annexe part of the newly overrun territory – the first significant addition to the Empire for ninety years.[1]

Soon after his first victory, Septimius took a remarkable step. He proclaimed himself to be the son of Marcus Aurelius. In the first bronze issue which give him the titles that celebrate his victories, one *sestertius* describes him as 'Son of the deified Marcus Pius'. This title is repeated later in the year. Simultaneously, or soon after, he took another step. His son Bassianus, now seven years old, was renamed after Marcus, and from henceforth was known as M. Aurelius Antoninus. There can be little doubt that he had already decided to make a break with Albinus. But he must have been supremely confident of the eventual outcome. It may be that he had already taken steps to dispose of his temporary ally. Herodian records that Albinus was 'acting more and more as if he were Emperor' and was receiving numerous letters from influential senators, 'who were trying to persuade him to come to Rome while Severus was absent, engaged on other matters'. Albinus, 'belonging to a noble family and regarded as being a good-natured man', was preferred to Septimius by the 'aristocrats'. Septimius was kept in-

[1] 'water': Dio 75.2.1–2, cf. F. STARK p. 255, who aptly compares the experiences of British troops in 1920 and 1943. – Dio's account: 75.2.3–4. – Candidus, Lateranus, Laetus, Gentianus, Anullinus: App. III. – Probus: the name was very common, cf. I. KAJANTO p. 253 (nearly 200 examples including nine senators). Those who wish may toy with the idea that he was Septimius's son-in-law. Unfortunately, it is clear that the Emperor had no daughters (cf. p. 90, above). – 'Syriac source': cf. *RE* Supp. 9 (1962) 1851. – 'proceeded to annexe': cf. esp. H. U. INSTINSKY (1942) pp. 212ff. on the title *propagator imperii*. But I do not accept that expansion of the Empire appealed mainly to hard-core conservatives in the Seante, see below, p. 285f.

formed of these developments. He therefore sent to Britain his most trusted couriers. They were to give his despatches to Albinus openly, and then to request a private meeting to hand over 'secret instructions'. Once they were alone with him they were to strike him down. In case this failed, they were given poison, 'so that if the opportunity arose they could persuade one of Albinus's cooks or cupbearers to administer a dose of it in secret'. Albinus's advisers were suspicious and warned him to be on his guard. The couriers were seized, and revealed their instructions under torture. The Augustan History has the same story in the mainly bogus *Life of Albinus*. The further details there supplied are probably derived from the author's own imagination (the number of messengers is given – five – and the place where they asked for the private conference is specified – a distant portico).

The whole story may have been put out as anti-Septimian propaganda. Certainly, it was not long before Septimius himself inspired anti-Albinian propaganda. In particular, it was probably at this time that it was first alleged that Albinus had instigated the murder of Pertinax. Since Didius Julianus's mother came from Albinus's home town of Hadrumetum, the story may have had a special air of plausibility – the fact that Julianus himself had had no part in the murder of Pertinax would, in the light of what subsequently happened, have been conveniently ignored.[1]

It may be that Herodian has preserved some portion of the truth in this story, when he notes that Septimius was unwilling to initiate hostilities against Albinus. At any rate, Septimius must have known that his self-adoption into the house of the Antonines and the renaming of his son were actions of which Albinus could not mistake the implica-

---

[1] 'Son of the deified Marcus': *BMC* V p. 136, with *Imp. V*. The main emphasis is with *Imp. VII, ib.* pp. 41, 140f. – Bassianus renamed: Only D. MAGIE p. 1541 accepts D. 8805 (quoted p. 187, below) from Aezani which gives the new names before 10 December 195 (others would emend the text to make it give the fourth, not third, *trib. pot.*). But Magie assumes that Bassianus already had the title Caesar, which is not in fact given in the stone. I prefer to believe that that came later. T. FRANK pp. 78, n. 39, 300, assumes that the whole affair was a device to usurp control of the Antonine family property. Cf. H. NESSELHAUF (1964) for a more sober appraisal of this point. – Albinus: Herodian 3.5.1–8; *HA Clod.Alb.* 7.2 – 8.3. – 'first alleged': cf. A. R. BIRLEY (1969) p. 266, discussing Eutropius 8.18.4, Victor *de Caes.* 20.9, *HA Alb.* 1.1, 14.2.6.

tions. There was no longer any question of the title of Caesar that he had accepted in 193 giving him any rights of succession. Indeed, Dio says that Septimius 'would no longer give him even the rank of Caesar'. When dedications were being made to Septimius ascribing to him divine ancestry back to Nerva and, incidentally, calling him the 'brother of the deified Commodus', it would only be a matter of time before his son would be designated as his eventual heir and successor. Albinus's only recourse was to gamble for the highest stakes. Before the end of 195 he must have sent troops across into Gaul and proclaimed himself Emperor. Septimius will not have been surprised by this move. There is little doubt that some at least of the troops brought east for the campaign were already on their way back to Europe before the end of the summer. A soldier of the Pannonian legion X Gemina died at Ancyra in Galatia on 3 September, 'returning from Parthia'. He must have been in Claudius Candidus's army.[1]

If it were possible to date the events of the year 195 more closely, some of the decisions that were taken might be easier to understand. But from what has been said already it follows that the bringing to an end of the eastern campaign cannot have been forced on Septimius by events in the west. The campaign must have been conceived from the start as a short-term punitive war, since the assumption of the dynastic claims – which came well before the fighting in Mesopotamia was over – was virtually an open challenge to Albinus, which – if accepted – would make Septimius's return to the west necessary. But he did not leave Mesopotamia until the news reached him that Byzantium had fallen, news that gave him exceptional pleasure, according to Dio.[2]

The siege had lasted for more than two years, and Dio's detailed account is preserved in full – it naturally interested Dio's epitomator Xiphilinus, whose eleventh-century Byzantine readers must have found this one of the most entertaining parts of the entire work. The late second-century Byzantines were evidently brave and resourceful,

---

[1] 'some . . . truth': Herodian 3.5.3. – 'Dio says': 75.4.1. – 'dedications': cf. G. J. MURPHY p. 102. A good example is *CIL* VIII 9317 (*trib.pot.III*, *Imp. VI*). – 'Before the end of 195': this is clear from Dio 75.4.2–7 (cf. p. 188 and n. 1, below). – 'soldier of X Gemina': *AE* 1941.166.

[2] Dio 74.14.2.

and the city only fell to Marius Maximus's besieging army when the people were starving – even then many escaped by boat, and the rest almost succeeded in getting away also. The city was treated in predictable fashion. Its walls were demolished, and its civic status annulled. It was annexed to its neighbour Perinthus. Dio, who had seen the city in its glory, with 'the seven towers extending from the Thracian Gates to the sea' that would pass on an echo from one to the other, comments sadly on what he later observed. The place 'looked as if it had been captured by some other people rather than by the Romans'.[1]

In recognition of the victory, Septimius now became Imp. VIII. An inscription preserves a letter that he wrote to the magistrates, council and people of Aezani, a city in Phrygia, in the eastern part of proconsular Asia. They had sent on to him the text of an honorific decree:

I have clearly understood from your decree the pleasure that you take in my successes and in the rise of my son Marcus Aurelius Antoninus with good fortune to the hopes of the Empire and to a position alongside his father. And I am pleased that you celebrated a public festival and made sacrifices of thanksgiving to your local gods, since you are a famous city and one that has been of value to the Roman Empire from of old. And when I saw that news of the victory had come to bear witness to my success, together with your decree, I was pleased. I sent my reply to you to be placed with your local gods. . . .

Septimius's titles are those of 195, except that he is already Imp. VIII. Clearly the embassy from the Aezanians had arrived in Mesopotamia at the same time as the news of the capture of Byzantium. The title Imp. VIII is not otherwise recorded until the beginning of 196. Thus the fall of Byzantium must belong late in the year 195, perhaps as late as December. Bassianus has already become M. Aurelius Antoninus, but he is not yet Caesar.[2]

[1] Dio 74.10.1 – 14.6. No mention of Maximus (App. II) – nor of the fact that Byzantium was later restored by Septimius (p. 212f. below).

[2] Imp. VIII: cf. *BMC* V pp. 111ff., 145ff. – Aezani: *IGR* IV 566 = D. 8805, cf. p. 185 n. 1, above.

The journey back to the west began at once, along the route taken the previous year. Meanwhile at Rome the Senate was obliged to declare Albinus a public enemy. This evidently took place in mid-December, to judge from a story in Dio's narrative. The realisation that another civil war was imminent – which can only mean that the breach had just been made open – caused dismay.

We senators kept quiet [says Dio], but the people of Rome showed their feelings in no uncertain fashion. An enormous crowd had assembled to watch the last chariot-races before the Saturnalia, in the Circus Maximus. When the six-chariot races were over, there was a demand for silence and then a sudden clapping of hands. There was a series of shouts, prayers for the welfare of the state. Then the people began to shout appeals to the goddess Roma, addressing her as 'Queen' and 'Immortal', and crying out: 'How long are we to endure such things?' 'And how long are we to go on waging war?' After shouting out further things of this kind, they finally ended, as suddenly as they had begun, with the cry 'So much for that' – and turned their attention to the horse-race.

Dio was there, as guest of one of the consuls, who was a friend of his. He professes to have been mystified by the affair, but there is little doubt that it had been organised by supporters of Albinus. But these supporters must have felt gloomy about Albinus's chances.[1]

---

[1] 'journey back': *HA Sev.* 10.1–3; Herodian 3.6.1–10 (mostly taken up by a speech of Septimius, 1–7, placed before the fall of Byzantium; since Herodian is unaware of the First Parthian War, of 195, this kind of slip is relatively trivial). G. ALFÖLDY, *Senat*, p. 118, shows that in a sense Albinus began the war, as *HA Sev.* 10.1 clearly asserts. But it is here argued that Septimius deliberately provoked Albinus into making an overt challenge. – 'Dio's narrative': 75.4.2–7, cf. Alföldy, p. 118, n. 44.

XIII

THE WAR AGAINST ALBINUS

Septimius now came racing back to the west with the same breathless speed that he had already shown in three campaigns. What arrangements were made for the administration and protection of the newly conquered area beyond the Euphrates can only be conjectured. The principality of Osrhoene seems to have been made into a province governed by an equestrian procurator straight after its annexation in the spring of 195. But the procurator, C. Julius Pacatianus, was back in the west in the following year, and it may be that Abgarus was restored to his throne before Septimius left Mesopotamia. The rest of the newly acquired territory, which was to become the province of Mesopotamia, can hardly have been given up as well, but it seems likely that the garrison it was given was minimal.[1]

Early in 195 Mantennius Sabinus had been replaced in Egypt by a new prefect, M. Ulpius Primianus. Fabius Cilo gave up his governorship in Bithynia, and went ahead to become governor of Upper Moesia. Claudius Candidus had already begun moving his Pannonian army back towards the Danube, and Marius Maximus now took his Moesian troops west from Byzantium, while a third special force was formed from the Dacian army and placed under the command of Ti. Claudius Claudianus, one of Septimius's new senators. He had been serving as legionary legate in Dacia under Geta. Steps were taken to recruit new legions in Italy. At Rome, Domitius Dexter opened the year 196 as one of the *consules ordinarii*. He was soon replaced as Prefect of the City by Cornelius Anullinus.[2]

[1] Pacatianus: App. III. Abgarus was restored to his kingdom, cf. *PIR*² A 8. – 'garrison . . . minimal': cf. p. 198, below.

[2] Cf. App. 3 for these persons, except Maximus (App. II) and Geta (App. 1 no. 30). – On the new legions cf. p. 191 n. 2, below.

On his way back Septimius stayed again at Perinthus, where he dedicated a temple that he had vowed during his first stay. One of the legionary commanders who had fought in the recent campaign, T. Statilius Barbarus, was appointed governor of Thrace. It may have been during his journey westwards that Pollienus Auspex, governor of Lower Moesia at this time, came out with one of his celebrated witticisms. He took the opportunity of congratulating Septimius on his self-adoption into the Antonine dynasty. ' "I congratulate you, Caesar," he said, "on finding a father." ' Cassius Dio explains the point of the story: the Emperor's real father had been so obscure that it had seemed that he did not have one.[1]

Only one point on his journey is recorded after Perinthus. At Viminacium in Upper Moesia on the Danube he proclaimed his son Caesar. There is no need to believe the story in the Augustan History that this move was made to put an end to the ambition of Septimius's brother Geta. But Geta was probably at Viminacium at the time – and so too may Marius Maximus have been, the probable source of the story. There may be something in it, therefore – but Septimius had no doubt decided on the move already. Only the time and place of the announcement could have been chosen for the purpose of deflating the ambitions of Geta. Meanwhile, in Noricum Claudius Candidus, on his way west with his Pannonian army task-force, had to engage in a hunt for 'public enemies'. Albinus must have had supporters in that province. Elsewhere too Septimius's rival was beginning to look more dangerous. He gained the support of the governor of Hispania Tarraconensis, Novius Rufus. But it would seem that Rufus failed to keep control of his single legion, VII Gemina, which remained loyal to Septimius. Albinus had gained control of Lugdunum, which he made his headquarters, and expelled the governor, T. Flavius Secundus Philippianus. But his attempts to seize the Rhineland failed, although he did defeat the governor of Lower Germany, Virius Lupus. His forces besieged Trier in Gallia Belgica, but the city held out, defended by part of the legion XXII Primigenia from Mainz, under its legate Claudius Gallus. Septimius had naturally taken steps to secure the

[1] Perinthus: *RE* 2A (1923) 1962. – Barbarus, Auspex: App. III. – The anecdote comes in Dio 76.9.4.

Alpine passes. A newly recruited legion was stationed under the command of Julius Pacatianus, in the Cottian Alps.[1]

Dio relates an episode from this period, which well illustrates the prevalent confusion in Italy. A schoolmaster named Numerianus set out from Rome for Gaul, pretending to be one of the senators appointed by Septimius to recruit troops. After collecting a small force together he entered Gaul and in a skirmish killed some Albinian cavalrymen. Septimius heard of his exploits and, under the impression that he was actually a senator, sent a message of congratulations and instructions to increase the forces under his command. Numerianus thereafter managed to capture the impressive sum of seventy million Sesterces. It was only after the war was over that he revealed his identity – and spent the rest of his life living in retirement on a pension from the Emperor.[2]

Septimius now proceeded to Rome, escorted by detachments under the command of Fabius Cilo. Coins were struck at Rome specially to commemorate his 'most fortunate advent'. Other coins from this time record imperial generosity to the people with a distribution of largesse and the holding of lavish games. The behaviour of the urban *plebs* the previous December will not have gone unnoticed. The other issues mainly emphasise the themes of war and peace – the martial prowess of the emperor and the peace that he would bring. It is worth noting at this point that during his first three years as Emperor Septimius struck no fewer than three hundred and forty-two different issues. Coins were now struck for his son also, advertising the 'perpetual security' and 'perpetual hope' that his proclamation as Caesar had

[1] Viminacium: *HA Sev.* 10.3, cf. App. II. 10.4–6 is contaminated: certainly 10.5 which derives from the same pointless invention that dominates *HA Geta*, that Septimius called his younger son as well as his elder son Antoninus. – Candidus, Lupus, Gallus, Pacatianus: App. III. – Defeat of Lupus: Dio 75.6.2. – Rufus: G. ALFÖLDY, *Reichsbeamte* p. 42f. – VII Gemina: *ib.* pp. 90ff. – Philippianus: D.1152, cf. G. ALFÖLDY (1967) p. 48, ID, *Senat* p. 142. Also A. R. Birley, *Gnomon* 40 (1968) p. 384. – Note also *CP* no. 226 (D. 1368) for the defence of the Alpine passes.

[2] Dio 75.5.1–3 (T. PEKÁRY, p. 476f. oddly assigns this episode to Galatia and draws unwarrantable conclusions). This serves to demonstrate that recruitment was in full swing, surely for the new *legiones Parthicae*, who would be raised mainly in Italy (cf. J. C. MANN [1963], p. 486).

brought. The boy now received the traditional title of heirs to the throne, *princeps iuventutis*.[1]

The coinage of Albinus for the most part merely echoes the claims of Septimius: Jupiter who brings victory, Mars, Minerva the peace-bringer and Peace herself announce his confidence in the forthcoming struggle. The 'spirit of Lugdunum', his capital, is also honoured, but there is no allusion to Africa. Septimius no longer felt the need to claim the loyalty of the army, but Albinus's coins proclaim the *fides legionum*. There are two reverse legends which emphasise Albinus's special claims. They refer to his *clementia* and *aequitas*. Neither quality was claimed by Septimius. The *aequitas* reverse of Albinus closely matches one that Pertinax had struck. These were the qualities that gained Albinus support among the Senate. There is one curious feature about his coinage. Some issues continue to give him the name *Sep.* or *Sept.*, which appeared on his coinage as Caesar, and which inscriptions show is the abbreviated form of *Septimius*. There is little doubt that he had taken the name as a compliment to Septimius in the year 193. Yet why did he now retain it when he was at war? There seems to be no logical explanation.[2]

How long Septimius spent in Rome is not recorded – Herodian seems to have been under the impression that he went straight to Gaul from the Danube, and neither the compressed account in the Augustan History nor the extracts from Dio preserve any record of this visit. One of his actions is attested by an inscription from the City. He made a dedication to 'The deified Nerva, his ancestor'. It is not improbable that this was done on 18 September, the hundredth anniversary of Nerva's accession in 96. The Code of Justinian preserves a relatively large number of rescripts of Septimius from the year 196. Whereas there is only one from 195 (early in March), one from 1 January 196 and one from 30 June, there are ten from the period 1 October to 29 December of that year. It is reasonable to infer that the news of Septimius's return to Rome produced a spate of legal business for his attention. Or at least, one may suggest that while in Rome

[1] Cilo: App. III. – Coins: *BMC* V pp. 5off., 15off. – 'Three hundred and forty two': T. PEKÁRY p. 456f.

[2] *BMC* V pp. civff.

he was able to give his personal attention to such matters.[1]

It may have been during Septimius's stay in Rome in that year that Cassius Dio took the opportunity of soliciting the Emperor's favour. As a native of Nicaea, a city that had openly and actively opposed Septimius two years earlier, he will have had many anxious months, wondering whether any of his friends or kinsmen, or he himself, would in any way be affected. While the Emperor was still in the east, he composed his first historical work, a pamphlet 'about the dreams and omens through which Severus was led to hope for the imperial power'. Dio and Septimius had in common a deep-seated belief in such things. He sent the Emperor a copy, and he, 'after reading it, sent me a long and complimentary letter'. Dio received the letter in the evening and soon after fell asleep. Then he himself had a dream, in which 'the Divine Power commanded me to write history'. He at once decided to write an account of the wars which followed the murder of Commodus.[2]

But Septimius cannot have remained at Rome for long. Once again he went to Pannonia, then crossed through Noricum and Raetia into Upper Germany. From here he moved south on Lugdunum with his army. It is significant that the roads in the region through which his armies had passed that year and through which he now went himself had been repaired in the previous year. This is further evidence that he had begun preparing for the campaign against Albinus in the year 195. Fabius Cilo probably escorted Septimius as far as Pannonia, remaining there as governor of the Upper Province. Septimius's elder son remained with Cilo.[3]

---

[1] Herodian 3.6.10 – 7.2. – Nerva: D. 418 – *Cod. Just.* 9.1.1 (195). The speech allegedly delivered by Septimius in the Senate on 13 June 195 (*Digest* 27.8.1) will of course have been read out by a *quaestor Augusti*, if not some higher magistrate. The fact that rescripts appear to be issued by two Augusti from 30 June 196 (*Cod. Just.* 4.19.1) is no real guarantee of Antoninus's status at this time, in view of the unreliability of the headings in the Code, cf. C. E. VAN SICKLE (1928b). However, H. U. INSTINSKY (1942) p. 215 n. 12 may well be right in his view that Antoninus was *imperator destinatus* before 197, cf. esp. D. 1143.

[2] Dio 72.23.1–2, cf. p. 7f., above.

[3] Route: this is largely an assumption. – Cilo: App. III. – The inscription of Porcius Optatus Flamma (D. 1143) shows that he was there. – The faithful Rossius Vitulus once more displayed his organisational talents, this time as *proc. ann(onae) ob exped(itionem) felicis(simimam) Gall(icam)*, cf. *CP* no. 224.

It is difficult to estimate what forces Septimius had amassed. Dio speaks loosely of 150,000 men being engaged on either side for the decisive encounter. But it is difficult to see how Albinus could have acquired anything like so large a force. Even if he had taken the entire army of Britain across into Gaul, that would not have amounted to more than 40,000 men at the most. He could of course have recruited further troops in both Britain and Gaul, and no doubt did so, but these will not have exceeded the number of his original force. In the three Gauls themselves the only regular military unit at all was the 500-man Urban Cohort at Lugdunum. It is unlikely that either side had more than 50,000 men. But in spite of the overwhelmingly greater size of the forces from which Septimius could draw, the army of Albinus could offer serious opposition. The Roman forces in Britain had never had the chance to grow slack from the absence of military action. They had fought in a major campaign just over ten years before. Not only that. Throughout the reign of Commodus they had been mutinous and discontented, seeking any opportunity to raise their own candidate to the throne. Now that they had their man, they would be ready to defend him with the 'courage and ruthlessness' of which Herodian speaks.[1]

The first encounter took place at Tinurtium, sixty miles north of Lugdunum. The Albinians were driven back to Lugdunum itself, where the final battle took place on 19 February. At first the Albinian left wing was defeated and fled back to its camp. But then the Septimian left wing fell into a trap. The Albinians had dug a series of concealed pits – the so-called *lilia* which the British army must have been skilled at making from their experience on the Antonine Wall – and the Septimians were lured into them by a feigned retreat. Septimius himself came up on horseback with the praetorians, but instead of saving the situation got himself into extreme difficulties and was thrown from his horse. Then, 'tearing off his riding cloak and drawing his sword', he rushed after his retreating troops and shamed them into making a stand. That at least was the official version. According to

[1] Dio 75.6.1. – '40,000 men': the three legions (II Augusta, VI Victrix and XX Valeria Victrix) would give 18,000 men. In AD 122 the auxiliary units had had a total paper strength of 25,500 (*CIL* XVI 65). There had been some changes since then. – Lugdunum cohort: *RE* Supp. 10 (1962) 1129f. – 'courage', etc.: Herodian, 3.7.2.

Herodian, he simply fled with the rest – and flung off the purple cloak which revealed his identity. At this critical moment – while the pursuing British troops were already raising the chant of victory – Septimius's general Laetus appeared with the cavalry and routed the Albinians. It turned out subsequently – or so it was alleged – that he had been waiting to see which side was winning before making a move, hoping that both leaders would be killed so that he could gain the throne for himself.[1]

Albinus's troops were pursued into Lugdunum, which was sacked and burnt by the victorious army. Albinus himself was trapped in a house beside the Rhône and committed suicide. His body was brought to Septimius ,who 'feasted his eyes on it', according to Dio. The version in the Augustan History, that Albinus was half alive when brought to Septimius (and the prophecy of the Pannonian augurs that was thereby fulfilled) perhaps ought to be rejected in the light of what Dio records. But the story may go back to a contemporary source. The head was cut off and sent to Rome. The Augustan History adds that 'the corpse was, by Severus's order, laid out in front of his own home, to be exposed to view, for a long time. Besides which, he himself rode over the body, and when the horse shied he spoke to it and loosened the reins, to make it trample boldly'. Finally the body was thrown into the Rhône, with the bodies of Albinus's murdered wife and sons. The Augustan History also records that the bodies of senators who had fought for Albinus were mutilated by Septimius's orders.[2]

A whole series of administrative moves now had to be made. Claudius Candidus was sent into Spain as governor of Tarraconensis, with the added mission of hunting down the remaining followers of Albinus. It was a task for which his previous missions of a like nature in Asia and Noricum had given him ample experience. Novius Rufus was executed. The legion VII Gemina, which under its legate Q. Mamilius Capitolinus had actively fought for Septimius, was rewarded with the title *pia* in recognition of its loyalty. In Spain and Gaul numerous

[1] Tinurtium: *HA Sev.* 11.1, cf. M. PLATNAUER p. 109 n. 2, who discusses various identifications. – The date is supplied by *HA Sev.* 11.7. – Cf. Dio 75.6.1–8, Herodian 3.7.2–6, *HA Sev.* 11.2. – Laetus: App. III.

[2] 'Pursued' etc.: Herodian 3.7.6–7; Dio 75.7.1–8; *HA Sev.* 11.6–9. – Tinurtium and Lugdunum seem to be the occasions for Imp. IX and X, cf *RE* 2A (1923) 1967.

leading men who had supported Albinus were put to death. It is no accident that Lollianus Gentianus, after serving on Septimius's staff at the battle of Lugdunum, conducted a special census of property in Gallia Lugdunensis. When Claudius Candidus's military operations in Spain were ended, Gentianus succeeded him there as governor, again with the mission of *censitor*. Meanwhile a *censitor* was appointed in Aquitania also. In both these provinces the executions had a direct effect on the economy. From this point a large amount of the Spanish olive oil production seems to have been taken over by the state. In Gaul the factories that produced *terra sigillata*, Samian pottery, were either destroyed, or went out of production when their owners were killed and their property confiscated.[1]

These were naturally not the only parts of the empire that were affected. The procurator Ti. Claudius Xenophon returned to the west from Asia to become *procurator ad bona cogenda* in Africa, 'to confiscate the property of the condemned'. Albinus had clearly had allies in his native province, even though less powerful than those of Septimius. Three procurators are later found administering such property, evidently at Rome. Here, naturally, the value of such confiscated wealth would be the greatest. Septimius was to institute a drastic purge of the Senate when he returned to Rome from Lugdunum.[2]

First, urgent measures were taken in the north-west. Marius Maximus was made governor of Belgica. Valerius Pudens was made governor of Lower Germany, replacing Virius Lupus. Lupus was made governor of Britain, and the defeated British legions were sent back with him, no doubt heavily reinforced with new manpower, necessary to restore losses – and their loyalty. Lupus faced an appalling situation. In the absence of the Roman garrison, the northern part of the province

---

[1] Candidus: App. III. – Rufus, Capitolinus: G. ALFÖLDY, *Reichsbeamte* pp. 42f. 90. – 'numerous leading men': *HA Sev.* 12.1, cf. G. ALFÖLDY, *Senat* pp. 119ff., ID, *HAC.* – Gentianus: App. III. There was also a *censitor* in Aquitania: M. Valerius Bradua Mauricus (cos. ord. 191) held two urban *curae* after his consulship before going to Aquitania, hence was probably there in 197 (D. 1128, *L'Albo* no. 506). – olive oil: cf. M. H. CALLENDER p. 56, etc. – Samian: cf. the views of E. Birley cited in J. A. STANFIELD p. xli.

[2] Xenophon: *CP* no. 222, cf. nos. 228, 239, 240. – 'allies in his native province': G. ALFÖLDY, *Senat* p. 120.

had been plundered by the Caledonians and Maeatae, joined by the Brigantes of the Pennines, it may be suspected. They had left a trail of destruction from the Antonine Wall to Hadrian's Wall and south as far as York itself, the home of the VIth legion. Herodian states that Septimius treated Britain as he had treated Syria, dividing it into two provinces. If this statement has any basis, the division cannot have been on the lines found twenty years later, with two legions in Upper Britain governed from London by a consular, and Lower Britain governed by the praetorian legate of VI Victrix. It may be that Upper Britain was assigned only one legion, II Augusta at Caerleon, under the Septimian dispensation. Certainly Lupus was a consular and operated entirely in Lower Britain. He had his work cut out. To begin with, he had to buy off the Maeatae, and then the work of rebuilding began. In the following year, Septimius's young kinsman Sex. Varius Marcellus was appointed procurator of Britain. It was an unusual appointment for a man who had only served in one post in the service, with immediate promotion to the higher rate of pay. But his duties were no doubt unusual. Only archaeology gives hints of confiscations in Britain. But measures of this kind must undoubtedly have been taken there also.[1]

Septimius did not go straight to Rome. Once more he seems to have gone via Germany and Pannonia. In Germany envoys came to him from the Senate, no doubt bearing congratulations and protestations of loyalty. One of these was a young man from Cirta in Numidia, the province from which so many of Septimius's henchmen had already been drawn. The Senate's choice of such a man was undoubtedly politic. The embassy went on into Pannonia to take messages of a similar nature to Antoninus. While in Germany Septimius ordered Claudius Gallus, the deserving legate of the legion XXII Primigenia, to

---

[1] Maximus: App. II. – Pudens, Lupus: App. III. – Marcellus: App. I (he was still *procurator aquarum* in a year not earlier than 198, hence S. S. FRERE p. 168 is mistaken in his statement that Marcellus went to Britain in 197). – 'an appalling situation': Dio 75.5.4. – York: cf. p. 246 n. 2, below. – Herodian 3.8.2 asserts that Britain was divided. A. J. GRAHAM argues that he is simply mistaken, J. C. MANN (1967) that he is probably correct but that the boundaries of the two new provinces were later rearranged. More evidence is needed to prove either case. – Confiscations: S. S. FRERE pp. 168, 275.

muster an army corps drawn from all four German legions and set out with it for the east. Laetus, the man who had saved the day at Lugdunum, was probably sent post-haste to Mesopotamia. Reports must have already reached Septimius – and they cannot have surprised him – that the Parthians had invaded his new province of Mesopotamia. Besides this, the Arabian legion III Cyrenaica had come out in favour of Albinus, and the cities of Side and Perge in Lycia-Pamphylia had even struck an issue of coins honouring him as Emperor.[1]

The Senate awaited Septimius's return with justifiable anxiety. Some, like Cassius Dio, had already gained Septimius's favour. But those who had had any dealings with Albinus must have trembled – Septimius had taken possession of Albinus's correspondence. Once again populace and Senate came out to greet him, as they had done four years earlier, with laurel branches. Once again, he made sacrifice in the Temple of Jupiter on the Capitol and went to the Palace. His first speech before the Senate caused dismay and terror. He now demanded the formal deification of Commodus, whose 'brother' he was constantly calling himself, as well as 'son of Marcus'. It seems that some senators, trying to hedge their bets, had put through a resolution in praise of Clodius Celsinus, a kinsman of Albinus. Septimius was incensed – it looked to him tantamount to recognition of Albinus – which was no doubt what those responsible had hoped Albinus would think if he won the war. The context of the story, in the Augustan History, suggests that the praise of Celsinus was coupled in some way with invective against Commodus. It is conceivable that it was this that led Septimius to demand the formal recognition of Commodus's deification. Although this is attested by inscription from as early as 195, it might otherwise never have been carried through publicly. The sources do not record whether he carried out the ornate and elaborate rituals that had been performed for Pertinax in 193. He openly praised the severity and cruelty of Sulla, Marius and Augustus, and criticised Pompey and Caesar for their clemency (the very quality that Albinus had claimed for himself on his coinage). He defended the character of Commodus

---

[1] 'Envoys ... Antoninus': D. 1143. – Gallus, Laetus: App. III. – Parthians: Dio 75.9.1. – III Cyrenaica: *HA Sev.* 12.6, cf. G. ALFÖLDY, *Senat* p. 119 n. 52. – Side and Perge: perhaps not genuine; cf. J. HASEBROEK (1921) p. 157.

and attacked the Senate for dishonouring him unjustifiably – since many of them lived worse lives.

'For if this was disgraceful, that he slew wild beasts with his own hands, yet only the other day at Ostia, one of you, a consular and an old man, was performing in public with a prostitute who imitated a leopard. Did Commodus fight as a gladiator, by Jupiter? And does not one of you fight as a gladiator? If not, how and why is it that some of you have bought his shields and those famous golden helmets?'

At the time he was making this speech some sixty-four members of the Senate were under arrest. Thirty-five were then released, but the remaining twenty-nine were executed. There were some famous names among them, including Sulpicianus the father-in-law of Pertinax, and Erucius Clarus, one of the consuls of the year 193. Clarus had been offered a free pardon if he would act as informer. But he preferred death. Another man was easily found to play the role, in return for his life – but was obliged to submit to torture so that his evidence could be verified.[1]

A striking passage in Dio well conveys the atmosphere in Rome either before or after the battle of Lugdunum. Everyone did their best to pretend to be loyal, but sudden news would catch men off their guard and their faces revealed their true feelings. 'And some, because they exaggerated their pretence, were recognised more easily.' It was ironic that one of the senators executed was Julius Solon. Four years earlier he had introduced the decree of the Senate that the Emperor should not put his peers to death without trial. Analysis of the names of the senators put to death reveals that more than a third of them were closely connected by birth or by property-ownership with proconsular Africa, and others were linked with Gaul and Spain.[2]

[1] 'Laurel branches', etc.: Herodian 3.8.3–4. – 'first speech': Dio 75.7.4–8.3 cf. Herodian 3.8.6. – Celsinus: HA Sev. 11.3 – regarded as spurious by Sir R. SYME (1968a) esp. p. 155f.; cf. G. ALFÖLDY, Senat p. 140. – Deification: HA Sev. 11.4, 8, etc. – 'openly praised . . .' etc.: Dio 75.8.1–3, HA Sev. 12.7. – Executions: Dio 75.8.4, HA Sev. 12.9 – 13.9, analysed by G. ALFÖLDY, HAC.

[2] Dio 75.8.5. – Julius Solon: Dio 74.2.2, HA Sev. 13.4, cf. G. ALFÖLDY, HAC, ID., Senat, p. 145. – Narcissus was also executed at this time: HA Sev. 14.1.

A natural corollary of this ruthless purge was the inflow of substantial funds to the Treasury. The procurators specially appointed to administer the property of the proscribed have already been mentioned. A more permanent step was taken with the transformation of the Privy Purse (*res privata* or *ratio privata*). Its operations were greatly extended by the setting up of regional offices throughout Italy. At this time the sinister Aquilius Felix was given the special task of revising the lists of Roman knights. Many changes will have been necessary – some sixty or more *equites* must have been serving as officers in the British army under Albinus. Few of these will have retained their rank, even if their lives were spared.[1]

One of Septimius's most important appointments had been made some time before but is first securely attested on 8 June 197. On that day three troopers of the *equites singulares* celebrated 'the return of the unit' – undoubtedly from the campaign in Gaul – by a dedication to 'Unconquered Hercules and the other gods and goddesses', for the safety of Septimius, of Antoninus, and of C. Fulvius Plautianus, Prefect of the Guard. Plautianus also has the title *clarissimus vir*, 'right honourable', and hence has been granted honorary senatorial rank. Septimius's energetic and strong-willed kinsman had been at his side during most of the last four years.[2]

Soon after this, if not before, Septimius ordered the Senate to confer on his son Antoninus the special title of *imperator destinatus*, 'emperor designate', and at the same time he was co-opted into the great priestly colleges. Septimius was awaiting an auspicious moment before making his son his full colleague. Measures were taken to ensure the favour of the urban populace at Rome with more lavish games and further distribution of largesse. Then he departed for his second war with Rome's eastern enemies.[3]

---

[1] *res privata*: cf. esp. H. NESSELHAUF (1964), who also deals with the career of Felix (*CP* no. 225).

[2] See now F. GROSSO (1968) esp. pp. 14ff., who shows that Plautianus was already Praetorian Prefect on 1 January, but not yet *C.V.* Cf. App. 1.

[3] *imperator destinatus*: cf. p. 193, n. 1, above. – priestly colleges: *BMC* V pp. 50, 52, etc. – 'lavish games . . .' etc.: Herodian 3.8.9 is not really a good source for this as his chronology is totally at fault. But cf. *HA Sev.* 14.11.

XIV

IN THE EAST AND AFRICA

This time Septimius went east by sea. Embarking at Brundisium he sailed directly across to Asia Minor, probably landing at the Cilician port of Aegeae. The bulk of the expeditionary force, including two of the three new legions, had been sent ahead. The other new legion, II Parthica, was left behind in Italy, in garrison at Albanum twenty miles south-east of Rome. Together with part of the Praetorian Guard, this would be an insurance against possible trouble during his absence. All three new legions were placed under the command of equestrian prefects, rather than senatorial *legati*. Considering that he had crushed his last opponent only a few months before, and that he must have made himself hated and feared by a large section of the Senate, his decision to go to the east is a little surprising. It is understandable that he preferred to absent himself from Rome after the purge of the Senate. But it might have been dangerous to place himself so far away, were it not that he had the right kind of associates to put into positions of high command. His friend Fabius Cilo ruled the key province of Upper Pannonia during the entire period of his absence; and it is not surprising that a high proportion of the other provinces with large armies were entrusted to men of African origins or connections at this time.[1]

Septimius was accompanied by his wife and sons and his kinsman Plautianus the Praetorian Prefect. On his arrival in Syria Septimius immediately mustered his forces and crossed the Euphrates, making

---

[1] 'by sea, etc.': *HA Sev.* 15.2. – II Parthica: *RE* 12 (1923) 1476ff., (and cf. *ib.* 1435f. 1539f. for the other two legions). – Cilo: App. III: where cf. the lists of military provinces (governed in a very high proportion of cases *ca.* 197-202 by men of certain or possible African origin).

for Nisibis, which Laetus had managed to protect from capture. The Parthians did not wait for Septimius's arrival, but withdrew at once. By the time that Septimius reached Nisibis it must have been late in the summer. The Parthians may have expected the Romans to wait until the following spring before attempting reprisals. But Septimius constructed a fleet on the Euphrates and probably in late September or early October began moving his troops south, partly by boat and partly on land. He was accompanied by a brother of the Parthian king.[1]

When the invading army reached southern Mesopotamia, they found Seleucia and Babylon (which was in any case a deserted city) abandoned by the enemy. By January 198 Septimius was outside the Parthian capital, Ctesiphon on the Tigris. There seems little doubt that he was able to choose his moment to assault and capture the city. The successful attack took place on 28 January, the hundredth anniversary of Trajan's accession. Ctesiphon was given over to the troops to plunder. Vast numbers of the enemy were killed, and according to Dio as many as a hundred thousand prisoners were taken. Vologaeses the king escaped but no attempt was made to pursue him and Septimius did not occupy the city. The capture of Ctesiphon was surely deliberately timed to coincide in date with the centenary of the accession of Trajan. It was the moment chosen by Septimius for the troops to proclaim his elder son Augustus. His younger son was now made Caesar, and he himself took the title Parthicus Maximus, 'greatest conqueror of the Parthians'. At the same time he accepted from the soldiers his eleventh and last acclamation as Imperator.[2]

The army once again was not standing up well to the unfamiliar conditions, and almost immediately Septimius led it back northwards. It is unlikely that he had had any intention of trying to reestablish

[1] Nisibis: Dio 75.9.1–3 (with an anecdote about a giant-sized wild boar); *HA Sev.* 16.1 (*aestate . . . iam exeunte Parthiam ingressus*).

[2] Dio 75.9.3–4; *HA Sev.* 16.1–5. The date is given by the *Feriale Duranum* col. i, l. 14, cf. C. B. WELLES p. 198. Its significance was brilliantly brought out by J. GUEY (1948). – *Imp. XI Part. Max.*: *BMC* V pp. 175ff., etc., cf. p. cxxixf. *Imp XII* is found sporadically from 198: clearly some people were under the impression that there were two acclamations, i.e. two separate victories, cf. A. A. BOYCE. (On *Imp. X* cf. p. 195 n. 2, above.) Note that the booty captured at Ctesiphon was probably immense, cf. p. 285, below.

Roman rule over all the territory once annexed by Trajan. His intention was to make certain that his newly created province of Mesopotamia was secure. The two new legions that he had brought with him, I and III Parthicae, were to form the main part of the province's garrison. As governor Septimius appointed a Prefect of equestrian rank, rather than a senator, on the analogy of Augustus's treatment of Egypt.[1]

There was one outstanding obstacle remaining, the city of Hatra, midway between Tigris and Euphrates, and well placed to threaten the new frontier. Its ruler Barsemius had given assistance to Niger, which was added reason for attacking the city. Besides, Trajan had failed to take it. Septimius made his attempt in the spring, but the siege was a failure. There were heavy casualties on the Roman side, and he was obliged to withdraw.[2]

During the siege there were two unpleasant episodes. A tribune of the Praetorian Guard, Julius Crispus, was overheard quoting some lines of Virgil which expressed the army's disgust at the siege, and its apparent pointlessness. His behaviour was reported to Septimius and he was executed. There was another victim. Julius Laetus, who had been with Septimius in the march on Rome, had served in Mesopotamia in 195, carried the day at Lugdunum, and rescued Nisibis, was also executed. He had become too popular with the soldiers: Dio says that they were refusing to go on campaign if Laetus did not lead them. No doubt after his death the story was circulated that he had hoped to seize the throne for himself at the battle of Lugdunum, and that he had deliberately held his troops back. Septimius gained considerable unpopularity among the army on account of the murder of Laetus, and tried to disclaim responsibility. It may well be, indeed, that the initiative to dispose of Laetus came from Plautianus, who was at this time actively engaged in a hunt for 'surviving supporters of Niger' – or this was the pretext. A number of Septimius's close associates lost their

[1] 'led it back': Dio 75.9.4–5. Herodian, apart from placing the war after the Saecular Games of 204, places the capture of Ctesiphon after an unsuccessful siege of Hatra. (3.9.1–12). – Prefect of Mesopotamia: none known by name from this reign, but cf. *CP* no. 281 for a procurator. And *AE* 1966. 495 indicates that L. Valerius Valerianus held a special financial post in the province.

[2] Dio 75.10.1.

lives at this time. Plautianus could not brook any rival.[1]

Two episodes which may belong to this time should be recorded here. After mentioning the death of Laetus, the Augustan History somewhat incongruously relates that when Septimius's 'sister, a woman of Lepcis, had come to see him, scarcely capable of speaking Latin, and the Emperor was greatly embarrassed about her, he awarded her son the *latus clavus* and gave her many presents, and ordered her to return to their home [*patria*, i.e. Lepcis] – with her son as well, who died shortly afterwards'. The story has no connection with what precedes or follows in the text. But with the Augustan History, this is not surprising. Its source no doubt supplied the context. It could well be that Septimia Octavilla was in the east with her husband. The husband may have been a Greek-speaker. After all, Septimius's wife was one. In that case, Octavilla's inadequate command of Latin could be the result of years spent in a Greek environment, and need not mean that her only language was Punic. This story is all that is known about her, except for the inscription set up after her death at Lepcis, which supplies her names; and also indicates that she died before Septimius and that her husband had had senatorial rank. (He may have acquired this from Septimius.)[2]

The other story is in Cassius Dio, again without a context. Dio records that as Emperor Septimius once more consulted the oracle at Apamea, which had given him a promise of greatness when he was in Syria as a legionary legate. This time the god's answer was gloomy. Instead of Homer, Euripides was quoted: 'Your house will utterly perish in blood.' It was probably in the course of 198 that Septimius was in Apamea.[3]

In the autumn Septimius made a renewed attempt to take Hatra, but it was no more successful. This time he had made more elaborate preparations, especially of siege engines. An engineer names Priscus, who had played an outstanding role in the defence of Byzantium, had

---

[1] Dio 75. 10.2–3. The quotation was evidently *Aeneid* 11.371–3: Laetus: App. III – Plautianus: *HA Sev.* 15.4–6. Cf. Dio 75.14.2.

[2] *HA Sev.* 15.7, cf. App. 1.

[3] Dio 78.8.6 (Euripides *Phoenissae* l. 20). This could have been in any of the years 198–202, in fact.

been reprieved by Septimius and taken on to his staff. Dio proudly noted that this man was a fellow Nicaean. Priscus's siege engines were the only ones that the enemy failed to destroy. Dio makes it clear that the failure to take Hatra was directly the fault of Septimius himself. He omitted to press home the attack when part of the outer wall had been breached. After only twenty days the siege was called off, and Septimius went to Palestine.[1]

Military operations may have dragged on to the year 199. It was apparently not until the end of that year that peace was officially concluded. But Septimius did not participate any further after the second siege of Hatra. In January he went from Palestine to Egypt.[2]

Fifteen years before, Septimius had chosen to go to Athens when he was in disfavour. His expressed motives for the choice were his interest in antiquities and his religious inclinations. Egypt offered him both these to the full. The Augustan History bears out this view. 'Subsequently, he always indicated that he had enjoyed this tour, because he had taken part in the worship of the god Serapis, had learned something of antiquity and had seen unfamiliar animals and places.' But there was also a serious need for administrative and economic reform. No Emperor had visited Egypt since Hadrian was there more than sixty years earlier. Egypt had twice recently joined in actual rebellion, with Avidius Cassius in 175 and with Niger in 193. There had been open and active discontent in the reign of Commodus, when in any case the administration can hardly have run as smoothly as it should – there had been as many as eleven different Prefects in thirteen years.[3]

[1] Dio 75.11.1 – 12.5.

[2] On Septimius's new frontier arrangements after the war see now especially D. OATES, pp. 76ff., – 'In January': I follow the dating by K. HANNESTAD (1944b), in spite of the criticism by W. L. WESTERMANN p. 30 (who does not go into detail). Even if some of Hannestad's arguments are weak – e.g. his use of dated rescripts in the *Cod. Just.* to deduce chronology of campaigns – in my view he shows that Septimius probably did enter Egypt well before the new Egyptian year beginning 30 August 199. J. GUEY (1959) p. 138 n. 3 accepts that this is quite possible, against Westermann.

[3] Athens: p. 119, above. – *HA Sev.* 17.3–4. Cf. also A. M. McCANN, esp. pp. 55f., 79f., 110f. She is surely right in the view that the Emperor's interest in Serapis existed well before his visit to Egypt. She shows that the famous Berlin tondo (K. A. NEUGEBAUER) has Septimius with the Serapis hair-style (cf. her coloured Plate A and pl. XXI), with corkscrew curls. It is reasonable to assume that the

Septimius entered Egypt at Pelusium. Here he made sacrifice at the tomb of Pompey, murdered there nearly two hundred and fifty years before. In making this gesture Septimius was following the example of Hadrian. But there may have been something more to it than an act of conventional piety and respect for a great Roman of the past. Pompey had been murdered by some treacherous Egyptians under the command of a renegade Roman who had once been in Pompey's service. According to Cassius Dio, 'their act brought a curse upon themselves and all Egypt'. Dio explains the nature of the curse by noting that they themselves died not long after, and that Egypt came under the rule first of Cleopatra and then of Rome. But there was a special reason why the superstitious Emperor may have wished to placate or propitiate the spirit of Pompey. The renegade Roman who had struck his former leader down was a certain L. Septimius. The Emperor could not have failed to know this. Even if there were no tie of descent to perpetuate any blood-guilt, he may have felt the need to make a personal act of reconciliation with the dead. Ironically, Marcus Aurelius, whose son Septimius now claimed to be, had been a remote descendant of Pompey. That act of sacrifice at Pompey's tomb was loaded with overtones.[1]

Since the time of the Pharaohs, the ruler of Egypt had been regarded as divine. At the same time, the Nile was a sacred river, the regular flooding of which controlled the prosperity of the country. For this reason, every year at the end of May a ceremony was held on the Upper Nile, at which the ruler of Egypt cast gold and silver gifts down into a rock cave near the river. During the Roman period this ceremony was carried out by the Prefect of Egypt, as the Emperor's Viceroy, except when the Emperor himself was present. There is little doubt that the deeply religious, or superstitious, Septimius took the opportunity of carrying out this *solemne sacrum*, at Philae (Aswan) in late May of the year 199.

---

portrait was painted during the imperial visit – but it is only an assumption. Cf. also p. 62f., above.

[1] Pelusium: Dio 75.13.1, cf. 69.11.1 and *HA Hadr.* 14.4 (Hadrian). – Pompey's murderer: *RE* 2A (1923) 1561f., known to Dio. – M. Aurelius and Pompey: A. R. BIRLEY (1966b).

It was also customary for the Prefect to hold his *conventus*, or assizes, on a regular basis, at three centres. In January and February he would be at Pelusium, in March and April at Memphis, and, after performing the *solemne sacrum* at Philae, at Alexandria in the summer. There is much to be said for the theory that Septimius took over in person the functions of the Prefect in the year 199, arriving at Pelusium in time for the *conventus* there in January, proceeding to Memphis in Upper Egypt in March, on to Philae in May, and only then coming to the great city of Alexandria in June. He will have sailed down the Nile to Alexandria just before the religious taboo began – which prevented the ruler of Egypt from sailing on the Nile while it was in flood.[1]

In the course of his visit he inspected the Pyramids, the Sphinx and other monuments. He was particularly interested in the 'singing statue' of Memnon at Thebes. In fact, his enthusiasm here seems to have been excessive. It was probably on his orders that the statue was repaired. As a result, the freak conditions that caused the stone to emit a musical sound when the temperature changed at sunrise were removed, and the statue was silenced for ever. His tour of Upper Egypt did not take him further than the region of Philae: Dio says that 'he could not cross the Ethiopian frontier because of a plague'.[2]

The ruthless power of Plautianus was demonstrated in Egypt. Dio instances his despatch of soldiers to steal 'horses with tiger-like stripes [presumably zebras] that were sacred to the Sun, from the islands in the Red Sea'. It is not clear from Dio's account whether it was in Egypt that Plautianus gave his daughter Plautilla an *entourage* of eunuchs, for this purpose castrating not only boys but married men, a total of a hundred 'Roman citizens', allegedly of 'noble birth'. His purpose was to ensure that she should have none but eunuchs in attendance on her, especially as teachers in music and the other arts. He was no doubt already planning to marry his daughter to Antoninus. Antoninus and Geta meanwhile were under the tuition of the eminent sophist Aelius Antipater of Hierapolis. Septimius, who had perhaps met Antipater at Athens in the 180s, had made this man his Greek

[1] Cf. K. HANNESTAD (1944 a and b).
[2] *HA Sev.* 17.3–4; Dio 75.13.1, 3–5. Memnon silenced: cf. M. PLATNAUER p. 123, J. HASEBROEK (1921) p. 123.

Secretary (*ab epistulis Graecis*). According to Philostratus in his *Lives of the Sophists* Antipater fulfilled his duties as Greek Secretary brilliantly – no one composed letters better than he did; 'like a brilliant tragic actor . . . his phraseology was always in keeping with the imperial *persona*'. Antipater used his influence with the Emperor to find a husband for his unattractive daughter, Philostratus also relates.[1]

The imperial party made a festive entry into Alexandria. There is an anecdote that the hot-tempered Septimius was enraged by an inscription on the city gate that the Alexandrians had imprudently omitted to remove: 'Niger is the Master of this City'. The Emperor's irritation may or may not have been assuaged by the excuse offered that, after all, he was Niger's master. While in Alexandria, Septimius inspected the tomb of Alexander the Great, and then sealed it permanently. Dio says that he wanted no one else after him to be able to look at Alexander's embalmed body. He also 'removed from almost all the shrines all the books that he could find containing secret lore' to prevent anyone else from consulting them.[2]

Soon after his arrival in Egypt Septimius replaced the Prefect Q. Aemilius Saturninus. Saturninus was evidently promoted to be the colleague of Plautianus as Praetorian Prefect. Plautianus clearly took extreme exception to receiving a colleague, and had Saturninus murdered. It is not clear whether any pretext was found. At the same time Plautianus took steps to prevent any other equestrians from aspiring to share his rank of Guard Prefect.[3]

While in Alexandria Septimius undertook a great deal of administrative reform. The principal change was the granting of a council to Alexandria and to other major cities. The right to have their own

[1] Plautianus: Dio 75.14.2-5. – Antipater: App. III, cf. Philostratus *v.soph.* 2.24-25.

[2] Entry: cf. J. HASEBROEK (1921) p. 123. – Niger: John Malalas 293. – Alexander, etc: Dio 75.13.2. I follow the chronology of K. HANNESTAD (1944b).

[3] Saturninus: Dio 75.14.2, cf. App. III. (he was still Prefect of Egypt in 199 or 200, cf. O. W. REINMUTH p. 106). See now F. GROSSO (1968), esp. pp. 23ff., who shows good reason to believe that Saturninus was succeeded in the Egyptian Prefecture by Alfenus Apollinaris; but that the latter was only in office for a few months. Grosso plausibly suggests that he may be the prefect condemned for forgery by Septimius (*Digest* 48.10.1.4). Quite possibly he was framed by Plautianus. Grosso also argues that the latter suffered a diminution in his power in 199, which he overcame by murdering Saturninus. See further App. 1, no. 8.

9   The central scene of frieze D from the Arch at Lepcis Magna: it is a *dextrarum junctio*, Septimius and his elder son joining right hands. The head of Geta in the center is restored, the original having been removed when he was murdered by his brother. See plates 8 and 10, for other portions of the same relief.

10 A portion of frieze D from the Arch at Lepcis Magna. The two figures belong to the right of the *dextrarum junctio* (plate 9). The left-hand man is
clearly a military man, holding a *rotulus* in the crook of his left arm. He
may well be the Praetorian Prefect, Plautianus.* The right-hand figure
cannot be certainly identified: he might be the Prefect of Rome, Fabius
Cilo, probably in Africa with the imperial party (see esp. Appendix I, under
Varius Marcellus) or possibly the Emperor's brother Geta, consul with
Plautianus in A.D. 203. (But there are no further alternatives.)

*This suggestion was made to me by J. B. Ward-Perkins, who was kind enough to supply a
photograph. Cf. E. Vergara-Caffarelli, pl. 44, for the fragment in its correct position.

11a Gold coin of A.D. 203 (*BMC* Sev., Car. no. 431) showing Septimius with the forked Serapis-style of beard and corkscrew curls.

11b The Arch of the Argentarii: this relief from the inner face of the east pier, showing Septimius and Julia sacrificing, originally included Geta also, on the right. The opposite (west) pier probably had a matching trio, Plautianus, Plautilla and Caracalla, of which only Caracalla now remains. See D. E. L. Haynes–P. E. D. Hirst, p. 33f. pl. IV.

12   The Arch in the Roman Forum.

council had been denied to the cities of Egypt alone among all the cities in the Empire, because of the extreme economic and strategic importance of the country and imperial suspicion of the volatile character of its inhabitants. The Alexandrians had continuously petitioned for a council to be granted them, and Septimius's action was therefore the rectification of an anomaly. Egyptians were also permitted to enter the Roman Senate, from which they had previously been excluded, whatever their personal qualifications. One of the first beneficiaries was a certain Aelius Coeranus, later described as a hanger-on of Plautianus (who may therefore have had a hand in this decision).[1]

Septimius showed his favour to Alexandria by initiating some building work, including public baths, a Gymnasium and a temple of Cybele. A number of papyri have been preserved which record legal and administrative decisions made personally by Septimius while in Egypt. One records an order designed to improve the lot of the peasantry. One particular papyrus contains a whole series of legal decisions made by Septimius. By the end of his stay here the most radical overhaul of the organisation of the province since its annexation had been made.[2]

Soon after Septimius left Egypt there was an outbreak of persecution against the Christians there. Some sources suggest that the Emperor personally initiated it and some scholars have rashly concluded that Septimius launched an Empire-wide persecution. There is no basis for this view. And the story in the Augustan History that he issued an edict prohibiting the Jews to proselytise and the Christians to make converts is a piece of fiction. There was no need for any such edict as far as the Christians were concerned. It had been long established that it was a capital offence merely to be a Christian. Active prosecution by the government or its agents was still avoided. Christians were arrested, prosecuted, and, if they refused to recant, executed.

---

[1] *HA Sev.* 17.2. Cf. J. HASEBROEK pp. 122ff. Coeranus did not however enter the Senate until later, cf. Dio 76.5.3–5 (made a senator in 212, it would seem). But he was given the important procuratorship *a libellis* by Septimius, before 205 when he was exiled. Cf. *L'Albo* no. 6.

[2] J. HASEBROEK p. 118ff. – 'one particular papyrus': W. L. WESTERMANN, revised by H. C. YOUTIE. – Cf. generally H. BRAUNERT (1964), esp. pp. 289ff.

only if and when local hostility to them led to individual denunciations.[1]

From Egypt the imperial party left by sea for Syria. Early in the year 201 Septimius decided to hold the consulship again the following year, with his elder son Antoninus as his colleague. Prior to this the boy, aged thirteen, was invested with the *toga virilis* and formally entered man's estate. None of the sources comment on the apparent anomaly that had been created of having a co-Emperor who was still a boy. Nor has any trace of criticism survived at the implied insult to tradition in making a thirteen-year old consul. There was little difference in the action of Marcus Aurelius, who had given the *fasces* to his son when Commodus was only two years older than this. But Marcus had given his son the *toga virilis* before making him either Emperor or consul.[2] The consulship was now an empty façade. But to be *consul ordinarius* still meant that the year was known by a man's name, and the office was therefore an honour which senators still greatly appreciated. Septimius adhered to tradition in his choice of *consules ordinarii*. The men so honoured were either members of the imperial family, Prefects of the City holding the office of consul for the second time – as Dexter had in 196 and Anullinus in 199 – or members of long established senatorial families. Within these limits, the choice of the men after whom the years would be named allowed the Emperor a useful means of conciliating particular interests. Thus in 197 one consul was the patrician Sextius Lateranus. His appointment could be construed as a gesture to an important party in the Senate, and an example of how those who threw in their lot with him were rewarded. The other was L. Cuspius Rufinus, a Greek senator from Pergamum in Asia, whose selection could have served to conciliate the notables of the east. In 198 one of the consuls was Martius Sergius Saturninus, a member of the recently decimated Gallic aristocracy. In the years 199 and 200 the sons of Marcus's friend Victorinus, who were also grandsons of Fronto, successively held office as consul. These men could be regarded as

[1] Cf. now T. D. BARNES (1968b) esp. p. 40f. The fictional nature of *HA Sev.* 17.1 is also demonstrated by K. M. SCHWARTE.

[2] 'by sea': *IGR* I 380 (20 Jan. 201, a dedication by the *praefectus annonae* Claudius Julianus: App. III). – consulship, *toga virilis*: *HA Sev.* 16.8 (misplaced). – Marcus: cf. A. R. BIRLEY (1966a) p. 256.

representing both the Marcan tradition and Septimius's strong reliance on Numidia, which at this time was undergoing radical development under the governor Anicius Faustus. The deference to the memory of Marcus was underlined by the other consul of 200, Ti. Claudius Severus Proculus, a grandson of Marcus and married to the same Emperor's grand-niece.[1] This example also serves to underline an anomaly of the Roman imperial dynasties. Although the reigning Emperor's person was as sacred as that of any absolute monarch, there was never any question of automatic hereditary succession. By the same token the son of Pertinax, still alive at this time, received no special honours whatever – for his father had refused to give him the title of Caesar. This explains why Septimius felt it vitally necessary to load his sons with titles and powers and honours as soon as it was humanly possible for the boys to accept them with some show of dignity. It was the only way to ensure the succession. Disaster had followed on almost every occasion in the Empire's history when the succession had not been firmly guaranteed in this way – as the fate of Caligula, Nero, Domitian and Commodus showed. Once an Emperor had a recognised successor, his own position was thereby immensely strengthened. Experience had shown that Emperors who had not chosen a successor and given him wide powers became the victims of conspiracy and revolt.[2]

Septimius and Antoninus inaugurated the year 202 as consuls at Antioch. It was by now not uncommon even for *consules ordinarii* to take office away from Rome, but it was probably rare for both to be absent. What is more, with the exception of the year 161, when Marcus Aurelius and Lucius Verus were consuls, there had never been an occasion before when two Emperors were consuls together – and Marcus and Lucius had taken office before their accession. This made the consulship of 202 a particularly rare occasion, and the honour done to Antioch thereby all the greater. Septimius had clearly decided to revoke the punishment inflicted on the city seven years previously. But

[1] Dexter, Anullinus, Lateranus, Faustus: App. III. – Rufinus: *PIR*[2] C 1638. – Sergius Saturninus: cf. G. ALFÖLDY, *Senat* p. 147. – Sons of Victorinus: *PIR*[2] A 1385, 1394. – Proculus: *PIR*[2] C 1028.

[2] 'person as sacred': the development of this aspect of the imperial position is documented brilliantly by A. ALFÖLDI (1934 and 1935).

it was announced that he did this at the request of Antoninus, thereby bringing his son into greater prominence and gaining him a fund of good will.[1]

The time had now come to return to Rome. On 9 April the tenth year of his reign would begin, and Septimius would celebrate his *decennalia*. He and his court probably set off from Antioch soon after the ceremonies on New Year's Day. Two anecdotes Cassius Dio records to illustrate the continuing increase in the power and arrogance of Plautianus probably belong to the beginning of this journey. At Tyana in Cappadocia Plautianus had fallen ill. Septimius went to visit him – but the soldiers guarding Plautianus made the Emperor go in alone, without his escort. Dio also mentions that Septimius 'tolerated seeing Plautianus lodge in better quarters than himself, and have better and more abundant food than he had himself'. Dio confirms this latter point by relating how 'at Nicaea, my native city, when Septimius once wanted a mullet – and the lake there produces large ones – he sent to Plautianus for one'. Plautianus, Dio adds, became a complete sensualist, gorging himself at banquets and freely indulging his lusts with both girls and boys. Yet his wife was kept more or less in purdah, and forbidden to see or be seen by anyone, even Septimius or Julia. Septimius was indeed finding his authority seriously diminished. When the *a cognitionibus* was asked by the Emperor to bring forward one of the cases due to be heard before the Emperor's tribunal, he replied: ' "I cannot do that unless Plautianus orders me to do so." ' Meanwhile Julia was treated by the Prefect with scorn and hatred, and he often abused her violently to Septimius. She took refuge in the company of sophists and the study of 'philosophy'.[2]

Meanwhile Plautianus had doubtless already persuaded Septimius that his daughter Plautilla should be betrothed to Antoninus. Not surprisingly, Antoninus loathed the man who treated his mother in this way and viewed the prospect of being married to his daughter with abhorrence. During this journey Antoninus was once again placed in a favourable light. He was given the credit by his father for the revocation of the penalties imposed on Byzantium in 195–196. This was no doubt

[1] *HA Carac.* 1.7, cf. generally G. DOWNEY p. 242f.
[2] Dio 75.15.3–7.

made public while the Emperors and their party were in Thrace. The route chosen took them on a tour of the Moesian and Pannonian armies. It is worth noting that the governor of Thrace at the moment of the imperial party's passage through the province was a Tripolitanian, a man from Oea, Q. Sicinius Clarus Pontianus. He was certainly a relative, probably the son, of Sicinius Pudens the loutish stepson of Apuleius, who had played a key part in the affair at Oea and the famous trial at Sabratha forty years and more previously. An inscription from Lepcis Magna may allude to the favour that Sicinius Clarus had enjoyed from Septimius. It is a metrical dedication set up by one Pudens. If the suggestion that this man is both the father of Sicinius Clarus and the stepson of Apuleius is right, his knowledge of Latin had improved a little – although his skill as a versifier left much to be desired.[1]

An inscription from Thrace records an action taken by Septimius in that province, carried out by Sicinius Clarus. It proclaims the setting up of a new community on the road from Adrianople to Philippopolis (Plovdiv), a small road-station called the *Emporion Pizos*, with a hundred and seventy-one settlers. 'Moved by concern for the road-stations,' the governor's edict proclaims, 'and wishing that their province should remain in the same state of prosperity throughout their lifetime, our Great and Most Divine Lords the Emperors gave orders that existing *emporia* should be improved and that new ones should be established.' Although the rest of the edict continues to emphasise the personal role of the Emperors in the establishment of the *emporia*, one is not entitled to deduce from this that the route of the imperial party took them through Pizos itself.[2]

A great many dedications and building inscriptions from the time

---

[1] 'already persuaded': cf. Dio 75.15.2, who says that 'the Emperor sought Plautianus's daughter on his son's behalf.' – Antoninus' attitude: cf. Herodian 3.10.7–8, etc. – Byzantium: *HA Carac.* 1.7 (not dated). – 'a tour of the . . . armies': this derives from Herodian 3.10.1. It is presumably correct, in spite of the hopeless muddle over chronology (it *might* however be a confusion with 196). But the elaborate reconstructions of the route followed are entirely hypothetical, cf. p. 214 and n. 2, below. – Clarus Pontianus: *L'Albo* no. 479, cf. the article by J. GUEY (1952) p. 25ff.; also ID. (1953) p. 341f. Cf. p. 48ff., above.

[2] *IGR* I 766.

of Septimius's visit in 202 have been preserved throughout the Danubian provinces. But no inscriptions of this kind offer any proof that Septimius actually visited the place where they were set up. In fact, the coming *decennalia*, the marriage of Antoninus and Plautilla, and indeed the successful conclusion of the Parthian war not long before, would have provided ample occasion for most of the dedications even without an imperial visit. But in any case, even if the Emperor did not visit a particular town in Thrace, for example, his presence somewhere in the province would inevitably cause the setting up of statues, altars, and other marks of honour. Anyone who hoped to gain the Emperor's favour would hasten to meet him on his route, no doubt armed with letters of recommendation which would not fail to mention that the petitioner had proved his loyalty and enthusiasm to the imperial house by the setting up of this or that monument.[1]

It was long thought that the heading of an imperial rescript preserved in the Code of Justinian showed that the Emperors were at Sirmium on 18 March. This would indeed give a helpful indication of the route that was followed. But there is no doubt that this heading is the result of a manuscript error, and there is thus no certainty as to the timing and direction of the journey. However, it is highly probable that the route followed was along the Danube. The welfare of the armies that had gained him the throne would never be closer to his heart than at the time when the anniversary of his proclamation was approaching. It is probable therefore that he visited Lower and Upper Moesia, perhaps Dacia also, and the two Pannonias. It may even be that he chose to return to Carnuntum on 9 April, the *dies imperii*, and that his journey back to Rome from there was timed to repeat the stages and the timing of his journey in 193. But this is purely speculation.[2]

The return to Rome was celebrated in high style. The urban *plebs* and the Praetorian Guards were given largesse – ten gold pieces each. It was the first *congiarium* to the *plebs* for five years, but the sum they

[1] Thus the reconstructions of the route by e.g. J. FITZ (1959) and G. MIHAILOV, while valuable in other respects, are not conclusive (cf. next note).

[2] *Cod. Just.* 2.31 (32).1. Cf. the important observations of J. KOLENDO pp. 127ff., who shows the fragility of attempts to work out the journey's stage in detail (cf. previous note). See now also F. GROSSO (1968) p. 38, who independently reaches the same conclusions about the rescript as Kolendo.

received was the highest ever. The total cost was two hundred million Sesterces. This evidently took place before the marriage of Antoninus and Plautilla. Dio says that 'Plautianus gave as much for his daughter's dowry as would have sufficed for fifty women of royal rank'. Dio himself watched the gifts being carried through the Forum to the Palace. He was also among the guests at the wedding banquet, which was 'partly imperial and partly barbaric in style'. The guests were given uncooked meat and live animals, as well as the normal presents of cooked meat, to take away. After the wedding, and to celebrate the Emperors' return, the *decennalia* and the Parthian victories – for which Septimius once again declined to celebrate a triumph; apparently he was already suffering from gout, which would have prevented him from standing up in the triumphal chariot – the spectacular shows lasted for seven days. On one occasion seven hundred beasts of all kinds – including bears, lionesses, panthers, lions, ostriches, wild asses and bison – were released into the arena simultaneously to be slaughtered.[1]

Dio chose the moment of Septimius's return to present him with his narrative of the *Wars that followed the death of Commodus*, begun five years before in obedience to the divine command in his dream. It won great approval with Septimius, as well as with others.

Therefore [Dio says] I decided not to leave my first historical treatise as a separate composition, but to incorporate it in the present narrative, so that in a single work I might write down and leave behind me an all-embracing history, from the beginning down to the moment that shall seem best to Fortune. This goddess gives me the strength to continue with my history when I begin to shrink from the task; when I grow tired of it and want to give it up, she brings me back to it through dreams. She gives me fair hopes that the future will allow my history to survive and never dim its lustre. It seems that she has been allotted to watch over the course of my life, and therefore I have dedicated myself to her.

[1] Dio 76.1.1-5. – 'declined . . . triumph': *HA Sev.* 16.6; but 16.7, the alleged 'Jewish triumph' for his son, is surely invented. R. BRILLIANT p. 93 believes it; but the other passages he cites, n. 26 (Tertullian *de habitu muliebri* 7, Herodian 3.10.1) prove nothing.

Dio was to spend the next ten years collecting the material for his history of Rome from Romulus to his own times, and the following twelve in composing his work.[1]

Septimius can scarcely have remained much longer at Rome on this occasion than on the previous three flying visits to the city – his triumphant entry in 193, when he spent less than thirty days there, and the visits in 196 and 197, before and after the conflict with Albinus. This time he planned a journey that must have been in many ways the most personally attractive and satisfying of all: a return to his native Africa. The stage was set for a triumphal passage of the first African Emperor through the land of his origin. He himself and his elder son were consuls in this year. For the following year the designated consuls were two other Africans, both natives of Lepcis Magna, his brother Geta and his kinsman and Prefect Plautianus.[2]

During the preceding five years Anicius Faustus, the governor of Numidia, had undertaken a whole series of measures designed to improve the security of the province. From Dimmidi in the west, more than two hundred miles south of modern Algiers, to Ghadames and Bu-Ngem in the east, deep in the desert south of Tripolitania, the frontiers of the empire had been extended and newly fortified. It is worth noting that Castellum Dimmidi, founded in 198, lies on the same latitude as Tasuni, where a reconnaissance party had penetrated in the year 174 – precisely when Septimius was serving as legate to the proconsul of Africa. Although his duties in proconsular Africa would not have been in any way concerned with the military undertakings in Numidia, Septimius cannot have failed to have heard reports of this mission. A quarter of a century later he was to order the advance of Roman garrisons to this latitude on a permanent basis.[3]

---

[1] Dio 72.23.3–5, cf. p. 7f. above.

[2] In spite of the doubts of P. ROMANELLI (1959) pp. 413ff., there seems no valid reason to doubt that the imperial family visited Africa at about this time. I accept J. GUEY's (1950) interpretation of *IRT* 292 (pp. 55ff.): this seems to show that Septimius was at or near Lepcis on 11 April 203.

[3] Cf. generally P. ROMANELLI (1959) pp. 395ff. – Dimmidi: G. CHARLES-PICARD (1949) esp. pp. 45ff. (n. 47 pp. 58ff. on Tasuni: *CIL* VIII 21567). – Ghadames, Bu-Ngem: cf. R. G. GOODCHILD (1949 and 1950); A. DI VITA (1964), esp. pp. 80ff.

It has not escaped notice that among the troops that constructed the fort of Dimmidi was a detachment from the Syrian legion III Gallica. It might seem at first sight surprising that men from the Syrian army should have been sent away from their base at the time of the Parthian war. But the deficiency was more than made good by the despatch of legionaries from III Augusta to Syria. In other words, there was an exchange of men. The motive was clearly to bring about a fruitful interchange of experience. The lessons learned by the men of the Syrian legion III Gallica in controlling a desert frontier would be invaluable when the new frontier was being created in Numidia. At the same time, as a disciplinary measure for men who had supported Pescennius Niger, a tour of duty in the Sahara could hardly have been bettered.

The legate Ancius Faustus was himself a man from Africa. His home was at the small town of Uzappa, near Mactar in Byzacena (central Tunisia). Faustus had been legate of III Augusta since 197. During the course of his five years command he was made consul, and his *de facto* province at last became *de iure* the separate province of Numidia. He was succeeded by Claudius Gallus, who had commanded detachments of the four German legions during the Parthian war. He too was probably from Africa.[1]

Once again the entire imperial family appears to have gone with Septimius – Julia and both their sons, and Plautianus and Plautilla. Fabius Cilo, now Prefect of the City of Rome, may also have accompanied them. At Rome, Julia Domna's nephew by marriage, Varius Marcellus, back from Britain and now director of the 'Private Fund' (*ratio privata*), was given authority to rule the City of Rome – or its garrison – as 'Acting Prefect of the Guard and the City'. The route taken can only be guessed at. It may be that they went first to Lepcis

---

[1] III Gallica: cf. G. CHARLES-PICARD (1949) esp. pp. 47ff. – Faustus, Gallus: App. III. – '*de iure* province': this is argued by H. G. PFLAUM (1957a). – It should be noted that the procurators Sallustius Macrinianus and Haius Diadumenianus (the latter dated 202) both governed the two Mauretanias simultaneously during the reign, while C. Julius Pacatianus was *pro legato* of Tingitana. All this points to special military undertakings in the Mauretanian provinces during the reign, cf. App. III for these men and the comments by Pflaum in *CP* nos. 227, 229; also P. ROMANELLI (1959) p. 408f.

Magna, but it is perhaps more probable that they landed at Carthage. This city, together with Utica, the original capital of the first Roman province of Africa, and by tradition the first Phoenician foundation in the country, were both given a new honour, receiving the *ius Italicum*, and thus immunity from provincial taxation. Lepcis Magna was likewise honoured, and the grateful people now called themselves the *Lepcitani Septimiani*. Septimius had ambitious plans for the embellishing of his native city. According to a cryptic remark in Philostratus's *Lives of the Sophists*, during his stay in Africa Septimius 'gathered together there men of talent from all over the world'. He may perhaps have invited some sophists to join him in Africa, but it is clear from the evidence of the buildings erected at Lepcis during his reign that it was above all architects and sculptors who came there, from Asia Minor. Work was begun on a huge new Forum and Basilica (completed in 216). On the far side of the Forum from the Basilica was a great new temple, which may be the one referred to in an extract from Dio, commenting acidly on Septimius's building activities: 'He also wasted a great deal of money repairing other buildings and building new ones; for example, he built an excessively large temple to Bacchus and Hercules.' No temple to Bacchus (i.e. Liber) and Hercules has been identified at Rome, and it may be that this is the temple at Lepcis. The expenditure of large sums of money at Lepcis may well have seemed wasteful to Dio. Apart from the Forum and Basilica, a monumental colonnaded street was planned, running between them and the Wadi Lebdah down to the harbour, which was now reconstructed on a vast scale. The water supply of the city was improved and the Circus enlarged and restored. Finally, a *quadrifrons* Arch over a major street intersection in the southern part of the city was – in some haste – decorated with reliefs depicting the Emperor's victories and the imperial family.[1]

Septimius and his court probably spent the winter of 202–3 at Lepcis.

[1] Marcellus: App. 1 (this dating is of course speculative). – honours to African cities: cf. P. ROMANELLI pp. 418ff. (R. M. HAYWOOD's [1940] thesis, that Septimius showed no special favour to Africa is in my mind effectively answered by Romanelli p. 435 n. 3. Haywood's reply [1962] adds nothing to his original case.) – Philostratus *v. soph.* 2.20.2. 'Asia Minor' (esp. Aphrodisias) this is the standard view, cf. e.g. J. B. WARD-PERKINS (1948, 1951); but also G. CHARLES-

Thus Plautianus and the elder Geta no doubt inaugurated the year 203 as consuls at their home town. In later winter or early spring Septimius undertook a campaign against the desert peoples to the south. It is hard to believe that he went right down to the heart land of the Garamantes, the Wadi el-Agial, but the fourth-century writer Aurelius Victor, himself an African, says unequivocally that 'he freed Tripolitania, the region from which he came, from fear of attack, by crushing most warlike tribes'. No doubt Claudius Gallus with part of the legion III Augusta and auxiliary troops from Numidia participated in the fighting, along with Plautianus and part of the Praetorian Guard. The campaign was evidently not quite over by 11 April, Septimius's fifty-eighth birthday. On that day a legionary centurion, T. Flavius Marinus, dedicated a thank-offering to the Syrian god Jupiter Dolichenus at Lepcis, 'for the safety and victory of our Lords the Emperors . . . and for the return of the Emperors to their own city'. The abbreviation for emperors used in this inscription – *Auggg.* – served to indicate that to Marinus there were three Emperors. In Africa, Geta was regarded as being equal to Antoninus as soon as he became Caesar.[1]

PICARD (1959a) pp. 335ff., who emphasises the role of African artists. – 'great new temple': Dio 76.16.3. No such temple is known at Rome and J. HASEBROEK (1921) p. 149f. reasonably enough conjectured that the reference is to Lepcis. – the Arch: See now A. M. McCANN pp. 74ff. She refers (p. 74 n. 7) to an unpublished excavation by A. Di Vita, who finds that the Arch itself was erected in the early second century; and that the reliefs were then 'attached in a hurry' to the existing structure. I see no reason to follow her dating of the visit to Africa to 206–7 (pp. 67, 75ff.) The iconography may look more appropriate to that date, but the historical evidence, such as it is, points to the year 203. On the art and architecture of Lepcis, cf. also J. GUEY (1950), pp. 73ff., D. E. L. HAYNES pp. 71ff., E. VERGARA CAFFARELLI. – It is possible that the statement in the HA, *Sev.* 18.3, etc., that Septimius gave free olive oil to the *populus Romanus* in perpetuity, which comes in the same sentence as the description of his military measures in Tripolitania (see below and next note), has some truth in it; if so, it was an act of magnanimity with which the Lepcitani then and later were probably not overjoyed – but on the other hand the Septimii will have amassed vast estates by now, and the whole affair may have been a matter for the *res privata*, not the *ordo* of Lepcis. J. HASEBROEK (1921) and R. M. HAYWOOD (1938) both ignore the passage, without giving reasons. Perhaps it was invented on the basis of Victor *de Caes.* 41.19.

[1] 'campaign': Victor *de Caes.* 20.19 = HA *Sev.* 18.3. Cf. J. GUEY (1952a) pp.

It was perhaps while the imperial party was at Lepcis that a rift was caused in Plautianus's immense power. For some reason Septimius became displeased with him. Dio and the Augustan History differ slightly about the details, which is not surprising. But what happened is clear enough. According to Dio, Septimius was annoyed at the number of statues that were set up to Plautianus. The Augustan History specifies that he was angry that Plautianus had 'set up his own statue among the statues of Septimius's kinsmen and relatives'. There cannot have been any city where there were so many statues of Septimius's relations as Lepcis, where his grandfather, father, mother, aunt, first wife, brother and sister were all honoured in this way, as well as himself, Julia and their sons – and Plautianus and Plautilla. According to Dio, Septimius had some bronze statues of the Prefect melted down, and from this act a rumour spread that he had been overthrown. As a result, some in official positions took appropriate action and themselves demolished the statues of Plautianus. One of these was the governor of Sardinia, Racius Constans, who later paid the penalty. This man, and others who had acted similarly, were tried and punished. The Augustan History, or its source, misunderstood what happened: the biography asserts that Septimius actually declared Plautianus to be a public enemy, and then relented. It is easy to understand that Septimius might have tolerated affronts from Plautianus elsewhere, but, at Lepcis alone, the Lepcitane Emperor would wish it to be shown that it was he, and not Plautianus, who was the greatest of the city's son.[1]

61ff., P. ROMANELLI (1959) pp. 398ff. There is no certain means of dating the campaign recorded by Victor, or of knowing whether Septimius was there in person. – Gallus: App. III. – Marinus: *IRT* 292 as interpreted by J. GUEY (1950) pp. 55ff. Cf. now also F. GROSSO (1968) pp. 40ff. – Cf. also p. 217 n. 1, above on possible warfare in Mauretania.

[1] Dio 75.16.2–5; HA *Sev.* 14.7 (misplaced, cf. App. II). On the dating of the 'rift' cf. also F. GROSSO (1968) pp. 38ff., who shows that W. JUDEICH's theory is unsatisfactory – but his own alternative is not the only possibility; cf. App. 1, no. 8. – The fact that the governor of Sardinia is the only named victim is no coincidence: that province would get news, or rumours, more quickly than most, whether from Rome or Lepcis, and Constans will have acted at once, before the rumour had been suppressed.

As well as Lepcis, Septimius no doubt visited other parts of proconsular Africa and Numidia. Inscriptions suggest that he was at Lambaesis, the base of the legion, in 203. Numerous other cities benefited from his patronage, but it is impossible to be certain whether he visited them. While the Emperor and his party were in Africa, the proconsul died. It may have been from natural causes. But the fact that Plautianus was there at the time makes one wonder. His duties were taken over by the procurator, Hilarianus. In his capacity as acting governor Hilarianus had some Christians, Perpetua and her companions, put to death. There is no sign that Septimius took any interest in this event. It happened that the day of the martyrdom was the fourteenth birthday of his son Geta, in the spring of 203. The imperial party would have been otherwise occupied. There is no clear evidence when they returned to Italy. But it was shortly before 10 June 203.[1]

[1] Lambaesis, etc.: cf. P. ROMANELLI (1959) pp. 413ff. – The proconsul: named variously as Minucius Timinianus and Minutius Oppianus in the Latin and Greek versions of the *Passio Perpetuae* 6.3. The point is not vital, but perhaps the real name was Opimianus, cf. *AE* 1906.80, a procurator (?) of Asia – nicius Opimianus; also the cos. 155 Opimianus. – The procurator: perhaps the same as P. Aelius Hilarianus, an *eques* from Aphrodisias in Caria (*PIR*[2] A 190), who is now known to have been procurator in Spain under Commodus, (unpublished: information from G. Alföldy). In that case, it is an interesting coincidence that sculptors from Aphrodisias are reckoned to have been active in Africa at this time, p. 218 n. 1, above. – Perpetua: cf. now esp. T. D. BARNES (1968a) pp. 521ff., ID (1968b) p. 41. – '10 June': cf. F. GROSSO (1968) pp. 40ff., re-reading *AE* 1935.156, which shows that the *equites singulares* were back at Rome on that day, after an *expeditio felic(issima)* – surely the African one, as Grosso argues.

XV

THE YEARS IN ITALY

Septimius's entry into Rome on his return from Africa will certainly have been festive. It may be that he decided to hold a minor triumph or *ovatio* for his military successes in Tripolitania. The Augustan History records that he entered the city after his reconciliation with Plautianus, 'as if celebrating an ovation'. But the author of that work has drastically abbreviated his source, probably the long-winded Marius Maximus. This notice about Plautianus is inserted out of place immediately preceding the mention of Septimius's departure for the east in summer 197. When the narrative in the Augustan History had brought Septimius to Egypt, the author found his basic source tedious and boring and turned to Aurelius Victor for a snappy summary of the entire reign, *quoniam longum est minora persequi*, 'since it is tedious to follow up minor details'.[1]

At any rate, Septimius did receive one public honour, a magnificent Arch, probably voted in his honour at the end of the first Parthian war, was dedicated in the year 203. It was set up in the north-east corner of the Forum, between the Rostra and the Senate-house, in front of the Temple of Concord. The monument towered more than seventy-five feet above the level of the *Comitium*, and was adorned with sculptured reliefs commemorating the *victoria Parthica*. The choice of position was carefully made. The Arch was placed on the spot where, in his dream in early 193, Septimus had seen Pertinax fall from his horse, and himself taken up on it. The imperial vision had already been commemorated by an equestrian statue of the Emperor. Now the massive Arch, the first major addition to the architecture of the Forum for

---

[1] *HA Sev.* 14.7 (misplaced.) – Victor: *ib.* 17.5, cf. App. II.

eighty years, gave a much more dramatic emphasis to this spot. Commemoration of the imperial dream was not, however, the sole reason for siting the Arch there. The *Comitium* was the site of the legendary encounter between Romulus and the Sabine king Titus Tatius, and then, for a time, the meeting place of the *comitia curiata*, the oldest assembly of the people. The Rostra, the *curia* of the Senate, the Temple of Concord, all had immense symbolic significance. Looming over the meetings of the Senate, but next to the Temple of Concord, the Arch was a powerful reminder of the Emperor's power but also perhaps a pointer to reconciliation. What is more, the Arch stands diagonally opposite the Arch of Augustus, erected to celebrate that Emperor's diplomatic success over the Parthians in 20 B.C. Thus Septimius would be linked with the first Emperor of Rome – and perhaps subtly be shown to have surpassed him. Besides all this, the Arch gave final definition to the architectural design of the Forum.[1]

The inscription on the Arch, honouring Septimius and both his sons, states that the Senate and People of Rome set it up to them, 'on account of the restoration of the Republic and the extension of the Empire of the Roman People by their outstanding virtues at home and abroad'. The 'restoration of the republic' can only refer, in a veiled *cliché*, to the defeat of Didius Julianus, and perhaps the other rival claimants. The 'extension of the empire' acclaims the new province of Mesopotamia, perhaps also the advance of the African frontiers. Further extension of the boundaries of Rome was yet to come.[2]

The year 204 was inaugurated by Fabius Cilo, as consul for the second time, and Annius Libo, a grandson of Marcus Aurelius's cousin of that name. Cilo's second consulship was the payment of a debt to a friend who had served Septimius well. Septimius's gratitude took tangible form also. Cilo was among the Emperor's friends whom he endowed with substantial wealth, according to a late fourth-century writer. His palatial mansion, the *domus Cilonis*, became a city landmark.

[1] The elaborate monograph by R. BRILLIANT supersedes all previous studies, and has been drawn on for this description.

[2] D. 425, cf. R. BRILLIANT pp. 91ff. (also H. U. INSTINSKY (1942) pp. 212ff., not cited by Brilliant. But Instinsky's views on the Senate's – rather than the Emperor's – enthusiasm for extending the Empire are unconvincing).

The choice of Libo as the other consul once again marked Septimius's proclaimed membership of the Antonine dynasty.[1]

In the course of A.D. 203 arrangements had begun to mark the year 204 with ceremonies and celebrations of the most striking kind known to the Romans, Saecular Games. The origin of these games was cloaked in legend and uncertainty even in ancient times. Augustus, the renovator of the Roman state and the Roman religion, had chosen to celebrate Saecular Games in 17 B.C. The year suited the political needs of his regime. It was possible to assert with some plausibility that these were the fifth in a series of games held at intervals of one hundred and ten years, the length of the Etruscan era or *saeculum*. All were ready to agree that the establishment of his rule marked a new age. With the ending of the civil wars, the final conquest of Spain, the fruitful marriage of his daughter Julia, the recovery of the legionary standards from the Parthians, Saecular Games could fittingly denote the close of one era and inaugurate a new golden age. For three nights and three days, from 1–3 June, sacrifices and games were conducted by the *quindecimviri sacris faciundis*, the Board of fifteen for performing sacrifices.

The next games, the sixth, should have been celebrated in 94. Claudius, impatient, found a learned excuse, no doubt, for holding his own in 47 – which also marked the eight hundredth year of Rome. Domitian ignored the Claudian Games and held the sixth in the series, but once again, with some impatience, six years early, in 88 – unless his reason was that the Augustan Games had been postponed (as well they might have been) from a date originally set in 23 B.C.[2]

Now two hundred and twenty years, two *saecula*, would have passed in the summer of 204 since the Augustan Games. What is more, by happy chance the time had come to celebrate the seventh in the series. The number seven carried magic significance to the superstitious – as it still does to some today – being the number of the planets. Septimius, whose own name in any case evoked *septimus*, seventh, assuredly was attached to the astral power of the number seven. That the celebration

---

[1] Cilo: App. III. – Libo: *PIR²* A 648.

[2] The standard work on the Games is that by J. B. PIGHI, to which reference should be made for what follows.

of these games was by tradition the task of the *quindecimviri sacris faciundis* may have been another factor of special interest to Septimius. His kinsman C. Septimius Severus had been one. It may well be that he himself had been co-opted to the College before becoming Emperor. Members of the great priestly colleges generally did their best to secure a priesthood for their relatives or protégés when vacancies arose. Or if a deceased priest had been respected by his colleagues, the man's own nominee would be given the place that he had vacated. Septimius may have replaced his kinsman. But certainly during Commodus's reign there must have been more than the usual number of vacancies, as the number of his victims continually rose.[1]

To the *quindecimviri* was entrusted the care of the Sibylline oracles and of foreign religious rites of which the worship was licensed at Rome. This included the cult of Isis and Serapis. If Septimius had indeed become a *quindecimvir* as a senator, he would have relished both aspects of his duties. It would not have required especial skill in sacred lore to establish that Saecular Games would soon be due. During the reign of Commodus the *quindecimviri* may well have pondered on what form that deranged Emperor would impose on the solemn ceremonies. The oracles in their guardianship were those carefully vetted by Augustus and housed in the temple of Palatine Apollo. Other oracles circulated under the name of the Sibyl, in the Greek east, composed by Jews. One of these prophesied the return of Nero and the fall of Rome in the year 195. That year had safely passed. The civil wars were over. The Parthians had been defeated and a new land added to the Empire of the Roman people. The Emperor had ruled for more than ten years, his elder son was his colleague and destined successor, there were now hopes, with Antoninus's marriage to Plautilla, of a third generation in the divine imperial house.[2]

At a meeting of the Senate in 203 – the exact date has not survived on the inscription, but it was March, June or July – the *quindecimviri* stood before the consuls' raised bench, and the Master of the College,

[1] C. Septimius Severus: App. 1. – 'relatives or protégés': cf. Pliny *Ep.* 4.8.3.

[2] On the *quindecimviri* cf. R. SYME (1958) pp. 65f. – 'the year 195': *Or. Sib.* 8.139ff., discussed by Syme p. 773. – 'hopes': cf. J. GAGÉ (however, I do not accept his arguments on the age of Antoninus or on the actuality of Plautilla's pregnancy; cf. p. 232 and n. 1, below).

Manilius Fuscus, read out a prepared speech. He recalled to the Senate that the time was at hand for holding the Saecular Games. He spoke of the Sibyl's prophetic song, that the longest span of a human life reached the hundred and tenth year. It was the duty of the Senate, in view of the happiness and joy of the human race, to render thanks for present benefits and to ensure their future continuance, by providing for the holding of these games.

> You should, with all worship and veneration of the immortal gods, for the security and eternity of the Empire, frequent the most sacred shrines, for the rendering and giving of thanks, so that the immortal gods may pass on to future generations what our ancestors have built up and the things which, after previously conferring them on our ancestors, they have granted to our own times as well.

A motion was then formally introduced by Calpurnius Maximus, that the Emperors and Septimius Geta the most noble Caesar should be requested to hold the Saecular Games, which were customarily held at intervals of one hundred and ten years, in the following year, and that the games should be held at public expense, and that there should be public holidays on the days when the games should be held. Lawsuits should be postponed for thirty days, likewise mourning by women should be prohibited for a similar period, and to commemorate the proceedings a record should be inscribed on marble. It is from the substantial surviving fragments of that marble inscription that this account is derived.[1]

Further arrangements were made at a meeting of the *quindecimviri* on the Palatine on 11 November, and in February or March 204. Then on 15 April the members of the College received a letter from the Emperors, which was read to them by the Master, Pompeius Rusonianus. They were to assemble in the Temple of Apollo on the Palatine on 25 May, 'to choose by lot the places in which the members, seated on tribunals, are to distribute means of purification to the people'. A second letter was also read out, informing them that if they decided on which days and nights the games should be held, and the

[1] J. B. PIGHI pp. 140ff. – Fuscus: App. III.

matrons should offer prayers and incense, the Emperors would so decree. The College duly met and drew lots on 25 May, and on the same day issued an edict announcing the arrangements for the games.[1]

On 26 May the *quindecimviri* took up their allotted positions on the Capitol, Palatine and Aventine hills, and distributed the incense and other purificatory materials. Probably three days later, on 29 May, the *quindecimviri* took up their positions again, this time to receive symbolic offerings of first-fruits from the people, after prayers, to Jupiter Best and Greatest, Juno Queen of Heaven, and Apollo Good and Beautiful, led by Septimius. On 31 May the solemn purificatory rites were undertaken in preparation for the solemnities. The Master of the *quindecimviri* Pompeius Rusonianus, purified the spot known as Terentum or Tarentum, on the edge of the Campus Martius, where the Saecular rites, once a private ceremony of the Valerian *gens*, had always had their focus. It was a place sacred to the gods of the underworld, whose share in the ritual had largely been taken by heavenly deities. The ritual purification of the people followed. Then came preparatory sacrifices, in the presence of the *quindecimviri* and the two senior Vestal Virgins, on the bank of the Tiber.

The following night, after midnight when the Kalends of June began, the Saecular rites proper were inaugurated with sacrifice and prayer to the *Moerae* or Fates, on the Campus Martius next to the Tiber. At the second hour of the morning were staged performances on a specially erected stage. Meanwhile Julia Domna, with one hundred and nine other married women, one for each year of the *saeculum*, held sacred banquets (*sellisternia*) on the Capitol in honour of the goddesses Juno and Diana.

Through the three days and two nights following Septimius and his sons performed all the traditional rituals of sacrifice and prayer, with games at intervals. On each occasion Septimius presided at the sacrifice, Antoninus led the prayer and Geta carried it on. The traditional formulas used by Augustus in 17 B.C. were faithfully followed. The god or goddess was invoked by name, then came these words:

As has been prescribed for you in these books, and by virtue of this

[1] J. B. PIGHI pp. 144ff. – Rusonianus: App. III.

let all good fortune attend the Roman People, the *Quirites*, let sacrifice be made to you with [the appropriate sacrifice for the particular deity]. I beg and beseech you that just as you have increased the empire and majesty of the Roman People, the *Quirites*, in war and in peace, so may the Latin always be obedient; that you may grant everlasting safety, victory and health to the Roman People, the *Quirites*; that you may protect the Roman People, the *Quirites*, and the legions of the Roman People, the *Quirites*; that you may keep safe and magnify the republic of the Roman People, the *Quirites*; that you may be favourable and propitious to the Republic of the Roman People, the *Quirites*, the College of the *Quindecimviri*, to me, my house, my household.[1]

As in 17 B.C., the final fames in the Circus were preceded by the hymn the *Carmen Saeculare*, sung first on the Palatine and then again on the Capitol, by two choirs of twenty-seven boys and twenty-seven girls. Augustus had been able to call on the services of the poet Horace to compose the hymn. The name of the poet of 204 has not been preserved, and cannot even be conjectured. Little of the hymn itself has survived, either. The few intelligible phrases witness to the invocation of Apollo and Diana, just as in the Horatian *carmen*. There is reference also to the shores and cities of the empire, to Bacchus and the golden fields, to ships sailing the seas, to the camps of the army, and, at the end, a prayer to protect 'our Leaders'. The mention of Bacchus is of special interest, for the god of wine is the same as Liber Pater, one of the two guardian deities of Lepcis Magna. However traditional the prayers and rituals may have been, there was clearly some modification in honour of the *di patrii* of Septimius, Hercules and Liber. The surviving portions of the *commentarium* do not contain any mention of them, apart from the name of Bacchus in the *carmen*. But the coins issued in commemoration of these games convey the impression that the two gods of Lepcis were the presiding deities of the whole occasion.[2]

[1] J. B. PIGHI pp. 146ff.

[2] J. B. PIGHI pp. 222ff. does his best with the fragments. Bacchus is mentioned in ll.67–68. – Hercules and Liber: cf. A. ALFÖLDI (1935) p. 153, who emphasises that the two gods were also the models with whom Alexander the Great – and, in imitation of him, Augustus – was compared. Through this means the Emperor was

Again in the tradition of the Augustan celebration, the three-day ceremony was followed by seven days of games, both stage performances and circus races. On the last day came the 'Troy Game', perfomed by boys of senatorial family. One of the boys, who bore an historic name, being a Calpurnius Piso, was severely injured. There were still a few surviving descendants of the ancient Republican nobility. They were kept well in the background. Augustus, mindful of the origin of the Saecular Games as a rite of the Valerii had given two distinguished members of the *gens* a role at the games of 17 B.C., as *quindecimviri*. As it happens, there were two men alive in the reign of Septimius whose nomenclature advertised descent from those noble and patrician Valerii, L. Valerius Messalla Thrasea Priscus, *consul ordinarius* in 196, and L. Valerius Messalla, who was to hold the same distinction in 214. Neither was even a *quindecimvir*.[1]

The composition of the College of Fifteen is indeed an interesting study in itself, not least for the contrasts and comparisons with 17 B.C. Then, together with Augustus himself, two Valerii Messallae, an Aemilius Lepidus, a Licinius Stolo and a Mucius Scaevola, noble names, balanced the *novi homines*, great soldiers and politicians such as Agrippa, Sentius Saturninus and Cocceius Nerva. This time there was little room for men of the first category, few though their representatives were by now. The bearers of great names among the *quindecimviri* of 204 had acquired them not from descent but from grant of citizenship to their ancestors – a Cassius, a Fabius, two Fulvii, a Manilius, a Pompeius. Some of the other *nomina* were redolent of provincial Italy: Gargilius, Ofilius, Pollienus, Vetina. But of the twenty-six *quindecimviri* recorded only one, Nonius Arrius Mucianus of Verona, is known certainly to have been the son of a consular. Few besides Mucianus were certainly Italian. Pollienus Auspex, the sarcastic friend of Septimius, was one. The Emperor, his sons and the Praetorian Prefect,

---

portrayed as a new Alexander – and the Alexander-mania of Caracalla becomes more intelligible (p. 277 and n. 1, below).

[1] Troy Game: J. B. PIGHI pp. 167, 173. – Piso: *PIR*² C 295, *L'Albo* no. 112 (not certain whether it was on this occasion). – The Messallae: *L'Albo* nos. 510–511. The Augustan XViri were M. Messalla Messalinus *cos. ord.* 3 B.C. and M. Potitus Messalla *cos. ord.* 29 B.C., cf. Pighi p. 236.

had several fellow-Africans in the College, perhaps as many as nine. The *magister* in 204, Julius Pompeius Rusonianus, has a *cognomen* that is otherwise certainly recorded only at Lepcis Magna. He was given a special role to play in the rites – the purification on 31 May. It would not be surprising if he was another Lepcitane.[1]

In the list of married women and boys and girls who participated in the rites in 204 the provincial names seem also to be dominant. Unlike the Augustan *commentarium*, which speaks only of the hundred and ten *matronae*, that of the year 204 specifies Julia Domna, *mater castrorum*, with the hundred and nine others who took part. Of the hundred and nine, ninety-one were wives of senators. The remaining eighteen equestrian ladies were headed by Julia's niece, Julia Soaemias, wife of Varius Marcellus.[2]

Of the three narrative sources only Herodian contains any mention of these games. Dio's account has obviously been omitted by his epitomator. The author of the Augustan History gives up any pretence at detailed narrative after the first six years of the reign. Herodian is brief and inaccurate, but one sentence does strike a true note: 'Heralds were sent out in Rome and Italy, calling all to come and see what they had never seen before and would never see again.' As it turned out, no one was ever to see Saecular Games again. These were the seventh and last in the series.[3]

In the course of 204, probably early in the year, Antoninus and Geta were designated to the consulship for the year 205. Thus the first year of the new *saeculum* would bear the names of Septimius's sons. Geta, who had probably received the *toga virilis* the previous year, was by now known generally as 'most noble Caesar'. For the past few years there had been some variation in his nomenclature: he had sometimes the *praenomen* Publius, sometimes Lucius. From now on he remained Publius officially. There must have been some reason for the change, although none of the ancient sources discusses it. It may be that when his elder brother changed his name to M. Aurelius Antoninus, Geta took Antoninus's original *praenomen* Lucius. Antoninus's original

---

[1] Cf. R. SYME (1939) p. 382 and the list in J. B. PIGHI pp. 232ff.; and App. III.
[2] Cf. J. B. PIGHI pp. 116f., 241ff., and App. I.
[3] Herodian 3.9–10.

praenomen is however unknown. Such a change of name would recall the action of Marcus Aurelius and Lucius Verus in A.D. 161, when Marcus took the name Antoninus and gave his original name Verus to Lucius. It could be that Geta's name, originally Publius, was changed to Lucius to avoid any confusion with the Emperor's brother P. Septimius Geta. Geta the elder remained in the background after his Dacian command. It is remarkable that the inscription on the base of a statue set up to him at Lepcis does not so much as mention his relationship to Septimius. Another inscription apparently in his honour, from Ancona where he had once served as *curator*, calls him *cognatus* of Septimius and *avunculus* of Antoninus and the younger Geta. *Cognatus* means 'relation by marriage' and *avunculus* means 'maternal uncle'. It may be that the people of Ancona – and indeed everyone else – were forbidden to call Geta the brother and paternal uncle (*patruus*), of the Emperors. The inaccurate description at Ancona may be the result of an evasion by people determined somehow to indicate that a man linked to their city was a kinsman of the imperial family. However this may be, in 204 the elder Geta died. On his deathbed, no longer restrained by his fear of Plautianus, he revealed all the facts about him to his brother. Septimius set up a statue to him in the Forum. And his attitude to Plautianus began to change. He stripped him of much of his power.[1]

The urban *plebs*, which had hardly had a chance to observe Plautianus during the years when he was building up his power, had soon commented on the Prefect's extraordinary preeminence. At the Circus on one occasion, Dio records, there was a shout: 'Why do you tremble? Why are you pale? You possess more than the Three!' 'Plautianus', says Dio, 'was in fact always pale and trembling because of his hopes and fears.' Quietly at work on gathering material for his projected history, Dio was much stirred by an event that he took to be an omen of impending change at the highest level. There was an eruption of Mount Vesuvius. The sound of the blast could be heard at Capua over twenty miles away, where Dio was living at the time on his estate.[2]

The marriage of Antoninus and Plautilla was not a success. In spite

---

[1] Cf. App. 1. – 'on his deathbed': Dio 76.2.4.
[2] Dio 76.2.1–3.

of this, some have deduced that Plautilla may have borne a child in 204. But the evidence thought to refer to such an event may indicate no more than the pious hopes of Septimius and the regime. The language of Cassius Dio allows one to doubt whether the marriage was ever consummated. As the bridegroom was only fourteen at the time of the ceremony, this would not have been surprising, especially as the youth loathed his wife and her father.[1]

Cassius Dio's account of the denouement of this unhappy affair has been preserved in some detail. In January 205 Antoninus felt confident enough to try a bold stroke. He persuaded the imperial freedman Euodus, who as his *educator* had supervised his early boyhood, to enlist the services of three centurions. The plan was carried out without a flaw. On 22 January, while the imperial family was about to begin dinner, after the *ludi Palatini*, the three centurions presented themselves to Septimius. They informed him that they and seven others had been ordered by Plautianus to kill both Emperors, and read out a letter which appeared to confirm their story. Septimius believed them, not least because of the dream he had had the previous night that Albinus was alive and plotting against him. He immediately summoned Plautianus. When the Prefect arrived at the palace, his followers were not permitted to go in with him – as had once been the case with Septimius at Tyana, as Dio notes. He was alarmed at this, but could not withdraw. When he entered Septimius spoke to him in a mild tone, but reproachfully, merely asking him why he wanted to kill them. He intended to give him the chance of making his defence. Antoninus could not endure the suspense. As Plautianus began to express his innocence in tones of amazement, he rushed up, seized the Prefect's sword and struck him with his fist. He wanted to kill him with his own hands, but Septimius restrained him. Antoninus then ordered one of the attendants to do the deed.

Someone plucked some hairs from Plautianus's beard and took them to Julia and Plautilla, who were together in another room and had not

---

[1] Dio 76.2.5, cf. Herodian 3.10.8 who explicitly states that Antoninus refused to sleep with Plautilla (or even eat with her). This makes the theory of J. GAGÉ that Plautilla produced a child, based mainly on a fragment of the Saecular Games inscription (J. B. PIGHI p. 142: I 21–22) and on coins (cf. *BMC* p. cliv), somewhat implausible.

known what was happening. 'Look at your Plautianus,' the man said. Julia was delighted, Plautilla, naturally, griefstricken. The body was flung out into the street, and only later buried at Septimius's orders.

The Senate was summoned to a special sitting. Septimius did not accuse his fallen favourite. He merely lamented the weakness of human nature. The honours given to the Prefect had been excessive. He blamed himself for loving and honouring the man so much. The three centurions were called in to testify, after some Senators whom Septimius did not fully trust had been removed from the *curia*. Many who had enjoyed Plautianus's friendship were now endangered. Some were put to death. One of his satellites, a procurator of Mauretanian origin, Opellius Macrinus, was saved by the intercession of Fabius Cilo. Septimius restrained the Senate from voting a decree in praise of Euhodus. It would be shameful, he told them, for an imperial freedman to be mentioned in a decree of the Senate in this way. The senators, many of whom must have been in a state of panic, chanted out Septimius's praises, even shouting, 'Everyone does everything well because you rule well.' Plautilla, presumably after being divorced – although this is nowhere stated – was banished to the island of Lipara with her brother. The names of Plautianus and his family were sedulously erased from all public monuments and his statues defaced. The immensity of his wealth, now confiscated, required the appointment of a special procurator *ad bona Plautiani* to administer it.[1]

At the meeting of the Senate, or soon afterwards, a detailed account of the 'plot' against the Emperors by Plautianus must have been circulated. Herodian shows that he for one swallowed it hook, line and sinker, although some of the details in his account are so implausible as to have been the product of his imagination rather than imperial propaganda. According to this version, Plautianus was unable to endure

[1] Dio 76.3.1 – 6.3. – Macrinus: 78.11.2. – procurator: *CP* no. 257. – Q. Anicius Faustus may conceivably have been one of those who suffered because of closeness to Plautianus: Septimius refused to let him ballot for the proconsulships when his turn came up, and it was not until Macrinus, specifically recorded as an ex-creature of the Prefect by Dio, became Emperor, that Faustus got his turn – an extra-long one. He had had an unusually long term as governor of Numidia, and was then legate of Upper Moesia, where his successor Marius Perpetuus probably arrived in 205; cf. App. III.

some diminution in his authority (caused in fact by the dying revelations of Septimius's brother, about which Herodian is silent). He determined to murder the Emperors. One evening, after everyone had gone to bed, he summoned a tribune, and with the promise of succeeding to the Praetorian Prefecture persuaded him to carry out the deed. The tribune asked to have the order in writing. When he got to the palace, he realised that he could not kill both Septimius and Antoninus, as they slept in different parts of the palace. He summoned the guards, asked to be taken to Septimius and confessed the story, showing the written instructions to prove it. Septimius did not believe him and summoned Antoninus, whom he suspected of concocting the affair. Antoninus swore he knew nothing about it. The tribune insisted on the truth of his story and asked to be allowed to send Plautianus the message that he had done the deed. Plautianus came, believing that the Empire was in his hands. The tribune saluted him as Emperor, and Septimius and Antoninus emerged to confront him. Plautianus replied to Septimius's reproaches with reminders of his past services – no reference to the incriminating written orders – and Septimius was beginning to believe him when the Prefect's robe fell aside, revealing his breastplate. This convinced Septimius that he was guilty and Antoninus then gave the tribune and other Praetorians the order to kill him.

The name of the tribune in this version is Saturninus, the same as that of one of the centurions in Cassius Dio's account. Herodian says the man was a Syrian – and this detail might be accurate. He might have been a protégé of Julia Domna. Equally, Saturninus may have been promoted to tribune as a reward for his services on this occasion. This may have confused Herodian. Perhaps the official version put out to save the credit of Antoninus did allege that Plautianus tried to use a tribune and was betrayed by him. In that case Herodian simply made the mistake of giving the tribune the name of one of the centurions actually involved. Dio and Herodian differ also on numerous details, for example, the time at which the affair took place. Dio clearly states that it was just before dinner, which would normally be at about 3 p.m. at that time of year. Herodian makes it happen after everyone was in bed and asleep.[1]

[1] Herodian 3.11.1 – 12.12, demolished by E. HOHL (1956b).

Dio, who was present at the special meeting of the Senate that followed Plautianus's death, must once again be preferred to Herodian. Yet Herodian was certainly in Rome at the time, and some aspects of his *History*, since it is preserved in full, supplement Dio's truncated text. Herodian is good at external description. He had clearly seen Plautianus, and his picture of the Prefect at the height of his power conveys a vivid impression that is worth quoting. 'He alone had the outward appearance of all-powerful authority. When he went out in public he was an object to fear. No one would approach him, and even those who came upon him by chance turned aside. The guards who preceded him did not allow anyone to stand near him or even look at him. They ordered people to step out of his path and keep their eyes fixed on the ground.'

There had never been a man like Plautianus among the ministers of the Caesars. Even Sejanus had not reached the same heights. Besides, Sejanus had built up his power when Tiberius let the reins of government slip out of his hands. Plautianus had been constantly at the side of Septimius. This was indeed the source of his strength. Alone among Septimius's generals and ministers he had been continuously with him since 193. But the hold that Plautianus had over Septimius up till the last minutes of his life may have had its origin in the Lepcis Magna of their youth. The truth will never be known.[1]

Little is recorded about the three years that followed the fall of Plautianus. During his reign Septimius did much to improve the appearance of the City of Rome, but most of his work had probably been done before the year 205. The Forum of Peace, destroyed at the end of Commodus's reign, was restored and a new version of the marble plan of the city, the *forma urbis*, was attached to the outside wall of its library. The Pantheon was restored in 202. The arch in the Forum has already been mentioned. Another striking arch in honour of Septimius and his family was erected in 204 by the *argentarii*, to form a monu-

---

[1] Herodian 3.11.2–3. – 'may have had its origin', etc: cf. p. 62, above. – Plautianus's power is amply documented by inscriptions, even though on most his names have been erased. He was made a patrician, pontifex (and XVvir), was *comes per omnes expeditiones* of the Emperors. Dio 75.15.1–2a says that Septimius's own position was inferior to that of Plautianus and that 'someone actually dared to write to him as a fourth Caesar'. Cf. *PIR*² F 554 and App. I, no. 8.

mental new entrance to the Forum Boarium. No trace now survives of a striking new building erected in 203, at the corner of the Palatine that faced the *via Appia*, the Septizodium. Nearly one hundred feet high and more than three hundred feet long, it resembled a *nymphaeum*, or theatrical *scaenae frons* and perhaps contained statues of the seven planetary gods, Saturn, Jupiter, Mars, the Sun, Venus, Mercury and the Moon. The central statue of the Sun, was quite probably depicted in the likeness of Septimius himself – looking south towards Africa, and welcoming travellers coming from Africa. The symbolism behind this great monument can only be guessed at. In the palace itself, Septimius also undertook rebuilding. New *thermae* were constructed and the front of the palace facing the Circus Maximus was extensively altered. Cassius Dio gives an interesting account of the interior decoration of part of the palace: the Emperor had 'the ceilings of the rooms where he heard lawsuits painted with the stars under which he had been born'. They were visible to everyone – 'except that portion of the sky which "observed the hour", as they call it, when he first saw the light of day'. This vital section was painted in different ways in two different rooms. Septimius did not want too much [to be] known about what the stars had ordained for him.[1]

The murder of Plautianus made necessary the appointment of a new Praetorian Prefect. Septimius now reverted to previous practice by giving command of the Guard to a pair of Prefects. The men chosen were Q. Maecius Laetus, who had been Prefect of Egypt from 200–203, and Aemilius Papinianus. Maecius Laetus was the senior. Little is

[1] Cf. the convenient list of buildings by H. W. BENARIO (1958a). – For the Arch of the *Argentarii* cf. M. PALLOTTINO. But his interpretation – that the reliefs in some way celebrate the Saecular Games, elaborated subsequently by others (cf. A. M. McCANN p. 73 with references), is questioned by G. CHARLES-PICARD (1962) who, rightly in my view, draws parallels with provincial reliefs and concludes that the imperial family is shown as 'bourgeois', and not as 'divine beings'. Septizodium: it is now known from the *Forma Urbis* that this, not Septizonium, was the official name, cf. A. M. McCANN p. 52, with references. I have not been able to consult the article she cites in n. 59, by N. Neuerburg in *Mem. Nap.* 5 (1965). But even if the name Septizodium, unlike Septizonium, has no connection with *septem*, seven, in the strict etymological sense, I feel sure that play was made with this; cf. the observations of J. GUEY (1946), written without knowledge of the new fragment of the *Forma Urbis*. – Dio 76.11.1, cf. A. R. BIRLEY, *HAC* p. 65f.

known of him, except that he enjoyed favour with Antoninus throughout the next ten years, which could be said of very few. He no doubt
had considerable military experience. Papinian was not a military man
at all, but a jurist. His experience went right back to the reign of
Marcus Aurelius, when he had been a legal adviser to the Praetorian
Prefects of the day. More recently, he had been serving in an important
legal position as *a libellis*. The Augustan History states that he was a
great friend of Septimius, 'and, as some record, related to him by
marriage, through his second wife'. The context does not make it
certain whether the second wife was that of Papinian himself or of
Septimius. But it would seem more probable that it refers to Julia
Domna. In that case, Papinian must have been a Syrian.[1]

Students of Roman law from the time of Justinian onwards have
concurred in rating Papinian highest among all its great classical ex-
ponents. This was indeed a great age of jurisprudence. A younger
contemporary of Papinian was Domitius Ulpianus, also a Syrian, from
Tyre. The third great name among the jurists, Julius Paulus, may also
have come from the east. What these jurists and their colleagues may
have lacked in elegance of style or clarity in comparison with their
predecessors of the previous generation, like Salvius Julianus, they
more than made up for by their voluminous output. During the
Severan age these men expounded and distilled an enormous quantity
of earlier material to produce the basis of the Roman Law codified by
the Emperor Justinian.[2]

Septimius himself took a keen interest in the administration of
justice. Cassius Dio, who as a member of the Emperor's *consilium*
could speak as an eye-witness, records with approval his patience in
court: 'He allowed the litigants plenty of time and he gave us, his
advisors, full liberty to speak.' Apparently he was particularly strict in
enforcing the law against adultery, to which he added. Dio says that
during his own consulship he happened to notice that there were as
many as three thousand cases pending. One piquant case is preserved

[1] App. III.

[2] The study by A. M. HONORÉ has some value; but many of his detailed
conclusions are invalidated by his uncritical acceptance of bogus passage in the
HA, e.g. on the careers of the three great jurists, cf. a forthcoming study by Sir R.
Syme.

in the *Digest*. A Senator named Claudius Gorgus accused his wife of adultery. He was then discovered to have taken her back. Septimius did not wait for a prosecution, and convicted the man of procuring. The *Digest* and other legal compilations preserved numerous decisions of his, covering the whole range of private and public law. They deal with the rights of women, minors and slaves, the obligations of *curatores* and *tutores*, or guardians, with testamentary law, with property disputes, and so on.

No attempt can be made here to deal with the complicated legislative and juridical activity of the reign. Let it suffice to say that the fourth-century historian Aurelius Victor called Septimius *conditor legum longe aequabilium*, 'the establisher of thoroughly equitable laws'. It was during his reign that the principle finally became openly admitted, that 'the Emperor is not bound by the laws' (*princeps legibus solutus est*). But at the same time, he and Antoninus in a joint pronouncement declared that 'Although we are not bound by the laws, nevertheless we live in accordance with them'.[1]

As far as the vast majority of the inhabitants of the Empire were concerned, the doctrine held good. The Senate, unfortunately, was still too much feared as a source of possible danger to be treated in this way. The murder of Plautianus did not bring to an end the executions of senators. Dio speaks of 'many being put to death, *some of them* after they had been formally arraigned before him, had made their defence, and had been convicted'. A number of instances are preserved in the excerpts from his *History*. Plautius Quintillus was the most eminent victim. A nephew of Lucius Verus and son-in-law of Marcus Aurelius, his only recorded political action had been in May 193. He had intervened forcefully against Didius Julianus's proposal that the Senate and Vestal Virgins should meet Septimius's advancing army as suppliants. He was now 'at the gates of old age, living on his country estate,

---

[1] A. M. HONORÉ p. 163 regrettably revives the mistaken idea that Septimius had been a pupil of Cervidius Scaevola, based on *HA Carac.* 83.3, shown by Mommsen, and then again by E. HOHL (1913) pp. 273ff. to be a 13th-century interpolation. – Dio 76.16.4 17.1. Cf. F. MILLAR (1964) p. 204, P. GARNSEY p. 57 (who thinks Dio may have tried some cases as consul). – Gorgus: *Digest* 48.5.2.6, cf. *PIR²* C 881. – Victor *de Caes.* 20.23. – 'principle': *Digest* 1.3.31. – 'pronouncement': *Inst.* 2.17.8.

interfering in nothing and doing nothing wrong'. Nonetheless he was informed against, and forced to suicide. He called for his funeral shroud, which had been made for him long before. It was by now tattered with age. ' "What is this?", he said, "we are late!" ' Preparing to die, 'he burned incense, and said: "I make the same prayer that Servianus made for Hadrian" ' – that is, that the Emperor should wish to die, but be unable to.

The other case Dio records is that of the proconsul of Asia, Apronianus. The man was condemned *in absentia*, while in Asia. The basis of the charge was the story that his nurse had once dreamed he would become Emperor. It was alleged that he had used magic to bring this about. A really remarkable scene occurred during the trial. Under torture, a witness had been asked who had told the story about the dream, and to whom. Among other things, the witness said that he had seen 'a certain bald-headed senator peeping in'. When the report, prepared by the Emperor himself, was read out, the senators were horrified. No name had been put down by Septimius, and everyone, even the ones who were only slightly bald and those who had never visited Apronianus's house, was frightened. No one could remain calm except those with plenty of hair. Dio gives a vivid picture of the humiliating and absurd position the senators were placed in.

> We all looked round at the men who were bald, and murmurs spread, 'It's So-and-So' – 'No, it's So-and-So'. I will not disguise what happened to me, ridiculous though it is. I was so taken aback that I actually felt the hair on my head, with my hand. A good many others found themselves doing likewise. We took good care to stare at those who were more or less bald, feeling that this would divert the danger from ourselves on to them.

Then evidence was read out that identified the bald senator as a certain Baebius Marcellinus. He stood up, came forward and said: ' "The man will of course recognise me, if he has seen me." ' The informer was brought in and gazed around for some while. Then someone – Dio does not say who it was – gave an almost imperceptible nod towards Marcellinus, and the informer identified him. He was led out straight away, said goodbye to his four children in the Forum, and was executed – before Septimius had even learned of his condemnation. Dio does add that Pollienus Sebennus, nephew of Auspex, who had laid the charge that caused Marcellinus's death, was later severely punished, although for a different offence – he only escaped with his life through the intervention of his uncle.[1]

Septimius' behaviour in January 205, and during the trials that followed, was hardly characteristic of the calm and ordered routine he followed in his Italian years. According to Dio he was always up and busy before dawn, and then would take a walk, on which affairs of state would be discussed. Then he would hold court, 'unless there were some great festival'. Dio's description of his patient and fair conduct of cases has already been quoted. At noon he would adjourn for a ride, 'as far as his health permitted, and then would exercise in a gymnasium and take a bath'. This would be followed by a substantial meal, taken alone or with his sons, and a siesta. After more official business, he would once again take a *passeggiata*, walking about and conversing in both Greek and Latin. Towards evening he would bathe again and then dine with his intimates. 'He very rarely invited guests to dinner, and only on days when it was unavoidable did he arrange expensive banquets.' It must have been one of those rare banquets that was witnessed and described by the writer Sammonicus Serenus. A sturgeon was brought in by servants [who were] garlanded with flowers, moving in time to the music of flutes.[2]

It was perhaps during this period that Septimius composed his autobiography. That he had not forgotten his struggle for power is proved by his dream about Albinus the night before the murder of Plautianus. The work dwelt on dreams and other portents that had told him of his destiny. And it vilified Albinus and Niger. There are no direct quotations preserved from it. It is not even known whether it was in Latin or Greek. If it was in Greek, Aelius Antipater may have helped him with it. If in Latin, perhaps the African lawyer Messius Saturninus gave some assistance. Saturninus was the holder of the new post *a declamationibus* (and had a very high salary). In this capacity he

---

[1] Dio 76.7.3–9.4.
[2] Dio 76.17.1–3. – Sammonicus: quoted by Macrobius, *Saturnalia* 3.17.4.

(a)

b)

13a Aerial view of Carpow, looking
    north: the confluence of the Earn
    and the Tay shows at the left. The
    north rampart of the fortress is
    marked approximately by the line
    of trees.

13b Carpow from the east; the fortress
    lies on the low hill in the middle
    distance, with the Tay estuary (ar-
    rowed) in the background.

13c Lead sealing from South Shields,
    showing the heads of Severus and
    his sons.

(c)

14a Coins of Plautilla (A.D. 202–205, left) and Caracalla (A.D. 202) found at Carpow, which first confirmed the Severan date of the fortress: cf. R.E. Birley (1962) p. 201.

14b Roofing tiles of *leg(io) VI Vic(trix) B(ritannica) p(ia) f(fidelis)* from Carpow: the upper stamp is on an *imbrex*, the lower on a *tegula*.

14c The Victoria Brit(annica) proclaimed on a gold coin of A.D. 211 (*BMC* Sev., Car. Get. no. 60)

15   Head of the emperor found in Rome (now in Museo Nuovo):
cf. A.M. McCann p. 128. (no. 4)

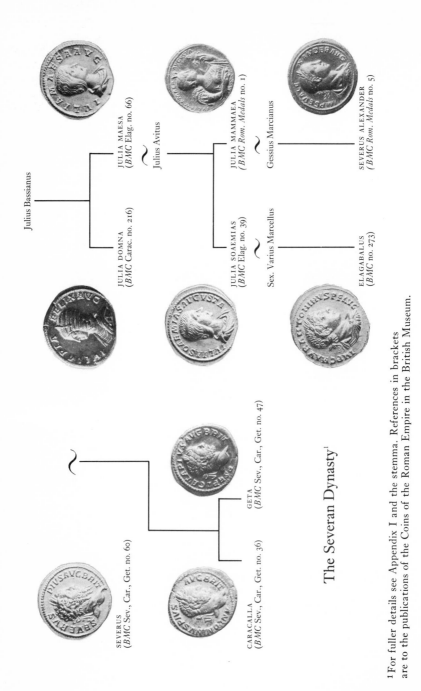

Julius Bassianus

JULIA DOMNA
(*BMC* Carac. no. 216)

JULIA MAESA
(*BMC* Elag. no. 66)

~ Julius Avitus

JULIA SOAEMIAS
(*BMC* Elag. no. 39)

Sex. Varius Marcellus

JULIA MAMMAEA
(*BMC Rom. Medals* no. 1)

Gessius Marcianus

ELAGABALUS
(*BMC* no. 273)

SEVERUS ALEXANDER
(*BMC Rom. Medals* no. 5)

SEVERUS
(*BMC* Sev., Car., Get. no. 60)

CARACALLA
(*BMC* Sev., Car., Get. no. 36)

GETA
(*BMC* Sev., Car., Get. no. 47)

The Severan Dynasty[1]

[1] For fuller details see Appendix I and the stemma. References in brackets
are to the publications of the Coins of the Roman Empire in the British Museum.

clearly drafted Septimius's speeches for delivery in court. Ulpian, quoting a letter of Septimius (and Antoninus) which gives the imperial decision (in a case involving acceptance of presents by a proconsul), describes it as 'very elegant'. A Greek proverb is quoted and the Emperor's judgement is pithily phrased.[1]

There were certainly plenty of literary figures at the court. For one thing, the Empress liked the society of such men. She had turned to this for consolation when Plautianus ousted her from her position of influence with her husband. That had been during their travels in the east. There is no reason to believe that she sent the Sophists packing when Plautianus went. The intellectual curiosity was genuine. Philostratus, who was with the Empress and her son in the east after Septimius's death, speaks of 'the circle around Julia'. The coherence of this 'circle' has perhaps been exaggerated. But certainly Philostratus himself was encouraged by Julia Domna to compose his curious *Life of Apollonius*, the wonder-worker of Tyana. And Philostratus calls her 'the philosopher'. Other members of the circle may be found. It would be uncritical, however, to assume that all the pagan writers of the age, from Diogenes Laërtius to Alexander of Aphrodisias, must have at some time danced attendance at the *salon* of the philosophical Empress. 'Philosophy' is in any case a courtesy term. To judge from the *Life of Apollonius* it meant a combination of religious superstition with somewhat pretentious erudition.[2]

Julia Domna had of course another reputation, in the fourth century at least, for promiscuity. Perhaps she did have lovers. Dio could hardly

---

[1] Autobiography: cf. p. 13, above. – Saturninus: *CP* no. 231; App. III. – Ulpian: *Digest* 1.6.3.

[2] Philostratus *v. soph.* 2.30; *v. Apoll.* 1.3. *Ep.* 73 is a feeble rhetorical 'appeal' to Julia to honour sophists. On Philostratus, *cf. RE* 20 (1941) 136; also Supp. 8 (1956) 719ff., on the Second Sophistic. I much regret that I have been unable to consult the forthcoming work by Professor Bowersock (cited by T. D. BARNES [1968c] p. 595 n. 3). See now G. W. BOWERSOCK (1969) pp. 101ff. – Cf. also Dio 75.15.7, 77.18.3. There is no other real evidence. But many, e.g. M. PLATNAUER pp. 144f. (and, even more excessive, A. DE CEULENEER p. 202f.) list all known literary figures as if they must have been dancing attendance on the Empress constantly. – Other aspects of Julia Domna also attract speculation, notably her religious position. The study by I. MUNDLE has served to correct exaggerated statements. However, cf. A. M. McCANN pp. 56ff.

have dwelt on this and Herodian was not interested in the subject of sex. Hence the only explicit accusation comes from much later times. But it is plausible enough, and it must be accepted as quite likely that the intellectual stimulus of Sophists may not have been enough to console her for the treatment she got from Plautianus.[1]

During these years in Italy Antoninus and Geta reacted to the removal of Plautianus as if they had been released from the charge of an oppressive schoolmaster. The two youths 'treated women shamefully, abused boys, embezzled money, hobnobbed with gladiators and charioteers'. In the meantime what may have begun as harmless rivalry ended as mutual hatred – which the coin issues advertising their 'harmony' might have led one to suspect, even if Dio did not explicitly report it. During a fiercely contested chariot race between them, Antoninus fell and broke his leg.[2]

In the meantime Italy was being subjected to a humiliating demonstration of how precarious was the recently re-established security and peace. A brigand named Bulla eluded capture again and again, and for two years 'ravaged Italy in the presence of the Emperors and a great host of soldiers'. Perhaps as a pun on the similarity of his name to the great Sulla, he also called himself Felix. 'He had a great many runaway imperial freedmen with him', Dio notes. 'Some of them had been paid very badly – and some had received no pay at all.' Dio had earlier mentioned that Septimius's strictness with his freedmen had won him praise – presumably from the senators. However, the ones who had joined Bulla would not have come from the Palace staff – they would be lowly employees on the imperial estates in Italy, now vastly increased in size by confiscation. Another element from which Bulla may have found support, although Dio does not specifically mention it, would be

[1] Victor *de Caes.* 21.3 = *HA Sev.* 18.8 calls her *famosa adulteriis* and accuses her of conspiracy. The latter charge at least was surely invented by Plautianus (if not by Victor or his source). Herodian 4.9.3 says the Alexandrians called her 'Jocasta': but there is no explicit mention of her alleged incest with Caracalla until Eutropius 8.20, etc., cf. *PIR*[2] J 663 (p. 315) for references. These late sources also mistakenly call Caracalla her stepson.

[2] Dio 76.7.1–3. – Antoninus performed at least one public duty at this time: in 206 he delivered a notable speech in the Senate on his father's behalf (*Digest* 24.1.32): the subject, the legal position of gifts between husbands and wives, was one in which he no longer had any direct interest.

the five thousand Praetorian Guardsmen discharged in June 193. But the men under Bulla's command did not number more than six hundred. The man was eventually captured through a trick.[1]

Until the year 204, Septimius had not spent more than twelve months at a time in Italy for forty years. Apart from the Saecular Games, he cannot have found his life there in the years 204-207 very much to his taste. The restlessness and impatience that marked his character were certainly exacerbated by the behaviour of his sons. The murder of Plautianus, the political trials, the frustrating Bulla Felix, must have made him yearn to be back with the armies. He was now over sixty. He was certainly convinced that he had not long to live, and certainly he would have wanted to end his life on a triumphant note. When the chance came, in 207, he took it eagerly.[2]

[1] Dio 76.10.1–7, cf. 6.2 (freedmen) and 74.2.4–6 (on the Guard: cf. E. BIRLEY. *Ep. Stud* p. 64f.). For the background cf. R. MACMULLEN (1963) pp. 50ff., ID. (1967) pp. 255ff.

[2] 'not long to live': Dio 76.11.1–2.

XVI

EXPEDITIO FELICISSIMA BRITTANNICA

News came from Britain in the year 207 that gave Septimius the way out of his dilemma. According to Herodian, 'the governor sent despatches, saying that the barbarians there were rebelling, overrunning the country, taking away booty and creating great destruction. There was therefore need of reinforcements to defend the threatened area, or else of an imperial visit.' For once, Herodian may be correct. Although the wording of the governor's despatches may be the product of his imagination, there is no reason to doubt that the military situation in Britain was troublesome. Proof of this is offered by the identity of the governor himself, L. Alfenus Senecio, not named by Herodian but recorded on seven or eight inscriptions in northern England. A Numidian from Cuicul (Djemila), Senecio's previous career is totally unknown except for one post: in the year 200 he had been governor of Syria Coele. Even after the division of Syria, the consular Syrian province was undoubtedly among the highest in prestige and importance, if not still highest of all. Besides, that he was governor while Septimius was in the east is perhaps an added indication of the esteem in which he was held. The fact that a man of this eminence was sent to Britain in or soon after 205 demonstrates the seriousness of the situation there.[1]

The real question that must have arisen in the year 207 was a matter of policy: where should the line of Rome's northernmost frontier be drawn? To understand the decision that Septimius had to make one

---

[1] Herodian 1.14.1. – 'threatened area': I. A. RICHMOND (1963) p. 57: Alfenus Senecio's 'report summing up the situation was realistic enough. "The need was either more troops to reinforce the frontier area, or an Imperial expedition." ' – Senecio: App. 1, cf. p. 171, above.

must look more deeply into the history of the British province. The invasion by Claudius had been undertaken as a major break with the Augustan policy. Augustus may have toyed with the idea of taking up the challenge that Caesar's two brief expeditions had left him. But he soon found compelling arguments for abandoning the idea. The officially stated reason was undoubtedly that to conquer and hold the island would represent an excessive drain on Roman resources. Events seemed to have proved him right. Claudius's main motive for the conquest lay in his desperate need for prestige. The size of his expeditionary force, four legions and numerous auxiliary regiments, amounted to a total of at least fifty thousand men. His advisers may have hoped that before long these numbers could be reduced, even if there was never any serious thought of limiting the standing garrison to the one legion that Augustan strategists had contemplated. But the pace of the subjugation of the island slowed down. The first reduction in the garrison did not come until the 80s, when Agricola's long series of campaigns had given Rome the impression that the whole of Britain had submitted. That impression was soon shown to be false. By the end of the first century Roman forces had almost completely pulled back to the Tyne-Solway line. Finally, in 122, Hadrian decided to give up any idea of further conquest, and to concentrate on the Romanisation of what territory could be economically held. The Wall and its related works formed the most elaborate frontier in the whole Empire.[1]

Yet no sooner was Hadrian dead in 138 than there was a reversion to the old expansionist policy. The Numidian general Lollius Urbicus, operating in the kind of hill-country that must have reminded him of his homeland, pushed forward to the shorter Forth-Clyde line. The thinking behind this change of policy is somewhat baffling. Either

---

[1] 'Augustan policy': cf. esp. C. E. STEVENS (1951). – 'Augustan strategists': Strabo 2.115f., 4. 200f., cf. A. J. GRAHAM p. 105 and n. 171. – On the Claudian invasion cf. S. S. FRERE pp. 58ff. – Agricola and after: I adopt the general view of E. BIRLEY (1953a) pp. 10ff., 20ff. Cf. also Frere pp. 119ff. J. E. BOGAERS and H. NESSELHAUF (1967) have shown that the Ninth Legion was not destroyed in Britain but transferred to Germany (by Trajan in Nesselhauf's view: in other words that Emperor reduced the garrison to two legions). Cf. now E. BIRLEY (1971). – '122': on the Wall cf. esp. E. BIRLEY (1961) with detailed bibliography. C. E. STEVENS (1966) postulates that the work began in 120, which is attractive.

Hadrian's Wall had failed, and it was decided that annexation was the only means of controlling the Scottish Lowlands – many of whose fighting men were now conscripted into the Roman army and shipped over to man the frontier in Germany – or it could be that Hadrian's Wall had appeared so successful that it was intended to repeat the experiment further north – perhaps with the ultimate intention of doing away with the need for a frontier altogether, the policy of Julius Agricola.[1]

But this policy was a costly failure. After less than fifteen years the new Antonine line had to be abandoned, and Hadrian's Wall once more became the frontier. Some have argued that the Antonine Wall was shortly thereafter recommissioned, and that the two Walls were held simultaneously. But the positive evidence for this view is slight and inconclusive and other evidence points in the opposite direction. The overall military situation in the 160s and 170s makes it inconceivable that the garrison of Britain could have been stretched so far. At the beginning of the reign of Commodus there was a military disaster to Rome in the north of the province. It seems that this time, when revenge had been exacted, the frontier was moved forward again. But when Albinus took the army of Britain away to Gaul in 196 the promises that he apparently exacted from the northern tribes were not honoured. They ravaged both Walls. It was no doubt the untamed Brigantians from the Pennines who took the opportunity of extending the damage as far south as York.[2]

[1] Urbicus: A. R. BIRLEY (1967b) p. 71f. – 'baffling': cf. J. P. GILLAM (1958) p. 66f. for a neat exposition of the various motives behind this. – 'shipped over': cf. now H. SCHÖNBERGER p. 167, who is cautious over the matter. – S. S. FRERE pp. 141ff. describes the new Wall.

[2] S. S. FRERE pp. 151ff. follows K. A. STEER (1964) in the view that both Walls were held simultaneously c. 158–181. I cannot accept Steer's arguments, cf. (briefly) A. R. BIRLEY, *Seventh Congress*. It is possible that the despatch of 5,500 Sarmatian troops to Britain was intended by M. Aurelius to prepare the ground for a new advance, as B. R. HARTLEY p. 14f. suggests; and that it was in carrying out this forward policy that the governor was killed c. 181 (cf. p. 120 above), a view I have developed elsewhere, cf. A. R. BIRLEY (1971), where it is also argued that the 'Wall' crossed by invaders then (Dio 72.8) was the Antonine Wall; that this Wall was reoccupied by Ulpius Marcellus c. 184 or soon after; and that in 196–7 both Walls were attacked and their installations damaged. The evidence of the samian makes this view rather difficult, as Mr Hartley kindly informs me; but it still seems

Virius Lupus was sent to Britain straight after Lugdunum. He was the logical choice, as governor of Lower Germany, even if his defeat at Albinus's hands the previous year suggests that he was no military genius. He had much on his hands. Not least, perhaps, the problems of administrative reorganisation, complicated by the division of the province into two. He himself, it would seem, was assigned to Britannia Inferior, comprising much of the Highland Zone and the whole frontier, with two legions, VI Victrix and XX Valeria Victrix. The legions must have needed massive drafts to bring them up to strength after the battle – and carefully chosen new officers at all levels to make sure of their loyalty to their new master. Lupus managed to gain a respite for the province by buying off the invaders, who are named by Dio as the Maeatae. Their territory evidently lay north of the Forth. He was just in time, for the Caledonians of the Highlands had been preparing to join them. Then he began the task of rebuilding, which proceeded slowly. His work is attested by inscriptions at Corbridge, the supply-base just south of Hadrian's Wall, and at two forts in the Pennines. How long Lupus remained in Britain is unknown. In 205 another governor, Valerius Pudens, in that year certainly near the end of his command in Britain, was still having reconstruction done in the Pennines. His successor Alfenus Senecio likewise undertook work there.[1]

But Senecio's presence is also recorded at Corbridge, at three forts on Hadrian's Wall, and north of the Wall at the outpost fort of Risingham. The Wall forts where his activity is known are widely spread out, and other building work on the line of the Wall is datable to the time of his governorship. What is unusual about two of the inscriptions which

---

to me the most satisfactory. – York: the latest evidence suggests that the old view is right (*contra* Frere p. 169, etc.), cf. *JRS* 58 (1968) p. 182: the *principia* 'was severely burnt in the late second century'.

[1] Lupus: App. III. – 'division of the province': I follow J. C. MANN (1967); cf. also A. R. BIRLEY (1971). – Maeatae: S. S. FRERE's statement (p. 164) that this people lived in southern Scotland is based on his identification of the 'Wall' in Dio 76.12.1 as Hadrian's. But even if that were right, other evidence points firmly to Strathmore and Strathearn, cf. I. A. RICHMOND (1963) p. 57, K. A. STEER (1958) p. 92. – Pudens and Senecio: App. 3. Cf. also *JRS* 59 (1969) p. 246 (an improved reading of *AE* 1963, 281, Bainbridge, by G. Alföldy and deductions therefrom).

name Senecio is that they also attest the involvement of the procurator of Britain in supervising the work. The procurator, Oclatinius Adventus, was not one of the administrators with financial expertise who would normally hold this post. He had risen from the ranks to be an officer in the secret police (*frumentarii*) and then to be the commander of that sinister body of men, before being transferred to procuratorial duties. One might in any case infer from the appointment to Britain of a procurator of this unusual background, that he had been given some special mission. The inscriptions which reveal his activity in the military zone of the province give a clue to its nature. The procurator's headquarters was at London. It looks as if Adventus, chosen as a man of the highest reliability, had been sent to Britain to report on the state of the frontier. He may perhaps have been asked to report on why it had taken so long to restore the northern forts. He may have been asked how the redistribution of garrisons had worked out – the British army had been badly knocked about at the battle of Lugdunum: although the three legions returned to their old bases, the auxiliary units had had to be reassigned. For one thing, no attempt was made to regain the territory north of Hadrian's Wall, except in so far as the outpost forts placed a small part of that area under Roman surveillance. However, it may not have been until Senecio's appointment that a firm decision was taken to make Hadrian's Wall the frontier once again. If the Antonine Wall had been the frontier from 184–196, official reluctance to give up Scotland now would be intelligible. Lupus and Pudens may well have been ordered to move Roman troops back to the Forth-Clyde line, but have found that mandate impossible to fulfil. If Senecio, a governor of exceptional seniority, and Oclatinius Adventus, playing an unusual role, both confirmed that there was no possibility of regaining Scotland, Septimius may, for the moment, have been prepared to order the re-commissioning of Hadrian's Wall. But the renewed outbreak of hostilities once more altered the situation.[1]

[1] Adventus: A. R. BIRLEY (1967b) pp. 78, 86; *CP* no. 247. *RIB* 1234 (Risingham) and 1462 (Chesters) attest his activity. Cf. also J. C. MANN (1967) p. 64 n. 39. – 'Headquarters': J. C. MANN (1961) p. 318. – 'redistribution': E. BIRLEY (1939) esp. pp. 216ff. – The four parallels cited by A. J. GRAHAM p. 98f. to prove that Adventus's activity was not unique are not really cogent: two deal with civil (not military) boundaries, one is an aqueduct inscription, the last a temple dedication. –

Senecio certainly had fighting to do at some time in the years 205–207 – and he had some success. At Benwell on Hadrian's Wall he made a dedication to 'The Emperors' Victory'. It is probably the campaigning of Senecio that is meant in a general statement by Dio: Septimius 'was angered that while he was winning wars in Britain at second hand, in person he was proving the inferior of a brigand in Italy [Bulla Felix].'[1]

He himself had never been to Britain, and one cannot point to any close adviser with British experience either. But this is merely the result of the defects in the sources. Polus Terentianus, once a key ally as governor of Dacia in 193, had commanded II Augusta in the 180s. There is no record of his advice being called on, but it is probable that he was consulted – if still alive – and he may have been asked to join Septimius's staff as *comes*. Julia Domna's kinsman by marriage, Varius Marcellus, had of course been procurator in Britain. But it is probable that he was now dead. Then there was Antius Crescens Calpurnianus, who had once served as *iuridicus* of Britain and then as acting governor in some emergency – perhaps the one early in Commodus' reign when the governor was killed in the north. He was still alive in 204, when he was one of the *quindecimviri* at the Saecular Games, and though he would no doubt have been of an advanced age if he survived until 207–8, his opinion would have been unusually valuable, even if he did not go in person. There were no doubt others who had served in Britain and would have been capable of giving their advice if called on.[2] Yet

---

'a firm decision': there are in fact numerous possible explanations for the delay in reconstructing Hadrian's Wall forts, without abandoning the view that there was destruction in 196–7.

[1] Benwell: *RIB* 1337 (*Victoriae* [*Au*]gg) omitted in error by A. R. BIRLEY (1967b) p. 79. It could of course be as late as 208 or 209, after the Emperors had begun campaigning in person. – Dio 76.10.6. – It may be that, as some now argue, Senecio had a very serious threat to face in or soon after 205; but this presumption, based on Herodian 1.14.1 (quoted p. 244, above) is quite insufficient to prove that there was no destruction in 196–7, but rather *ca*. 205 – followed by immediate reconstruction under Senecio (cf. the comment in the previous note). I refer to this because it seems to have become fashionable to deny the 196–7 destruction – yet the case against it has never been cogently argued (in print, at least). I await it with interest, although a careful and repeated examination of the evidence makes me doubt whether a real case can be made. [Cf. now J. P. GILLAM (1970).]

[2] Terentianus: App. III. – Marcellus: App. I. – Calpurnianus: A. R. BIRLEY (1967b) p. 75f., cf. App. III. – 'Others': especially Lupus and Pudens (App. III).

Septimius very probably had formed a clear idea already of what measures were necessary. It might seem over-speculative to guess that he might have read the *Agricola* and *Histories* of Tacitus. But the governorship of Agricola in Britain was well known to Cassius Dio, and another contemporary, Tertullian, had read Tacitus. It would indeed have been surprising if Septimius's grandfather Severus had not brought back to Lepcis copies of some of the literary productions of his contemporaries. As a pupil of Quintilian, he cannot fail to have revered the greatest orator of his day and he may well have purchased copies of his historical works. About one composition of that era there can scarcely be any doubt: the first Septimius Severus surely had his own copy of Statius's *Silvae*. His family may, it is true, have ignored everything in that modest collection except the *Ode Lyrica ad Septimium Severum* in the fourth book. But there is a chance that Septimius knew the *Laudes Crispini Vetti Bolani filii* in the fifth book. Here he could have read 'how Crispinus's mighty father [i.e. Vettius Bolanus] entered Thule, that sets a limit to the western waves, where Hyperion is ever weary, bearing the commands of Caesar'. Statius asks where the young Crispinus will serve:

> But if the land curbed by your mighty parent receives you . . . what glory will exalt the fields of Caledonia! when some ancient dweller in that savage land shall tell you: "Here did your father dispense justice, from this mound did he address the cavalry . . . these gifts, these weapons did he dedicate to the gods of war . . . this breastplate did he himself put on when battle summoned, this one did he take from the breast of a British king."

(Vettius Bolanus's activity as governor of Britain in the years 69–71 is portrayed less romantically in the pages of Tacitus.) In the eyes of Cassius Dio, Septimius was motivated by the desire for glory in his eastern campaigns. He also had an insatiable curiosity. Who can say that ten years later he may not have been influenced by a line of Statius – *quanta Caledonios attollet gloria campos*?[1]

[1] Agricola: Dio 66.20. – Tertullian: cf. *Apol.* 16, *ad nat.* 1.11, 2.12. – Quintilian: cf. p. 36f., above. – Bolanus: Statius *Silvae* 5.2.54ff., 132ff., esp. 142; contrast Tacitus

This may be mere fanciful speculation. But it is at least worth remembering that his brother Geta's service in Britain in the 160s, as tribune of II Augusta, must have made an impression on him as a young man. During the entire reign of Commodus, Britain and the Roman army of Britain must have attracted a great deal of interest. And he had had only too close a personal experience of that army's fighting prowess at the battle of Lugdunum in 197. Whether or not he had made his final decision before reaching Britain, Cassius Dio states un-ambiguously what that decision was: 'he desired to subdue the whole [of Britain]'. In other words there was to be a return to the Agricolan policy. The frontier problem would be solved for ever – for no artificial frontier would be needed.[1]

Before Septimius could leave Italy, he must have taken steps to ensure that the situation in Rome and the rest of the Empire was well under control. There is in fact evidence that there was some trouble at this time, but its nature is somewhat baffling. Two inscriptions from widely separated points, Ephesus in proconsular Asia and Sicca Veneria in proconsular Africa, refer in very similar language to the defeat of 'insidious plots'. The first of these inscriptions is not precisely dated, the second was set up in 208. Both inscriptions suggest that some insurrection had been defeated. It may be that the activity of one of the legates of the German legions has some bearing on this. At about this time, C. Julius Septimius Castinus (very possibly a kinsman of Septimius), legate of the Bonn legion I Minervia, was commanding a force drawn from all four German legions, 'against defectors and rebels'. Coins issued in the same year honour 'Jupiter the Victorious'. It might be suggested that this refers to Alfenus Senecio's British campaigns. But there is also an inscription from Arrabona in Upper Pannonia, dedicated to the 'Victory of the Emperors and of the legion

---

Agr. 8, 16 (and *Hist.* 2.65, 97; 3.44). But see E. BIRLEY (1953a) pp. 10ff. – 'desire for glory': Dio 75.1.1.

[1] Geta: p. 68f., above; App. 1 no. 30. – Dio 76.13.1 is unambiguous: 'ὁ δ' οὖν Σεουῆρος πᾶσαν αὐτὴν καταστρέψασθαι ἐθελήσας ἐσέβαλεν ἐς τὴν Καληδονίαν. From 76.12.5 it seems clear that αὐτήν refers to ἡ Βρεττανία (but even if it looks forward, referring to Caledonia, it makes little difference. The subjugation of Caledonia would have been a major step towards the conquest of all North Britain.)

I Adiutrix' by the governor Egnatius Victor, which might point to fighting on or near the Danube. It is not impossible that Antoninus had in fact participated in military action in that area. The coinage of 207 certainly accords great prominence to his martial prowess.[1]

The precise nature of the events of 207 outside Britain must remain conjectural. What can be established in part are the arrangements that Septimius made for the administration of the Empire. Examination of the men placed in key commands at this time is revealing. In 208 the experienced Marius Maximus, the future biographer of the Emperors, was governing Syria Coele. It is not known how long he had been there. This area was always important, and one of Maximus's recorded actions as governor was to arrange for the passage of an envoy from the Parthian king to the Emperors. Before the death of Septimius he had been replaced – but not by another senator. The financial procurator seems to have been deputising as governor. The same situation is found in Dacia, where the procurator Herennius Gemellinus is recorded as acting governor. It is impossible to believe that Marius Maximus was dismissed because he was feared as a potential danger, for his brother

[1] Ephesus: D. 430 (*ubivis spes parricidiales insid[iatorum ?sustulerunt]*). – Sicca: D. 429 (*ob conservatam eorum salutem detectis insidiis hostium publicorum*). G. J. MURPHY pp. 38ff. argues that some major insurrection was in progress in 207. But cf. M. HAMMOND (1950) pp. 194ff., who shows the weakness of Murphy's case. The two inscriptions could well refer back to the overthrow of Plautianus, or the executions for 'treason' that followed it (pp. 233ff. above). – Castinus: App. III. The suggestion in *RE* Supp. 11 (1968), 67f., that he was fighting surviving Albinians – near Aquincum – is curious. His mission was surely in the Rhineland. – Jupiter: *BMC* V p. 262. – '*Imperator XII*' is recorded sporadically from 198 onwards, cf. A. A. BOYCE, who plausibly argues that there was uncertainty in that year and thereafter whether or not this title had been assumed. There is no reason to connect its occasional appearance in or soon after 207 with any event in that year. – I Adiutrix: *CIL* III 11082. The 'Victory' might of course have been the Parthian victory of 198, recalled nine years later. (But the suggestion of R. O. FINK p. 140 that the occasion was simply the festival of the Vestalia is hardly convincing, in view of the explicit dedication to *Victoria*.) I. A. RICHMOND (1963) p. 57f. has indeed suggested that Antoninus had been sent ahead to Britain, following Mattingly, *BMC* V p. clx. There is no real evidence. Mattingly also (p. clix) suggests an imperial visit to Africa in 207, an idea that appeals to A. M. McCANN pp. 67, 75ff. (cf. p. 218 n. 1, above). – 'martial prowess': *BMC* V pp. 265ff., 348f. See also J. FITZ (1962) p. 97f., who argues that the Lower Pannonian legion II Adiutrix was absent *ca.* 206–211, perhaps in Britain. Did Antoninus go to the Danube to gather part of the expeditionary army?

Marius Perpetuus was governor of Upper Moesia at the same period. More probably, when Maximus's normal term of office came to an end, he was simply not replaced. Of the other governors about whom comment can safely be made, one should particularly note the Prefect of Egypt, Subatianus Aquila, who held office from at least 206 to 210. Aquila was from the same town in Numidia – Cuicul – as Alfenus Senecio, and Aquila's kinsman Subatianus Proculus was governor of his native Numidia in the years 208–210. These three men clearly enjoyed imperial favour and confidence. Septimius Castinus, who has already been mentioned as a possible kinsman of Septimius, was made governor of Lower Pannonia at about this time.[1]

A single medallion of 207 proclaims the arrival of Septimius in Gaul. It is not impossible that he and his *entourage* left Rome before the start of 208, even though that year was inaugurated once more by a joint consulship of Antoninus and Geta, holding office for the third and second time respectively. Dio notes that Septimius took an immense sum of money with him. He also collected a sizeable expeditionary force to strengthen the British army. This force must have been built round the Praetorian Guard, a large part of which certainly accompanied him, together with one of the Prefects, Papinian. Among those selected to join the military staff were Julia Domna's kinsman Julius Avitus Alexianus, who had just been serving as governor of Raetia, and a widely experienced African senator, Junius Faustinus.[2]

The coins of 208 show Septimius riding off to war. But Herodian notes that 'for most of the journey he was carried in a litter'. He was increasingly troubled by a painful condition in his legs or feet, variously

---

[1] The point is that senators could not be trusted, except in a few cases, to be left in command of large armies when the Emperors were to be in the far west. J. B. Leaning has suggested to me that the rivalry between Antoninus and Geta (p. 242, above, p. 261f. below) made it impossible to agree on governors acceptable to both: this was certainly a major factor when Septimius was in poor health. If – as actually happened – he were to die in Britain, each of his sons would bid for support from the army commanders. Better if these were men of equestrian status for the most part. – The Marii: App. II. Note that there was a change of ruler in Parthia in 207–8: *RE* Supp. 9 (1962) 1852. Aquila, Proculus, Castinus: App. III.

[2] 'medallion': *BMC* V p. clxxvf. Cf. F. GNECCHI p. 73: '*Lo cito con molto riserva*'. – 'money': Dio 76.11.2. – 'expeditionary force': Herodian 3.14.3. – Papinian: Dio 76.11.5. – Alexianus: App. I.; Faustinus: App. III.

described or translated by modern writers as gout or arthritis. But in spite of this, and his age – in 208 he reached 'the grand climacteric', his sixty-third birthday – he 'was more vigorous in mind than any youth'. And he had not lost that remarkable capacity for speed. Once again the rapidity of his arrival disconcerted the enemy. According to Herodian the British tribes at once sued for peace through envoys. But Septimius had no intention of accepting. He wanted to avoid an early return to Rome, and he wanted an actual victory.[1]

Far-reaching plans had been made to supply the expedition. At South Shields on the south side of the Tyne estuary the fort had been completely transformed into a stores-depot, containing twenty-two granaries: the normal accommodation had been demolished to make way for an extra twenty *horrea*. The depot could hold enough corn to supply more than 40,000 men for three months. From South Shields the grain was shipped up the coast to the Forth at Cramond. For the purpose of this shipment, no doubt to avoid diverting the *classis Britannica* from its regular naval duties, detachments – if not the whole fleets – from the Rhine and Danube flotillas were transferred to the command of the Prefect of the British fleet. Meanwhile supplies were also sent forward on land. An inscription from Corbridge on Tyne, an important centre of communications and supply in the Hadrian's Wall zone, records a religious dedication made by an official in charge of the granaries 'at the time of the most successful' – or 'most fortunate' – 'British expedition', *tempore expeditionis felicissi(mae) Brittanic(ae)*. Vast rebuilding schemes had begun at Corbridge, either to create a great new stores complex, or to turn it into a new legionary base.[2]

---

[1] coins: *BMC* V pp. 208ff., 349ff., esp. no. 568, p. 270, no. 854, p. 350. – litter, gout: Herodian 3.14.3. On gout cf. also Dio 76.13.4, *HA Sev.* 23.3, etc. and the comments of F. MILLAR (1964) p. 24 and n. 3 – 'climacteric': A. Gellius, *Noctes Atticae* 15.7.3. (a letter of Augustus). – see now the plan in *TheNinth Pilgrimage of Hadrian's Wall* (1969) p. 3, fig. 1 – 'sudden arrival': Herodian 3.14.5.

[2] S. Shields: – *classis: CP* no. 259. – Corbridge: cf. E. BIRLEY (1959) esp. pp. 12ff.; also M. G. JARRETT (1965), who rightly lays emphasis on the changes of policy regarding the British frontier. His conclusions about York are some-what speculative and – as far as the fortress's fate in 197 is concerned – seem-ingly no longer valid, cf. *JRS* 58 (1968) p. 182, quoted p. 245 n. 2, above. Frere p. 172 is illogical: since the granaries official was clearly there during the expedition, it is hard to see why the evidence from Shields shows that 'the original plan'

To Dio – whose account is in any case pitifully truncated – and even more so to Herodian, North Britain was an almost legendary area, and the narrative they provide is heavily laced with travellers' tales about the inhabitants. The actual campaigning was in any case – inevitably – difficult to describe, for the Caledonians and Maeatae were waging guerilla warfare, avoiding pitched battles. Coins of Septimius struck in 208 show a bridge, with a boat under sail beneath it. A single coin of Antoninus of this year appears to show a bridge of boats. This evidence accords with the statement of Herodian, that 'the army crossed over the rivers and fortifications that marked the limits of the Roman Empire', and with Dio's description of the hardships Septimius experienced in his advance, 'cutting down forests, levelling hills, filling up swamps and bridging rivers.'[1]

The impression given by Dio's fragmentary account and by Herodian's vague narrative is that there were two separate campaigns. Dio seems to indicate that the second campaign only took place because the northern tribes rose again, after submission. It is difficult to be sure of the chronology. All that is certain is that at the end of 209 Septimius and his sons took the title Britannicus.[2]

It is probable that the first campaign in fact began in 208 and lasted into 209. During this first stage Geta was left behind in what Herodian calls 'the section of the province under Roman control', to gain experience of administration. Septimius and Antoninus went with the armies. Dio gives a hair-raising picture of the enemy and of the Roman reverses, a curious compound of fact and myth. Both Maeatae and Caledonians were said to 'inhabit wild and waterless mountains and

---

(supplies assembled at Corbridge for transport north up Dere Street) had been changed. It is quite reasonable to argue that supplies were gathered at both Corbridge and Shields (and no doubt elsewhere) for simultaneous despatch north. Indeed new evidence makes it quite certain that Dere Street was a major supply-route, cf. esp. J. K. ST JOSEPH, 119 and p. 257f. below.

[1] Coins: *BMC* V pp. 269, 353, cf. p. clxxiv; S. S. FRERE pp. 173ff. and plate 4 nos. 8 and 9. – Herodian 3.14.10 (cf. 5–6), Dio 76.13.1.

[2] 'two campaigns': cf. Dio 76.13.4 and 15.1, also Herodian 3.14.9–10 and 15.1. – *Britannicus*: the title does not appear on the coins until the second issue of 210, cf. *BMC* V pp. 361ff., 363f., 365f., 397, 400: and it is not on the earliest record of Geta's elevation to Augustus (p. 264 below). But it does appear on some inscriptions of 209, cf. D. 431 (Rome: an official dedication; *AE* 1965, 338 (*ib.*).

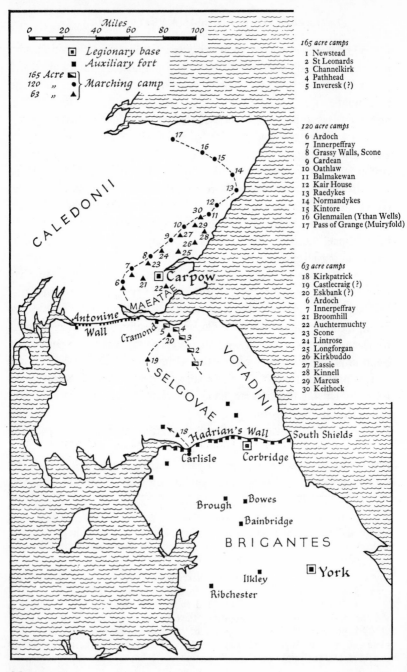

Map 3

NORTHERN BRITAIN AND THE SEVERAN CAMPAIGNS

desolate and marshy plains'. Pastoralists, with no knowledge of agriculture, living in tents, sharing their women in common, they were tough and intrepid fighters. Among other remarkable feats they could allegedly live immersed in swamps with only their heads above water, for many days at a time, and they could subsist on special iron rations – 'a small portion about the size of a bean, of this special food, prevents them from feeling either hunger or thirst'. Their expertise in guerrilla tactics caused Roman losses of some 'fifty thousand men' – surely an exaggeration.

But nothing daunted, Septimius pressed on almost to the northernmost extremity of the island, where he 'observed most accurately the variation of the sun's motion and the length of the days and the night, in both summer and winter'. After this, the Britons were forced to come to terms. It is clear that Roman losses cannot have been so immense as Dio alleges – and equally, the Caledonians and Maeatae must have received a severe battering.[1] The nature of the campaign is only now beginning to be understood in the light of archaeological discoveries. Two series of marching-camps have been traced by air photography over a large area of Scotland, which both appear to date to the time of this expedition. One series is of camps each of some 63 acres in size. Those in the second series are mostly of 120 acres, but the southernmost examples are even larger – 165 acres. The first of these is at Trimontium (Newstead) in the Eildon Hills, close to the fort which had been a Roman base, at intervals, since Julius Agricola's day. Its vast extent makes it large enough to have included a major part of the Roman army of Britain within its ramparts. No doubt other camps were set up further south, in which the army and its supply-train could halt on the way from Corbridge, a distance of over fifty miles (passing on their way Habitancum [Risingham], one of the forts where Senecio had had work done). But no camps as large as Newstead have yet been spotted along the Cororidge road. Newstead was perhaps the point

[1] Geta: Herodian 3.14.9. There is no real basis here for regarding him as actual governor of Britain, cf. A. J. GRAHAM, p. 94 and n. 33. – 'hair-raising': Dio 76.12–13. G. W. CLARKE suggests that the 'proof that Britain was an island' (72.12.5) made at this time may have been proof of something that was only doubted in rhetorical exercises. Still, Dio's comments here hint at an interest in Julius Agricola's campaigns (cf. 39.50.4 and 66.20).

where Septimius and his generals concentrated their forces for the big push into hostile territory. Three more of these giant-sized camps, with perhaps one more at Inveresk on the south side of the Firth of Forth, show the line of advance, slow but menacing. Beyond the Firth more have been detected, now reduced in size by a quarter to 120 acres, perhaps because part of the army had been detached to proceed by ship. The 120-acre camps begin at Ardoch, a few miles south of Agricola's old base Pinnata Castra (Inchtuthil). More have now been detected for miles further north, showing the expeditionary force swinging on across the Earn and the Tay and around the foothills of the Grampians into the Dee valley, then right up as far as Muiryfold, a dozen miles south of the Moray Firth.

This alone represents a campaign on a truly massive scale, fully confirming the evidence of Dio and Herodian on the heavy expenditure in men and money that was poured in by Septimius. But there is much more. The other series of camps has now been detected as far south as Kirkpatrick in Dumfriesshire, some seven miles north of Aballava (Burgh-by-Sands) at the western end of Hadrian's Wall, and two possible examples to the north-east of this indicate that there was an advance into Scotland by the western route as well, which then moved across, skirting the Pentlands, towards the Forth. Further examples have been picked up beyond the Forth, the first example again being at Ardoch. Beyond Ardoch there seem to be two parallel lines of them, which may represent the traces of a single army, returning by a slightly different route, or perhaps indicate that there were two parallel columns marching forwards simultaneously. From Ardoch the westerly line goes north-eastwards across the mouths of the glens that run south-east out of the Highlands. The other, first detected at Auchtermuchty in the Ochils, goes on to Carpow on the south bank of the Tay, which must have been crossed here by a bridge of boats. Here a polygonal enclosure some 70 acres in size, bounded on the north by the steep descent to the river, must represent a base where the army could link with the fleet and be supplied by vessels plying from Tyne and Forth. On the north side of the river was a small fortified post, no doubt to guard the bridge. From here an army went on north-east via Longforgan, Kirkbuddo and Kinnell to Keithock, which also seems to be the goal of the line of 63-acre camps beginning at Ardoch. Only excavation, particularly at Ardoch, where the 120-acre and 63-acre camps intersect, can determine which series came first. But it looks already as if the literary evidence, which indicates that there were two separate campaigns, has been confirmed in the field, or from the air.[1]

That the intention of the Emperor was to do something more than merely lay waste the country of the Maeatae and Caledonians and then to return to the line of Hadrian's Wall, might in any case be suggested by the ambitious scope of the operations that these marching-camps reveal. The proof has been supplied by the evidence from Carpow. Within the polygonal enclosure already described a smaller, permanent base was begun, a fortress measuring 24 acres internally and 27.6 acres over the ramparts. It was of more or less orthodox plan, with a *principia* of standard type and an elaborate *praetorium* well equipped with baths. Its size made it too small for a whole legion, far too large for any auxiliary unit. At least two legions took part in its construction, for the Sixth is represented on over two hundred stamped tiles, while the Second's emblems are carved on the side of the monumental inscription from the *porta praetoria*. The Sixth legion carries a new title, for it is styled LEG VI VIC B P F. *Victrix Pia Fidelis* it had been for 120 years, but B is new and must mean B(*ritannica*), a title given it, presumably, when the Emperors took the name Britannicus.

Although the fortress was never to be completed, the nature of its masonry alone shows that the occupation was intended to be permanent: the walls of the *principia* were over three feet thick, and the floors were of high quality *opus signinum*. The unusual size of the fortress suggests that it was designed for a composite force, perhaps legionary vexillations together with auxiliaries. The base may not have

---

[1] See now J. K. ST JOSEPH, whose paper became available only after this work had gone to press. I had previously relied on Dr St Joseph's summary in the *Cambridge University Reporter* for 8 May 1968. I must add that the account here given, while using the evidence Dr St Joseph has now published, represents my own conclusions – he himself refrains from speculation, on the whole, although he quite firmly states his belief that both series of camps are Severan. – S. S. FRERE (whose map pp. 173–4 must now of course be extensively revised), states on p. 111 that the 63-acre camp at Ardoch ('65-acre' in his text, and of course still thought to be Flavian) seems earlier than the 120-acre one there. [In *Britannia* (1970) pp. 167ff. Dr St Joseph shows that the 63-acre camp was indeed the earlier.]

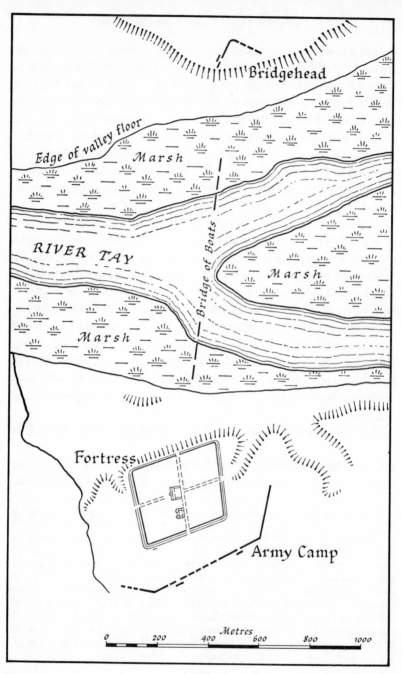

Bridgehead

Edge of valley floor

Marsh

RIVER TAY

Bridge of Boats

Marsh

Marsh

Fortress

Army Camp

Metres

0   200   400   600   800   1000

Map 4   CARPOW

been popular – however beautiful the views across the Tay to the north, westwards to the Highlands and south to the looming hills beyond Abernethy, the place can be damp and cold. Situated on a level shelf just east of the confluence of the Earn with the Tay, the ground is well-drained, certainly, but there are reed-beds on the north where the river floods from time to time at high water. It is not surprising that the army rations included wine infused with horehound, a remedy, or an alleviation, for chest-complaints. But it looks as if Septimius intended to leave a force there when the expedition had brought the enemy to submission.

The coins struck in 208 give some tantalising clues as to how the military activity proceeded, as already mentioned. The one of Antoninus showing a bridge of boats with the legend *traiectus* surely records the crossing of the Tay at Carpow. The bridge shown on the coins of Septimius may therefore commemorate a march across the Forth. It may be that Antoninus and Septimius commanded separate armies in this year (208), and that while the young Emperor pressed rapidly north with a smaller force his father brought another army, with heavy equipment, more slowly up the central route from York and Corbridge to Newstead. The coins of 209 continue to have naval themes, with references to Neptune and Ocean. One issue shows Oceanus with a sea-horse.[1]

Dio has one or two stories to illustrate the campaign. Antoninus evidently continued to cause Septimius anxiety because of his lack of self-restraint – and his obvious wish to kill his brother if he could get the chance. He had a row with the freedman Castor, who had a leading role

---

[1] Carpow fortress: R. E. BIRLEY (1962, 1963) and A. R. BIRLEY (1967c) report on the initial excavations which located and dated the site. Further work, by J. D. Leach and J. J. Wilkes, is in progress: cf. *JRS* 55 (1965) p. 208f., 56 (1966), 199, 57 (1967), 175, 58 (1968), 177f., 59 (1969), 202. For *VI Vic. B.p.f.* cf. also *ib.* 52 (1962) p. 197 and 53 (1963), 164, which also reports an example from York, the legion's base. And I have suggested elsewhere that *ILAlg* I 539.1 (Zattara in Numidia) may show the title on the tombstone of a veteran of VI *Victrix Britannica pia fidelis* cf. A. R. BIRLEY (1971). – II Augusta: R. P. WRIGHT (who dates the very fragmentary inscription to 212, but cf. J. C. MANN [1967] p. 64, where it is shown that it may be earlier). – 'horehound'; *JRS* 53 (1963), 166. – coins of 208: cf. p. 255, n. 2, above; of 209: *BMC* V pp. 356ff. – Oceanus and sea-horse: *ib.* p. 357 no. 5.

in Septimius's household. He burst out of his tent, yelling that Castor had 'wronged him'. The thing was a put up job – he had primed a group of soldiers beforehand to join in his shouts and raise an outcry. Another episode was more serious yet. Septimius and Antoninus were riding forward to meet the Caledonians to discuss terms. The two Emperors were out in front, with the army following. The enemy army was arrayed on the other side. Antoninus suddenly reined in his horse and drew his sword. It looked as if he was going to strike his father in the back. Their attendants shouted out a warning, and he refrained from making the attempt. It seems incredible that he should have been so senseless as to try and kill his father in the presence of thousands of Roman soldiers. If Dio gave no further details it would have been natural to assume that a movement by Antoninus had been misunder-stood. But that was not the end of the matter. Septimius turned when he heard the shouts, and saw his son's sword, but remained silent. After the negotiations with the Caledonians were completed, and they had returned to headquarters – perhaps at Carpow – he summoned Antoninus, Papinian and Castor. He ordered a sword to be placed within easy reach and then reclining on a couch, gave his son a tongue-lashing – not only for daring to try such a thing at all, but for trying it in the face of both armies. Then his tone changed to sarcasm. ' "But if you really want to kill me, do it here. You are strong and I am an old man, and am lying down. If you don't shrink from doing this, but hesitate to kill me with your own hands, there is Papinian the Prefect standing beside you, and you can order him to put me to death. For he will surely do anything that you command, since you also are an Emperor." '

Nonetheless, Septimius refrained from taking any action against Antoninus – even though, according to Dio, he had now realised that his plans for the succession were less wise than he had thought. 'He had often blamed Marcus for not removing Commodus – and he had often threatened to do this to his son.' But his love for Antoninus outweighed his love for his country – yet to spare Antoninus was to betray Geta, 'for he well knew what would happen'.[1]

No reliable source gives any details about how Geta was spending

[1] Dio 76. 14. 1-7.

his time, apart from Herodian's generalised statement that he was entrusted with duties in the Roman part of Britain. But some have thought it possible Geta may be the 'most impious Caesar' referred to in the earliest manuscript of the *Passio* of Alban, the first British martyr: 'Without an order from the Emperors the most impious Caesar ordered the persecution to cease, reporting to them that slaughtering the saints was causing Christianity to flourish, rather than suppressing it.' The martyrdom is generally placed much later, during the so-called 'Great Persecution' under Diocletian, but there is no intrinsic reason why this should be so. If the identification of the Caesar with Geta can be accepted, it provides one of the very few pieces of evidence for the character or actions of Septimius's younger son.[1]

The Augustan History is almost useless as a source for these campaigns. Great emphasis is placed there – following Aurelius Victor – on Septimius's achievement in building Hadrian's Wall. With no apparent knowledge that the work carried out under Septimius was merely a reconstruction of the Hadrianic frontier, the Wall is described as the greatest glory of the reign. Jerome's *Chronicle*, which has the same basic story, dates the work of building to the year 207 – which is correct enough, for Alfenus Senecio had certainly still been at work on the Wall in that year. It looks as if later propaganda, after Septimius's death, asserted that the purpose of his expedition all along had been the strengthening of the existing frontier fortifications, in conjunction with a punitive campaign.[2]

But the evidence of Cassius Dio leaves little doubt that Septimius's intention was much more far-reaching. He wanted to conquer the whole island, and the evidence of archaeology confirms that his plans had progressed some considerable way. Whether the treaty concluded with the Maeatae and Caledonians in 209 had in fact formally laid down the annexation of the remaining portions of free Britain cannot be determined. But there is no question but that these peoples ceded large portions of territory to Rome. Closer inspection of the Scottish

---

[1] This is the theory of J. MORRIS (1968), who is followed by S. S. FRERE, p. 332. But the dating and identification are very doubtful.

[2] *HA Sev.* 18.2, cf. Victor *Caes.* 20.18, etc. – propaganda: if so, it was remarkably successful, cf. p. 17 n. 2, above.

Highlands may have led Septimius to renounce any claims he may have intended to pursue north and west of the Great Glen. But in Britain as elsewhere – in the east and in Africa – Septimius showed himself to be a *propagator imperii*.[1]

At the conclusion of the campaign he assumed the title Britannicus, together with his sons. No imperatorial salutations were registered, no doubt for the simple reason that no real battles had been fought. At the same time, as far as can be determined, Geta was raised to the rank of Augustus. The news had reached Athens by December 209 or January 210 – at the end of the Attic month Poseidon. The Council of the Areopagus, the Council of Five Hundred, and the People of the Athenians decreed that a festival and public sacrifice should be held to celebrate this good news;

> since the most sacred and perfect of all days, longed for by all, on account of the undying concord of the Sacred Emperors, Lucius Septimius Severus Pertinax Augustus . . . and Marcus Aurelius Antoninus Pius Augustus . . . has been announced by a joint proclamation to all men by the great Emperors, in which, by their heavenly decree and judgment, they have made the most divine Emperor Publius Septimius Geta Pius Augustus an equal partner in the imperial rule, establishing the rule of the world in their whole family.

The promotion of Geta was surprisingly belated, considering that he was less than twelve months younger than his brother – he had waited more than ten years before being given equal rank. The motives are not clear, either for the delay, or for the timing of the decision when it was finally made. One may suspect that Antoninus's murderous behaviour had something to do with that. Equally, Septimius must have had a good idea that he had not long to live – all the sources emphasize the painful nature of his illness. He was obviously convinced of the wisdom of sharing the imperial position between two partners, in the manner of Marcus Aurelius. If he neglected to promote Geta himself,

[1] Cf. p. 251 n. 1, above. – 'ceded': Dio 76.13.4. – *propagator*: cf. p. 184 and n. 1, above.

Antoninus would be unlikely to take this step when Septimius died.[1]

Considering how genuinely superstitious Septimius was, it is likely that his belief that his days were now numbered was strengthened by a number of omens. In the version now preserved, Cassius Dio only has one of these, which occurred shortly before his departure from Rome in 208. Lightning struck an inscription on the gate through which he planned to march out of the city, erasing the first three letters of his name. The remaining three formed the Greek work 'ΗΡΩ. This was interpreted to mean that after three years he would die, and be deified – becoming a *hero*. The Augustan History, in its perverse fashion, after neglecting to give any details about the campaigning, records four omens that may be assigned to the end of the year 209 – if they are not the product of the author's own imagination. The first purports to be a dream that Septimius had about his own deification. The second apparently took place at games in honour of the victory in the north. They will have taken place at the main base, perhaps Carpow. Three plaster figures of the goddess Victory were set up, one each for Septimius and his sons. The central one, bearing a globe inscribed with his name, was struck by a gust of wind, and fell down from the podium. The one honouring Geta was blown over and totally shattered, while Antoninus' Victory lost its palm and barely remained upright.

The third and fourth omens, which seem to be part of the same story, belong to Septimius's journey southward to winter-quarters. The text at the beginning of this passage is difficult to translate and is perhaps corrupt – it has been variously emended to try and make it produce some coherent meaning. But in fact the text can be understood perfectly well as it stands, in the light of evidence from Britain.

After giving a Moor his discharge from the army, on the Wall [this would be something quite normal at the end of a campaign] when he returned to the nearest *mansio* [halting-place], not merely as victor but having established eternal peace, and turning over in his mind what sort of man should meet him [or 'what omen he should meet with'] a certain 'Ethiopian' (black man) from the military *numerus*, with a wide reputation as a buffoon, and always noted for his jokes,

[1] *Britannicus*: p. 255 n. 2. – Augustus: *IG* II/III 1077.

met him with a garland made from cypress-boughs. When he ordered that the man should be removed from his presence, in a rage, being upset by the man's colour and the ill-omened nature of his garland, the man is said to have called out, as a joke: 'You have overthrown all things, conquered all things, now be a conquering god!' When he reached the town and wanted to make sacrifice, by a mistake on the part of the rustic soothsayer, in the first place he was taken to the Temple of Bellona, and then the sacrificial victims that were provided were black. Then, when he had abandoned the sacrifice in disgust, and had withdrawn to the Palace, through the attendants' carelessness the black victims followed him right up to its doors.'

The story could be easily rejected as a feeble concoction. But curiously enough, at the fort of Aballava (Burgh-by-Sands), west of Luguvalium (Carlisle) on Hadrian's Wall, the garrison in the third century included a *numerous Maurorum*, a unit of Moors. An army unit of this kind may well have had black soldiers in its ranks. That Septimius should have used Burgh-by-Sands as a *mansio* is perfectly plausible. The fort guarded two important fords across the Solway Firth,[1] and the marching-camp at Kirkpatrick now shows that the western route was used at this time by the army. Septimius, returning from Scotland, may have used one of these fords. As for the shrine of Bellona, there was certainly one in the close vicinity, for a dedication to the goddess has been found at the fort of Olerica (Old Carlisle) some ten miles away. The town may have been Luguvalium itself, although Eburacum (York) might seem likelier, in view of the mention of a 'Palace'. No such building is known at Carlisle.

It is not unlikely that Septimius was on his way to York at the time. No other evidence can be cited to prove that he was in north-west England, but it is quite plausible to suppose that if he had gone to Scotland by sea up the east coast, he may have wished to return by land – or indeed, he may have taken ship from the Clyde to the Solway on

---

[1] Edward I was to die at Burgh in 1307, while waiting for an opportune moment to cross into Scotland.

the way back.[1] He was certainly at York on 5 May 210, if the heading of a rescript in the Code of Justinian is accurate. On that day a reply written 'at Eboracum' was sent in the names of Septimius and Antoninus in response to the enquiry of a lady named Caecilia. (The case concerned the ownership of a slave.) There are eighteen rescripts from the years 208–210, all of which, except three from February 208, were no doubt issued from Britain. This is a salutory reminder that Septimius could not relax his attention. Once a man was Emperor his subjects would constantly crave his attention. An inscription from Ephesus records how an ambassador from that city came to Britain to petition Septimius and Antoninus.[2]

Dio has a pleasant story which shows that the Empress found some intellectual diversion in the island. In conversation with the wife of a Caledonian named Argentocoxus, after the treaty had been concluded, Julia joked with her about the sexual customs of her people, referring to their women's freedom in having intercourse with men. The Caledonian woman showed a biting humour in her reply: 'We fulfil the demands of nature in a much better way than you Roman women. We have intercourse openly with the best men – you allow yourselves to be seduced in secret by the worst of men.'[3]

The peace that Septimius had imposed did not last long. The Maeatae broke out into revolt, and were soon joined by the Caledonians. It may well be that the Maeatae had one of their tribal centres very close to the fortress of Carpow – the later Pictish capital of Abernethy is only a mile or so away, and the Maeatae may be regarded as 'proto-Picts'.

---

[1] Dio 76.11.1–2. – *HA Sev.* 22.1–7 (cf. App. II). – Burgh: *RIB* 2042. – Bellona: *RIB* 890. – *Eburacum*: cf. E. BIRLEY (1966) p. 727 quoting a note by J. C. Mann. – Carlisle: it may have been Septimius that created a new *civitas*, of the Carvetii, of which Luguvalium was probably the *caput*; it is first attested *c.* 260 (*JRS* 55 [1965] p. 224; cf. *RIB* 933, 2283 and S. S. FRERE p. 187).

[2] '5 May': *Cod. Just.* 3.32.1. – 'eighteen rescripts': *ib.* 8.25.2, 2.11.9, 3.28.4; 6.35.2, 8.13.4, 2.11.10, 6.53.4, 8.40.3 (208), 7.62.1, 7.74.1, 8.18.1, 7.8.3 (209); 3.32.1, 8.53.1, 6.4.1, 8.44.3, 8.37.2, 3.1.2 (210). The issue of 6.37.3 (28 April 211) which bears his name may have been delayed because of his death. – Ephesus: J. KEIL.

[3] Dio 76.16.5. It could be that this was as close as Dio dared to get to hinting at the sexual license of the Empress (p. 241f., above). Argentocoxus and his wife may have been hostages, given under the terms of the treaty.

They may have taken some months to realise that the Romans were settling down permanently in their heartland. Septimius decided on a campaign of extermination, quoting the Homeric Agamemnon's exhortation to slaughter the Trojans:

Let no one escape utter destruction,
Let no one escape our hands, not even the babe in its mother's
    womb,
If it be male – let not even this escape utter destruction.

The second campaign was evidently conducted by Antoninus alone. Septimius, crippled by his illness, remained behind, probably at York. Once again a massive army was taken up into Scotland. Its route could be that indicated by one of the lines of camps already described. According to Herodian, Antoninus paid little attention to the war, but concentrated on winning the personal allegiance of the soldiers. Certainly Dio notes that Septimius began preparing to take over the command again in person after the Caledonians joined the revolt. But his illness got worse during the winter, and on 4 February 211, at York, he died. Dio notes that Antoninus was said by some to have hastened his death and Herodian states outright that he had tried to bribe his father's doctors and nurses to bring this about. Septimius's last words of advice to his sons – Dio claims to 'give them exactly, without any embellishment' – were, ' "Do not disagree between yourselves, give money to the soldiers, and despise everyone else." ' Aurelius Victor, whose fault as an historian is simply incompetence – rather than fraud as in the case of the Augustan History – reports that at the end of his life Septimius uttered the despairing remark that 'I have been all things, and it has profited nothing.' The Augustan History's attempt at originality in the description of his death is better disregarded. Cassius Dio hits a convincing note: 'He showed himself to be a man of such energy that even as he expired he gasped: "Come, give it to me, if we have anything to do." '[1]

[1] 'revolt': Dio 76.15.1–2, Herodian 3.15.1. – 'proto-Picts': cf. A. R. BIRLEY (1967c) p. 4f. also *Northern History* 3 (1968) p. 190f. – 'camps': cf. pp. 258ff., above. – last advice: Dio 76.15.2. – last words: 76.17.4; Victor *Caes.* 20.29, cf. *HA Sev.* 20–21 (demolished by J. STRAUB).

XVII

EPILOGUE: DEGENERATION OF A DYNASTY

The body of the dead Emperor was cremated at York. The ashes were placed in an urn of 'purple stone' (no doubt Derbyshire Blue John). Septimius had apparently sent for the urn shortly before his death. After handling it he said: 'You will hold a man that the world could not hold.' Antoninus and Geta at once [began preparations] to leave for Rome. Antoninus's preparations involved the execution of a number of members of the imperial household. Among them were the court doctors, who, Herodian says, 'had refused to obey his orders to hasten the old man's death', and the freedmen who had been the princes' tutors, 'because they continued urging him to live at peace with Geta'. Euodus, who had helped him to overthrow Plautianus, and Castor, whom he hated, were two of the victims. In secret he began bribing the officers, wanting them to induce the soldiers 'to accept him as sole Emperor'. But the soldiers refused to take any step. Although Herodian is not explicit here, he must mean that Antoninus made an immediate attempt in Britain to have his brother killed by the army. The context indicates that Antoninus made these approaches to the troops in the north, having left Geta and Julia at York. The soldiers' loyalty to Geta was partly inspired by 'his very close resemblance to his father in appearance'.[1]

---

[1] 'purple stone': Dio 76.15.4 (who quotes Septimius). Herodian (3.15.7) says 'alabaster'. Blue John, some of which looks pinkish, and which was readily available, would explain the discrepancy. (The *HA Sev.* 24.2 says the urn was gold – an ignorant guess.) – 'preparations . . . York': Herodian 3.15.4–5, Dio 77.1.1. One of the officers bribed may be the cavalry prefect Tineius Longus (*RIB* 1329 cf. A. R. BIRLEY [1967b] p. 82). – 'resemblance to his father': Dio 77.1.3. There are few surviving portraits of Geta (other than those on coins).

269

In the face of this refusal to cooperate, Antoninus made peace with the enemy, withdrawing from their territory and abandoning the forts in it – including the newly begun base at Carpow. He returned to York, where Julia made an attempt, backed by the *comites* of the Emperors, to reconcile him with Geta. He made a show of agreement, and the imperial party then left Britain in haste. The outcome was obvious all the time. Even on the journey the brothers had separate quarters. In Rome the Palace was physically divided. After jointly carrying out the ceremony of deification for their father, they led entirely separate existences. The months following saw a battle for support, the majority of the Senate favouring Geta, who was apparently showing himself to be a cultivated person or posing as such. Antoninus preferred the role of a rough and uncultured military man. There may have been a proposal to divide the Empire, Geta taking the east, Antoninus the west. Julia is said to have fought successfully against this.[1]

The end was not long in coming. Antoninus's hostility was open and at the end of the year, it turned to violence. He no doubt had it in mind to remove Geta before the oath of loyalty was renewed on 3 January, 212. He seems to have been successful, though the exact date has not

---

[1] 'made peace . . . Carpow': Dio 77.1.1 and Herodian 3.15.6 make it quite clear that he withdrew from Scotland. In spite of the arguments of R. P. WRIGHT, who published it, the new fragmentary inscription from Carpow need not be dated as late as 212, cf. J. C. MANN (1967) p. 64: there is no need to assume that a further campaign in Scotland in 211 was passed over in silence by hostile historians, nor do the coins prove that it took place. The reconstruction of the Hadrianic frontier that followed this withdrawal is well described by I. A. RICHMOND (1940) pp. 94ff. (whose views on the 'campaign of 211' should however be rejected). – 'He returned . . .' to end of paragraph: cf. esp. Herodian 3.15.6 – 4.4.2; Dio 77.1.1–6. – The boundaries of Britain were certainly re-arranged after Septimius's death. Perhaps the province was first divided into two then, cf. A. J. GRAHAM. Alternatively, an earlier division (made 197 or soon after) which had left two legions in Inferior and one in Superior, was altered, putting leg. XX at Chester in Superior: cf. J. C. MANN (1967). For the diminished importance of the northern part of Britain after 211 cf. e.g. A. R. BIRLEY (1966c) citing E. Birley's identification of the future Emperor Gordian I as governor in 216 from *RIB* 1049 and 1279 (to which *RIB* 590 should be added, cf. A. R. BIRLEY, reviewing *RIB* in *Erasmus* 18 [1966] p. 101: ID [1967b] p. 87; also T. D. BARNES [1968c] p. 591). Gordian was perhaps one of those 'sent to uncongenial provinces whose climate would harm their health, etc.' (Dio 77.11.6–7). – For a commemoration of the British victory cf. C. BOUBE-PICCOT.

been established. Persuading Julia to summon them both for a re-conciliation, he had his brother stabbed to death in her arms.

He went post-haste to the camp of the Guard, claiming hysterically that he had escaped an attempt on his life. He told the praetorians to rejoice, 'for now I can do you favours'. When he had told them his version of what had happened, he made an appeal to them:

> 'I am one of you, and it is because of you alone that I want to stay alive – so that I may bestow many benefits on you, for all the treasuries are yours. I pray above all that I may live with you, but if not at least that I may die with you. For I am not afraid of death in any form and I want to end my life in war – there is where a man should die, if anywhere.'

In the Senate on the following day he proclaimed an amnesty. But at the same time there was a holocaust of Geta's supporters. Dio says twenty thousand, both men and women of all ranks were put to death at Rome. Papinian was one prominent victim. Others included the son of Pertinax, a surviving sister of Commodus, and one of his own cousins. Fabius Cilo narrowly escaped, after the Urban Cohorts and sections of the *plebs* had made an outcry at the sight of that great man under arrest.[1]

A systematic campaign was carried out to obliterate the memory of Geta [for ever]. All his portraits were defaced. His name was pains-takingly erased from inscriptions. Sometimes, where the defacement would have been a constant reminder of what had been removed, the space was filled up by new titles for Antoninus. Monuments of the imperial family from which Plautianus and Plautilla in 205, and now Geta in 212 had been removed, looked very different from the originals. It was as if Geta had never existed. Even those inscriptions that did not actually name him, but presumed his existence by the abbreviation *Auggg.* to show three Emperors, were emended by the removal of the final *g*. The result has been that little is known about him. Dio and

---

[1] Dio 77.2.1 says that Antoninus wanted to murder Geta at the Saturnalia, but failed to carry it out. For an excellent study of the dating question cf. T. D. BARNES (1968a) p. 514f. The murder is described by Dio 77.2.2–6, Herodian 4.4.3, *HA Carac.* 2.4. What follows is given by Dio 77.3.1 – 77.5.2, Herodian 4.4.4 – 4.6.5, *HA Carac.* 2.4 – 4.10 (some of which is re-used in *Geta* 6.1–8).

Herodian suggest that his character was considerably pleasanter than his brother's. But that does not say much. In any case, he never had the opportunity to impress his personality on the course of events.[1]

The sole reign of Antoninus lasted just over five years. History knows him as Caracalla, or Caracallus, from the nickname the *plebs* gave him. It was a Celtic or German word for the hooded cloak that was one of his favourite costumes. Dio, when he comes to describe the reign, calls him variously Antoninus, Caracallus, or Tarautas 'from the nickname of a gladiator who was very small and extremely ugly, and of most violent and bloodthirsty character'. Dio's hatred of him was so strong that his account of the reign is of questionable value. But there is little evidence with which to correct it. Herodian has one or two good words to say for him. He could grasp the essentials of a case quickly in court, and could give judgment quickly. His attachment to the soldiers led him to share their burdens: 'If a ditch had to be dug, the Emperor was the first man to dig . . . grinding corn with his own hand, one man's ration, he made a loaf, baked it in the coals and ate it. He scorned luxuries and used what was cheapest and issued to the poorest of the soldiers.' He marched with the men, and sometimes even carried the legionary standards – 'a heavy burden even for the strongest soldiers'. This behaviour won him the admiration of the troops, and Herodian concedes that 'for a small man, the performing of such efforts was praiseworthy'.[2]

Dio also has an account of this soldierly conduct. The trouble was, in his view, that even if Caracalla was a good soldier he made a hopeless general. True to the concept of the Emperor's role that his father had held, he soon went to the armies. In 213 he campaigned on the Danube where his British experience was perhaps put to good use. A stone wall was erected along the western part of the Raetian frontier, where it diverged from the Danube. In the following year he left for the east, taking the northern land route. He was never to return to Rome. There was a Civil War in prospect in Parthia, and he intended to take

[1] Character of Geta: cf. Dio 77.1.3 (no indication of Dio's own opinion seems to be anywhere explicit, however); Herodian 3.3.2–3 emphasises the affability and 'Gemütlichkeit' of Geta. The *HA* elaborates this theme (but must be disregarded).

[2] 'Caracallus': cf. e.g. Dio 78.3.3. – 'Tarautas': Dio 78.9.3, etc. – 'Herodian has . . . to say for him': 4.7.4–7.

advantage of it. Even the course of events is hard to establish. The years 214 and 215 were spent in travel through the eastern provinces, and in the latter year there was some kind of massacre when the Emperor came to Alexandria. The Alexandrians had angered him, and bloody reprisals were taken. In 216 he began a Parthian expedition. Little had been achieved when in April 217 one of the Praetorian Prefects, Opellius Macrinus, had him murdered.[1]

One action of Caracalla's that is mentioned only in passing by Cassius Dio, is ignored by Herodian and barely alluded to in the Augustan History, has won him praise in later times. Some time after his brother's murder, he issued an edict granting Roman citizenship to all free inhabitants of the Empire. Cassius Dio includes this edict in a list of fund-raising measures. The motive, he says, was in fact to increase the revenues from certain taxes paid only by citizens – which he simultaneously doubled. Modern scholarship has debated both his motives and the exact scope of the award. It is clear that some failed to gain the rank of *civis Romanus*. But for practical purposes, Dio's statement that 'he made all the people in his Empire Roman citizens' scarcely exaggerates. The actual effect may not have been great – not least for his fund-raising: those with enough money to pay substantial taxes will mostly have been Roman citizens already. The legal privileges belonging to a Roman citizen by this time had been greatly diluted. But in symbolic terms, as the consummation of a long process, its value was high. Later, at least, it gave a sense of unity to the inhabitants of the Empire. Rome really was now the *communis patria*.[2]

---

[1] 'Dio also has . . .': 77.13.1–2. For Dio's account of the reign (the best), contained in 77 and 78.1–9, cf. the useful discussion by F. MILLAR (1964) pp. 150ff. (on the famous Edict cf. below and next note).

[2] The date of this measure, traditionally assigned to 212, has been questioned by F. MILLAR (1962) who argues for 214, But J. F. GILLIAM (1965) has shown that Millar's new date will not really fit the evidence. 212 still seems most likely (W. SESTON [1966b] argues for 213. This is not particularly convincing). The scope of the measure is the subject of great debate. The monograph by C. SASSE and the paper by E. CONDURACHI, which both appeared in 1958, are still valuable, but new ideas appear every year (or old ideas with new, or re-stated, arguments in support). Matters are not helped by the non-publication, more than eleven years after its discovery, of an important inscription from Mauretania Tingitana, which could presumably throw much light on the whole question of

His motives are perhaps unimportant. It is not hard to believe, in any case, that the idea was not his own, but that it emanated from one of the brilliant lawyers of the time. Ulpian and Paulus were continuing their work, even if Papinian had been removed. It may well have struck a legal mind that the work of magistrates and jurists would be greatly simplified if some at least of the variations in status were swept away. Why the step appealed to Caracalla may remain an enigma, with no great loss. Always unstable, he became seriously unbalanced after the killing of Geta. For all that he appreciated one essential part of the Emperor's role, the urgent necessity for continuous contact with the soldiers, his removal can hardly be regarded as a catastrophe for Rome.[1]

The murder of Caracalla was an act of self-preservation by Macrinus. The Prefect had intercepted a letter to the Emperor which would have seriously endangered his own position. The affection in which the army held Caracalla made it necessary to conceal his own role in the murder, and to proceed with caution. To appease the troops, Macrinus took the name Severus, and gave his son, Diadumenianus, still a boy, the name Antoninus. He did not wait for recognition from the Senate but assumed the titles and roles of Emperor. Julia Domna, who had been constantly by the side of her son, as his sole adviser, was treated with cautious respect by the usurper. But she was not content to withdraw into the background. Macrinus was obliged to make her leave Antioch when she began intriguing. The sense of helplessness which this induced, combined with the shock brought on by the news that her son's death had been greeted with rejoicing at Rome, led her to suicide.[2]

But her sister Julia Maesa was not prepared so easily to surrender the high position that her status as the sister of an Empress had given her for nearly a quarter of a century. She was now at Emesa. Macrinus was finding difficulty in establishing himself. Dio speaks of him with studied contempt. He was the first Emperor who had not even been a senator when he gained the throne. He showed himself incompetent in

---

citizenship, if available to scholars. J. CROOK (1968) gives a useful analysis of the benefits and duties of citizenship in his recent book, esp. pp. 255ff.

[1] The study by W. REUSCH still has some value, especially on the *HA vita*, in the absence of a modern account of the reign.

[2] Cf. esp. Dio 78.4.1 – 23.6: Herodian 4.12.1ff. does not add much. The *vita Macrini* in the *HA* is almost worthless (cf. App. II, p. 321f.).

war – an ignominious peace was made with Parthia – and incompetent in administration. Dio was horrified by the way in which he flouted age-old rules of rank and precedence in making appointments. By the winter of 217–218 the troops in the east were thoroughly discontented.

A means of redress lay to hand. The eldest of Julia Maesa's grand-children, Varius Avitus Bassianus, a youth of about fourteen, was now fulfilling the role of hereditary priest of Elagabalus, the Emesene God. He closely resembled the murdered Caracalla, his mother's first cousin. It was suggested that the boy should be presented as Caracalla's illegitimate son, and dressed in clothes that his alleged father had worn as a child. The idea, appropriately enough, came from an actor, a certain Eutychianus. His connection with the family is unknown – the manuscript of Dio is damaged here, but the context suggests that he may have been the lover of the widowed Julia Maesa. Actor or not, he showed considerable daring. The boy was taken to the nearest military base in his borrowed robes. At dawn on 16 May he was displayed to the troops, and acclaimed as Emperor under the name of Marcus Aurelius Antoninus.[1]

It took less than a month to oust Macrinus, who was defeated in battle near Antioch on 8 June. His reign of just under fourteen months could thus be regarded as a mere interlude. At Rome the Senate dutifully prayed that the new Antoninus, of whose character its members must have been for the most part quite ignorant, should be like his alleged father, whose memory they almost unanimously abhorred. The boy-Emperor was to become known as Elagabalus, after the god whose priest he was. For good reason. He was a fanatical devotee, and he quite literally brought his god – the black stone of Emesa – with him to Rome. From Nicomedia in Bithynia, where he spent the winter of 218–219, he sent ahead a portrait of himself in his exotic priestly robes. The painting was ordered to be hung in the Senate-house, above the altar of Victory. The magistrates were directed to call first on Elagabalus in their official prayers.[2]

In the early autumn of 219 Emperor and god arrived at Rome. The

---

[1] Cf. esp. the account in Dio Bk. 78, analysed well by F. MILLAR (1964) pp. 166ff. Cf. App. 1 no. 37 for Elagabalus.

[2] Cf. previous note.

two and a half years that followed were perhaps the most bizarre in the entire history of Rome. Julia Maesa was evidently powerless to control the Emperor she had created, and the boy's mother Soaemias pandered to his extraordinary tastes. After the religious fanaticism, foremost among these were his sexual perversions, which no serious historian could avoid mentioning. Cassius Dio and the Augustan History expatiate on them, to the virtual exclusion of anything else for many pages at a time. It would be inaccurate or oversimplified to describe him as a homosexual. On the strength of Dio's account, he was an invert, with strong leanings to transvestism. But, although he had male lovers, he was sufficiently bi-sexual to have intercourse with women, including at least three wives. Little of this might have mattered, had it not impinged on his public life – one of his Empresses was a Vestal Virgin up till the time of her marriage, for example. This imperial marriage was complemented by the summoning from Carthage of a statue of Caelestis to be the bride of the Emesene Ba'al, a marriage of sun and moon. Another of the Empresses was a descendant of Marcus Aurelius, whose names the Syrian Emperor so unworthily bore. This seems a strange irony. But the marriage with Annia Faustina was contracted in 221, when the prestige that her name carried was desperately needed. Even Herodian's account, which passes over the sexual deviations in almost total silence, lays emphasis on the exhibitionist tendencies – 'he had no wish to sin in secret. He appeared in public with his eyes made up and rouged cheeks' – adding characteristically that the cosmetics spoiled a naturally handsome face.[1]

The soldiers were not impressed by the religious charades, and were disgusted by the effeminate conduct. The Senate watched in numbed horror as actors, dancers, charioteers and athletes were advanced to positions of power and prestige, after gaining the favour of the Emperor by their sexual prowess. Julia Maesa saw that things could not go on in this way indefinitely. In reserve, as it were, she had another grandson, the child of her other daughter Mammaea and of Gessius Marcianus. On 26 June 221 the boy, Gessius Bassianus Alexianus, was formally

---

[1] Space does not permit detailed annotation. See generally Dio Bk. 79 and F. MILLAR (1964) pp. 168ff. Also Herodian Bk. 5. Some of the *vita Heliogabali* in the *HA* (the first part) is more or less factual.

adopted by Elagabalus as his son and heir. His name was changed to Marcus Aurelius Alexander and he was given the title Caesar. The boy had been deliberately shielded by his mother from the excesses of his cousin. Elagabalus soon became jealous when he saw that he had a rival in popular favour, and tried to have him killed. This was too much for the enraged soldiery. The 'false Antoninus', as Dio calls him among other names, was murdered, with his mother Soaemias, on 12 March 222, and Alexander became Emperor. He at once took the additional name Severus, becoming M. Aurelius Severus Alexander. The name Antoninus, now irrevocably associated with Caracalla and Elagabalus, he shunned. But he too was proclaimed a bastard son of Caracalla, 'the deified Antoninus the Great'. And the name Alexander was itself a piquant reminder of Caracalla, whose obsession with Alexander the Great had been pathological.[1]

Alexander can scarcely have been older than fourteen at his accession – he had assumed the *toga virilis* only the previous year, on the day he became Caesar. It is probable that he had then only reached his twelfth birthday. The day and the month, but not the year of his birth are known, and reports of his age at death differ. He was to reign for thirteen years. This alone was a remarkable achievement. The opening of the reign augured well enough. Ulpian was appointed Praetorian Prefect. The Emperor chose as his colleague – or rather, was advised to do so – in the consulship of 223 none other than Marius Maximus. Maximus had served Severus, Caracalla and Macrinus in a remarkable series of offices. He was soon to begin his biographies of the Emperors from Nerva to Elagabalus. Cassius Dio, who had had the good fortune – or good sense – to remain in the east throughout the reign of Elagabalus, belatedly began a career in imperial service. After being proconsul of Africa, a position that normally marked the close of an official career, he became governor successively of Dalmatia and Upper Pannonia, and was rewarded with a second consulship in 229 as the Emperor's colleague. But by then things had taken a turn for the worse. Ulpian was murdered only two years or less after becoming Prefect of the Guard. In the east, there was an ominous change. The Parthian King

[1] See previous note. – Alexander: App. 1 no. 10. – Caracalla's Alexander mania: cf. esp. Dio 77.7.1 – 9.1 and F. MILLAR (1964) pp. 151, 214ff.

Artabanus V was killed in 224, and his successful rival Artaxerxes, or Ardashir, was crowned in 226 as King, not of Parthia, but of the revived Persian Empire. In the closing pages of his History Dio records with concern the dangerous rebirth of the aggressive power of the Persians (after five and a half centuries of submergence under alien rule).[1]

Julia Maesa did not survive long into the reign of Alexander, but, as long as there was no threat to the frontiers of the Empire, Julia Mammaea and her son made acceptable rulers. At length the presence of the Emperor in the east became mandatory. In 230 Ardashir invaded Roman Mesopotamia and threatened Syria. Diplomacy had no effect, and in 231 Alexander was obliged to set out with an expeditionary force. Further attempts to negotiate, made from Antioch, were no more successful. In 232 Alexander entered Mesopotamia. The campaign was not markedly successful, but apparently Ardashir was obliged to withdraw. The situation had at least been restored to the status quo. More might have been attempted, but now a threat on the northern frontiers was reported. The Germans were taking advantage of the absence of some of the garrisons in the east. Alexander returned to Rome in 233, and in 234 he left for the Rhine. Early in 235 all was ready for a campaign beyond the Rhine. But once again, Alexander tried to avoid war if possible, and began negotiations. The troops did not like it. Negotiation was almost bound to mean Roman payments to the barbarian chiefs – to be construed pejoratively as 'Danegeld', otherwise as a subsidy to an ally – when a treaty had been made. The troops preferred to fight and receive the money themselves as bounty. Alexander was murdered by his own men on 21 March 235. The Severan dynasty had thus lasted for forty-two years, less nineteen days. The following fifty years are rightly reckoned the darkest in the history of Rome. But that is another story.[2]

[1] The reign of Alexander is very imperfectly recorded. Modern accounts have in many cases been wrecked by incautious reliance on the *HA vita*, the most elaborate and most untrustworthy in the entire collection. The monograph by A. JARDÉ still has some value. *CAH* XII pp. 517ff. is more or less sound in most places. The date of death of Ulpian is now fixed by new data on the career of his murderer, cf. App. III, p. 342f.

[2] Cf. e.g. *CAH* XII pp. 68ff. for a slightly more detailed account. The *Res Gestae* of the Persian King Sapor throw a little more light on the eastern campaigns and their aftermath, but it would be exceeding the scope of the present work still further to go into this or other details.

XVIII

CONCLUSION

The Emperor's relationship with the Senate was the dominant theme of imperial historiography for more than two hundred years. How an Emperor treated that august assembly mainly governed the verdict of the ancient writers.[1] It is no surprise that some of the most favourable judgments on Septimius Severus come from three men – Galen, Tertullian and Aurelius Victor – whose interests lay for the most part far from senatorial circles at Rome. Septimius Severus had a number of senators executed during his reign. Only one is known in the first two years, Asellius Aemilianus (there were doubtless a few others), twenty-nine after the battle of Lugdunum. Nine or ten more names can be added, killed at other times. Good reasons, even justification, can be offered for the majority of these executions. The twenty-nine who died in 197 had no doubt committed treason – they had given active support to the losing side in a civil war, an unforgivable offence (but Dio says that another thirty-five were pardoned at that time).[2] Yet it is no good counting heads. On two occasions, the Augustan History and Dio, respectively, do not name names. At the time of the second Parthian war 'many' were put to death on the grounds that they had consulted astrologers about the length of Septimius's life. If the evidence of the Augustan History is regarded as weak, what of Dio? According to Xiphilinus's *Epitome*, Dio said that as well as Plautius Quintillus, 'many others senators' were put to death – *some of them* after a formal trial.[3] It was not quite like the terror under Domitian, however. There

---

[1] See notably the paper by J. MORRIS (1963).

[2] Dio 75.7.4, cf. pp. 198ff. above.

[3] *HA Sev.* 15.5, cf. p. 203f., above. – Dio 76.7.3 (205 or a little later) cf. p. 238f., above.

is no hint of that from Dio. Nor again was it like the terror under Commodus. Going further back, the reign of Tiberius seems to be echoed: an all-powerful Praetorian Prefect, as a result of whose influence many are executed, then his death, which brings another purge. But the parallel is superficial.[1] The author of the Augustan History invokes Sulla and Marius: some allegedly called him the Punic Sulla, others the Punic Marius. And Dio reports that Septimius himself openly introduced the behaviour of these men, in favourable mention, into his speech in the Senate in 197. Curiously, the label 'Punic Sulla' has found greater acceptance among modern writers. One wonders why. Is it because that person is himself universally condemned? The cruelties of C. Marius are regarded as a blot on a fair name. The dictator Sulla is loathed as a reactionary who waded to power through blood, in an abortive attempt to reverse the trend towards 'democracy' – a trend that Marius, not least, had set in motion. Septimius invoked another name in his oration of 197: Augustus, the first Emperor.[2] Here surely is a true parallel, if one has to be sought. If any man was a butcher of the Senate it was he. But he had one extenuating factor in his favour: he came on the scene after more than a generation of intermittent civil war. In addition, he was young. More than one hundred senators were put to death by the Triumvirs; others were executed after Philippi. Later, the blame could be conveniently shifted to M. Antonius. But some of the Antonians were executed after Actium. Other men – conspirators (of course) – were suppressed from time to time throughout the reign. Yet when men thought back to Marius and Sulla, or remembered his earlier self, the principate of Augustus did not seem all that bad in comparison.[3] Septimius Severus followed the 'five good Emperors', after the insane and frightful interlude of Commodus. The Senate aspired to return to the spirit of M. Aurelius, which in 193 they could all remember personally. To take another example, Septimius rates low in comparison with Vespasian, an Emperor who gained power

[1] Dio himself makes the comparison betwen Plautianus and Sejanus in 58.14.1: in his view Plautianus had the greater power.

[2] *HA Pesc. Nig.* 6.4: *ab aliis Syllae Punici, ab aliis Marii nomen accepit.* I think that the context requires that *Punici* be applied to both names. – Dio 75.8.1. – S. N. Miller in *CAH* XII p. 24 duly brings out 'Punic Sulla'. But it is invention.

[3] It will be sufficient to cite R. SYME (1939) *passim.*

through the legions. At his door few charges of murdering senators can be laid. But Vespasian did not have four years of civil war: his struggle for power was achieved in less than six months.[1]

This is not a justification of judicial murder. But it is an explanation. Too many have written as if the behaviour of Septimius in this respect was outrageous and shocking in its novelty and extremity. It was much more normal than historians of Rome like to remember. Another charge requires examination: that 'he forced himself on the senate, and the recognition of his power was voted by the senate under military pressure'. The account in the Augustan History of his attendance at the Senate on 10 June 193 does give that kind of impression. And in a sense it is true to the spirit of what had happened. But it ignores the fact that the Senate had already declared Septimius Emperor on 1 June. Besides, if the choice – a free choice – had been between Didius Julianus and Septimius, it is hard to believe that a majority would have opted for Didius Julianus, after the murder of Pertinax. But how else had some of his predecessors gained recognition from the Senate? Did not Augustus, and Claudius and Vespasian, at least, 'force themselves on the Senate' and gain recognition by military power? And Trajan and Hadrian might not have gained the imperial office without the convenient support of thousands of legionaries.[2]

It has been amply shown by careful research that Septimius did not stuff the Senate with Illyrians, Mauretanians and Syrians. The Italians continued to form the largest single component of that body.[3] Numerous Italians may also be found in positions of some authority. It is sufficient to cite the names of Sextius Lateranus and Lollianus Gentianus. Men from the Roman west are also found – Fabius Cilo, Cornelius Anullinus, Manilius Fuscus, all from Spain. Similarly, the men of established

---

[1] It may be that Vespasian's hand was held by a desire to avoid any appearance of emulating Nero. And he may have been the first to swear the oath not to execute senators without a trial before the Senate. Cf. A. R. BIRLEY (1962). Dio, quite reasonably, dwells on the mockery made of Septimius's taking of this oath in June 193 (74.2.1–2) by his subsequent actions. The value of that oath was already diminished by the behaviour of Commodus (who surely took it, when raised to the rank of Augustus in 177, cf. Birley, p. 197).

[2] The quotation is from M. ROSTOVTZEFF (1957) I p. 401.

[3] Cf. esp. G. BARBIERI (1952) and the same scholar's analysis in *L'Albo* pp. 432ff.; and note also M. HAMMOND (1957).

families continued their almost exclusive hold over the eponymous consulship.[1] When one looks more closely, it is clear that men from Africa and, to a lesser extent, Syria and the east, played a particularly important role once his power had become established. That was natural. He could trust them. The two Praetorian Prefects who held the post between them for the best part of fifteen years, Plautianus and Papinian, were an African and a Syrian (both kinsmen of the Emperor). The origin of the senatorial *viri militares* is not always ascertainable. But the governors of the military provinces were probably more often than not African. One need recall only the names of Alfenus Senecio, Anicius Faustus and Claudius Claudianus; while Subatianus Aquila, who served an exceptionally long term as Prefect of Egypt, was also African.[2] Even if Septimius had been an Italian, however, the prominence of Africans in his reign would have been predictable. Africa was the richest province in the west, Carthage the second city after Rome. The accession of Septimius was a symptom not a cause of the rise of the Africans, which had begun long before. These Africans were not very different, in any case, from their Italian counterparts, whatever their families' ultimate origin. And what does it mean to speak of 'Orientals'? It is pointless – or at least misleading – to describe men like Papinian and Ulpian in these terms.[3]

In the next highest grade in the administrative service, the procurators, a marked change is detected with the accession of Septimius. From the time of Hadrian down to the year 192, just over half the places available were filled by Italians. From Septimius onwards, sixty per cent were taken by Africans and men from the Greek east. Besides this, many more procurators were now men promoted from the centurionate. There was another significant change: an increase in the number of

[1] See App. III for the men named. J. MORRIS (1965b) esp. p. 91 draws attention to the prominence of two particular Italian senatorial families in this period. Cf. generally G. ALFÖLDY, *Senat*, esp. pp. 127ff.

[2] App. III.

[3] See the comments of F. MILLAR (1964), esp. p. 9, n. 7. G. BOWERSOCK p. 470 criticises Millar's use of the term 'Greek' in preference to 'oriental' and has some useful remarks on the subject. However, the latter term has certainly acquired a patronising, if not pejorative, tone in current English usage, and is better avoided. See further Millar pp. 182ff.

procurators. Before Septimius there were about one hundred and thirty-five. By creating over forty new posts, a net increase of over thirty, Septimius at last produced a real promotion pyramid. Perhaps most significantly, as many as ten new posts were established in the highest grade of all, that of *trecenarius*. Formerly only the *a rationibus*, the Financial Secretary, had enjoyed this rank. Most of these new procurators functioned in Rome and Italy. Meanwhile, as if to indicate that the status of Rome was no less respected than in the past, a procurator from this period is attested, holding a post in what he describes as *sacra urbs*, 'the Sacred City'.[1]

If Septimius did not swamp the Senate with men from the Danubian provinces – indeed not a single name is known – it was for a very good reason. That region was the source of his power. From its armies he derived his new garrison for Rome and Italy. And the Danubian armies themselves remained the strongest in the Empire. It would not have done to place, in command of those armies, generals who were compatriots of the soldiers.[2] Septimius's military policy is of considerable importance. Cassius Dio ascribes to him the dying advice to his sons which appears to sum up his attitude: 'Give money to the soldiers and despise everyone else.' Dio and the other sources wax eloquent on the barbarous soldiery that filled the streets of Rome. Herodian actually asserts that he quadrupled the garrison there. He certainly increased the pay of the army and granted the soldiers new privileges. Many sweeping judgments have been passed on the basis of these facts and of deductions from the epigraphic evidence. A new study of the Septimian army reforms now provides the opportunity to see the facts in their proper perspective.[3]

The garrison of Rome – and Italy – was indeed heavily increased. Probably not quite fourfold, as Herodian in his typically vague fashion would have it. But at least threefold. The Praetorian Guard and the

---

[1] Cf. esp. H. G. Pflaum's useful analysis in *RE* 23 (1957) 1240ff., esp. 1255ff., based on his classic treatment in his 1950 work on the procurators and on *CP*. (The new evidence on the *ratio privata* necessitates minor modification of his tables. Cf. p. 16, above.) – *sacra urbs: RE l.c.* 1259 (*CP* no. 228).

[2] This is the shrewd conclusion of G. BARBIERI (1952) p. 35f.

[3] 'A new study': by E. BIRLEY, in *Ep. Stud.* What follows is based mainly on that article, where reference will be found to the work of numerous other scholars.

vigiles were both doubled in size. The Urban Cohorts were tripled. Only the *equites singulares*, a thousand strong, retained their original establishment. The new legion II Parthica stationed at Albanum close to the City added a further six thousand men. The total strength of these forces thus amounted to 30,000 men, against the previous number of 11,500. To the 30,000 must be added the unknown number of men in the *castra peregrina*, which included Moors and Osrhoenian archers. What was the purpose of this vast increase in the military establishment? To cowe the Senate and citizenry? Surely that would have been ludicrously excessive. It is far more intelligible to explain this new concentration of forces as the creation of a mobile field army, or at least, of the nucleus of such an army. Septimius, who grew to manhood in the reign of Marcus Aurelius, will have seen the shunting backwards and forwards of entire legions from one war to another; and then the abandonment of this system – which had prevailed from Augustus onwards – in favour of the use of detachments, vexillations. He himself had formed army corps by brigading together vexillations from each of the legions in a particular province, during the civil wars. But that system was not ideal. It was far better if the Emperor could bring a really large force to the theatre of war without weakening the defences of other frontiers. That had been done before on a small scale; the Praetorian Guard had gone with the Emperor on numerous occasions. But now there was indeed something resembling an army reserve.

What of the barbarization of these units, and the exclusion of Italians from the Guard? This too must not be exaggerated. The new Urban Cohorts, 6,000 strong, were larger than the old Guard had been, and continued to take Italian recruits. The new *vigiles*, 7,000 strong, formerly manned by freedmen, now accepted free-born – Italian – recruits as well. Service in the Guard was of course better paid and more prestigious, and offered better prospects of promotion. But the Italians were certainly not excluded from a role in policing the capital.

It was once concluded that until the time of Septimius the legionary centurions were preponderantly of Italian origin; and that equestrian officers who commanded the auxiliary regiments, likewise, before his reign, were in the majority Italian. From the reign of Septimius onwards, it is asserted, Italians were excluded from commissions in both these branches of the service. Their places were supposedly taken by provincials of an increasingly untraditional type – 'Asiatics', Africans, Illyrians. But it has been shown that these views are invalidated by the evidence. Plenty of legionary centurions and equestrian officers before the reign of Septimius were provincial; and the provincial officers at the higher level of the equestrian *militiae* even seem to have been dominant in the mid-second century. Any prominence of provincials from Septimius onwards is therefore hardly surprising, and is in no way a radical and deliberate change of policy.

It is true, however, that there were some changes. The army officers from the time of Septimius were of lower social standing. More of them came from the frontier areas. Equestrian commissions were now given to ex-rankers. If the army officers had all been of this type, there might have been some truth in the idea that there was a deliberate policy of excluding the provincial upper classes (who were in any case, it was alleged, decimated by mass executions). But enough Italians and municipal notables from the provinces can be found to make this point of view untenable.

Improvement in pay and conditions for serving soldiers – about which authorities ancient and modern have complained – is something for which one may cheerfully give Septimius credit. The pay was increased, perhaps mainly to take account of inflation. And soldiers were allowed to marry.

It was not only in Rome that Septimius expanded the army. There were the other two new legions, I and III Parthicae. And some new auxiliary units, perhaps a large number, were also raised. Changes seem to have been introduced into the internal organisation of both legions and *auxilia*. These measures were not gratuitously undertaken.[1] Septimius had a frontier policy that demanded more troops. He was an expansionist, extending the frontiers of the Empire in all four quarters: in the south, a new frontier, from the Atlantic to the Libyan desert; in the east, a new province, Mesopotamia, with two legions; in the north, the borders of Dacia were extended. In the far west, in Britain, he

---

[1] 'It was once concluded' . . . 'it was asserted', etc.: by A. v. DOMASZEWSKI, in various places. See E. BIRLEY in *Ep. Stud.*, also ID. (1953a) pp. 104ff., 154ff. for judicious analysis.

attempted to do away with the necessity for any frontier at all. Opinions differ as to the wisdom of some of these actions. The weakening of Parthia, which the annexation of northern Mesopotamia brought about, was perhaps unfortunate, in one way. Within a generation the Parthians succumbed and the far more dangerous Persians became Rome's new adversary in the east. Cassius Dio questions the motive anyway – it was simply 'desire for glory'. That could be, of course. But it may be argued that the Parthian expedition brought an immense amount of booty, especially gold, into Roman hands staving off an economic crisis; and that the new province was a valuable protection for Syria.[1] As for the British policy, that was no doubt misconceived. It is possible to argue that Britain was a millstone round the necks of successive Roman Emperors. From the campaigns of Agricola to the troubles under Commodus, the province had created a disproportionate amount of difficulty. And before that there had been the bloody massacre led by Boudicca.[2] Many other factors require consideration in assessing the reign of Septimius. But it would be beyond the scope of a biography to analyse the economic and social developments in the provinces. They were, after all, for the most part not susceptible to direct policy decisions of the Emperor himself.[3]

Galen, writing not long before his death, early in the reign of Septimius, speaks lyrically of the beneficence of 'the Emperors'

[1] Dacia: cf. *RE* 13 (1926) 645. – 'staving off a crisis': cf. T. PEKÁRY p. 458. Cf. also p. 202, above. Other frontiers, and the policy, are discussed at various points above, cf. e.g. pp. 181f., 216. Cf. also A. R. BIRLEY, *Seventh Congress*.

[2] Cf. p. 243f., above.

[3] The classic treatment is that by M. ROSTOVTZEFF (1957). But, as is well known, his work was dominated by some strong preconceptions. The article by T. PEKÁRY is the most detailed recent examination. But he tends to accept somewhat too readily the judgments of his predecessors, e.g. p. 478 where he follows T. FRANK p. 85: 'I venture the opinion that if we had a reliable history of the third century, we should arrive at the conclusion that Septimius Severus dealt the fatal blow to the Empire by his confiscation and his centralizing the ownership of vast estates under imperial control.' Large private landowners were not much better, and their holdings continued to increase: cf. A. H. M. JONES (1964), esp. pp. 556f., 1045. Such questions as the *annona*, *congiaria*, debasement of the currency, etc., are all covered by Pekáry, with full bibliography. (Cf. also G. WALSER pp. 81ff.) The new evidence for the existence of the *ratio privata* before 193 (above p. 16 n. 2) renders some of this obsolete. On the much discussed *annona militaris* cf. the judicious remarks of F. Millar (1964) p. 152 n. 3.

(Septimius and his elder son), which resembled that of the gods. They wanted a share in happiness for all, to the greatest possible extent – a positively Benthamite sentiment. They believed that the main part of their imperial role lay in bringing 'health' (or 'safety') to all. But one cannot take the great physician too seriously. The flattering sentiments form an introduction to a story about how his own services were called upon by the Emperors, to attend the ailing Antipater, Greek Secretary and imperial tutor.[1] Tertullian could be cited as another favourable witness. Addressing himself to the men of Carthage he says that he rejoices in their present felicity. The tone is of course sarcastic – the peace and prosperity of the times gives them enough leisure to be critical judges of dress. Later in the same work – the *de pallio* – he waxes eloquent on the blessed state of the Empire: 'What a great part of the world has been changed by the present era! What a great number of cities have the threefold virtues of the present Emperors created, amplified or restored!' He speaks of the favour of God being shown to the Emperors; and 'in truth the world is the cultivated garden of this Empire, all poisonous weeds of external hostility have been eradicated, the cactus and briar of conspiracy at home has been uprooted, and it is more pleasing than the orchard of Alcinous or the rose garden of Midas.' He would hardly have expressed himself in this way if the picture was totally false. Of course life in Africa was no doubt pleasanter than in most other parts of the Empire. Yet this has little relevance to any assessment of Septimius Severus. Africa was highly prosperous before his accession. The favours that he bestowed – except at Lepcis Magna – were honorific rather than material.[2]

Recourse must be had to another fellow-African, Aurelius Victor, for wholehearted praise: *quo praeclarior in republica fuit nemo*, which might be rendered as 'No man in Roman history has been more distinguished than he'. Victor has his word of criticism – for the cruelty exhibited in mass executions, for example. But he goes on to call him wise and successful, especially in war – 'so much so that he left no battle except

---

[1] Galen 14.217f. K. Some curious interpretations of this passage lurk in the pages of otherwise sound historical works. [On Galen cf. now G. W. BOWERSOCK (1969) pp. 59ff].

[2] Tertullian *de Pallio* 1.1, 2.7.

as victor'.[1] This impressed Herodian also. No battles or victories of the past could compare, in his view, with those of Septimius Severus, even those of Caesar against Pompey, Octavian against Antony and the sons of Pompey, or Sulla against Marius. 'Here is a single man who over-threw three Emperors who were already in power, who gained control over the Praetorian Guard by a trick, who succeeded in killing Julianus, the Emperor in the Palace, Niger who ruled the people of the East and had been saluted as Emperor by the people of Rome, and Albinus, who had already the title and authority of a Caesar – this he did by virtue of his courage. One could not easily name his equal.'[2]

In the last analysis recourse must be had to Cassius Dio, the only witness who knew the Emperor personally. As has been pointed out, 'this will not in itself help very much in considering Severus's place in the history of the Empire; but it will show how he stood with a man who was both a respectable contemporary senator and a typical re-presentative of Graeco-Roman culture'.[3] Dio introduces Septimius with a description that other sources confirm: of the three rivals that faced Didius Julianus, he was the most intelligent. The obituary notice with which he ends Book 76 is respectful, almost affectionate in tone.

He was a small man, but physically strong (although he did become very weak from the gout). His mind was extremely keen and vigorous. He did not get as much of an education as he wanted, and because of this he was a man of few words, although he had plenty of ideas. He did not forget his friends. His enemies he treated with a very heavy hand. He took a great deal of thought over all his plans; but he never gave a thought to what was said about him. For this reason he raised money from every source – except that he never killed anyone to get their money – and he met all necessary expenditures unstintingly.

[1] Victor, de Caes. 20.6, 10. Cf. p. 13f., above. The personal characteristic for which he was most remembered was his hot temper, cf. Julian, Caesar 312 D.

[2] Herodian 3.7.7–8. As a matter of fact, Septimius was not a military genius – second Hatra shows this only too well, cf. p. 205, above. Herodian was aware of this (cf. 3.9.12; 'by luck rather than judgement'). But the quality that he admired was something rather different (perhaps it was just success that really impressed him).

[3] F. MILLAR (1964), p. 138.

So warm is this verdict (the touch of condescension over his limited education notwithstanding) that one might be tempted to infer that Dio wrote this passage in the lifetime of Caracalla, when unfavourable comment would have been badly received. But Dio went on to criticise his wasteful building programme, and his habit of inscribing his own name on buildings that he had merely restored, 'as if he had erected them himself from his private funds'. Suspicion about Dio's frankness is in any case removed by something he records elsewhere. After the death of Septimius he had a dream. He saw the entire Roman army arrayed on a great plain. The Emperor was standing on a tribunal addressing the men. When he saw Dio standing near and trying to hear what was being said, he spoke to him: ' "Come nearer, Dio, so that you may learn accurately everything that is being said and done, and write an account of it." ' This story reveals something interesting: Dio could hardly have had a dream like this, or, at least, he would have omitted to record it, if the Emperor had not been 'a respected and authoritative figure' in his eyes.[1]

At his first proclamation, Septimius Severus proclaimed himself the avenger of Pertinax. Some would regard that as a pose. Yet he never chose to abandon the name of Pertinax. Indeed, he seems to have emphasised his deference to that memory by inserting the additional name or title *Pius* between Severus and Pertinax: that connoted above all loyalty. Pertinax had for his part proclaimed his intention of reviving the policies and practice of Marcus Aurelius. It is almost superfluous to comment that Septimius attempted to follow suit – and at the same time, in the light of the civil wars and the various grisly episodes that disfigured his reign, it is easy to decide that his fictitious self-affiliation to the philosopher Emperor was a cynical and calculating fraud, and no more. Yet, however unworthily, Septimius did make an attempt to emulate that paragon. His relentless capacity for hard work is one example of this. Another is his determined elevation of his son to

---

[1] 'obituary': Dio 76.16.1–4. Herodian seems to be contradicting the statement that 'he never killed anyone for their money' in 3.8.7–8. – 'so warm': cf. F. MILLAR (1964) p. 139 and G. BOWERSOCK (1965) p. 473f. for diverging viewpoints; and cf. p. 6f., above. – 'a dream': Dio 78.10.1–2. – 'reveals something interesting': as pointed out by F. MILLAR (1964) p. 180 (from which the quotation at the end of this paragraph is taken).

the rank of Augustus. Yet another is his abandonment of Rome in favour of the armies. And the expansionist frontier policy was in the Marcan tradition also. The consular Fasti of his reign are redolent of the age of Marcus – an Aufidius Victorinus sharing the *fasces* with a Claudius Severus, grandson of Marcus, a Fronto, an Annius Libo, a Claudius Pompeianus. Perhaps it was all cold calculation and an empty façade. He was a clever man. But he was capable of passion, and compassion. There surely was a real and conscious effort at emulation. Sadly, the model was unique, and the times had changed.[1]

The changes were not necessarily for the worse. It depends on the point of view. To some he has seemed the destroyer of the existing social order.[2] But there is another view: 'It is not excessive to say that the Roman Empire and – in general terms – the Mediterranean world were never more democratic than under the "Dominate" of the Lepcitane Emperors.'[3] It is one of the fascinations of this period of Roman history that such divergence of opinion continues to be possible.

[1] The seriousness of the allegiance to Pertinax is discussed by A. R. BIRLEY (1969) p. 273. One of the main aims of the first part of the present work has been to underline the links between Septimius and Pertinax. I hope that neither this chapter nor what precedes it will be construed as an attempt to 'whitewash' a man who has been described quite legitimately as 'cruel and insensitive' (Sir R. SYME [1968a] p. 200). But such defects of character were not, after all, a novelty, especially on the imperial throne. These were not his only characteristics either. There has been a tendency to regard the accession of Septimius Severus as a major watershed in Roman history. That may be valid. But he himself was above all a product of the Antonine era, and that has perhaps been unduly neglected in favour of generalisations about the 'Punic' aspects of his personality and policies.

[2] J. HASEBROEK (1921) p. 99.

[3] G. CHARLES-PICARD (1959a) p. 145. Cf. also the interesting observations of M. PALLOTTINO p. 100f. on the transformation of the Empire: '*Ciò avvenne soprattutto altraverso i seguenti ordini di fatti: (1) provvedimenti a favore dell' esercito; (2) indebolimento del Senato e delle classi urbane e tentativo di instaurare anche sul piano giuridico una più vasta giustizia sociale; (3) orientamento verso una politica provinciale che dovera culminare nell' editto di Caracalla.*'

APPENDICES
ABBREVIATIONS
BIBLIOGRAPHY
INDEX

APPENDIX I

THE FAMILY OF SEPTIMIUS SEVERUS
(AND *STEMMA*)

The attached stemma contains the names of some thirty-eight persons. The relationship of a few of these to Septimius is hypothetical or imprecisely known, and is marked accordingly. This list below, which is in alphabetical order (by *nomina*), briefly resumes the salient biographical data about each. Many of them have been discussed by the present writer in two articles: 'The *coups d'état* of the year 193' in *Bonner Jahrbücher* 169 (1969) and 'Some notes on *HA Severus* 1–4' in *HAC 1968*. The arguments there presented are not repeated here in detail, but reference is made to them and to the principal discussions of the persons concerned.

1. *C. Cl(audius) Septimius [A]per*. Known from *IRT* 316, a dedication at Lepcis in honour of *Antoninus Pius*, not datable more closely than to that reign. Surely a kinsman. The editors of *IRT* read the *cognomen* as *[A]fer*. In view of the nomenclature of nos. 26 and 27 on this list, *Aper* would seem probable. Cf. A. R. Birley, *HAC*, p. 64f. and ID. (1969), p. 258, no. 70. It would be reasonable to guess that nos. 26 and 33 might be the sons of this man, the elder taking the father's *cognomen*, the younger his *praenomen*, and, perhaps, the *cognomen* of his uncle (no. 35). In that case, *C. Claudius Septimius Aper*, if that was his correct name, would have been over sixty when he dedicated *IRT* 316. But it must be emphasised that this is purely speculative. The man may have been a quite distant kinsman. (Or it is not impossible that he is the same as the *cos*. 153, *P. Septimius Aper*: if that man had been adopted by a *C. Claudius*, he might well have borne the names *C. Claudius Septimius Aper* for a time, and then have reverted to his original style.)

2. *Flavia Neratia Septimia Octavilla*. Known from *CIL* VI 1415, from Rome, an inscription she set up to her father (no. 4). She is described as *c(larissima)* *p(uella)*. There is no indication of date. The last two names of this girl point clearly to kinship with *Septimius*' sister (no. 24).

293

3. (*L. Flavius ?Aper*). The father of no. 4 was presumably an *L. Flavius*. It is here suggested, purely hypothetically, that he may have been the husband of *Septimia Octavilla*, sister of *Septimius* (no. 24). That lady was married to a senator, whose identity is not known. The *cognomen Aper* of no. 4 may have been derived from the *Septimii* (cf. no. 27). There was a senatorial family of *Flavii Apri*, cf. *PIR²* F. 206, 208, 209 (210 would seem not to be connected with them); but 208 and 209 were *M. Flavii*.

4. *L. Flav(ius) Septimius Aper Octavianus*. Known only from *CIL* VI 1415. Father of no. 2, son of no. 3, perhaps also of *Septimia Octavilla* (no. 24). The only basis for this assumption is the last two names of his daughter, no. 2. The inscription records the following career: *Xvir stlitibus iudicandis, sevir turmae II equitum Romanorum, quaestor provinciae Cypri, sodalis Hadrianalis, tribunus plebis*. It is not impossible that this man is identical with the *cos. ord.* 207, *L. Septimius Aper* (no. 26). Cf. *PIR²* F. 365; *L'Albo* nos 2237, 466. In view of the second *cognomen* of his daughter, it is likely that his wife was a *Neratia*. Several senators of this name are known from the period, cf. *L'Albo* nos. 2062–6.

5. *Fulvia Pia*. Mother of *Septimius*. Known from *HA Sev.* 1. 2 and *IRT* 415 and 416, set up not earlier than 198. There is no information about the date of her death. *Fulvia* was presumably a kinswoman of *Plautianus* (no. 8). On this and on the other links of the *Fulvii*, cf. A. R. BIRLEY, *HAC*, p. 64f., and ID. (1969) p. 256.

6. *Fulvius Pius*. Maternal grandfather of *Septimius*. Known only from *HA Sev.* 1.2. Cf. under no. 5.

7. *Pu(blia) Fulvia Plautilla* (Augusta 202–205). Daughter of no. 8, wife of no. 28. Cf. *PIR²* F 564. It seems unlikely that she had any children, cf. p. 232 and n. 1, above. Put to death by her former husband after the death of *Septimius*.

8. *C. Fulvius Plautianus*. The *damnatio memoriae* and consequent erasure of his inscriptions has made it difficult to recover the details of Plautianus's early career. He is securely attested as Praetorian Prefect and *clarissimus vir* on 9 June 197 (D. 2185) and was probably sole Prefect, except for a brief period in 199 when Q. *Aemilius Saturninus* (App. III) was made his colleague, until his murder on 22 January 205. He received consular *ornamenta*, was *consul ordinarius* in 203, as *cos. 'II'*, was made a patrician, pontifex and claimed to have been *comes* of the Emperors *per omnes expeditiones eorum*. Cf. *PIR²* F 455 for details. His daughter married *Antoninus* in 202 and he became *socer Augusti* and *consocer Augusti* thereby. But even before this he could claim to be a kinsman of *Septimius*. Herodian 3.10.6 states somewhat

diffidently that he was related to the Emperor, and there is little doubt that
he was from the same family as the Emperor's mother (no. 5). There have
been several attempts to detect his early career on inscriptions, cf. *PIR*² F
for some of them. G. BARBIERI's (1957) effort to identify him with the
man whose career is known from an inscription at Ostia (also handled in
CP no. 271+*add.*, without mention of Plautianus) was rightly criticised by
R. MEIGGS p. 565. For Herodian 3.10.6 states that *Septimius* 'raised him
ἐκ μικρᾶς καὶ εὐτελοῦς τύχης, etc.' Another possibility is that he is
the man in *IRT* 572, as the Editors there suggest. This person was certainly
one of the *Fulvii* of Lepcis, brother of *Fulvia Nepotilla*, who, with her
husband *Q. Fulvius Dida Bibulianus* and her two sons, set up the stone to
her *fratri pio*, whose names have been erased. In lines 6–8 two offices the
man held are preserved: *praefectus vehiculorum* and *procurator XX heredita-
tium*, of which the second is the more senior, cf. *CP* no. 238. It is not
impossible that *Plautianus* was given one of these posts by *Pertinax* in 193,
as a favour to *Septimius*: Dio 73.15.4 (*Exc. Valesiana* 334) speaks of a man
named in a marginal gloss as Φλούβιος, i.e. surely Φούλβιος, who, having
been condemned by *Pertinax* when the latter was proconsul of Africa, was
τότε δὲ ἐν τοῖς πρώτοις ὑπ' αὐτοῦ ἐκείνου τῇ τοῦ Σεουήρου χάριτι
ἀπεδέδεικτο. This surely has the natural sense: 'was then appointed,
among the first [in a chronological sense] by that same person [i.e. *Pertinax*]'.
The story of his condemnation by *Pertinax* fits what Herodian 3.10.6 says,
that in his youth *Plautianus* 'had been banished after being convicted of
treason and many other crimes.' Cf. Boissevain in his edition, III, p. 320.

Much new light on *Plautianus* has been shed by F. GROSSO (1968).
He has shown convincingly that his name may be recognised, erased, on
CIL XIV S. 4380 (pp. 14ff., and plate 1), as Prefect of the *vigiles*: the date
is 195, and not later than the summer, for *Septimius* is *Imp. V.* Grosso has
further shown that *Plautianus*' name, as Prefect of the Guard, but not yet
clarissimus vir, may be detected on *AE* 1935.156 (pp. 17ff., and plate 2):
the date is 1 January, 197. I cannot however accept Grosso's interpretation
of some of the consequences. He argues that Dio 73.15.4 must mean that
Plautianus was given a high position (taking ἐν τοῖς πρώτοις as 'among the
foremost') in 193, and by *Julianus*, not *Pertinax*, citing the analogy of
Flavius Juvenalis and *Veturius Macrinus* (App. III), and arguing from the
context of the excerpt. I do not think that this follows necessarily. The first
point – which allows Grosso to argue that *Plautianus* was in fact made
Prefect of the *vigiles* (by Julianus) in 193 – conflicts with Herodian 3.10.6.
It also, as Grosso recognises, creates a little difficulty with the phrase *comes*

per expeditiones omnes, for if he was commanding the *vigiles* in spring 193 and still in spring or summer 195, he cannot have participated in the *expeditio orientalis* of 193–4 or in the Parthian campaign that followed it in 195. I prefer to believe that *Pertinax* gave *Plautianus* a junior post in 193 (perhaps the supervision of the *vehicula*, a key role at that time, giving him control of the *cursus publicus*) and that *Septimius* then promoted him swiftly (perhaps first to be *proc. XX hered.*); that he went to the east in 193–4 and returned to Rome to command the *vigiles* at a time when *Septimius* was preparing for the break with Albinus. This is no less speculative than Grosso's hypothesis, but seems to me to create fewer difficulties. Grosso also handles the later career of Plautianus. His thesis that the appointment of *Saturninus* as co-Prefect of the Guard was the product of the first 'rift' between the Emperor and the Prefect (pp. 24ff.) is persuasive, although J. HASEBROEK's (1921) theory (pp. 109, 131f.) of two 'rifts' and two reconciliations before the final downfall is based on a strict interpretation of *HA Sev.* 14.7, part of a passage so mangled as to be rather an unsafe foundation for any theory. Indeed, W. JUDEICH denied that there was more than one 'rift', but Grosso rejects his arguments. Grosso may well be right over this. However, I prefer the date adopted above (p. 219) for the major row, over the statues, rather than early as argued by Grosso. He also argues that the omission of Plautianus's name in the *Acta* of the Saecular Games – only the title *pr. pr.* is given – shows that he was already in disfavour after the revelations of the dying *Geta* the elder (Dio 76.2.4). This may well be (although there is no need to believe that *Geta* died as early as Grosso would have it). It may be mentioned finally that Herodian's description of Plautianus as πρὸς γένους αὐτῷ ὑπάρχοντα (3.10.6) would seem to be confirmed by the term οἰκεῖος ἡμῶν in lines 47–48 of *P. Columbia* 123 (in spite of the doubts of W. L. WESTERMANN, *ad loc.*). On the death of Plautianus cf. esp. E. HOHL (1956b).

9. *C. Fulvius Plautius Hortensianus*. Son of no. 8. His second *nomen* was surely *Plautius* (as Dio 77.1.2) rather than *Plautus* as in *PIR*² F 555. On the *Plautii* of Lepcis cf. A. R. BIRLEY (1969) p. 256f. His last name suggests that his mother, kept totally out of the public eye by *Plautianus* (Dio 75.15.7) may have been a *Hortensia*, although that name is not yet attested at Lepcis. His fate was similar to that of his sister (no. 7). His tribe, Quirina, is recorded by *CIL* XIV 4392.

10. (*?M. Julius*) *Gessius Bassianus Alexianus*=*M. Aurelius Alexander Caesar*=*Imperator Caesar M. Aurelius Severus Alexander Augustus*, etc. Son of nos 11 and 13. Dio attests the *cognomen Bassianus* (78.30.3; 79.17.2;

18.3), Herodian gives *Alexianus* (5.3.3; 7.3), and both are probably right. He might be the same as *M. Julius Gessianus Bassianus*, an Arval Brother in 213 and *magister* in 214, although as Herodian says that he was only twelve years old in 221 (5.7.4), which might be correct, he would surely have been too young in 213 to be an Arval Brother. In that case the Arval Brother may be an elder son of no. 11, although none is recorded; and if so, must surely have died before *Alexander* was made *Caesar*. Cf. *PIR*² A 1610 and J 342; also p. 277f., above.

11. *Gessius Marcianus*. From Arca Caesarea in Syria Phoenice. Second husband of no. 13, father of no. 10 and of a daughter, murdered with her husband in 218 (Dio 78.31.4). It looks as if his own murder, by an officer of *Macrinus* in 218 (after *Elagabalus'* proclamation on 16 May) was described in a fragmentary passage of Dio (78.33.2–34.1²): ... κιανω .... τω/...... Μακρῖνον/........ μενω../ (ὁ γὰρ Μάρκελλος ἐτεθνήκει), τοῦτον μὲν ἀπέκτεινεν, αὐτὸς δὲ ἀτολμήσας περαιτέρω χωρὶς τοῦ Μακρίνου προχωρῆσαι, μετεπέμψατο αὐτόν. He had a career as a procurator, not specified, according to Dio in an earlier passage (78.30.3), before and after which (30.2 and 4) he specifically records the deaths of nos. 16 and 37. By implication therefore this man was still alive at the time of *Elagabalus'* rising. At all events, he was surely dead by 222, or else he would have played some part in his son's elevation. He is mentioned by implication in *Digest* 1.9.12 (cf. under no. 13). See also *PIR*² G 171 (no mention of the passage quoted from Dio).

12. *Julia Domna* (from 193 *Augusta*). It is not impossible that she is the *Julia Domna* who inherited property from her great-uncle *Julius Agrippa*, a *primipilaris* (*Digest* 32.38.4), in spite of the doubts in *PIR*² J 662. The name *Domna* is the same as the Aramaic *Martha*, meaning 'wife of a king'. The name was clearly given her because of her *genitura*, of which *Septimius* had heard (*HA Sev.* 3.9, etc.) – it is absurd to argue, as some have, that the *genitura* was invented to account for the name. For the falsity of the story that she was stepmother, not mother, of *Antoninus*, cf. J. HASEBROEK (1921), p. 12, M. PLATNAUER p. 49f. The date of her birth is unknown. Since her sister *Maesa*'s elder daughter *Soaemias* (no. 15) was probably born before 180, and she herself was not married until 187, it is probable that she was the younger sister. Cf. in general *PIR*² J 663.

13. *Julia Avita Mammaea* (from 222 *Augusta*). Younger daughter of nos 12 and 16. First married to a man of consular rank, cf. *Digest* 1.9.12, recording that her cousin *Antoninus* as Emperor allowed her to retain the rank of a consular's wife when she married a second husband, of lower status,

i.e. *Gessius Marcianus* (no. 11), who seems to have remained an equestrian. She presumably married for the second time not later than 204, if she was the mother of *Marcianus*'s married daughter murdered with her husband in 218 (cf. under no. 11). Her second *cognomen* is generally spelt *Mamaea* on coins and inscriptions. Cf. *PIR²* J 649.

14. *Julia Maesa* (from 218 *Augusta*). Sister of no. 12, mother of nos. 13 and 15, and perhaps of no. 17, wife of no. 16. Probably the elder sister, as her daughter *Soaemias* was probably born before 180. Cf. *PIR²* J 678.

15. *Julia Soaemias Bassiana* (from 218 *Augusta*). Elder daughter of nos. 14 and 16, wife of no. 38, mother of no. 37 and of at least one other child (cf. D. 478, the sarcophagus of her husband set up at Velitrae by herself *cum filis*). Born probably before 180, cf. C. HUELSEN p. 371, whose arguments are accepted in *PIR²* J 704. Her son (no. 36) was probably born in 203 or 204. She was still equestrian at the Saecular Games in June 204.

16. *Julius Avitus* (*?Alexianus*). Husband of no. 14, father of nos. 13 and 15, perhaps of 17. Dio calls him *Julius Avitus* (78.30.2) and describes him as a consular. He apparently died in Cyprus, where he had been sent by *Antoninus* on a special mission from Mesopotamia (hence presumably in 216) after being proconsul of Asia, probably in 214–215, as predecessor of *L. Marius Maximus* (cf. Appendix II). His consulship (suffect) should thus fall *c.* 199. He may have been adlected into the Senate by *Septimius* shortly before this (see under no. 17). He was not the *cos. ord.* 209, who was a *Lollianus Avitus*, cf. J. ŠAŠEL. Dio says that he died of 'old age and sickness'. Herodian calls the grandfather of *Severus Alexander* (no. 10) *Alexianus* (5.7.3). In view of the nomenclature of no. 17, it is likely that this man originally had two *cognomina*. The name *Alexianus* suggests that he may have been a kinsman of his wife: cf. *C. Julius Alexio*, father of *C. Julius Sampsigeramus* of Emesa, *PIR²* J 143 and 542, and *Julius Alexander* of Emesa, *ib.* 134; also *Alexander*, prince of Emesa and Arethusa, executed by Caesar, *PIR²* A 497.

17. *C. Julius Avitus Alexianus*. The career of this man has been brilliantly reconstructed by H.-G. PFLAUM (1962b). As governor of Raetia he dedicated an altar to the god of Emesa at Augsburg, *c.* 207 at latest. The rest of his career is supplied by an inscription from Salonae in Dalmatia, where he was governor *c.* 221. He began as an equestrian officer, held a minor procuratorship, and then was adlected into the Senate, where he served as *praetor* and legate of a legion before his Raetian governorship. This was followed by the consulship and an appointment as *comes* of the Emperors

in Britain. Thereafter he was Prefect of the *alimenta*, *comes* of *Antoninus* (in Germany or Mesopotamia), again Prefect of the *alimenta*, and governor of Dalmatia. In that post he was appointed proconsul of Asia, not later than 222. His name was erased on the inscription at Salonae, no doubt because of his kinship and favour with *Elagabalus*, which he presumably failed to retain with *Severus Alexander*. Pflaum, p. 92, suggests that he was a '*cousin germain*' of no. 16, noting that he was too young to be the same as that person, whose career in any case was different. But there is no reason why he should not have been the son of no. 16. The only argument against this is his initial equestrian rank. However, no. 16 may well have been an equestrian also, until the accession of *Septimius*. The procuratorship, which Pflaum restores as [*proc.*] *ad annonam Augg. Ostiis*] may in fact have been held before 198, as *procurator Augusti*, not *Augustorum*. Father and son could have been elevated to the Senate simultaneously. His *tres militiae* began with the prefecture of a cohort of Petraeans, but the details of the other two stages are missing on the Salonae inscription. It must be borne in mind that he could have been serving as prefect of cavalry in the army of his (presumed) uncle by marriage in 192-3. Cf. also *PIR*² J 192, where Pflaum's results are summarised.

18. (*Julius*) *Bassianus*. Father of nos. 12 and 14. Priest of the Emesene god, named only in *Epit. de Caes*. 21.1; 23.2. The name *Bassianus*, borne by two grandchildren and two great-grandchildren of his (nos. 10, 15, 27, 36) evidently derives from the priestly title *basus*, cf. A. v. DOMASZEWSKI (1909a), pp. 209ff.

19. *Paccia Marciana*. First wife of *Septimius*, whom she married probably in 175. She died at latest in 187, evidently childless. Cf. A. R. BIRLEY, *HAC*, p. 71 and ID. (1969), p. 258, on this woman and her family, clearly native in origin, enfranchised (at Lepcis) in the first century AD. Perhaps distantly related to no. 5, her mother-in-law.

20. *M. Petronius Mamertinus cos*. 150. The hypothesis that this man may have been connected by marriage with the *Septimii* of Lepcis is put forward by A. R. BIRLEY (1969) p. 259f. It is no more than a guess, based initially on the second *cognomen* of this man's son (no. 22). It may be noted that this family of *Petronii* could well have had their home in Africa. The *cos*. 150 is probably the nephew of the homonymous Praetorian Prefect, in office 139-142. A further argument in favour of this man having married a *Septimia* is the fact that both he and no. 34 were *XVviri s.f.* The birth of his elder son, *cos. ord*. 182, need not have been earlier than 149; that of the younger could have been as late as 158, if he was only thirty-two when *cos*.

ord. 190 (which is likely, as he was patrician, cf. *CIL* VI 1979, line 11, 1980, line 9). If the postulated *Septimia* were the second wife of *Mamertinus*, mother only of the younger son, she could have been a daughter of no. 34. But a sister is perhaps more likely. Cf. also under no. 22.

21. *M. Petronius Sura Mamertinus cos. ord.* 182. Son-in-law of *M. Aurelius*, son of no. 20. For the identity of his wife – *Cornificia* – cf. H.-G. PFLAUM (1961), p. 36f. *Sura Mamertinus* was executed by *Commodus* in 190 or 191. *Cornificia* subsequently remarried: her husband, undoubtedly chosen by *Septimius*, was *L. Didius Marinus*, who Pflaum, in *CP* (no. 295, p. 769) argues was probably Syrian, hence no doubt a protégé of *Julia Domna*. It should be noted that in his 1961 article Pflaum mistakenly calls this man and no. 22 sons of the Praetorian Prefect: cf. A. R. BIRLEY (1969), p. 259f.

22. *M. Petronius Sura Septimianus cos. ord.* 190. Executed by Commodus at the same time as no. 21 under whom, and no. 20, see further details on this man. Here two points may be added, which are discussed by A. R. BIRLEY (1969), p. 259f. First, the link between *Petronii* and *Septimii*, which this man's names attest, may have already existed before the postulated marriage of his father to a *Septimia*. The procurator *L. Septi-- Petro---*, whose complete name is most likely to have been *L. Septimius Petronianus*, had a career dated by Pflaum in *CP* (no. 146 *bis*) to the general period 125–165. His names suggest a marriage between a *Septimius* and a *Petronia*. Second, it is just possible that the favour enjoyed by the *cos. ord.* 190 helped to obtain the consulship in that year for *Septimius* (no. 36), although a likelier explanation is of course judicious bribery of *Cleander*.

23. (*Septimia*). See under nos. 20 and 22.

24. *Septimia Octavilla.* Her names are attested by *IRT* 417, where she is described as *c(larissimae) m(emoriae) f(eminae)* and sister of *Septimius*, who has the title *Parthicus maximus*. This indicates that she had been married to a senator (in view of *HA Sev.* 15.7, on which see below); and that she died at some time in the years 198–211 (or perhaps, 198–209, as *Septimius* would have had the title *Brittannicus* after 209). The only other mention of *Septimius*'s sister comes in *HA Sev.* 15.7, where it is stated that she came to him (the context suggests that this was during the second Parthian war) and caused him embarrassment because of her inadequate command of Latin; and that he gave her son the *latus clavus* and sent her back to Lepcis, where the boy died soon after. T. D. BARNES (1967a) p. 96f. doubts the veracity of this story on the grounds that the woman is unlikely to have been in the east. However, it is perfectly plausible to suppose that her husband held some official position there at the time. If her husband was

already a senator, it would have been unnecessary for *Septimius* to give her son the *latus clavus*. If the expression means what it says, one may assume that her husband was then an equestrian, who was raised to senatorial rank before her death. (Cf. p. 204 above). It is suggested above that she may be the mother of no. 4, hence wife of no. 3, a *L. Flavius*. In that case no. 4 would hardly be the boy referred to in *Sev.* 15.7, but another son. Her *cognomen* suggests that one of her grandmothers was an *Octavia*.

25. *Septimia Polla*. Aunt of *Septimius* (no. 36), sister of no. 29, whom she pre-deceased. Her death must therefore fall not later than 171. Known only from *IRT* 607, the base of the silver statue set up after her death by her brother and heir. On the great wealth indicated by the cost of this statue, cf. A. R. BIRLEY (1969) p. 259, citing R. P. DUNCAN-JONES p. 57. No husband is mentioned on *IRT* 607, and it is reasonable to assume that she did not marry.

26. *L. Septimius Aper cos. ord.* 207. Known only from his consulship, cf. *FC*, p. 58, *L'Albo* no. 466, where Barbieri notes that he is probably identical with *Antoninus'* cousin '*Afer*', murdered in 212 (*HA Carac.* 3.6–7). The suggestion that he is also identical with the cousin '*Severus*' whom Herodian (4.6.3) says was put to death at this time is possible, though Herodian is quite likely to have got the name wrong. Cf. *L'Albo* no. 470 and no. 32 below. It is suggested here that he may be the same as L. *Flav(ius) Septimius Aper Octavianus* (no. 4). If not, he should probably be regarded as a grandson (rather than son) of the *cos.* 153 (no. 27).

27. *P. Septimius Aper cos.* 153. Described as *patruus* of *Septimius* in *Sev.* 1.2, on which see A. R. BIRLEY, *HAC*, p. 64f. and ID. (1969) p. 258f. He was more probably a *frater patruelis* of *Septimius'* father (no. 29). Perhaps son of no. 1. The only inscription attesting his consulship spells his *nomen* as *Septumius* (D. 5423), but this does not indicate that he himself used this form. As consul in 153, he can hardly have been born earlier than 110 (cf. R. SYME [1958], pp. 653 on the age for the consulship).

28. (*L.?*) *Septumius Bassianus* (*Caracalla*)=*M. Aurelius Antoninus* (from 195; from 196 *Caesar*, from 198 *Imperator Caesar ... Augustus*). Born 4 April, 188, cf. M. PLATNAUER (1918), pp. 50ff., T. D. BARNES (1967a), p. 93, n. 48, for the year of his birth (some sources suggest an earlier year). Son of no. 12 (not stepson, cf. under no. 12) and no. 35. Named after his maternal grandfather (no. 18). His original *praenomen* is nowhere recorded, but it is likely that it was *L.*, or perhaps *P.* It is suggested under no. 31 that this brother *Geta* was originally *P.*; and that *Geta* took *Bassianus'* praenomen *L.* when *Bassianus* became *M. Aurelius Antoninus*, a

move reminiscent of that by *L. Verus* in 161 (cf. A. R. BIRLEY (1966), p. 153). His marriage to no. 7 was probably childless. Cf. *L'Albo* no. 467.

29. *P. Septimius Geta.* Father of the Emperor. Known from various inscriptions and from *HA Sev.* 1.2, *Geta* 2.1 where only the cognomen is given. Cf. A. R. BIRLEY, *HAC*, p. 60 and ID. (1969) p. 259.[1]

30. *P. Septimius Geta cos. II ord.* 203. Brother of the Emperor. Information about this man has been greatly increased by *IRT* 541, originally published by G. M. BERSANETTI (1942). But some problems remain, in particular whether he was the elder or younger brother. In the present work it is taken that he was the elder brother (and that he was legate of Lower Moesia before the death of *Commodus*). But there is no secure means of proving this. For a discussion, cf. A. R. BIRLEY (1969) p. 262f. His senatorial career has some importance for the reign of *Septimius*: the contacts he had made were clearly of value to his brother. They have mostly been mentioned above (cf. e.g., pp. 68, 135). Note that the proconsul of Crete–Cyrene under whom he served as quaestor was *Q. Caecilius Rufinus*, an African, for

---

[1] No career, local or imperial, is recorded on any of the inscriptions honouring the Emperor's father (or on *IRT* 607, which he himself set up). However, this does not prove absolutely that he had no public office. It is just conceivable that the story found in Victor *de Caes.* 20.28, Eutropius 8.8 and – derived from Victor – in *HA Geta* 2.4, that *Septimius* had been *advocatus fisci* and *tribunus militum (augusticlavius)* before entering the Senate, grew out of a statement in Marius Maximus's *vita Severi*. There is no doubt that *Septimius* himself did not hold these posts. M. HAMMOND (1940) pp. 152ff. tries to justify its accuracy. And recently A. M. HONORÉ p. 163 simply accepts it (and worse: he believes the gloss in *HA Carac.* 8.3, that *Septimius* was a pupil of *Cervidius Scaevola*, etc.; cf. p. 238 n. 1). But see J. HASEBROEK (1921) p. 6 and T. D. BARNES (1967a) p. 91f., where it is rightly rejected. But *Marius Maximus* devoted some space to *Septimius*'s father (cf. *HA Geta* 2.1 and p. 313f., below). Is it possible that Victor, and, following him, Eutropius and the author of the *HA*, misunderstood a passage in Maximus' *vita*? (Or the error may have been made by the author of the so-called '*Kaisergeschichte*', on which cf. R. SYME [1968a] p. 105f.) In *Geta* 2.3–4, it is alleged that *Septimius* owed these equestrian appointments to *Antoninus Pius*, which is made the excuse for a piece of fiction about the name Antoninus being given to his son, *Geta*. It could be that Septimius's father *Geta* held an equestrian tribunate and was advocate of the fisc under Pius, and that Maximus recorded this in words which were later misunderstood. Certainly, it is not fiction by the author of the *HA*—Victor and Eutropius must have got the information from somewhere. The absence of any mention of the posts on inscriptions of *Geta* senior is not a difficulty. It would have been better to suppress the record of such minor functions when the man's son was Emperor. (It was another matter with the grandfather's distinctions. They were held much earlier, and some were intimately connected with the city of Lepcis.)

whose family cf. H. G. PFLAUM (1957), correcting *PIR*² C 36, 47, 74–77 (cf. Appendix III, below). As legate of I Italica he may have served under *Pertinax*. As a *fetialis*, he will have known *C. Aufidius Victorinus*, on whom cf. G. ALFÖLDY, *Reichsbeamte* pp. 38ff., *Q. Aurelius Polus Terentianus* and *L. Marius Maximus* (see Appendix III). The date of his death was after his second consulship at the beginning of 203, and before – evidently some while before – the death of *Plautianus* in January 205, to judge from Dio 76.2.4. Cf. *L.Albo* 469 and A. R. BIRLEY (1969) p. 263., where the enigmatic *P. S . . . G . . .* of D. 441 is identified with him (*contra:* J. GUEY [1951a], pp. 170ff. and *L'Albo* 452).

31. *P.* (*L.*) *Septimius Geta* (*Caesar* from 198; *Imperator Caesar . . . Augustus* from 209) *cos. ord.* 205, *II ord.* 208. Younger son of nos. 12 and 36. Born in 189. There is some difficulty about the day and month, both of birth and death. See most recently T. D. BARNES (1968a), pp. 522ff., who argues that he was probably born on 7 March (189) and murdered on 26 December (211). It is not easy to understand why he was not given equal rank to his brother for over ten years, considering that he was less than a year younger. (In Africa, and occasionally elsewhere, he was described as *Augustus* from 198 onwards, cf. A. R. BIRLEY (1969) p. 262, n. 94.) It has been suggested above that his original *praenomen P.* was altered to *L.* when his brother became *M. Aurelius Antoninus*; partly perhaps to distinguish him from no. 30; and that he reverted to *P.* after the latter's death (cf. p. 229f., above). Apparently unmarried – perhaps his brother's experience deterred him.

32. (*Septimius*) *Macer*. Known only from *HA Sev.* 1.2. See A. R. BIRLEY, *HAC* p. 65 and ID. (1969) p. 256, where it is suggested that he might have been *proavus paternus* of the Emperor, hence father of no. 35 and possibly of no. 1.

33. (*Septimius*) *Severus*. Known only from Herodian 4.6.3. In *L'Albo* no. 470 it is suggested he may be identical with the *cos. ord.* 207 (no. 26 above). He could be a son of no. 31, but descent from no. 34 is one of several other possibilities. He could even have been a *Fulvius* (cf. for example *IRT* 572).

34. *C. Septimius Severus, procos. Africae* 174. The inscription from Lepcis Magna published by G. DI VITA-ÉVRARD (1963) revealed the existence of this man, and made virtually certain the identification with *-mius Severus* (originally read as *-rius Severus*), a proconsul honoured on *ILAlg.* I 1283, which gives his full *cursus*. Equally, he must be the man described as *patruus* of *Septimius* in *HA Sev.* 1.2. Cf. A. R. BIRLEY, *HAC*, p. 64f., where it is argued that he and no. 26 are more likely to have been *fratres patrueles* of

Septimius's father. As proconsul of Africa in 174, probably for the year 173–174, his consulship should have been *c.* 158. Consuls are known in both 155 and 160 who might be identical with him (*FC* p. 44f.), but the *cognomen* was so common that it is unnecessary to confine the choice to these two years. The suggested link between this man and *C. Septimius C. f. Pup. Severus* on an inscription from Praeneste (CIL XIV 3004), raised among others by G. DI VITA-ÉVRARD (1963) pp. 407ff.; and by T. D. BARNES (1967a), p. 89, should be discounted. Also the idea that there was ever 'an Italian branch of the family'. The *Septimii* were clearly enrolled in the Quirina, as were other pre-colonial *cives Romani* at Lepcis. Cf. A. R. BIRLEY, *HAC*, p. 63f. and ID. (1969), p. 254. See also nos. 20–22, above.

35. *L. Septimius Severus.* Grandfather of the Emperor. Cf. A. R. BIRLEY, *HAC*, pp. 63, 75ff., and ID. (1969) p. 253ff., above for a defence of the view that the grandfather (*IRT* 412–413) is the same as *Septimius Severus* of Lepcis, a Roman knight and friend of the poet Statius (*contra*: J. GUEY [1951], T. D. BARNES [1967a]. It would be superfluous to repeat the arguments here. Cf. also A. R. BIRLEY, (1969), p. 255f. where it is suggested that this man's father may have been enfranchised *c.* 79, taking the *nomen* of the legate of III Augusta *Septimius Flaccus*. The father may have been no. 32. No. 35 need not have been born earlier than 70.

36. *L. Septimius Severus=Imperator Caesar L. Septimius Severus Pertinax Augustus,* etc. It would be superfluous to repeat details about the Emperor's career and relations here. But this is a good opportunity to note the development of his titulature. This is briefly discussed by G. J. MURPHY, p. 102f. The cognomen *Pertinax* was assumed from the outset. *Pius* appears in 195. *Parthicus Arabicus Parthicus Adiabenicus,* assumed in that year also, from 198, being replaced by *Parthicus Maximus* (although they make frequent re-appearances). *Brittannicus Maximus* appears in 209. *dominus noster* and the full filiation back to Nerva are commonly found. Other titles include *fortissimus* and *felicissimus.* Cf. indices to *CIL*, etc. (Note the convenient discussion of *dominus noster* by G. M. BERSANETTI [1946].)

37. *Varius Avitus Bassianus=Imperator Caesar M. Aurelius Antoninus Augustus.* Son of nos. 15 and 37, born probably in 203. Priest of the Emesene god before his elevation to the throne. His *cognomina* were taken from nos. 16 and 18. Cf. *L'Albo* no. 963 + Agg.; *RE* 8A (1955) cols. 391ff. His original *praenomen* is unknown.

38. *Sex. Varius Marcellus.* From Apamea in Syria Phoenice. Father of no. 36, husband of no. 15. The fullest treatment is by H.-G. PFLAUM in *CP*

(no. 237) and cf. also B. E. THOMASSON, II, pp. 205ff. The career may be set out here, as some discussion is necessary: *procurator aquarum C; procurator provinciae Britanniae CC; procurator rationis privatae CCC, vice praefectorum praetorio et urbi functus; C.V.; praefectus aerari militaris; legatus legionis III Augustae praeses provinciae Numidiae.* He is attested in the first of these offices by D. 8687, which from the description of *Antoninus* as *Augustus* and *Geta* as *Caesar* cannot be earlier than 198. He may well have been holding the post for several years at the time of the inscription. He died before 218 (D. 478 and Dio 78.30.2). Some help is given by the Fasti of Numidia. He cannot have been governor before 201, when *Q. Anicius Faustus* is last attested, or in the years 208–210 (or strictly, between 1 August 208 and 4 April 210) when *Ti. Claudius Subatianus Proculus* was governor. Three other governors must be assigned to the years 201–208: *Claudius Gallus*, clearly governor before January 205, *Q. Cornelius Valens*, who may alternatively have been governor in the years 210–211, and *Pontius*, governor at some time in the years 201–209 (cf. Appendix III). Further help is given by the *Acta* of the Saecular Games, on which his wife heads the list of ladies of equestrian rank. Thus his promotion to the Senate, recorded on D. 478 by the laconic abbreviation *C.V.*, cannot have taken place before June 204 at earliest. H.-G. PFLAUM and B. E. THOMASSON follow E. BIRLEY (1950), p. 63, in placing the Numidian governorship early in the reign of Caracalla. At least two governors are already known from that six-year reign (Thomasson, II, pp. 207ff.), so there is not much more room then. However, since Marcellus died without being even consul designate, it is fair to assume that he died in office, perhaps after a short tenure only. Pflaum argued that his post as *proc. rationis privat.* and Acting Praetorian and Urban Prefect belonged to the years 208–211. It is clear that it must have been held during the absence of the Emperors. However, it is now known that one *Q. Cerellius Apollinaris* was procurator of the *ratio privata* during those years: he was *praefectus vigilum* on 13 April 212 (his predecessor in this post still being in office on 4 April 211: *PIR*² J 511), having had charge of the *ratio privata* immediately before, cf. J. M. REYNOLDS (1962). Hence it is unlikely that *Marcellus* held this post in the years 208–211. It is perfectly reasonable to suggest the following timetable for his career: 196 (or earlier)–198, *procurator aquarum*; 199–201, procurator of Britain; 202–204, procurator of the *ratio privata* and Acting Praetorian and Urban Prefect; 204, made a senator and appointed Prefect of the Military Treasury; 207, perhaps 208, governor of Numidia, for a short time only. The occasion for his special post at Rome would be the absence of the Emperors and

Prefects in Africa in 202–203. But this remains speculative.

One further person may perhaps have been a kinsman, *C. Julius Septimius Castinus* (*PIR*² J 566). He was certainly entrusted with responsible posts by both *Septimius* and *Caracalla* and was a close friend of the latter (Dio 79.4.3). Cf. Appendix III, below, p. 348f.

THE FAMILY OF SEPTIMIUS SEVERUS

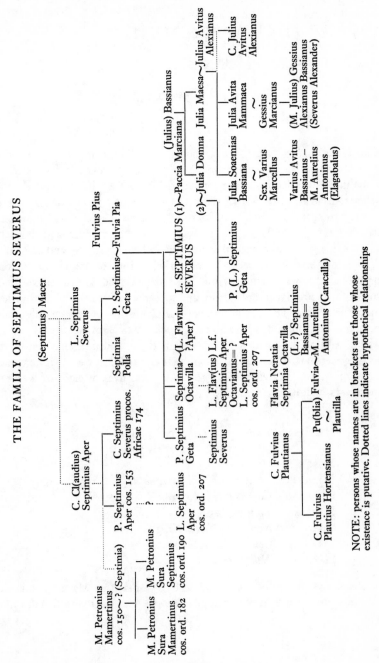

NOTE: persons whose names are in brackets are those whose existence is putative. Dotted lines indicate hypothetical relationships

APPENDIX II

MARIUS MAXIMUS

The *Historia Augusta* contains a good deal of factual information on the period covered in the present work (see pp. 10ff., above). It is clearly of some interest to determine the source of this material. For a century most scholars have accepted that the hard facts in the first part of the *HA* were derived from the biographies of Marius Maximus. The case was argued at length by J. J. MÜLLER in 1870, and refinements were added by J. PLEW in 1878 (who argued that for much of the work, the author of the *HA* used Maximus at second-hand). Both wrote before H. DESSAU unearthed the basic nature of the *HA* itself in 1889, and to that extent some of their arguments are invalid; and subsequent research and discoveries make further modifications necessary. Marius Maximus is known only from mentions in Ammianus Marcellinus, the scholiast on Juvenal, and the *HA*, where he is cited as a source twenty-eight times, and mentioned on three further occasions. The scholiast on Juvenal 4.53 makes it clear that he wrote a life of *Nerva*. The citations in the *HA* attest lives of eight of Nerva's successors, written by Maximus:

> Trajan: *Sev. Alex.* 48.6; 65.4
> Hadrian: *Hadr.* 2.10, 12.4, 20.3, 25.4;
>   *Ael.* 3.9, 5.5; *Sev. Alex.* 30.6
> Pius: *Ant. Pius* 11.3
> Marcus: *M. Ant.* 1.6, 25.10; *Avid. Cass.* 6.6–7, 9.5, 9.9
> Commodus: *Comm.* 13.2, 15.5, 18.2ff.
> Pertinax: *Pert.* 2.8, 15.8
> Severus: *Sev.* 15.6; *Clod. Alb.* 3.4, 9.2, 9.5, 12.14;
>   *Geta* 2.1; *Sev. Alex.* 5.4
> Elagabalus: *Heliog.* 11.6

In *Quad. Tyr.* the author of the *HA* notes (1.1–2) that Marius Maximus did not write separate lives of usurpers (*tyranni*) but dealt with them in the

Life of the relevant Emperor. He describes Maximus as *homo omnium verbossimus, qui et mythistoricis se voluminibus inplicavit*. In *Probus* 2.7 he classes Maximus as one of those *qui haec et talia non tam diserte quam vere memoria tradiderunt*. (The other mention is in *Sev. Alex.* 21.4, where Maximus is said to have reported in many of his *Lives* the practice of dismissing Praetorian Prefects by 'kicking them upstairs' into the Senate.) Ammianus Marcellinus couples Maximus with Juvenal as the favourite – indeed sole – reading-matter of the aristocracy of his own time: *quidam detestantes ut venena doctrinas Iuvenalem et Marium Maximum curatiore studio legunt, nulla volumina praeter haec in profundo otio contrectantes : quam ob causam non iudicioli est nostri* (28.4.14). He obviously took a dim view of Maximus.

There is little doubt that Maximus wrote a second *Twelve Caesars, a fine Suetonii Tranquilli*; Nerva, Trajan, Hadrian, Pius, Marcus, Commodus, Pertinax, Didius Julianus, Severus, Caracalla, Macrinus, Elagabalus. In the reign of Severus Alexander such an opportunity presented itself for the first time. And historical writing had a vogue. Cassius Dio had been at work for twenty years on his great *History* (see pp. 7ff., above), and another writer, Asinius Quadratus, was attempting something similar at the same time (see F. MILLAR [1964], pp. 62, 192). Maximus may have felt the need to provide a Latin alternative to these two Greek works.

Maximus is generally identified with the *cos. II ord.* 223, L. Marius Maximus Perpetuus Aurelianus. This man's career is known in great detail. The names are admittedly common enough (hundreds of Marii in Italy and the western provinces; and I. KAJANTO, p. 275f., records the existence of over fifteen hundred men with the cognomen Maximus from the imperial period). But it is reasonable to identify the biographer with either the *cos. II ord.* 223 or with his (presumed) son L. Marius Maximus, *cos. ord.* 232. A citation in the *Commodus* (13.2) is thought to favour identification with the first of these: *versus in eo* (the *tumor* of Commodus) *multi scripti sunt, de quibus etiam in opere suo Marius Maximus gloriatur*. This is held to mean that Maximus himself wrote some of these satiric verses, and boasted about them in his work (cf. *RE* 14 [1930] col. 1831). But A. O'Brien-Moore, in the Loeb translation of the *HA*, renders the passage as follows: 'Many verses were written alluding to this deformity; and Marius Maximus prides himself on preserving these in his biography of Commodus.' (vol. I, p. 297) Similarly F. GROSSO (1964), p. 378 n. 4, prefers to take *gloriatur* in the sense of '*fare sfoggio*'. But he does not question the identification of the biographer with the elder Marius Maximus. There is no real means of deciding. However, even if one does not interpret *gloriatur* to mean 'boasts', which would make the identification between the *cos. II ord.* 223 and the biographer almost certain, it still seems likelier that the biographer was a contemporary of Commodus. On the other hand, if one were to allow for the possibility that the biographer were the son of the *cos. II ord.*, the latter's career would still be of importance. Items in the *HA* that the *cos. II ord.* would seem to have been particularly well qualified to record, could reasonably enough have been passed on to his son, or another kinsman.

Of some incidental interest, although not strictly relevant to this enquiry, is the origin of these Marii. H.-G. PFLAUM in *CP* (no. 168) assumes the family to be Italian, in fact '*Romains de Rome*'. G. BARBIERI in *L'Albo* (no. 1100) describes the *cos. II ord.* as '*assai probabilmente italico*'. Sir R. Syme in *Ammianus and the HA* (1968), p. 89 n. 4 enters a useful caution, suggesting that origin in Spain or Africa is more likely. His suggestion is pursued further by A. R. BIRLEY (1969), p. 276f. It is there argued that African origin is plausible. A stemma of the family is provided by Pflaum in *CP*. It is convenient to set that out here, adding against each name the principal references.

L. Marius Perpetuus, *scriba quaestorius* (*ILAfr.* 591)
|
L. Marius Perpetuus, *procurator Augusti* (D. 1369, cf. *CP* no. 168)

L. Marius Maximus Perpetuus Aurelianus *cos. c.* 198, *II ord.* 223 (D. 2935–6, *CIL* X 6567, 6764, *AE* 1955, 188, *IGR* IV 1287, *Forsch. Ephesos* III, p. 118, no. 30, *Dura Final Report* V.1, pp. 217ff. no. 56, Dio 78.14.3, 79.2.1. *L'Albo* no. 1100)

L. Marius Maximus, *cos. ord.* 232 (*L'Albo* no. 1099)

L. Marius Perpetuus *cos. c.* 202 (D. 1165, 5899, *IGL Syr.* 39–40, etc. *L'Albo* no. 357).

L. Marius Perpetuus, *cos. ord.* 237 (*L'Albo* no. 1101)

Maria Aurelia Violentilla, *Perpetui cos. filia* (see *PIR*² E 31, under her husband Q. Egnatius Proculus. She may be daughter of the *cos. c.* 202, rather than of the *cos. ord.* 237)

The following should also be noted:

Q. Venidius Rufus Marius Maximus L. Calvinianus, *cos. c.* 201 (*L'Albo* no. 519; and cf. A. R. BIRLEY (1969) p. 277); Claudia Maria Maxima Martia Secunda, *clarissima femina*, wife of P. Attius Pudens Rufinus Celsianus (cf. *PIR*² C 1107); L. Marius L. lib. Doryphorus, *anulos aureos consecutus a divo Commodo, scrib. aedilic. et tribunic.*; etc. (D. 1899).

The first known member of the family, the *scriba* L. Marius Perpetuus, was on the staff of a proconsul of Africa *c.* 137–138 (cf. Sir R. SYME (1965), p. 343). The procurator Perpetuus's career probably belongs to the reign of Pius, or to the years 169–176, in view of his description as procurator of one emperor on D. 1389. That inscription was set up at Lugdunum, when he was procurator of Lugdunensis and Aquitania. His previous career had been entirely at Rome, in various financial posts. The career of his elder son, the first Marius Maximus, may be set out as follows:

> *IVvir viarum curandarum*
> *tribunus legionis XXII Primigeniae*
> *tribunus legionis III Italicae*
> *quaestor urbanus*
> *tribunus plebis candidatus*
> *adlectus inter praetorios*
> *curator viae Latinae*
> *curator reipublicae Faventinorum*
> *legatus legionis I Italicae*
> *dux exercitus Moesiaci apud Byzantium*
> *et apud Lugdunum*
> *legatus Augustorum* (*duorum*) *pro praetore provinciae Belgicae*
> *consul*
> *legatus Augustorum* (*duorum*) *pro praetore provinciae Germaniae*
>   *Inferioris*
> *legatus Augustorum* (*duorum*) *pro praetore provinciae Syriae Coelae*
> *proconsul provinciae Africae*
> *proconsul provinciae Asiae iterum*
> *praefectus urbi*
> *consul iterum ordinarius*
> He was also a *fetialis*

The command at Byzantium may be certainly dated to the summer of 193, and that at Lugdunum to February 197 (cf. pp. 175, 189ff. above). He is attested in Syria in the year 208 (cf. p. 253f., above) and is recorded as proconsul of Asia apparently in 215 (IGR IV 1287), which was the first of his two years in that position. He had already, pace B. E. THOMASSON, II, pp. 114ff., been proconsul of Africa (cf. E. Birley, reviewing Thomasson, in *JRS* 52 [1962], p. 224). He was made Prefect of the City in place of Oclatinius Adventus, by Macrinus, when Adventus proved incapable of behaving with decorum in that office.[1] His second consulship, as colleague of Severus Alexander when that Emperor was consul for the first time, was thus the crown of a long and distinguished career. His first consulship must have come soon after his appointment to Belgica, in 198 or 199. It is reasonable to assume that he held it at the age of about forty – hardly much younger, possibly a little older (cf. Sir R. SYME [1958], pp. 653ff.). This would give the year 158 as his approximate date of birth, and it would be reasonable to suppose that he began his two military tribunates at about the age of twenty, hence that he served during the second Marcomannic War of 178–180 (cf. A. BIRLEY [1966a], pp. 283ff.). His quaestorship would fall in about 182 or 183, and his tribunate and adlection to praetorian rank during the years of Cleander's domination (cf. pp. 122ff., above). He was clearly serving as legate of I Italica at the moment of Septimius's proclamation in April 193. (In view of all the evidence available for the career of Maximus, it is surprising, to say the least, to find W. SESTON [1966] commenting that '*de sa vie nous ne savons guère que son nom, L. Marius Maximus Perpetuus Aurelianus, et la fin de son cursus; il a été consul deux fois, en 198 et en 223; entretemps, Macrin en avait fait un préfet de la Ville.*' [p. 88of., n. 5] Seston adds, *ibid.*, that '*de son oeuvre nous ne connaissons que ce qu'en a conservé l'Histoire Auguste qui s'y reporte explicitement 19 fois, mais qui lui a certainement beaucoup emprunté sans le dire,*' evidently unaware of the scholiast on Juvenal 4.53. '19', may be a misprint for '29'.)

The career of Maximus's brother Perpetuus was also successful. The inscriptions which record it are unfortunately defective in some respects, but this much is known:

> *tribunus legionis IV Scythicae*
> *quaestor candidatus*
> *legatus legionis XVI Flaviae*
> *legatus Augustorum (duorum) pro praetore provinciae Arabiae*
> *consul*
> *curator reipublicae Urbisalviensium*
> *item Tusculanorum*
> *legatus Augustorum (duorum) provinciae Moesiae superioris*
> *legatus Augusti pro praetore provinciarum trium Daciarum*

Only the last post is securely dated, to 214 (cf. A. STEIN [1944], p. 67). But it seems that he was promoted from commanding the legion XVI Flavia to be governor of Arabia in 200 (cf. *CP*, p. 442f.). This makes it virtually certain that he was in Rome, going through the urban magistracies, in the years 191–193. It is quite possible that his service as tribune of IV Scythica was at the time when Septimius commanded that legion and Pertinax was governor of Syria. As consul *c.* 202, he should have held the military tribunate about twenty years earlier. A contact of this kind may have had some weight in the year 193.

Between them, the members of this family had a wealth of experience. One would expect, *a priori*, that some of this at least would have been made use of in the biographies by Maximus; and, *a fortiori*, that some of it would be apparent in the *HA* also, if that work is based on Maximus to any considerable extent. An obvious omission is the siege of Byzantium, which Maximus himself directed. But this is not surprising. The author of the *HA* would not have been willing to incorporate a detailed account of a city that he clearly despised (*Gall.* 6.9, cf. W. HARTKE, p. 293f.). Dio's account of the siege is flattering to the Byzantines (74.10.1ff.) and there is no reason why the man who took more than two years to capture the city (cf. p. 187f., above) would have underrated their virtues, or the excellence of their city. A major error in the account of the civil wars in *Severus* is the assertion (9.1) that Niger was killed at Cyzicus. In fact, he was killed fleeing from Antioch to the Euphrates (Dio 74.8.3), in the outskirts of the city according to Herodian (3.4.6). But the error in the place-name is also found in Aurelius Victor 20.8 and Eutropius 8.18.4. It may have crept into the *HA* from there: the author was careless; and he was about to abandon his good source in favour of Victor (*Sev.* 17.5). The account of the civil wars in the *HA* is scrappy and confused. But there are details there which show the murky outlines of a well-informed source. Only the *HA* knows of the battle of Tinurtium by name (*Sev.* 11.1). Particularly interesting, the *HA* has some details about the Emperor's brother Geta. Not only was Geta, as governor of Moesia Inferior (cf. Appendix I, above, no. 28), Maximus's commanding officer. They were fellow-members of the college of *fetiales*. The *HA* has two stories about Geta, belonging to the years 193 and 196 (*Sev.* 8.10, 10.3). The second of these follows the account of the elevation of Septimius's elder son to the rank of Caesar, which only the *HA* localises, at Viminacium. Maximus may well have been there, with the *exercitus Moesiacus*. Maximus may also have learned from Geta the details about the father of Geta and Septimius that he recorded in his Life of *Severus*, *satis copiose* (*Geta* 2.1). Copious details on the *vita* and *mores* of this man would have been hard to come by. The account of the events of 31 December 192 and 1 January 193 is particularly good. The *HA* knows, for example, that Pertinax was involved in the plot to murder Commodus (*Pert*, 4.4). Maximus is explicitly cited as the source of the remarkable anti-*adclamationes* against the murdered Commodus (*Comm.* 18.2ff.). There are other details; Pertinax had to sit waiting in the Temple of Concord, as the janitor of the *curia* could not be found; and Claudius Pompeianus came to see him there (*Pert.* 4.9–10); and so on. Maximus was not, of course, an eye-witness (as F. MILLAR [1964], p. 134 and n. 10 implies). He was in Lower Moesia. But he no doubt heard a graphic account from his brother – or perhaps from the freedman L. Marius Doryphorus, who may well have been holding one of his posts as clerk to the magistrates at this time (D. 1899). The picture of Pertinax conveyed by the *HA* is far less favourable than that of Dio and Herodian (cf. *Pert.* 6.7, 7.9, 9.4ff., 12.1ff.). Maximus may have had cause for resentment against Pertinax, who ordered *eos, qui praeturas non gessissent sed allectione accepissent, post eos esse, qui vere praetores fuissent* (*Pert.* 6.10). This won Pertinax *grande odium* – perhaps from Maximus also, who was affected by the measure.

A number of items crop up elsewhere, that might suggest that Maximus incorporated in his work knowledge gained in public service by himself or his family. Thus, the *origo materna* of L. Verus (*Ael.* 2.9, *Verus* 1.9) would have been familiar to a *curator* of Faventia. The list of barbarian tribes that 'conspired' against Rome in the Marcomannic wars (*M. Ant.* 22.1 – at least seventeen names, although the text is somewhat corrupt) should have been familiar to one who served in a legion of Upper Germany and of Raetia at the end of those wars. The *HA* has a few minor details that Maximus could well have supplied. Didius Julianus's service in XXII Primigenia, as governor of Belgica (about which the *HA* has some specific information) and of Lower Germany (*Did Jul.* 1.6–9) matched Maximus's own (except that Julianus was legate, not tribune, of leg. XXII). His brother Perpetuus was tribune of the legion that Septimius commanded (and quite possibly served under him). From Perpetuus, or indeed from his own experience as governor of Syria Coele, Maximus could have gained some of the details given in *Sev.* 3.6, 3.9 (cf. *Geta* 3.1; also *Sev. Alex.* 5.4, where Maximus is explicitly cited for this information) and 9.4. More items of this kind could be brought forward. But it is time to turn to the objections raised against viewing Maximus as the main source of the first part of the *HA*.

Serious doubts were first raised by G. BARBIERI in 1954, but although he was cited from time to time, it was almost always in disagreement. However, in 1968, in his book *Ammianus and the Historia Augusta*, pp. 89ff., and in two articles, published in the *Bonner HAC.* (pp. 131ff.) and in *Hermes* (pp. 494ff.). Sir R. SYME, has taken up Barbieri's arguments and reinforced them (the article in *Hermes* does not go further than the article in *HAC*, and Syme's arguments will be cited from the latter place alone, for the most part). He argues that there was another source, whom he designates '*Ignotus*', and gives seven arguments 'that tell against Marius Maximus' (*HAC*, p. 146f.):

1. 'Citations of Maximus have been grafted into the main source.' The item he instances, *M. Ant.* 1.6, the ultimate ancestry of Marcus Aurelius, is the only one where this does appear to be certain. Yet caution is necessary. Maximus was extremly longwinded, according to the *HA* (*Quad. Tyr.* 1.2). There is no reason why he might not have introduced the mythical ancestors of M. Aurelius separately, after detailing the other ancestors and then the date and place of birth. For example, it might have had relevance to an omen noted at the time of birth. Suetonius, whom Maximus emulated, has far longer accounts of the *origo* of his twelve Caesars than is preserved in the *HA* for any of those dealt with by Maximus. Yet one need not doubt that Maximus would have provided an account just as lengthy as those of Suetonius. Besides, in the Life of *Vespasian*, Suetonius introduces mention of the mythical origin of the *gens Flavia* in the middle (*c.*12) of the *vita*, many pages after recording the historical ancestry. In any case, to say of Maximus, as does Barbieri, that '*egli crede ingenuamente che Marco Aurelio discenda da Numa*' (p. 263) is absurd. One has only to compare Suetonius *Galba* 2 and *Vitellius* 1.2 to see that a reasonably sober biographer could introduce this kind of detail, without believing it himself. How this kind of story would then be used by the author of the *HA*, whose 'product is hasty and careless' (in these early lives: Syme, *Ammianus and the HA*, p. 183), is another matter. Syme follows Barbieri (who in turn follows Schulz, Lecrivain and Kornemann) p. 43, in the view that '*le citazioni di M.M. sembrano come chiuse tra parentesi e si possono eliminare senza danno, anzi spesso con vantaggio del contesto.*' This is unreasonable. In truth, the same could be said of numerous passages in the *HA* for which no source is given. It is simply a reflection of the incompetence and haste with which the author has excerpted his material. For example, the single citation of Maximus in the *Pius* (11.3) could, certainly, be removed without damage. But so could any other of the sentences in that chapter. In other cases, the

citation of Maximus appears to be a thoroughly integral part of the context (e.g. in *Pertinax* 2.8).

2. 'Many of the citations are trivial in content or scandalous.' Hardly a valid criticism when one compares passages in the excellent Suetonius. Trivia and scandal were in the very nature of the genre. What opinion would one have of the worth of Suetonius if the original had perished, and he were known only for citations of *Div. Aug.* 70, *Tiberius* 43ff., *Gaius* 24.1, *et hoc genus omne*? Besides, how many of the *fragmenta* of Maximus really deserve the label of triviality or scandal? *Sev. Alex.* 21.4 is a reference to imperial practice in dismissing Praetorian Prefects, by giving them the *latus clavus*. *Pius* 11.3 is a comment on the authorship of that Emperor's speeches (this kind of subject interested Tacitus: *Ann.* 13.3.2). *Severus* 15.6, Septimius's denial of his responsibility for the execution of (Julius) Laetus, is neither trivial nor scandalous. The scandal is there of course: for example, Plotina's influence gaining Hadrian a bride against Trajan's real wishes (*Had.* 2.10); Hadrian's cruelty (20.3); Faustina's implication in the rising of Cassius (*Av. Cass.* 9.9.) – but it is mostly political scandal. The *tetrapharmacum* (Hel. 5.5, *Sev. Alex.* 30.6) and the *iocularia* at Elagabalus's vintage festival (*Heliog.* 11.6) are certainly trivial. But it would be excessively severe to classify many of the other comments in this way (the number of Albinus' sons, *Alb.* 9.5, the *genitura* of Julia Domna, *Sev. Alex.* 5.4, and so on).

3. 'Orations in biography . . . An innovation, and not reassuring.' Sir Ronald argues that his '*Ignotus* stood by his model, Suetonius.' If it could be proved independently that a biographer who supplied speeches – two are mentioned as supplied by Maximus (*M. Ant.* 25.10 and *Pert.* 2.8), but not quoted *verbatim* – could not have provided sober facts also, this criticism might be valid. As it is, this is not an independent argument. It is based on an assumption. Both speeches, incidentally, were put in the mouth of Marcus Aurelius: one commending Pertinax, the other castigating the Antiochenes as *seditiosi*. Both belong to the same period, 175 (the second could belong to 176). It could be that the remarks derive from one and the same speech. Another point should be noted. Marcus Aurelius, unlike most emperors, left behind him literary productions – the *Meditations*, and his letters to Fronto. It could be that the speech, or speeches, of Marcus reported by Maximus belonged not to the genre of the ancient historian's speech in the Thucydidean manner, but to the category of documentary evidence. In other words, Maximus may have had published speeches of the Emperor to draw on, perhaps collected and published after his death by his admirers

– although speeches delivered during a civil war are likely to have been circulated at the time, as a weapon of propaganda.

4. The preceding comments lead to the next argument: 'Marius Maximus appended documents ... There is no sign that the basic source adopted this practice.' In citing documents *verbatim*, Maximus was following Suetonius, in whose biographies many examples may be found – including part of an oration, that delivered by Caesar as the *laudatio* for his aunt (*Div. Jul.* 6.1). (Maximus's introduction of orations into biography was hardly 'an innovation', therefore.) In any case, is there really no sign that 'the basic source' adopted the practice? What of the passage in *Commodus* 11.13–12.12? Is this not in essence the citation of a document listing events in Commodus's life, dated by the new names of the months? See F. GROSSO (1964), p. 374f. and H. NESSELHAUF (1965), pp. 127ff.

5. 'Opinions expressed by Maximus clash with the basic text. The main trend of the *Vita Hadriani* is favourable to that ruler. Maximus, three times out of four, is hostile.' In chapter XVII of *Ammianus and the HA*, Sir Ronald modifies this slightly: 'There are unfriendly stretches, insertions, or comments. For some of them Marius Maximus is expressly cited.' (p. 91). In fact, examination of this *vita* reveals a whole series of comments and anecdotes that show the same hostile tendency as those three passages expressly attributed to Maximus (2.10, 20.3, 25.4: 12.4 is neutral in tone).

They may best be examined by a simple listing:

1.5   the label *Graeculus*, surely pejorative

2.1   reported criticism of his passion for hunting

2.6   Servianus inspires Trajan to hate Hadrian by revealing the latter's debts

3.3   he toadies to Trajan by imitating his hard drinking

4.1   he gets his Syrian command through Plotina's influence

4.5   he corrupts Trajan's freedom and abuses his *delicati*

4.10   his adoption by Trajan was faked

7.1   his unpopularity after the murder of the four consulars

7.6   his spending of *infinita pecunia* to gain popularity

9.1–6   his abandonment of Trajan's conquests on the pretext that he was following Trajan's orders
          his wish to murder his former guardian and Prefect Attianus, and his dismissal of those who had gained him the throne

11.3–7   his sacking of Suetonius and others and his prying *per frumentarios*. His adulteries and homosexual affairs

317

13.10   the belief that he incited accusers against provincial governors and procurators

14.5–7   his 'womanish' mourning for Antinous and the rumour that the latter's death was a *devotio*

14.8–11   his excessive addiction to poetry and his boasted talents at singing and flute-playing; his excess *in voluptatibus*, and the general verdict *severus laetus* . . . etc.

15.2–13   his mean treatment of his friends and his desire to seem more learned than the *professores omnium artium*

16.1   his *famae cupido* and his autobiography published under the names of his freedmen

16.7   his addiction to astrology

23.2–9   the deaths of Servianus, Fuscus and Sabina; the Emperor's hatred for his former friend Platorius Nepos and for Terentius Gentianus

23.10–11 the adoption of Ceionius Commodus, *forma commendatum*

25.7   his death *invisus omnibus* (if this means 'hated by all')

25.8   the death of Servianus again

27.1   the Senate's unwillingness to deify him

These passages, together with those for which Maximus is explicitly cited, or for which he can be supplied as a source from a citation in the *Aelius* (viz. *Ael.* 3.9, basically the same as *Hadr.* 16.7), form a substantial portion of the *vita*. Not merely 'hostile stretches'. If one were to assess what percentage of the *vita* they amounted to, a conservative estimate would be at least 25%; and they are spread uniformly throughout. The answer is, that Maximus, like Cassius Dio, was not uniformly hostile to Hadrian. Hadrian was too complex a figure for any simple verdict. He was not easy to like as a person (cf. Fronto, *ad M. Caes.* 2.1=Haines 1.110) but it would have been absurd to withhold favourable judgment on all his actions (cf. Dio 69.5.1ff. and the comments by F. MILLAR [1964], p. 66). In fact, SYME himself had summed up the complexity of Hadrian better than anyone in his 1965 paper 'Hadrian the Intellectual'.

6. 'The Vita Veri. As has been shown above, this biography must no longer be left among the Nebenviten. It belongs to the main series. Now a Verus written by Maximus will not concord with the total of twelve rulers from Nerva to Elagabalus. The life and actions of that person (it follows) were recounted in the Life of Marcus by Maximus. That biography, so at least the *HA* asserts, comprised two volumes (Avid. 6.7; 9.5).' To Syme's own

proof that the *Verus* cannot be regarded as one of the Nebenviten (*HAC*, p. 133f.) should be added the article by T. D. BARNES in *JRS* (1967), to which he refers. There can be no gainsaying this proof. This Life cannot be included with the *Aelius, Avidius Cassius, Niger, Albinus, Geta* and *Diadumenianus*, as it was by Mommsen (quoted by Syme, l.c.), under the general description '*nicht etwa eine getrübte Quelle, sondern eine Kloake*'. It is full of excellent factual material, and lacks the characteristic fabrications of the Nebenviten, faked letters, verses and the rest. But does it necessarily follow that the material in it could not have derived from a Life of Marcus by Marius Maximus? Maximus was, after all, *homo omnium verbosissimus*. Yet the Lives in the *HA* are fairly short. The *vita Marci* is hopelessly muddled. 15.3–19.12 is interpolated into the basic version. It is based on Eutropius 8.11–14. There is little doubt that the author of the *HA* lost patience with his basic source – surely because it was becoming too lengthy to excerpt with ease (cf. p. 328, below, on *Severus* 17.5). It would have added to his confusion if he had already messed up his source by extracting all the details he could find on Verus to form a separate *vita* of that Emperor. It is significant that in the *Marcus* there is no mention of one of the key events of the reign, the invasion of Italy – which occurred soon after the death of Verus (probably in 170, cf. A. R. BIRLEY [1968]). Examination of the *Verus* in detail does not conflict with the hypothesis that most of the information in it could have derived originally from a *vita Marci* – at least from an exceptionally lengthy *vita Marci*, such as Maximus evidently wrote. 1.1–6 is of course the author of the *HA*'s own introduction. But 1.7–2.7 and 2.10–3.7 could well have been included in a Life of Marcus, introducing the character of Verus in some detail. In what follows, it is noteworthy how frequently Marcus rather than Lucius appears as the subject (3.8, 4.1, 4.3, 4.11, 5.6, 6.7, 7.7, 9.2, 9.4, 9.7 and 9.11.2). In fact, comparison of the Lives of Marcus and Verus in the *HA* shows that the material in the *Verus* could perfectly well have fitted into an original Life of Marcus. For example, most of *M.Ant.* 7.5–11 and *Verus* 3.8–4.4, the accounts of their accession, could be amalgamated with little overlapping (the passages from the *Verus* are italicised):

M. Ant. 7.5   'post excessum divi Pii a senatu coactus regimen publicum capere fratrem sibi participem in imperio designavit.

Verus   4.1   *Dato igitur imperio et indulta tribunicia potestate, post consulatus etiam honorem delatum, Verum vocari praecepit, suum in eum transferens nomen, cum ante Commodus vocaretur.*

M. Ant. 7.5 quem Lucium Aurelium Verum [Commodum] appellavit
–8.3 Caesaremque atque Augustum dixit. atque ex eo pariter
coeperunt rem publicam regere, tuncque primum Romanum
imperium duos Augustos habere coepit, (cum imperium sibi re)
lictum cum alio participasset. Antonini mox ipse nomen recepit.
et equasi pater Lucii Commodi esset, [et Verum eum appellavit
addito Antonini nomine] filiamque suam Lucillam fratri
despondit. ob hanc coniunctionem pueros et puellas novorum
nominum frumentariae perceptioni adscribi praeceperunt.
actis igitur quae agenda fuerant in senatu pariter castra praetoria
petiverunt et vicena milia nummum singulis ob participatum
imperium militibus promiserunt et ceteris pro ratis. Hadriani
autem sepulchro corpus patris intulerunt magnifico exsequiar-
um officio. mox iustitio secuto publice quoque funeris
expeditus est ordo, et laudavere uterque pro rostris patrem
flaminemque ei ex adfinibus et sodales ex amicissimis Aurelia-
nos creavere. adepti imperium ita civiliter se ambo egerunt ut
lenitatem Pii nemo desideraret, cum eos Marullus sui temporis
mimographus, cavillando impune perstringeret. funebre munus
patri dederunt. dabat se Marcus totum et philosophiae, amorem
civium adfectans.

Verus 4.2–3 *Lucuis quidem Marco vicem – reddens si quid susciperet obsecutus*
ut legatus proconsuli vel praeses imperatori. iam primum enim
Marcus pro ambobus ad milites est locutus, et pro consensu imperii
graviter se ad Marci mores egit.

Verus 3.8 is merely a paraphrase of *M.Ant.* 7.5, or rather, it would be better
to say that both are paraphrases of the same original. *Verus* 3.8 has a phrase
lacking in the Life of Marcus: *cum illi* (sc. *Marco) soli senatus detulisset*
imperium. The words placed in square brackets above, in *M.Ant.* 7.5 and
7.7, are surely glosses by the author of the *HA*. In *Verus* 4.3 *Marcus*
is supplied as a conjecture by Lenze (cf. the Loeb edition, vol. I,
p. 214; the Teubner edition is silent on this, although it prints the
conjecture).

Similar treatment could be adopted with the rest of the *Verus*. There are
a few overlapping passages, notably *M.Ant.* 8.10–11 *et Verum quidem . . . ad*
eum videndum contendit and Verus 6.7 *profectum eum . . . ad eum visendum*
frater contendit. But only enough to give continuity, of a kind. Otherwise,
the whole of the *Verus* could with profit be chopped up, and distributed –

or re-distributed – in the pages of the *vita Marci*. Marius Maximus would have found no guidance in his model Suetonius when he came to the reign of two Augusti. But there was an obvious way to proceed: to introduce Verus, with a sketch of his origin and upbringing (to supplement what had been said already *à propos* of Hadrian's succession arrangements) and comment on his elevation to the rank of Augustus; then an account of the Parthian war, followed by a description of Marcus's activity at Rome in the early 160s; then the triumph, and an analysis of Verus's behaviour, contrasted with that of Marcus – making a nice pendant to the details about the plague; finally, the departure of the two Emperors for the northern war, their actions in that quarter, Verus's death and obituary notice. It is hard to see why the *Verus* in the *HA* could not have been extracted from details of this kind in a Life of Marcus. But the process may have tired and confused the author of the *HA*. Hence perhaps the omissions in the *M.Ant.* and the impatient recourse to a chunk of the convenient *Breviarium* of Eutropius.

7. 'The *Vita Macrini*. If the *HA* had been using Maximus, there was no reason to drop him at this point. On the contrary. Yet the *Vita* reveals no trace of the particulars which Maximus was in a position to furnish, for example, the origin and career of Macrinus … The consular biographer was appointed *praefectus urbi* by this emperor (Dio LXXVIII 14.3); and later, after his defeat, received a despatch from him (36.1; LXXIX. 2.1). Maximus, pursuant to his practice (Comm. 18.1; Pert. 15.8), would hardly fail to subjoin such a document to his *Vita Macrini*. The *HA* happens to quote an *epistula Macrini* sent to the Senate after his proclamation (6.2ff.). It is pure invention.' This argument is the most powerful of all, and is hard to answer. It is a sad reflection on the situation that obtained before DESSAU's epoch-making paper that the bogus documents in the *HA*'s *Macrinus* convinced J. J. MÜLLER that that Life did indeed derive from Maximus (pp. 102ff.). However this may be, Müller refused to concede that Maximus provided these details in a *vita Macrini*. In his view (pp. 21ff.), Maximus did not write such a Life: Macrinus was disqualified from inclusion, as he did not reign at Rome. The opening of the Macrinus in the *HA*, where the author bewailed the lack of information on that Emperor, indicated to Müller (p. 98f.) that he had no Life by Maximus available. The documents that Müller was prepared to accept, as derived from another Life by Maximus, may cheerfully be rejected out of hand. But what is the solution? Did Maximus fail to provide a *Macrinus* – thus failing to round out the desired number of Twelve Caesars? It may have been so. Maximus was, of course, especially well-informed, there can be no doubt, about

certain aspects of Macrinus's reign – but so would a large number of his readers have been. Once the Prefect had read out the Emperor's letters to the Senate, they were public knowledge. As Maximus was in Rome throughout the brief reign, his detailed knowledge of what was happening in the east would in fact have been markedly inferior to that of many observers with first-hand evidence. This may have deterred him from going into any detail. But this is not the point. Marius Maximus, the *cos. II ord.* of the year 223, a pillar of the new regime of Severus Alexander, may well have wanted to avoid reminding his contemporaries of the role he had played in bolstering the tottering throne of Macrinus. It would have been convenient to allot a Life of contemptuous brevity to Macrinus, treating it as a mere interlude. In that case, the author of the *HA* will have found little material to interest him and will have had recourse to his own imagination. This answer is admittedly incomplete. But it is at least worth emphasising that Marius Maximus, however well-informed about affairs of state under Macrinus, is likely to have wished to avoid parading this fact. It is by no means obvious that 'he would hardly fail to subjoin' to his *vita Macrini* a despatch he had received from that Emperor. A professional historian would have leaped at the chance. But Maximus was a politician.

The arguments against Marius Maximus having been the principal source of the good information in the *HA* Lives from Hadrian to Elagabalus are therefore far from compelling. One or two further points may be looked into here, to investigate the structure and contents of Maximus's Life of Septimius, so far as they may be recovered from the remains in the *HA*. (But this investigation is not of course intended to be comprehensive.) In the *Geta* 2.1 a clue is given: *Geta dictus est vel a patrui vel avi paterni, de cuius vita et moribus in vita Severi Marius Maximus primo septenario satis copiose rettulit.* The meaning of *septenarius* is discussed by G. BARBIERI (1954), pp. 272ff. He concludes that the word means a book divided into seven sections or chapters, following a suggestion by T. BIRT. Birt supposed that Septimius's autobiography might have been divided into sections in this way. Septimius, the builder of the Septizodium, who celebrated his *decennalia* with games lasting seven days at which seven hundred beasts were slaughtered, may well have done this, for superstitious reasons. But it is unnecessary to assume this. Barbieri (p. 274f.) points out that had Maximus's Life of Septimius contained only two *libri septenarii*, strict usage would have required *priore septenario* in *Geta* 2.1; and he suggests, reasonably enough, that there were three books in the Life, thus making it even longer than the two-volume Life of Marcus (*Av. Cass.* 9.5). Suetonius covered his Twelve Caesars in eight books, allowing only one for Galba, Otho and Vitellius, and one for the three Flavians. The Julio-Claudians were allotted one book each. It is fair to assume that Maximus, while spreading himself for Marcus and Septimius – to allow ample space for L. Verus and Avidius Cassius, and for Niger and Albinus – may have cut down elsewhere. Nerva and Trajan may have been put into a single book, with Nerva's brief reign the prologue to that of Trajan. Pertinax and Didius Julianus may have shared a book. Likewise Caracalla, Macrinus and Elagabalus. Barbieri (p. 273) handles severely a theory ('*l'assurda ed erronea ipotesi*') that *septenarius* might mean 'covering seven years'. That theory supposed that *primo septenario* might have been a volume covering the first seven years of the reign, 193–200. Barbieri rightly notes that 200 is not a significant year and that the reign of Septimius does not divide into multiples of seven (p. 273, n. 1). However, the first seven years were in fact 193–199, and the latter year saw the end of the Parthian wars. Although the years 193–211 at first sight do not form a convenient multiple of seven, it could be that Maximus covered the reign in three books which each in a loose sense dealt with seven years. The first might have dealt with the years 193–199, or more precisely, have covered the period from Septimius's accession to the end of the second Parthian war, part way through 199. The second would have run from 199 to the fall of Plautianus early in 205; the third would then have covered the rest of 205 and the years 206–211. Each of the three books could thus have included an account of events during seven years; and at the same time a proper historical balance would have been gained. But in certain respects this division would have been unsatisfactory. The first period would have needed more detailed treatment, the pre-imperial career of Septimius, and accounts of Niger and Albinus as well as five campaigns.

The question of the exact nature of the *libri septenarii* must therefore be left unresolved. It remains to attempt an analysis of the contents of the *vita* as a whole. For a start, it is clear that the first chapter in the *HA Severus* is drastically abbreviated (cf. A. R. BIRLEY, *HAC*, p. 64f.). As it stands, the text is confused and erroneous in any case (cf. Appendix I, above), and the author of the *HA* has omitted details about the Emperor's father (*Geta* 2.1). Mention of the paternal grandfather and other kinsmen and kinswomen may also have been included. In *Severus* 4 the author of the *HA* has surely tampered with his source, misplacing the Pannonian command and introducing a command of the *exercitus Germanicus* in its place (4.2, 4.4–5, 5.1); and the story in 4.5 is clearly bogus, cf. T. D. BARNES

(1967a), p. 93 n. 48. In 6.9 the invention about Albinus having been made Caesar by Commodus, elaborated in the *Albinus* 2.1–3.2, 6.4–5, 13.4–14.6, is clearly an insertion by the author of the *HA*. In 8.1–3 the story about Septimius's daughters and their husbands is best regarded as another invention. 8.4–5 are also suspect. Cf. J. HASEBROEK (1921), p. 49f. At some stage in his account of the year 193 Maximus will certainly have included a mention of Septimius's offer of the title Caesar to Albinus, and its acceptance, perhaps a biief sketch of the origin and career of Albinus also, and an account of the origin and career of Niger. It is reasonable to assume that the inadequate sentence in 6.9 *eodem tempore* (i.e. as he was approaching Rome) *de Clodio Albino sibi substituendo cogitavit* represents the remains of Maximus's description of the grant of the title Caesar. In *Niger* 4.7 and *Albinus* 3.4–6, this account is repeated, worded differently: *in vita sua Severus dicit se, priusquam filii sui id aetatis haberent, ut imperare possent, aegrotantem id in animo habuisse, ut si quid forte sibi accidisset, Niger Pescennius eodem et Clodius Albinus succederent, qui ambo Severo gravissimi hostes extiterunt.* (*Nig.* 4.7); *nec negari potest, quod etiam Marius Maximus dicit, hunc animum Severo primum fuisse, ut, si quid ei contingeret, Pescennium Nigrum et Clodium Albinum sibi substitueret. sed postea et filiis iam maiusculis studens et Albini amori invidens sententiam mutasse atque illorum utrumque bello oppressisse, maxume precibus uxoris adductus. denique Severus eum et consulem designavit, quod utique nisi de optimo viro non fecisset, homo in legendis magistratibus diligens.* (*Alb.* 3.3–6). The addition of Niger here is clearly the work of the author of the *HA*. Otherwise, the substance of Maximus's version may be recognised. Severus made Albinus Caesar (this simple fact has been omitted from its right place in the *HA*, in favour of the ridiculous story about Commodus and Albinus, although a trace still survives in *Albinus* 3.2–3. It is only mentioned explicitly in *Albinus* 10.3 *Severus ipse Caesarem suum eundem appellari voluerit et, cum de successore cogitaret, hunc primum habuerit ante oculos.*) In his autobiography (cf. pp. 13, 241, above) Septimius stated that he genuinely intended Albinus to succeed him if anything should happen to himself. And he designated him to the consulship (with himself, for 194). Maximus will have added, either here or later, Septimius's reasons for changing his mind later – the influence of Julia, and his chagrin at Albinus's popularity. (Barbieri's attempt [pp. 45ff.] to dispute the view that the reference to Septimius' autobiography is lifted from Maximus is not persuasive). Maximus will not have failed to give some account of who Albinus was. Some of this may survive in the *HA*, although opinions differ as to how much. The following passages may perhaps be genuine: *fuit autem Clodius Albinus familia nobili, Hadrumetinus ex Africa* (*Alb.* 1.3). *dein per Commodum ad Galliam translatus, in qua fusis gentibus transrenanis celebre nomen suum et apud Romanos et apud barbaros fecit* (6.3). *consul a Severo declaratus est eo tempore, quo illum sibi paraverat Pescennio subrogare, ad imperium venit natu iam grandior et maior Pescennio Nigro, ut Severus ipse in vita sua loquitur.* (*Alb.* 6.8–7.1). See G. ALFÖLDY (1968) for a defence of the accuracy of the Hadrumetine origin, and for evidence of a governorship of Lower Germany by Albinus (presumably emended by the author of the *HA* to *Gallia*). As for Niger, there is little about him that has any verisimilitude, which is not merely a repetition of passages in the *HA Severus* or *Didius*. On this, and on the Lives of Niger and Albinus in general, of J. HASEBROEK (1916). It is possible that *Niger* 1.5 *pervenit, ut exercitus Syriacos iussu Commodi regeret, suffragio maxime athletae qui Commodum strangulavit, ut omnia tunc fiebant* may be an extract from Maximus. Two other passages could perhaps be defended: *et Pescennius quidem eo tempore quo Lugdunensem provinciam regebat amicissimus fuit; nam ipse missus erat ad comprehendendos desertores, qui innumeri Gallias tunc vexabant* (*Nig.* 3.3–5); *a Commodo denique Pescennius consul declaratus Severo praepositus est, et quidem irato, quod primipilaribus commendantibus consulatum Niger mereretur* (4.6).

Throughout the account of the civil wars in *HA Severus* there are serious omissions and confusions that can readily be explained as the result of drastic abbreviation. A particularly obvious example comes in *Sev.* 6.11, where the summoning of the praetorians is described, but not their fate. The error in the *HA* about the final battle with Niger has already been mentioned (cf. p. 315, above). On the *Pannoniciani augures*, a story explicitly said to derive from Maximus (*Sev.* 10.7, cf. *Alb.* 9.5), see G. ALFÖLDY (1960). On the actions of Septimius at Rome after the battle of Lugdunum, see G. ALFÖLDY in *HAC* (1969). On the *ratio privata* (*Sev.* 12.4), cf. H. NESSELHAUF (1964). The father of Marius Maximus had been a financial procurator at Rome (D. 1369), though not of the *ratio privata*. Septimius's measures no doubt interested Maximus, who may have expatiated on them at length, confusing the author of the *HA* into the belief that Septimius created this department *ab ovo*. The list of names in *Sev.* 13.1–8 has clearly been augmented by the author of the *HA*. As Alföldy points out, 12.9 *post hoc de sua clementia disseruit, cum crudelissimus fuerit et senatores infra scriptos occiderit,* looks like a direct and deliberate contradiction of Dio 75.8.1. It may go back to Maximus; but this is far from certain. However, 13.8 *horum igitur tantorum ac tam inlustrium virorum ... interfector ab Afris deus habetur* is certainly a comment by the author of the *HA*

325

(a dig at Victor, cf. Sir R. SYME [1968a] p. 201 n. 6, quoted above, p. 14 n.1). Alföldy may be right in arguing that the genuine names in the list derive from Dio's original. But Maximus would surely have given the names also. At this point the *HA Severus* begins to disintegrate. 14.5–10 is mainly an account of Plautianus, out of chronological order. The narrative (interspersed with obvious fiction, viz. 14.13 and 17.1) is then resumed, up to the end of the second Parthian war and the visit to Egypt. There follows the statement at 17.5 *et quoniam longum est minora persequi* which introduces the extract from Aurelius Victor, going on till 19.3. Clearly Maximus's narrative had become too boring and verbose to abbreviate. He was, after all, *homo omnium verbosissimus*. But the author of the *HA* extracted, from the section of Maximus that he had jettisoned, some comments on Plautianus, inserting them out of place in 14.5–9. After the extract from Victor comes a heterogeneous collection of material filling out the rest of the *vita*. On 19.4, cf. J. HASEBROEK (1921), p. 146f. 19.5, on the Septizonium may derive from Maximus, but a late source, or the author of the *HA*'s own contribution, is likelier. 19.6–10 is entirely worthless, although the assertion about the African accent in 19.9 may be accurate enough (cf. p. 63, above). 20.1–21.12 is worthless fiction, cf. J. HASEBROEK (1921), p. 147f. and J. STRAUB (1964). The *omina mortis* in 22.1–7 are probably genuine, or largely genuine, and there is no reason why they should not derive from Maximus. Having abandoned him in favour of Victor, and essayed some original composition, the author could have been ready for some more Maximus to end off with. The same may apply to 23.1 J. HASEBROEK (1921), p. 148f., assumes that the source must be Dio. 23.2 is a repeat from 8.5 (see above, p. 170). The whole of the remainder looks bogus, 23.3–24.5. Only 24.1 *corpus eius a Brittannia Romam usque cum magna provincialium reverentia susceptum est* can be regarded as sound. See J. HASEBROEK (1921), p. 146 and 150.

Thus little idea can be gained from the *HA* of the *Vita* by Maximus as a whole. In view of the sketchiness of Herodian, and the fragmentary nature of Cassius Dio, the loss is serious. The author of the *HA*, having had a foretaste of the delights of free composition in the Nebenviten, was now looking forward to his grand design. He had almost had enough of Maximus, and there was not much Maximus left. A little on Caracalla, and the same kind of detail on Elagabalus that is supplied by Dio, remained to be used.

APPENDIX III

SEPTIMIUS SEVERUS AND THE AFRICANS

Two views are current on this question. A quotation from a single proponent of each will serve to illustrate their divergence. H.-G. PFLAUM, in *CP* (p. 644) writes as follows: '*L'avènement du Lepcitain Septime Sévère au trône des Cesars améne l'arrivée de toute une équipe africaine et surtout lepcitaine . . . les Romains d'Afrique forment sous ce régne une coterie nombreuse,*' (and cf. p. 614: '*cette équipe d'Africains qui firent leur fortune à Rome grace à la protection de l'empereur lepcitain*', etc.). On the other hand T. D. BARNES [1967a], p. 107) concludes that 'as emperor Severus was little influenced by his African origin – except for a sentimental attachment to Lepcis, his *patria*. He exhibited no excessive generosity either to Africans or to Africa.' The opposition between the views of these two scholars must not be exaggerated. Pflaum is of course speaking of procurators, some of them men of relatively lowly status. Barnes acknowledges (p. 98f.) that some of Septimius's supporters were Africans; 'among the most powerful of Severus's early allies certain Africans can be discovered.' But these statements have been selected because they are sober, considered judgements. And a dichotomy between them remains, even allowing for a certain watering down of their positions.

But what is the question at issue? When a man gains supreme power, or something approaching that, over millions of his fellow-citizens, he has to have associates to carry out his policy. (Velleius Paterculus put it clearly for the Roman Empire: *etenim magna negotia magnis adiutoribus egent* [2.127.2].) Where will he turn? Surely to those he knows already, and can trust, in the first instance. It is in no way surprising or shocking that in the years 1960–1963 a higher proportion of Americans of Irish extraction were found in positions of high trust in the United States than at other times (similarly with natives of Texas in the period 1964–1968). *A priori*, one would expect that Septimius Severus would have chosen – at first, at least – for important posts men whom he already knew at the time of his accession.

Some he will have met during his senatorial career. Others would be known to him on the recommendation of his family and friends. *A fortiori*, it would be little short of amazing if men from Africa and Syria had not cornered the lion's share of the key positions during his reign. This does not prove any narrow chauvinism, any racism, any despising of Italians in favour of Romans of Semitic origin. A man of Lepcis may have viewed the people of Lepcis's neighbour Oea with some contempt or ill-feeling, it is true, rather than with special favour. But did this – well-attested – inter-city rivalry have any meaning among the upper echelons of provincial society? In any case, inter-city rivalry was very localised.[1] Lepcis and Oea might be deadly enemies, or Nicomedia and Nicaea. But Lepcis and Carthage – for example? Or Cirta and Cuicul? On the contrary, the evidence here shows some close contacts, cf. *CIL* VIII 20144. Similarly Cuicul and Carthage had ties (cf. AE 1916, 32–37; *Libyca* 3, pp. 169ff.).

A man raised in proconsular Africa would undoubtedly take pleasure in the society of fellow-Africans at Rome. The evidence is unambiguous for the orator Fronto (cf. H.-G. PFLAUM [1964]). Furthermore, they might gather in one region: 'a fashionable resort near Rome such as Tibur with its villas might congregate a whole cluster of magnates from one and the same province' (R. SYME (1958), p. 602: referring to men from Spain, cf. *ib.*, n. 5).

A problem remains. It is not always easy to determine a man's origin. Where there is no direct evidence, one can only use the clues provided by nomenclature. Two classic descriptions of the method are given by E. BIRLEY (1953a), pp. 154ff., and W. KUNKEL, pp. 8off. G. BARBIERI in *L'Albo*, p. 432ff. shows that he is aware of the possibilities. (But in a number of cases he is inclined to label a man as '*probabilmente italico*' on purely negative evidence.) To the classic tools essential for such enquiries (the works of W. KUBITSCHEK (1889) and W. Schulze on tribes and *nomina* respectively) there has now been added the monograph on *cognomina* by I. KAJANTO (1965). None of these obviates the necessity of going through the Indices of *CIL* and the other epigraphic collections, to test the distribution of names.[2]

[1] The classic source is the work of Dio of Prusa. In spite of the friction between Lepcis and Oea in 70 (p. 31f, above), there is no need to assume that the citizens of African towns had the same phrenetic rivalries as the turbulent Greeks of Asia.

[2] It must be emphasised that the comments on the *origo* of the persons discussed in this Appendix are in many cases consciously negative. Often one cannot prove a precise *origo*. But one can, and should, cast doubt where the evidence is less certain than has been assumed.

It must also be asked, who qualifies for the label of 'important associate'? What constituted a 'key position'? Here one can only be pragmatic. Importance is not always measured by the actual positions held. But at least an analysis of the holders of important military posts will provide a basis. To this other persons may be added, such as those mentioned specifically in the literary sources as men of influence; and the *XVviri sacris faciundis* who participated in the Saecular Games of 204.[1] G. ALFÖLDY, *Senat* and A. R. BIRLEY (1969) deal with many of the relevant persons. Here, they are listed according to office, with a miscellaneous category at the end. There follows an alphabetical list, in which the evidence for origin is discussed.

1. *Military provinces*
   These are as follows:

3 legion provinces: Britain, Pannonia Superior.
2 legion provinces: Germania Inferior, Germania Superior, Dacia, Moesia Superior, Moesia Inferior, Cappadocia, Syria Coele, Syria Palaestina, Mesopotamia.
1 legion provinces: Hispania Tarraconensis, Raetia, Noricum, Pannonia Inferior, Syria Phoenice, Arabia, Egypt, Numidia.
Others: Mauretania Tingitana, Mauretania Caesariensis.

This categorisation is of course misleading to some extent, as the governors of some provinces within a particular category were of differing status (viz. the Prefect of Mesopotamia was an *eques*, not a consular; the governor of Tarraconensis was a consular not a praetorian; the prefect of Egypt was an *eques*, not a praetorian). But it is convenient enough for this purpose.

Britain For the evidence, cf. A. R. BIRLEY (1967b), pp. 79f. (note that *RIB* 1151 could be *Pudens*, not *Senecio*; and that *RIB* 1337 is omitted by error from the evidence for Senecio).

The attested governors are:

197/8	*Virius Lupus*
205	*C. Valerius Pudens*
205/207	*L. Alfenus Senecio*
(?Severan	*Pollienus Auspex*)

---

[1] It may be that it is totally misleading to include the XVviri. However, in view of the undoubted importance given to the Saecular Games (cf. pp. 224ff. above), and the fact that the Emperor controlled the membership of the College, I think it is fair to regard them as important and favoured persons.

Pannonia Superior   For the evidence, cf. W. REIDINGER (1956), pp. 96ff.
(on *Protomachus*, cf. J. FITZ [1963], p. 280).
The attested governors are:

197–201[1]	*L. Fabius Cilo*
c. 201	*Ti. Claudius Claudianus*
207	*Egnatius Victor*
210	*C. Fulvius Maximus*
(?Severan	*Ti. Pomponius Protomachus*)

Germania Inferior   For the evidence, cf. E. RITTERLING, pp. 76ff. (on
Fulvius Maximus, cf. G. ALFÖLDY *Senat*, p. 142, *Reichsbeamte*, p. 93).
The attested governors are:

196	*Virius Lupus*
198	*C. Valerius Pudens*
c. 200	*L. Marius Maximus*
205	*Q. Venidius Rufus*
before 210	*C. Fulvius Maximus*
211	*Lucceius Martinus*
(210/212	*ignotus CIL* XIII 8050)
(Severan	*ignotus CIL* XIII 10804)

Germania Superior   For the evidence, cf. E. RITTERLING, pp. 33ff. (for
Memmius Fidus, ib., p. 88f.)
The attested governors are:

?193	*C. Memmius Fidus*
c. 200	*T. Statilius Barbarus*
209	*Q. Aiacius Modestus*
198/211	*C. Caesonius Macer*
(Severan	*-ilinus*)

Dacia   For the evidence, cf. A. STEIN (1944), pp. 58ff. (on *Terentianus*,
cf. now A. R. BIRLEY [1969] p. 267f.; on *Gallus*, cf. B. E. THOMASSON
II, p. 202f.).
The attested governors are:

193	*Q. Aurelius Polus Terentianus*
195	*P. Septimius Geta*
200–201	*L. Octavius Julianus*

[1] Note that in these lists an oblique stroke between two dates, e.g. 205/207, indicates 'within the period limited by these years', whereas a horizontal stroke, e.g. '197–201', indicates 'attested in office in these particular years'.

204	*L. Pomponius Liberalis*
202/209	*(P. ?) Mevius Surus*
c. 205/209	*Claudius Gallus*
198/209	*C. Julius Maximinus*
198/211	*Herennius Gemellinus proc. agens v. p.*
(Severan ?	*Pollienus Auspex)*

Moesia Superior For the evidence, cf. A. STEIN (1940), pp. 50ff. (for (*?Vettule)nus Pompeianus* cf. A. R. BIRLEY (1966b), pp. 251ff.; for *Gabinius Barbarus*, cf. *Srpski Spomenik* 71 (1931), p. 81, no. 186 (Timacum minus): E. Birley points out to me that the *C. Gabinio* in this inscription should be a governor; on the family to which the man presumably belonged, cf. *CP* no. 265, with stemma, p. 711, for the Caracallan procos. Asiae *C. Gabinius Barbarus(?) Vindex Pompeianus.*

The attested governors are:

195	*(? Vettule)nus Pompeianus*
196	*L. Fabius Cilo*
(199	*(?) C. Gabinius Barbarus)*
202/211	*Q. Anicius Faustus*
205/211	*L. Marius Perpetuus*

Moesia Inferior For the evidence, cf. A. STEIN (1940), pp. 81ff.
The attested governors are:

193	*P. Septimius Geta*
193/198	*Pollienus Auspex*
198	*Cosconius Gentianus*
198–201	*C. Ovinius Tertullus*
202/205	*L. Aurelius Gallus*
198/209	*C. Junius Faustinus*
198/209	*L. Julius Faustinianus*
209/212	*Flavius Ulpianus*

Cappadocia For the evidence, cf. D. MAGIE, p. 1593.
The attested governors are:

197/198	*C. Julius Flaccus Aelianus*
(199(?)	*L. M——ius*
(Severan (?)	*Claudius Hieronymianus)*

Syria Coele For the evidence, cf. J. F. GILLIAM (1958).
The attested governors are:

| 200 (?) | *L. Alfenus Senecio* |
| 208 | *L. Marius Maximus* |

209/211   *Minicius Martialis, proc. agens v. p.*
(Severan (?)   *Gemellus*)

Syria Palaestina   The only governor attested with any degree of certainty
is:
not later than 196 *M. Ulpius Arabianus*

On this man cf. *L'Albo* no. 532+Agg. (but Barbieri is inaccurate when he
asserts, *ib.*, p. 604, that this province was normally governed by '*legati di
grado pretorio*'. The governors were consulars from the reign of Hadrian
onwards, cf. *RE* 12 [1925], col. 1591).

Mesopotamia   The names of none of the Prefects from this reign are known.

Hispania Tarraconensis   For the evidence, cf. now G. ALFÖLDY, *Reichsbeamte*, pp. 42ff.
The attested governors are:
(193/197   *L. Novius Rufus*)
197   *Ti. Claudius Candidus*
198/209   *Q. Hedius Rufus Lollianus Gentianus*
198/209   *M. Maecius Probus*
206/211   *M. Nummius Umbrius*
Severan (?)   *T. Flavius Titianus*

Raetia   For the evidence, cf. E. RITTERLING, pp. 117ff. (for Alexianus,
cf. H.-G. PFLAUM [1962]).
198/209   *P. Porcius Optatus Flamma*
198/209   *A. (Olus) Terentius Pudens Uttedianus*
c. 207   *C. Julius Avitus Alexianus*
(Severan (?)   *Ap. Claudius Lateranus*)

Noricum   See now G. WINKLER pp. 80ff.
201   *M. Juventius Surus Proculus*
206   *Pollienus Sebennus*
206/208   *P. Catius Sabinus*

Pannonia Inferior   For the evidence, cf. J. FITZ (1963), pp. 281ff.
193 (?)   *C. Valerius Pudens*
193/199   *Ti. Claudius Claudianus*
199   *L. Baebius Caecilianus*

198/209	*Q. Caecilius Rufinus Crepereianus*
209/211	*C. Julius Septimius Castinus*

Syria Phoenice There is no recent work dealing with the governors of this province. The four known are *L'Albo* nos. 347, 519, 18+Agg., and 128.

194	*Ti. Manilius Fuscus*
198	*Q. Venidius Rufus*
Severan (?)	*Aetrius Severus*
(Severan	*-etianus*)

Arabia For the evidence, cf. H.-G. PFLAUM (1957).
The attested governors are:

193/194	*P. Aelius Severianus Maximus*
before 198	*M. Caecilius Fuscianus*
194/200 (?)	*Q. Scribonius Tenax*
200 (?)	*L. Marius Perpetuus*
before 209	*Q. Aiacius Modestus*
(209/211	*ignotus AE* 1939, 255)

Egypt For the evidence, cf. O. W. REINMUTH, pp. 105ff. On Apollinaris see now F. GROSSO (1968) pp. 26ff.
The attested Prefects are:

193–194	*L. Mantennius Sabinus*
195–196	*M. Ulpius Primianus*
197–199	*Q. Aemilius Saturninus*
(199/200 (?)	*Alfenus Appollinaris*)
200–203	*Q. Maecius Laetus*
204–205/206	*Claudius Julianus*
205/206–210	*Subatianus Aquila*

Numidia For the evidence, cf. B. E. THOMASSON, II, pp. 195ff. (for *Pontius*, cf. *AE* 1967 p. 571; for *Marcellus*, cf. App. 2, above no. 38).
The attested governors are:

193	*L. Naevius Quadratianus*
194	*C. Julius Lepidus Tertullus*
197–201	*Q. Anicius Faustus*
201/208	*Pontius*
201/208, 210/212	*Q. Cornelius Valens*
201/205	*Claudius Gallus*
204/208, 210/217	*Sex. Varius Marcellus*
208–210	*Ti. Claudius Subatianus Proculus*

Mauretania Caesariensis For the evidence, cf. *CP*, p. 1096f. (and nos. 262a, 233, 227, 253, 229, 342).
The procurators attested are:

195	*Cn. Nunnius Martialis*
197/198	*C. Octavius Pudens*
201	*P. Aelius Peregrinus Rogatus*
202	*Cn. Haius Diadumenianus*
1932/11	*Q. Sallustius Macrinianus*
198/209	*M. Aurelius Heraclitus*
(205/217	*C. Julius Pacatianus*)
(Third century	*Aurelius Januarius*)

Mauretania Tingitana For the evidence, cf. *CP*, p. 1098f. (and nos. 229, 227, 342).
The procurators attested are:

c. 198	*C. Julius Pacatianus*
200	*C. Sertorius Cattianus*
202	*Cn. Haius Diadumenianus*
198/209	*Q. Sallustius Macrinianus*
(Third century	*Aurelius Januarius*)

2. *Praetorian Prefects* For the evidence, cf. L. L. HOWE, pp. 68ff. to be supplemented by *CP* nos. 179 *bis*, 354 add., 219, 220.
The known Prefects are:

193	*D. Veturius Macrinus*
193	*Flavius Juvenalis*
197–205	*C. Fulvius Plautianus*
c. 200	*Q. Aemilius Saturninus*
(*c.* 200/205 (?)	*M. Aurelius Julianus*)
205	*Q. Maecius Laetus*
205–211	*Aemilius Papinianus*

3. *Prefects of the City* For the evidence, cf. G. VITUCCI, pp. 119ff.
The known Prefects are:

(193	*Bassus*)
193–196	*C. Domitius Dexter*
198	*P. Cornelius Anullinus*
203	*L. Fabius Cilo*

4. *The XVviri sacris faciundis of* 204 For the evidence, cf. J. B. PIGHI, esp. pp. 240ff., 246ff.

Q. Aiacius Modestus
M. Antius Crescens Calpurnianus
Atulenus Rufinus
(L.?) Cassius Pius Marcellinus
Sex. Cocceius Vibianus
M. Fabius Magnus Valerianus
Fulvius Fuscus Granianus
C. Fulvius Plautianus
Julius Pompeius Rusonianus, magister 204
Ti. Manilius Fuscus, magister 203
M. Nonius Arrius Mucianus
Ofilius Macedo
Pollienus Auspex
L. Pullaienus Gargilius Antiquus
Saevinius Proculus
(L. Cornelius?) Salvius Tuscus
Q. Venidius Rufus
Vetina Mamertinus
Ulpius Soter
(C——— (?))
(———lian———)
(———rnus pr———)
(———rom———)

5. *Miscellaneous*
Generals:
Julius Laetus (cf. p. 346, below)
Laetus (cf. p. 346, below)
Q. Mamilius Capitolinus (cf. p. 350, below)
T. Sextius Lateranus (*L'Albo* no. 477+Agg.)
Jurists:
Arrius Menander (W. KUNKEL, p. 233f.)
Callistratus (*ib.*, p. 235)
Claudius Tryphoninus (*ib.*, pp. 231ff.)
Domitius Ulpianus (*ib.*, pp. 245ff.)
Julius Paulus (*ib.*, p. 244f.)
Messius (*ib.*, p. 229f.)

Procurators:
Aelius Antipater (*CP* no. 230)
L. Cominius Vipsanius Salutaris (*CP* no. 235)
Cn. Marcius Rustius Rufinus (*CP* no. 234)

Aelius Antipater   From Hierapolis in Phrygia (prov. Asia). *ab. epistulis Graecis*, and tutor of the sons of Septimius. Later made senator, and governor of Bithynia. *CP* no. 230.

P. Aelius Peregrinus Rogatus P. f. Pap.   Origin not attested: *P. Aelius* indicates provincial extraction; *Papiria* is found for over twenty African towns, also two in Mauretania Caesariensis, against eleven in all other provinces and nine in Italy (W. KUBITSCHEK, p. 271); *Rogatus* is a predominantly African *cognomen* (I. KAJANTO, p. 297: 650 in Africa out of a total of 714). This man was procurator of Caesariensis in 201 and then *a cognitionibus Auggg., perfectissimus vir. CP* no. 233.

P. Aelius Severianus Maximus   Probably from Perinthus in Thrace. Governor of Arabia in 193–194, under Pertinax and Septimius. G. ALFÖLDY, *Senat*, p. 133, *L'Albo* no. 10, *PIR* A 260, etc.

Aemilius Papinianus   Generally reckoned Syrian on account of *HA Carac.* 8.2: *P. amicissimum fuisse imperatori Severo et, ut aliqui loquuntur, adfinem etiam per secundam uxorem, memoriae traditur.* W. KUNKEL, pp. 225ff. is more cautious, noting that the 'second wife' could be Papinian's, not Septimius's. But if not a kinsman of Julia Domna, his wife was related to Septimius, hence African. (Unless the story is rejected as fiction by the author of the *HA*.) *A libellis*, then Praetorian Prefect 205–211. *CP* no. 220, *PIR²* A 388, etc.

Q. Aemilius Saturninus   Origin not attested. The *cognomen Saturninus* was especially popular in Africa but was extremely common everywhere (I. KAJANTO, p. 213: 1163 in Africa out of a total of 2507). Prefect of Egypt 197–199/200, Praetorian Prefect *c.* 199–200, murdered by Plautianus (O. W. REINMUTH, p. 106; L. L. HOWE, p. 70, etc.; also p. 296, above). See now also F. GROSSO (1968) esp. pp. 23ff.

Aetrius Severus   Origin not attested: G. ALFÖLDY, *Senat*, p. 133, shows that he is certainly Italian, probably from Sentinum. Cf. also *L'Albo* no. 18+Agg. *praetor tutelarius* 193/198, later governor of Syria Phoenice. Thought by some to be 'Aetius', alleged son-in-law of Septimius; cf. p. 90, n. 2, above.

Q. Aiacius Modestus Crescentianus Origin not attested, but his tribe *Stellatina* was confined to Italy (W. KUBITSCHEK, p. 272). G. ALFÖLDY, *Senat*, p. 133f. notes that *Aiacii* are known only in Rome and northern Italy. *XVvir s.f.* in 204, governor of Arabia, and Germania Superior under Septimius; later *cos. II ord.* 228. Cf. also *L'Albo* no. 22, *PIR*² A 470, etc. His presumed daughter, *Junia Aiacia Modesta*, married a kinsman of *Q. Aradius Rufinus Optatus Aelianus*, almost certainly a native of Bulla Regia in Africa (cf. *PIR*² A 1016–1017 and A. R. BIRLEY [1967b, p. 83].[1]

L. Alfenus Senecio Certainly from Cuicul in Numidia, cf. *CP* no. 176 on the homonymous procurator (presumably his father, though it is not impossible the procurator is the same as this man, promoted into the Senate), said to have helped *coloniae suae* on a stone at Cuicul. The tribe *Quirina* is correct (W. KUBITSCHEK, p. 271f.) and the priesthood of Neptune is also appropriate (*CP*, p. 443f.). This man was legate of Syria Coele in 200 (cf. *CP* pp. 441ff. for the date) and of Britain 205/207 (A. R. BIRLEY [1967b], p. 81). Cf. also G. ALFÖLDY, *Senat*, p. 134, *L'Albo* no. 25 (where Spanish origin is suggested, unconvincingly), *PIR*² A 520–521, etc.

Q. Anicius Faustus Origin now known almost certainly as African, from Uzappa near Mactar (A. BESCHAOUCH, pp. 209ff.). Governor of Numidia 197–201, later of Moesia Superior. Cf. B. E. THONASSON II, pp. 197ff, *L'Albo* no. 27, *PIR*² A 595, G. ALFÖLDY, *Senat*, p. 134, etc.

M. Antius Crescens Calpurnianus Origin not attested. Perhaps from Ostia, where he held a priesthood. *XVvir* in 204. Cf. A. R. BIRLEY (1967b) p. 75f., R. MEIGGS, p. 209, *L'Albo* no. 34, *PIR*² A 781, etc.

Arrius Menander Origin not attested. W. KUNKEL, p. 233f. favours the Greek east in view of the *cognomen*, but does not commit himself. A jurist and *consiliarius*. *PIR*² A 1100.

Atulenus Rufinus Origin not attested. Perhaps the same as '*Apuleius*' *Rufinus*, consular colleague of Septimius in 190. *L'Albo* no. 67, *PIR*² A 1372.

L. Aurelius Gallus As *cos. ord.* 198, son of the *cos. ord.* 174, grandson of

---

[1] *Q. Aradius Rufinus* cet. himself was perhaps not the husband of *Modesta* (as suggested in *PIR*²). His wife was another person as G. Bowersock kindly informs me (on the basis of an unpublished inscription from Bulla Regia). It is possible, of course, that Rufinus was married more than once. On Modestus, of now *AE* 1968, 518ff.

the *cos.* 146, great-grandson of a man *cos.* 129/132, his family's ultimate origin is perhaps immaterial. But he is generally reckoned a descendant of the homonymous *signator* of the decree of a proconsul of Sardinia in 69 (D. 5947); and his tribe, *Quirina*, would accord with Sardinian origin, cf. W. KUBITSCHEK, p. 271f. But *Quirina* is also found in eight Italian towns and very frequently in Spain and Africa, *ib.*, Cf. H.-G. PFLAUM (1962b), pp. 108ff., G. ALFÖLDY, *Senat*, p. 135. Probably *leg. leg. I Adiutricis* in 193; governor of Moesia Inferior *c.* 202. A rare example of a fourth-generation consular *vir militaris*.

M. Aurelius Heraclitus   Origin not attested. *Nomen* indicates provincial (or perhaps freedman) extraction, *cognomen* the Greek-speaking part of the Empire. Evidently procurator of the *portorium vectigalis Illyrici* in 201, subsequently procurator of Caesariensis; probably not the same as *Aurelius Septimius Heraclitus*, the Prefect of Egypt executed by Caracalla (O. W. REINMUTH, p. 111), cf. *CP* no. 253. But there is no reason why he should not be identified with the *Heraclitus* sent by Septimius *ob optinendas Brittannias* in April or May 193 (*HA Sev.* 6.10), cf. p. 159, above, in spite of the doubts expressed in *PIR*² H 88–90.

Q. Aurelius Polus Terentianus   Origin not attested: it is argued by A. R. BIRLEY (1969), p. 267f., that he was probably African (citing *inter alia* 18 *QQ. Aurelii* in *CIL* VIII, against e.g. only 8 in *CIL* VI – excluding *Symmachi* – and less in other volumes; ten African examples of the rare *cognomen Syriacus* borne by his son), although no certainty is possible. Legate of XXII Primigenia and then of II Augusta under Commodus, also a *fetialis* (cf. G. ALFÖLDY [1967], p. 44, n. 229 for the best text of the new Mainz inscription); governor of Dacia in 193 (A. STEIN [1944], p. 56); later proconsul of Asia (*AE* 1964, 232).

L. Baebius Caecilianus   Origin not attested. G. ALFÖLDY, *Senat*, p. 136 suggests 'vielleicht Afrikaner', citing a *B(a)ebius C(a)ecilius* in Mauretania (*CIL* VIII 21718) – 'jedoch unsicher'. It should be noted that *Baebius* and *Caecilius* were very common names in Spain (cf. R. SYME [1958], p. 783). Governor of Pannonia Inferior in 199. *L'Albo* no. 85, *PIR*² B 14, etc.

M. Caecilius Fuscianus Crepereianus Flor(i)anus   Certainly African, from Theveste, cf. D. 6839, a *Q. Crepereius Pap. Rufinus* citizen of that place. The relationships of the various Caecilii Crepereiani and *Rufini* are established by H.-G. PFLAUM (1957), improving on *PIR*² C 47: the father of this man (and of the next on this list) was very probably proconsul of

Crete-Cyrene when *P. Septimius Geta* was quaestor there (App. I, no. 29). Governor of Arabia before 198, at a critical time, cf. p. 198, above.

Q. Caecilius Rufinus Crepereianus Brother of the preceding, *q.v.*, African. Governor of Pannonia Inferior *c.* 203/208. Cf. G. ALFÖLDY, *Senat*, p. 136, *PIR*² C 76, *L'Albo* no. 96.

C. Caesonius Macer Rufinianus Generally reckoned Italian; although in Regio I his tribe *Quirina* is found only at Antium (W. KUBITSCHEK, p. 271), which weakens the arguments of Dessau, *ad CIL* XIV 3902, that he was from Campania. Nor is it the tribe of Tibur where his funerary inscription, D. 1182, was found. He had a long career beginning under *M. Aurelius*. Perhaps legate of VII Claudia in 193. Later governor of Germania Superior, etc. *PIR*² C 210, *L'Albo* no. 106, G. ALFÖLDY, *Senat*, p. 137, *Reichsbeamte*, p. 146f.

Callistratus Origin not attested, presumably eastern, cf. W. KUNKEL, p. 235. The jurist.

(L. ?) Cassius Pius Marcellinus Origin not attested. Tribune of II Adiutrix; quaestor designate and *XVvir* in 204, perhaps the same as *L. Cassius Marcellinus*, governor of Pannonia Inferior and *cos. des.*, cf. J. FITZ (1960), p. 405, (1963), p. 286. Fitz also argues that this man is the *ignotus* from Sufetula (*AE* 1952, 95); and see *RE* Supp. 9 (1962), col. 19, also by Fitz. This is less certain than he asserts. If it could be accepted, African origin would then be probable. But more evidence is required before Fitz' arguments completely convince.

P. Catius Sabinus Probably from northern Italy, cf. G. ALFÖLDY, *Senat*, p. 137f. who notes that *PP. Catii* are found exclusively there. Tribune of XIII Gemina (*AE* 1956, 204), quite probably in 193. Probably the governor of Noricum who succeeded *Pollienus Sebennus*, *q.v.*, and prosecuted him. Later *cos. II ord.* 216, therefore clearly a friend of Caracalla. Cf. also *PIR*² 571, *L'Albo* no. 126.

Ti. Claudius Candidus Quite possibly Numidian, cf. J. FITZ (1966), p. 832f., G. ALFÖLDY, *Senat*, p. 139 (hardly 'a Greek of Asia' as T. D. BARNES (1967a) p. 101 and n. 113, for no good reason). On his career, of which the years when he was *dux* of the *exercitus Illyricus* 193–197 are the most interesting, G. ALFÖLDY, *Senat*, p. 139, *Reichsbeamte*, pp. 43ff., is the most acceptable. Cf. also J. FITZ [1966], pp. 831ff., *L'Albo* no. 143, *PIR*² C 823. He evidently lost favour at some time in the reign, and later regained it; he may even have been executed and posthumously pardoned. His names were first erased, and then restored on his cursus inscription, D. 1140.

Ti. Claudius Claudianus From Rusicade in Numidia: cf. D. 1146=*ILAlg.* II 29, etc. Cf. most recently J. FITZ (1961), pp. 74ff., (163), pp. 282ff., modified by G. ALFÖLDY, *Senat*, p. 139. Made a senator, and *praetor candidatus*, probably in 193, then legate of the two Dacian legions and *praepositus* of vexillations from the Dacian army, governor of Lower Pannonia, consul *c.* 199, governor of Upper Pannonia. Cf. also *PIR²* C 834, *L'Albo* no. 147, etc.

Claudius Gallus Origin not attested. G. ALFÖLDY, *Senat*, p. 139, suggests that he was a close kinsman of the preceding, whose sister was named *Claudia Gallitta*, as was the daughter of *Gallus*, cf. *AE* 1957, 123 (which renders previous discussions obsolete); and notes that the *cognomen Gallus* was common in Africa, citing I. KAJANTO, p. 195 (who also notes that six out of twelve *Gallittae* are African). Governor of Numidia and Dacia.

Claudius Julianus Origin not attested, and the names are much too common to make any suggestions about it. The newly attested Prefect of Egypt 204–205/206 of this name (O. W. REINMUTH, pp. 106ff.) is presumably the same as the *praefectus annonae* of 201 (D. 1346; perhaps also D. 6987).

Ti. Claudius Subatianus Proculus From Cuicul in Numidia: cf. D. 9488. Presumably brother, son or other close kinsman of *Subatianus Aquila*, *q.v.* Entered the Senate as quaestor after the *tres militiae equestres* and service as subprefect of the Misenum fleet; was *candidatus* as tribune and *praetor*. *Inter alia*, governor of Numidia 208–210. Cf. B. E. THOMASSON, II, pp. 203ff., *CP* no. 242, *L'Albo* no. 173, etc. *AE* 1966. 488 appears to show him as proconsul of Cyprus. If this is Procalus, it was probably after Numidia that he went there (there is no reason to date the inscription early in the reign).

Claudius Tryphoninus Origin not attested, but clearly provincial and presumably eastern, cf. W. KUNKEL, pp. 231ff. Jurist and *consiliarius*, *ib.* He received a rescript from Caracalla in 213 which is concerned with Antioch-on-Orontes, and he may well therefore have held some official position in Syria Coele at that time.

Sex. Cocceius Vibianus Origin not attested, but he was patron of an African town (*CIL* VIII 84, cf. 11226, Thamalla) and the names of his presumed grandson (*PIR*² A 600) suggest a link with *Q. Anicius Faustus*, *q.v.* (viz. that the son of *Faustus* married this man's daughter). Hence perhaps African. *XVvir* in 204. Cf. *PIR*² C 1232, *L'Albo* no. 185.

L. Cominius Vipsanius Salutaris   Origin: City of Rome (D. 1406: *domo Roma*). *A cognitionibus, perfectissimus vir*, perhaps before 198, after posts in Rome, Italy, Sicily and Spain. Cf. *CP* no. 235.

P. Cornelius Anullinus   From Iliberris in Baetica (D. 1139). Friend of Septimius, who enriched him (*Epit. de Caes.* 20.6), perhaps known to him since *c.* 170, when he was proconsul of Baetica, cf. G. ALFÖLDY, *Reichsbeamte*, p. 122f, *Senat*, p. 146, and, following him, A. R. BIRLEY (1969), p. 270. Proconsul of Africa in 193, *dux* against Niger in 194 and the first Parthian war, Prefect of the City and *cos. II ord.* 199. Cf. also *L'Albo* no. 191, *PIR*² C 1322, etc.

Q. Cornelius Valens   Probably Numidian, cf. *L'Albo* no. 194a, where *CIL* VIII 18269 is cited, on which cf. *PIR*² C 1470; perhaps from Thamugadi, cf. D. 2752. Governor of Numidia, B. E. THOMASSON, II, p. 205f., (and cf. App. 1, no. 38, above).

Cosconius Gentianus   Origin not attested. Regarded as Italian in *L'Albo*, no. 195, but G. ALFÖLDY, *Senat*, p. 141, notes that Cosconii are also found in southern Gaul and Africa. Governor of Lower Moesia in 198.

C. Domitius Dexter   Origin not attested. Not necessarily Italian in view of the commonness of his names, even if a kinsman of *Ser. Calpurnius Domitius Dexter*, as argued by Barbieri (*L'Albo* nos. 203, 980). For one thing, the daughter of that person seems to be a descendant of *Aemilia Severa*, mother of *C. Julius Flaccus Aelianus*, *q.v.*, and an African, as Barbieri shows in the *Aggiunte*, p. 614 (no. 911a). Governor of Syria in 183, perhaps when Septimius was still commanding IV Scythica. Prefect of the City in 193, *cos. II ord.* 196. Cf. also *PIR*² D 144.

Domitius Ulpianus   From Tyre in Syria Phoenice, as he himself writes (*Digest.* 50.15.1.*pr.*). On the *consilium* of *Aemilius Papinianus*, *q.v. Praefectus annonae*, later Praetorian Prefect, in 222. Hardly a *libellis*, as alleged by *HA, Pesc. Nig.* 7.4, cf. J. HASEBROEK (1916), cited by Pflaum in *CP*, no. 294, where the other relevant texts are collected and discussed. A. M. HONORÉ makes use of this suspect passage in the *HA* and draws very dubious conclusions from it. On the date of his death, cf. now O. W.

REINMUTH, p. 113, who shows that (*M. Aurelius*) *Epagathus*, his murderer who was sent to Egypt after Ulpian's death 'ostensibly as governor' (Dio 79.2.4), was already Prefect of Egypt in May or June 224. Thus Ulpian was Praetorian Prefect for only two years at the most.

Egnatius Victor Origin not attested: 'Italico' according to Barbieri in *L'Albo*, no. 206 (likewise *PIR²* E 35). But cf. G. ALFÖLDY, *Senat*, p. 141: '*vielleicht jedoch aus Thibilis in Numidia, wo ein* Q. Egnatius M. fil. Q(uirina) Victor *belegt ist* (*CIL* VIII 5574): It may be added that I. KAJANTO p. 278 states that there are 771 examples of the name *Victor* in Africa out of a total of 1568. Governor of Pannonia Superior in 207.

L. Fabius Cilo From Iluro in Baetica, cf. H. U. INSTINSKY (1944b). By his full nomenclature *L. Fabius M. f. Gal. Cilo Septiminus Catinius Acilianus Lepidus Fulcinianus. Cos. suff.* in 193, after a career which may have brought him into contact with Septimius at various points. The stages in the career are all more or less clear, and, from 193 onwards, can be dated closely. All that is really uncertain is at what stage he was *curator* of various towns (D. 1141, *AE* 1926, 79). He was perhaps *curator* of Nicomedia at the same time as he governed Bithynia-Pontus, or immediately before, when Nicomedia but not the rest of that province was in the hands of the Severan army; although it may have been under Commodus. It is conceivable that he was *curator* of Graviscae and Interamna Nahars immediately after his consulship; and thus may have been there in May 193. He would have been very useful then. For the various – very numerous – pieces of evidence for his career, cf. *PIR²* F 27, *L'Albo*, no. 213, G. ALFÖLDY, *Senat*, p. 141f., etc.: he commanded vexillations at Perinthus in 193, was *comes* of Septimius, governor of Bithynia-Pontus and Moesia Superior (195–196), commander of vexillations in Italy (196), governor of Pannonia Superior, City Prefect, and *cos. II ord.* 204. 'Enriched' by Septimius and described as his friend, according to *Epit. de Caes.* 20.6. Almost murdered by Caracalla in the last days of 211 or early 212, after the death of Geta.

M. Fabius Magnus Valerianus Origin not attested. Barbieri in *L'Albo*, no. 215, suggests that he is from Narbonensis, but notes that his tribe, *Quirina*, is not found there. No doubt a descendant of *Q. Fabius Barbarus Valerius Magnus Julianus cos.* 99, as Barbieri notes, but hardly a connection of *M. Iallius Bassus Fabius Valerianus*, as he also suggests (the sole reason for the hypothesis of Narbonensian origin): *Fabius* and *Valerius* and their derivatives are too common to prove this. The *cognomen* Barbarus borne by the *cos.* 99, though not uncommon elsewhere, was found more in Africa than in other provinces: I. KAJANTO, p. 312 ('in Africa 41 out of 98'). In view of this, and of his tribe, Africa or Spain must be regarded as likelier homes for this man. He seems to have had a break in his career under Commodus: having evidently been legionary legate before 180, he was *curator operum publicorum*, etc. in 193 (D. 1138, 5920), hence presumably consul not long before that. *XVvir* in 204. Cf. also *PIR²* F 23.

Flavius Juvenalis Origin not attested, but perhaps African if identical with the homonymous centurion of III Augusta from the year 162 (VIII 18065, line 18) or son of that man, cf. *PIR²* F 300. Note also his choice of a young man from Lambaesis for his *officium* (D. 2428). Praetorian Prefect in 193. Cf. also L. L. HOWE, p. 69.

T. Flavius Titianus Origin not attested; perhaps brother of Pertinax's wife, if so from Praeneste in Italy, cf. G. ALFÖLDY, *Reichsbeamte* p. 45f. Evidently governor of Tarroconensis.

Flavius Ulpianus Origin not known, but certainly provincial from the names; and senatorial *Ulpii*, at least, in the third century, were mostly from the east, cf. the index of names in *L'Albo*, p. 771. Governor of Cilicia 202, later governor of Moesia Inferior, 209–211. Cf. also *PIR²* F 402; *L'Albo* no. 247. Hardly identical with *T. Flavius Aristus Ulpianus* (*L'Albo* no. 735) – whose names are certainly indicative of eastern origin – as that person was still a *clarissimus puer* in 197; but perhaps a kinsman.

Fulvius Fuscus Granianus Origin not attested, and none suggested. But it should be noted that there are several examples of the not very common *nomen Granius* at Lepcis Magna, one bearer of which was a senator (*Q. Granius Caelestinus, IRT* 532; cf. also 642, 708, 709). This suggests that he may have been one of the *Fulvii Lepcitani*, which would explain his position as *quaestor Augg.*, and *XVvir*, in 204. Cf. *PIR²* F 539, *L'Albo* no. 250.

C. Fulvius Maximus Origin not attested, but probably Italian, cf. G. ALFÖLDY, *Senat*, p. 142, *Reichsbeamte* p. 93. Governor of Dalmatia, Germania Inferior, and Pannonia Superior (in 210).

C. Fulvius Plautianus From Lepcis Magna in Africa, cf. Appendix I, no. 8, above.

Cn. Haius Diadumenianus Probably from Puteoli, where a man of almost identical name (except that the *cognomen* is recorded as *Diadumenus*) is known, cf. *PIR²* H 8. See further *CP* no. 178 *bis*, where Pflaum cites five bearers of this *nomen* (sometimes spelt *Ahius*) from that city and three others from Campania (p. 1003). As he notes, the name is rare elsewhere. The man was procurator of Mauretania Caesariensis and Tingitana simultaneously in 202.

Q. Hedius Rufus Lollianus Gentianus The specific origin of the *Hedii* is unknown, but they owned lands in Liguria; and the rare *nomen* is common only in central Umbria, cf. *PIR²* H 34–44, *stemma*, p. 52, discussion of the *origo*, p. 57. This man is H 42. His father (H 40) was the patron of Pertinax's father (*HA Pert*, 1.5, cf. *Epit. de Caes.* 18.4). His brother (H 41) is now known to be the *cos. II ord.* 209 (cf. J. ŠAŠEL). He himself is a rare example of a patrician *vir militaris*. He served as legionary legate under Commodus (XXII Primigenia), and as *comes ter* of Septimius, i.e. was on the Emperor's staff in three expeditions (presumably 193–4, 195 and 196–7), and was later governor of Tarraconensis among other posts. Cf. also *L'Albo* no. 267, and G. ALFÖLDY (1967), p. 43f., *Senat*, p. 143, *Reichsbeamte*, p. 47f. (A different view is possible on the order of his career from 197 onwards; and of that of his son.)

Herennius Gemellinus Origin not attested, but cf. *PIR²* H 109, where E. Birley deduces origin in Germany on the basis of his sons' names (*CIL* III 7901). H.-G. Pflaum in *CP*, no. 254, regards him as Italian. Procurator of Dacia Apulensis and acting governor of Dacia, perhaps at the time of the British expedition.

C. Julius Avitus Alexianus From Syria Phoenice, probably Emesa. Cf. Appendix I, no. 17, above.

L. Julius Faustinianus Origin not attested, and seemingly undiscoverable. There is no particular reason why he need have been a native of Larinum in Italy, as suggested by Barbieri in *L'Albo*, no. 292: this town honoured him after his death as its patron (he had clearly been useful, cf. E. BIRLEY [1953a], pp. 172ff., showing that the town was made a *colonia* by Septimius; and that one of its citizens, who bore the famous names *A. Cluentius Habitus*, became an equestrian officer in Britain). Governor of Moesia Inferior 209–211 and later. Cf. *PIR²* J 304.

C. Julius Flaccus Aelianus Origin not attested, but possibly African: his mother *Aemilia Severa* seems to have come from an African family, cf. *PIR²* J 666, p. 317, where the arguments are given. Besides this, G. ALFÖLDY, *Senat*, p. 144, cites three *Julii Flacci* in *CIL* VIII. There can, however, be no certainty, in view of the commonness of all three names

(*Julius* common everywhere; 128 known *Aeliani* and 163 *Flacci*, according to I. KAJANTO, pp. 139, 240, who does not mention any special concentration of either in any one area). Governor of Cappadocia in 197/198, cf. *PIR²* J 311, *L'Albo* no. 293.

Julius Laetus Origin not attested and seemingly undiscoverable. The problem here is to identify various prominent *Laeti* who figure in the years 193–199, who are to be distinguished from *Q. Aemilius Laetus* the Praetorian Prefect and murderer of Commodus (cf. chapters 10 and 11, above, *passim*) and from *Q. Maecius Laetus*, Praetorian Prefect in 205, *q.v.* A *Laetus* is mentioned in five significant contexts, as follows:

1. By *HA Did. Jul.* 8.1: *et Crispinus quidem cum occurrisset praecursoribus Severi, Iulio Laeto auctore a Severo interemptus est.* This is the only time when the *nomen Julius* is given. The reference is to the murder of Julianus's Prefect *Tullius Crispinus* when he went out to meet the advancing forces of *Septimius* in May 193. This *Laetus* was presumably commanding the advance-guard and as such should be a senator, cf. Tacitus, *Hist.* 3.2ff. and 3.59; the Flavian march into Italy was led by *Antonius Primus* and *Petillius Cerialis* led an advance-party across the Appennines.

2. A general in the first Parthian war named *Laetus* is mentioned by Dio 75.2.3.

3. At the battle of Lugdunum a general named *Laetus* saved the day for Septimius, but almost left it too late; cf. Dio 75.6.8; Herodian 3.7.3ff.; also *HA Sev.* 11.2, apparently the same episode: Herodian notes that this *Laetus* was later put to death for this affair; Dio and Herodian both say that he had hoped to be made emperor himself; the *HA*, without naming *Laetus*, says that *alius iam paene imperator ab exercitu diligeretur*.

4. A general named *Laetus* rescued Nisibis from Parthian siege in 197, according to Dio 75.9.1, who says that as a result 'Laetus acquired a still greater reputation, although he had already shown himself an outstanding man in both war and peace.'

5. At the first siege of Hatra, in 198 (or perhaps 199), Septimius put to death *Laetus* 'because he was proud and was loved by the soldiers, who used to say that they would not go on another campaign unless *Laetus* led them' (Dio 75.10.3). In *HA Sev.* 15.6 the same episode is alluded to: several persons were killed at the time of the second Parthian war, including friends of the Emperor and suspected rivals (*ib.* 15.4–5). After their death, *Septimius* made excuses, denying that he had ordered it, *quod de Laeto praecipue Marius Maximus dicit.*

345

M. Fluss in *RE* 2A (1923), col. 1969 argued quite reasonably that the general at Lugdunum could well have been sent post-haste to the east to cope with a particularly dangerous situation. Indeed, this could have been one of several occasions when the troops refused 'to go on another expedition unless *Laetus* led them', Dio, *l.c.* J. HASEBROEK's (1921) statement, p. 34, n. 5 that *Julius Laetus* must have been an *eques* is quite untenable, especially in view of the parallels from 69, cited above. There is therefore no objection to identifying him with any of the other Laeti. The man at Lugdunum and the man at Nisibis were clearly of the utmost distinction, *capaces imperii*; and the context of *HA Sev.* 15.5-6 makes it clear that the man murdered during the second Parthian war was also in this category. All things considered, it makes excellent sense to regard all five *Laeti* as one and the same man, in spite of the almost unanimous verdict to the contrary, cf. *L'Albo* nos. 297a and 323a, *PIR*² J 373, G. ALFÖLDY, *Senat*, p. 144, etc. The reason why the *nomen Julius* is given in *HA Did. Jul.* 8.1 and not in *Sev.* 15.6 is obvious: the other famous *Laetus*, the murderer of Commodus, had just been mentioned (*Did. Jul.* 6.2) before the first item, and confusion would have resulted otherwise. J. B. Leaning has kindly drawn my attention to Herodian's statement (3.7.4) that the only general put to death by Septimius was the man who won Lugdunum for him – which, if accepted, would clinch the identification with the man murdered at Hatra. Mr Leaning further suggests that if regarded as *capax imperii* in 197 Laetus ought to have been consular in 193, perhaps governor of Upper Germany. I am less convinced on this.

C. Julius Maximinus Origin not attested. Perhaps from the same family as *C. Julius Maximus Mucianus* of Philippi in Macedonia, as suggested by G. ALFÖLDY, *Senat*, p. 144, but the *nomen* and *cognomen* are so common that no certainty is possible. Governor of Dacia *c.* 197/200. Cf. also *PIR*² J 419, *L'Albo* no. 300, etc.

C. Julius Pacatianus Generally reckoned a native of Vienna in Narbonensis, where a statue was set up in his honour (and still survives; cf. D. 1353) by the colony of Italica in Baetica. For the details of his long career, cf. *CP* no. 229 add., *PIR*² J 444. Pflaum in *CP*, p. 607, believes that he was prefect of *legio Parthica* (no number given – Pflaum assumes that it was *leg. I Parthica*) before 196-7, after having been procurator of Osrhoene in 195. It was probably in 196-7 that he was procurator of the Cottian Alps. *Pace* Pflaum, p. 608, there is no reason why he should not have been *comes* of the Emperor at Lugdunum in 197, in spite of the phrase *adlecto inter* *comites Auggg. nnn.*, cf. the abusive use of *Auggg.* on D. 1146 and *IRT* 541, for posts held well before 197. He was then procurator of Mauretania Tingitana, *pro legato*, indicating that he had legionaries under his command, held two further procuratorships, was procurator of the other Mauretania, commander of vexillations in the east and Prefect of Mesopotamia, the last three posts under Caracalla. The fact that he was made *comes* was most exceptional for a knight, but is perhaps explained by his origin: a man from Vienna would have been an invaluable staff officer before the battle of Lugdunum. Certain problems remain about the early part of his career; it is not impossible that he commanded the *leg. Parthica* in Italy in 196, for one thing. Septimius may have met this man when governor of Lugdunensis in the 180s.

Julius Paulus Origin not attested, and quite undiscoverable in the absence of further evidence as W. KUNKEL, p. 244f. rightly points out. The famous jurist. In *PIR*² J 453 it is noted that there is no good evidence for his having held any particular office (though he very probably did hold one or more): all statements attributing tenure of office to him are in suspect passages of the *HA*.

Julius Pompeius Rusonianus Origin not attested; but I. KAJANTO, p. 154, has only discovered two other bearers of this name (he also notes that there were three senators called *Rusonianus*: it would seem that two are this man, variously *Julius Pompeius* and *Pompeius* only; and that the other is derived from a restored – and uncertain – reading of Philostratus, *v.soph.* 2.25.2, cf. *L'Albo* nos. 304 and 446). The other two *Rusoniani* are attested by *IRT* 396, 750, both from Lepcis Magna. The first, Commodan in date, was a local magnate; the second is on a stone 'not seen' by the editors of *IRT*, but of good second-century lettering (autopsy). Although this evidence is slight, it is not improbable that the man was a compatriot of *Septimius*. Certainly he must have been in high favour, as *magister* of the XVviri in 204. Cf. also *PIR*² J 476.

C. Julius Scapula Lepidus Tertullus Origin not attested; possibly from Spain, cf. G. ALFÖLDY, *Senat*, p. 144f. (Barbieri, in *L'Albo*, no. 298, notes the theory of Pallu de Lessert that he was African. But there is no evidence for this). Governor of Numidia (strictly: legate of III Augusta) in 194. Cf. also *L'Albo*, no. 298, *PIR*² J 554 (and nos. 552–3, 555–7, his kinsmen).

C. Julius Septimius Castinus Origin not attested, but perhaps a kinsman of

Septimius and in any case quite probably African, cf. G. ALFÖLDY, *Senat*, p. 195, who notes that sixteen *Julii Casti* are recorded in Africa, very few elsewhere (and cf. I. KAJANTO, p. 251 for the popularity of *Castus* in Africa: 125 out of a total of 289. *Castinus* is rare, only nine men apart from this person, *ib.*, p. 252). After other posts, *dux* of vexillations of the four German legions *adversus defectores et rebelles* and legate of I Minervia. In spite of G. ALFÖLDY (1967), p. 51, *Senat*, p. 145, it is quite possible that these two posts were cumulated. Later governor of Pannonia Inferior and (under Caracalla) of Dacia. Cf. *L'Albo* no. 308, *PIR*² J 566, etc. G. Alföldy suggests to me that Castinus's service as tribune of I Adiutrix and V Macedonica could well have been under Septimius and Geta as governors of Upper Pannonia and Dacia. This would seem very plausible on chronological grounds, and as Dr Alföldy points out to me, lends weight to the view that he was their kinsman.

C. Junius Faustinus Placidus Postumianus African origin is demonstrated by *CIL* VIII 597 (+p. 2927) and 11763; cf. esp. G. ALFÖLDY, *Senat* p. 145, *Reichsbeamte* pp. 49ff. Alföldy's arguments in the latter place have led me to revise an earlier view (A. R. BIRLEY [1967b] p. 83f.) that the two inscriptions refer to different men, and to accept a (mainly) Severan date for this career. After commanding I Adiutrix, he was governor of Lusitania and Belgica; consul; governor of Lower Moesia and *comes* of two Augusti, presumably during the British expedition 208–211. Thereafter he was governor of Britain (presumably Britannia Superior) and Tarraconensis.

M. Juventius Surus Proculus From Brixia in Italy, cf. *PIR*² J889, *L'Albo* no. 319, etc. Governor of Noricum in 201.

Laetus See *Julius Laetus*.

L. Lucceius Martinus Origin not attested, and seemingly undiscoverable. Governor of Germania Superior in 211. *L'Albo* no. 336, etc.

Q. Maecius Laetus Origin not attested, and seemingly undiscoverable. Prefect of Egypt 200–203 (O. W. REINMUTH, p. 106), Praetorian Prefect 205. Earlier on he had been procurator of Arabia. Cf. CP no. 219. He was later *cos. ord.* 215, (described as *cos. II*, having perhaps been adlected *inter consulares* before that rather than actually holding a first consulate); cf. *L'Albo* no. 341.

M. Maecius Probus Origin not attested; possibly African according to G. ALFÖLDY, *Reichsbeamte*, p. 46, citing *CIL* VIII 18065d 13. *Praefectus alimentorum*, and governor of Tarraconensis, where he died. Cf. also *L'Albo* no. 343. Possibly the general in the First Parthian War (Dio 75.3.2).

Q. Mamilius Capitolinus   Origin not attested, but G. ALFÖLDY, *Senat*, shows that there is some reason to regard him as African. Cf. especially G. ALFÖLDY, *Reichsbeamte*, pp. 90ff. on his role in Spain 196–7, as *dux* of *leg. VII Gemina*; D. 2299, *L'Albo* no. 2054, etc.

Ti. Manilius Fuscus   Origin not attested, but very probably Spanish, cf. G. ALFÖLDY, *Senat*, p. 146. legate of XIII Gemina in 191, perhaps still in April 193, governor of Syria Phoenice in 194. *Magister* of the *XVviri* in 203. Later proconsul of Asia and *cos. II ord.* 225. Cf. also *L'Albo*, no. 347.

L. Mantennius Sabinus   Origin not attested, but married to a woman from Praeneste; cf. A. R. BIRLEY (1969), p. 268f., for the evidence. It is there suggested that he was a friend of Pertinax and for that reason made Prefect of Egypt in 192. Retained office for a while under Septimius in 194, in spite of having given (no doubt only nominal) support to Niger.

Cn. Marcius Rustius Rufinus   From Beneventum in Italy, cf. *CP* no. 234+ add. He rose from being centurion *ex equite Romano* to (apparently) being Praetorian Prefect in 210 or 212. Prior to this he had served as a legionary centurion, centurion in two of the three major units at Rome, and in the *equites singulares*, chief centurion of III Gallica in Syria, then tribune of the *vigiles* (in 190), and of the other two major units in turn. He was thus very probably a praetorian tribune in June 193, one of these who cooperated with *Septimius* in dismissing the old Guard. He then became *primus pilus bis* of III Cyrenaica in Arabia, raised recruits in Transpadana (probably in 196), a post followed by the procuratorship of Syria Coele, command of the two Italian fleets and the charge of the *annona* (no doubt in the second Parthian war). He is recorded in 205 and 207 as Prefect of the *vigiles*, and finally seems to have been made Praetorian Prefect. Unless he commanded the *vigiles* for some years before 205, he would seem to have had a period from 200 onwards without employment. This could well be, for *Plautianus* took steps to dispose of potential rivals, cf. p. 208, above.

L. Marius Maximus   Perhaps African. Cf. Appendix II, above, p. 309.

L. Marius Perpetuus   Perhaps African, cf. Appendix II, above, p. 309.

C. Memmius Fidus Julius Albius   From Bulla Regia in Africa, cf. *L'Albo* no. 367, G. ALFÖLDY, *Senat*, p. 147, etc. Governor of Noricum and *cos. des.* in September 191. Perhaps governor of Germania Superior in 193, certainly of some province, after his consulship and an urban *cura*, cf. D. 1110.

Messius=(?) *P. Messius Saturninus. Saturninus* was from Pheradi Maius in proconsular Africa, cf. *ILTun.* 250 and *CP* no. 231. After two posts in the equestrian *militiae* he went on to an outstanding career in the imperial service, all of it specifically as a lawyer or legal adviser, ending up in the highest category, *trecenarius*, as *a declamationibus Latinis*. Pflaum, in *CP*, pp. 617ff., shows that this official *'doit avoir préparé, sinon redigé les déclamations latines de l'empereur'* – i.e. his legal pronouncements. Pflaum cites *HA Sev.* 18.5: *philosophiae et dicendi studiis satis deditus, doctrinae quoque nimis cupidus*, which he translates *'assez adonné aux études de philosophie et de rhétorique, même trop avide de science juridique'*. This interpretation of the career of *Saturninus* justifies the identification with the jurist *Messius* (p. 619), mentioned once in the *Digest*. W. KUNKEL, p. 229f., who does not mention *Saturninus*, suggests identification with the *cos. II ord.* 217, *T. Messius Extricatus*. This is of course possible (that person, incidentally, was almost certainly from Africa, cf. I. KAJANTO, p. 352: 161 out of 178 bearers of the *cognomen* were from Africa).

P. (?) *Mevius Surus* Origin not attested; G. ALFÖLDY, *Senat*, p. 148 notes that the *nomen* is common only in central Italy (24 examples) and Africa (42, including *PP. Mevii*). Governor of Dacia *c.* 202–5. Cf. also *L'Albo* no. 373, etc.

Minicius Martialis Origin not attested. The *cognomen* was popular in Africa (I. KAJANTO, p. 212: 324 out of a total of 771), but there is nothing conclusive. Apparently acting governor of Syria Coele while the Emperors were in Britain, cf. J. F. GILLIAM (1958), p. 230.

L. Naevius Quadratianus Origin not attested. G. ALFÖLDY, *Senat*, p. 148 suggests he could have come from Mastar, but acknowledges that this is very uncertain. Legate of III Augusta in 193 under Pertinax. He held office only briefly and was perhaps of suspect loyalty – on the other hand he might have been needed elsewhere. Cf. also B. E. THOMASSON, II, p. 195f., *L'Albo*, no. 378.

M. Nonius Arrius Mucianus From Verona, with connections in Brixia, cf. *L'Albo* no. 379. *cos. ord.* 201, *XVvir* in 204.

M. Nummius Umbrius Primus Senecio Albinus Evidently Italian, cf. G. ALFÖLDY, *Senat*, p. 148, *L'Albo*, no. 386, etc. *Cos. ord.* 206, governor of

Tarraconensis 206/211. A brother or half-brother of Didius Julianus according to Barbieri and Alföldy, following E. Groag in *RE* 17 (1937), col. 1413f.

Cn. Nunnius Martialis   Origin not attested. *Nunnius* is rare: 35 in *CIL* VI, 14 in VIII, none in II, IX, XII, XIII; 7 in X and 11 in XI. *Martialis* is common, especially in Africa (I. KAJANTO, p. 212: 324 out of a total of 771). Known only as procurator of Mauretania Caesariensis in 195 (*CP*, p. 1096).

Ofilius Valerius Macedo   Origin not attested; but connected in some way with *Martius Verus* and *Sergius Saturninus*, who were probably from Tolosa in Gaul, cf. G. ALFÖLDY, *Senat*, p. 147. Curator of the Tiber in 198, *XVvir* in 204. Cf. *L'Albo* no. 390.

L. Octavius Julianus   Origin not attested, but probably of the family of the jurist (*L. Octavius Cornelius*) *P. Salvius Julianus* from Hadrumetum in Africa, cf. *L'Albo* no. 389, G. ALFÖLDY, *Senat*, p. 149. Governor of Dacia 200–201.

C. Octavius Pudens Caesius Honoratus   Apparently from Auzia in Mauretania Caesariensis, the province he governed as procurator with the added function *a censibus*, cf. *CP* no. 262a. But Pflaum (*ib.* p. 705) quotes E. Birley's suggestion that his citizenship of Auzia (D. 1357) may have been honorary. However this may be, the *cognomen Honoratus* points to North African origin (I. KAJANTO, p. 279: in Africa 495 out of a total of 666).

C. Ovinius Tertullus   Origin not attested, but G. ALFÖLDY, *Senat*, p. 149 points out that *Ovinii* are recorded here and there in Italy and Spain, and commonly in Africa; *CC. Ovinii* are found only in Rome and Africa. Governor of Moesia Inferior 198–202, cf. also *L'Albo* no. 391.

Pollienus Auspex   Origin not attested, but clearly Italian, cf. A. R. BIRLEY (1967b), p. 8of. There is much controversy over this man's career. The view here followed is set out in *op. cit.* Seemingly governor of Dalmatia *c.* 193, and of Moesia Inferior *c.* 194–6. *XVvir* in 204. Cf. also G. ALFÖLDY, *Senat*, p. 150, *Reichsbeamte*, pp. 53ff. and (for a different view), *L'Albo* nos. 412–413.

Pollienus Sebennus   Italian (nephew of the preceding person). Governor of Noricum in 206, prosecuted for corrupt government (and saved from the death penalty by his uncle). Cf. *L'Albo* no. 414, G. ALFÖLDY, *Senat*, p. 150f.

L. Pomponius Liberalis   Origin not attested, and seemingly undiscoverable. *Nomen* and *cognomen* were both common. Governor of Dacia 204. *L'Albo* no. 424.

Pontius   Origin not attested. His name is unknown, but his son was called *Pontius Surus Ju——*, and his wife was *Claudia Proculina*, cf. *AE* 1967.571. Note *L'Albo* no. 1137, *Pontius Proculus Pontianus cos. ord.* 238, perhaps a kinsman of *Junius Pontius Proculus junior*, recorded at Philippi in Macedonia: Barbieri deduces origin there from this. Note also *M. Juventius Surus Proculus*, *q.v.*, from Brixia. For the dating of his governorship of Numidia, cf. Appendix I, no. 38, above.

P. Porcius Optatus Flamma   From Cirta in Numidia, cf. *L'Albo* no. 432, G. ALFÖLDY, *Senat*, p. 151, etc. Envoy to Antoninus in Pannonia in 197, later governor of Raetia *c.* 210.

L. Pullaienus Gargilius Antiquus   Apparently African, in spite of his tribe *Velina* (found only in Italy and Tarraconensis, cf. W. KUBITSCHEK, p. 272), cf. *PIR*² G 80, also 77–79, *L'Albo* no. 441. It could of course be that the family, originally Italian, had large estates in Africa, on which some members settled permanently, adopting a new tribe (*Arnensis*, cf. D. 9404, *CIL* II 4120, etc.), while others stayed, mainly, in Italy. *XVvir* in 204 (and patrician).

Saevinius Proculus   Origin not attested. Italian according to Barbieri in *L'Albo*, no 457 (cf. 846) but this is doubtful.[1] *trib. lat.* of *leg. III Augusta* in 199, and *curator* of Thamugadi, when *Q. Anicius Faustus*, *q.v.*, was governor. *XVvir* in 204.

Q. Sallustius Macrinianus   Origin not attested and seemingly undiscoverable. Procurator of both Mauretanian provinces simultaneously under *Septimius*. Cf. *CP* no. 227.

(L. Cornelius?) Salvius Tuscus   Origin not attested, but if the *XVvir* of 204, *Salvius Tuscus*, is the same as the *L. Cornelius Salvius Tuscus* made a *salius Palatinus* in 181 (cf. *L'Albo* nos. 461, 717), then presumably from the family of (*L. Octavius Cornelius*) *Salvius Julianus* of Hadrumetum, the jurist (W. KUNKEL, pp. 157ff.)

---

[1] Barbieri assumes him to be a descendant of a senator mentioned in Tacitus *Histories* 1.77. However, the name *Saevinius Proculus* in that passage is the result of a conjecture rejected by E. Groag, *RE* 1A (1920) 1727, and the person probably never existed. It remains true that the *nomen Saevinius* is extremely rare, and scarcely attested outside Italy.

Q. *Scribonius Tenax*   Origin not attested, and seemingly undiscoverable. Governor of Arabia under Septimius. Cf. *L'Albo* no. 462, H.-G. PFLAUM (1957), p. 137 etc.

P. Septimius Geta   Brother of the Emperor. Cf. Appendix I, no. 29, above.

C. Sertorius Cattianus   Origin not attested, but *Catii* (or *Cattii*) are very common in northern Italy and Gaul, rare elsewhere, cf. G. ALFÖLDY, *Senat*, p. 138. Governor of Mauretania Tingitana in 200 (*AE* 1953, 80).

T. Sextius Lateranus   Italian, cf. *L'Albo* no. 477, etc. A general in the first Parthian war and friend of *Septimius* who 'enriched' him (*Epit. de Caes.* 20.6). *Cos. ord.* 197.

T. Statilius Barbarus   Origin not attested. Cf. A. R. BIRLEY (1969), p. 277 where the possibility of African origin is scouted. Fought in the first Parthian war, later governed Thrace and Germania Superior. Cf. *L'Albo* no. 483.

Subatianus Aquila   Presumably brother or other close relative of *Ti. Claudius Subatianus Proculus*, *q.v.*, hence from Cuicul in Numidia. Prefect of Egypt 205/6–210 (O. W. REINMUTH, p. 109).

A. (Olus) Terentius Pudens Uttedianus   From Carthage, cf. *L'Albo* no. 499. Legate of XIII Gemina, governor of Raetia.

M. Ulpius Arabianus   From Amastris in Pontus, cf. *L'Albo* no. 532, Governor of Syria Palaestina *c.* 196.

M. Ulpius Primianus   Origin not attested, but certainly provincial in view of the nomenclature. Note *CIL* III 5114 (near Celeia, Noricum) for a boy named *Ulpius Primianus*. The *cognomen* is not very common (I. KAJANTO, p. 291, records the existence of 48). Prefect of Egypt 195–6 (O. W. REIN-MUTH, p. 105f.).

Ulpius Soter   Origin not attested, but presumably eastern from his names, cf. *L'Albo* no. 538. *XVvir* (and *cos. des.*) in 204.

Sex. Varius Marcellus   From Apamea in Syria Phoenice, cf. Appendix I, no. 38, above.

C. Valerius Pudens   Origin not attested. G. ALFÖLDY, *Senat*, p. 153, suggests he may be African, citing evidence, but admits that the names are too common to allow any probability. Governor of Pannonia Inferior, probably in 193 (J. FITZ [1961] pp. 71ff.), Germania Inferior, and Britain

(*AE* 1962, 260: 205), later proconsul of Africa. Cf. also A. R. BIRLEY (1967b) pp. 79, 101.

Q. Venidius Rufus Marius Maximus L. Calvinianus Generally reckoned Italian, but cf. A. R. BIRLEY (1969) p. 277f., where various *Venidii* (including *Q Q.*) in Africa are cited, and p. 276f., where it is argued that his kinsman *L. Marius Maximus* may have been African (and cf. Appendix II, above, p. 310f.).[1] Legate of I Minervia, probably in 193, then governor of Cilicia, Syria Phoenice (in 198) and Germania Inferior. Curator of the Tiber and *XVvir* in 204. Cf. *L'Albo* no. 519, G. ALFÖLDY, *Senat*, p. 153, etc.

Vetina Mamertinus 'Senza dubbio italico' according to Barbieri in *L'Albo* no. 521. *XVvir* in 204.

(Vettule?)nus Pompeianus If this person existed – cf. A. R. BIRLEY (1966b), pp. 215ff. – he was Italian. The governor of Moesia Superior in 195 was [—]*n. Pompeianus*, restored as [*Vettule*]*n.* in *op. cit.* Cf. G. ALFÖLDY, *Senat* p. 153.

D. Veturius Macrinus Origin not attested and seemingly undiscoverable. Procurator of Mauretania Tingitana 180, Prefect of Egypt 181–3, Praetorian Prefect 193. Cf. *CP* no. 179 *bis*.

Virius Lupus Origin not attested. Generally reckoned Italian, cf. G. ALFÖLDY, *Senat*, p. 154, although Gallic origin is possible, cf. A. R. BIRLEY (1967b), p. 79. Governor of Germania Inferior 196–7, and of Britain 197/8. Cf. also *L'Albo* no. 528.

This list comprises a total of 106 names. It may be helpful to arrange these in categories, by origin. First, those whose *origin appears quite undiscoverable* may be eliminated:

Atulenus Rufinus
Claudius Julianus
C. Domitius Dexter
L. Julius Faustinianus
Julius Laetus
Julius Paulus
L. Lucceius Martinus

[1] I regret that in my 1969 paper, *l.c.*, I failed to note that Sir R. Syme had already suggested an African origin for this man in *Historia* 5 (1956), p. 210f., citing *CIL* XIV 2939 (M. Venidius Rogatianus: cf. now I. KAJANTO, p. 297 for the overwhelmingly African distribution of that *cognomen*).

Q. Maecius Laetus
L. Pomponius Liberalis
Q. Sallustius Macrinianus
Q. Scribonius Tenax
D. Veturius Macrinus
(12)

Second, those who are certainly, or almost certainly, *Italian*:

Aetrius Severus
L. Aurelius Gallus
P. Catius Sabinus
L. Cominius Vipsanius Salutaris
T. Flavius Titianus
C. Fulvius Maximus
Cn. Haius Diadumenianus
Q. Hedius Rufus Lollianus Gentianus
M. Juventius Surus Proculus
Cn. Marcius Rustius Rufinus
L. Mantennius Sabinus
M. Nonius Arrius Mucianus
M. Nummius Umbrius cet.
Pollienus Auspex
Pollienus Sebennus
T. Sextius Lateranus
Vetina Mamertinus
(Vettule)nus Pompeianus (if he existed)
(18, or 17)

Third, those more or less certainly of *eastern* origin:

Aelius Antipater
P. Aelius Severianus Maximus
Aemilius Papinianus
Arrius Menander
M. Aurelius Heraclitus
Callistratus
Claudius Tryphoninus
Domitius Ulpianus
C. Julius Avitus Alexianus
M. Ulpius Arabianus

Ulpius Soter
Sex. Varius Marcellus
(12)

Fourth, those more or less certainly from *Africa* (in the broad sense, including Numidia and Mauretania).

P. Aelius Peregrinus Rogatus
L. Alfenus Senecio
Q. Anicius Faustus
M. Caecilius Fuscianus cet.
Q. Caecilius Rufinus cet.
Ti. Claudius Claudianus
Ti. Claudius Subatianus Proculus
Q. Cornelius Valens
C. Fulvius Plautianus
C. Junius Faustinus cet.
C. Memmius Fidus cet.
P. Messius Saturninus
L. Octavius Julianus
C. Octavius Pudens cet.
P. Porcius Optatus Flamma
L. Pullaienus Gargilius Antiquus
(L. Cornelius) Salvius Tuscus
P. Septimius Geta
Subatianus Aquila
A. Terentius Pudens Uttedianus
(20)

Fifth, those who are more or less certainly from *Spain*:

P. Cornelius Anullinus
L. Fabius Cilo cet.
C. Julius Scapula cet.
Ti. Manilius Fuscus
(4)

Other:
C. Julius Pacatianus (Narbonensis)
(1)

This comprises a total of 67 persons, for 55 of whom more or less certain knowledge about their *origo* obtains. In the above discussion there has been speculation about the remaining 39. In some cases, a strong probability points to one particular region, as follows:

1. *Italy:*
M. Antius Crescens Calpurnianus
(1)

2. *The east, or Greek-speaking area:*
Flavius Ulpianus
C. Julius Maximinus
Pontius
(3)

3. *Africa:*
Q. Aurelius Polus Terentianus
Ti. Claudius Candidus
Claudius Gallus
Sex. Cocceius Vibianus
Egnatius Victor
Fulvius Fuscus Granianus
C. Julius Flaccus Aelianus
Julius Pompeius Rusonianus
C. Julius Septimius Castinus
M. Maecius Probus
Q. Mamilius Capitolinus
L. Marius Maximus cet.
L. Marius Perpetuus
C. Ovinius Tertullus
Q. Venidius Rufus cet.
(15)

4. *Gaul and Germany:*
Herennius Gemellinus
C. Sertorius Cattianus
(2)

This makes a total of 21. The remaining 18 cannot easily be categorised. Not all would agree, of course, on what constitutes certainty or probability, but the attempt has been made to conduct the enquiry as objectively as possible. The 106 persons here discussed may be regarded as a reasonable selection of the men most prominent during the reign of Septimius Severus.

357

Of the 76 for whom origin is known or can be guessed with some confidence, 19 seem to be Italian, 35 African, 15 eastern, 7 from Gaul and Spain. Of the 18 'uncertain' cases, none looks at all eastern; for about half of these men, African origin looks possible. Counting heads can be misleading, of course, even though here the attempt has been made to select the most prominent persons. Further selectiveness may be more instructive. Examination of the governors of three legion and two legion provinces, for example. There are 41 known with certainty (40 excluding (*Vettule*)*n. Pompeianus*). The origin is more or less certain in 16 cases, as follows (by provinces):

Italy
Fulvius Maximus (Pannonia Superior and Germania Inferior)
(Vettule)nus Pompeianus (Moesia Superior)
Pollienus Auspex (Moesia Inferior)
L. Aurelius Gallus (Moesia Inferior)
(5, or 4)

Spain
L. Fabius Cilo (Moesia Superior and Pannonia Superior)
(2)

East
M. Ulpius Arabianus (Syria Palaestina)
(1)

Africa
L. Alfenus Senecio (Britain and Syria Coele)
Ti. Claudius Claudianus (Pannonia Superior)
C. Memmius Fidus (Germania Superior, probably; or another province)
P. Septimius Geta (Dacia and Moesia Inferior)
L. Octavius Julianus (Dacia)
Q. Anicius Faustus (Moesia Superior)
(8)

Others
nil

Of the remaining 25 governors (22 men, three of whom governed two provinces), as many as 18 may well have been African; but, equally, some 15 could have been Italian. Further conclusions from this analysis are drawn in Chapter 18.

ABBREVIATIONS

AE   *L'Année Épigraphique. Revue des publications épigraphiques relatives a l'antiquité romaine* (1888ff.)

BMC   H. Mattingly, *Coins of the Roman Empire in the British Museum*: IV, *Antoninus Pius to Commodus* (1940); V, *Pertinax to Elagabalus* (1950) *BMC Rom. Medals* H. A. Grueber, *Roman Medallions in the British Museum* (1874)

CAH   *The Cambridge Ancient History*: XI, *The Imperial Peace AD 70–192* (1936); XII, *The Imperial Crisis and Recovery AD 193–324* (1939)

CIL   *Corpus Inscriptionum Latinarum* I–XVI (1863ff.)

CP   H. G. Pflaum, *Les carrières procuratoriennes équestres sous le Haut-Empire romain* (1960–1961)

D.   H. Dessau, *Inscriptiones Latinae Selectae* (1892–1916; repr. 1960)

FC   A. Degrassi, *I Fasti Consolari dell'Impero romano* (1954)

IG   *Inscriptiones Graecae*

IGSyr.   L. Jalabert and R. Mouterde, *Inscriptions grecques et latines de la Syrie*, I–V (1929ff.)

IGR   R. Cagnat, *Inscriptiones Graecae ad res Romanas pertinentes*, I, III, IV (1901–1921)

ILAfr.   R. Cagnat, A. Merlin, L. Chatelain, *Inscriptions latines d'Afrique* (1923)

ILAlg.   S. Gsell, *Inscriptions latines de l'Algérie*, I (1923); II–1, ed. H. G. Pflaum (1958)

ILTun.   A. Merlin, *Inscriptions latines de la Tunisie* (1944)

IRT   J. M. Reynolds and J. B. Ward Perkins, *Inscriptions of Roman Tripolitania* (1952)

JRS   *The Journal of Roman Studies* (1910ff.)

L'Albo   G. Barbieri, *L'Albo senatorio da Settimio Severo a Carino* (193–285) (1952)

PIR²   *Prosopographia Imperii Romani, saec. I, II, III*, 2nd ed. by E. Groag and A. Stein, continued by L. Petersen: I (A–B: 1933); II (C: 1936); III (D–F: 1943); IV 1 (G: 1952); IV 2 (H: 1958); IV 3 (I–J: 1966)

RE   *Realencyclopädie der classischen Altertumswissenschaft*, ed. Pauly-Wissowa-Kroll-Mittelhaus-Ziegler (1893ff.)

RIB   R. G. Collingwood and R. P. Wright, *The Roman Inscriptions of Britain*, Vol. I, *Inscriptions on Stone* (1965)

The main editions of the three principal ancient sources are as follows:

Dio: *Cassii Dionis Cocceiani Historiarum Romanarum Quae Supersunt*, ed. U. P. Boissevain, 5 vols. (1898–1931; repr. 1955) is the standard text. There is a Loeb translation, in 9 vols., by E. Cary (1927; repr. 1955). The numbering of Dio's books I have adopted is that of Boissevain.

Herodian: *Herodiani ab excessu divi Marci*, ed. C. Stavenhagen (1922; repr. 1967) is the standard text
There is a recent translation into English by E. C. Echols (1961).
Vol. 1 of a translation in the Loeb series has just appeared (1969), by C. R. Whittaker, with valuable introduction and notes.

The Augustan History (abbreviated *HA*): *Scriptores Historiae Augustae*, ed. E. Hohl (corrected ed. 1965) is the standard text.
There is a Loeb translation by D. Magie (assisted by A. O'Brien-Moore), in 3 vols. (1921–1932 and reprs.)

BIBLIOGRAPHY

ABT, A., *Die Apologie des Apuleius von Madaura und die antike Zauberei. Beiträge zur Erläuterung der Schrift* de Magia (1908, reprint 1963).

ALFÖLDI, A. (1934), 'Die Ausgestaltung des monarchischen Zeremoniells am römischen Kaiserhöfe', *Mitteilungen des deutschen archäologischen Instituts: roemische Abteilung* 49 (1934), 1.

ALFÖLDI, A. (1935), 'Insignien und Tracht der römischen Kaiser', *Mitteilungen des deutschen archäologischen Instituts: roemische Abteilung* 50 (1935), 1.

ALFÖLDY, G. (1960), '*Pannoniciani augures*', *Acta antiqua academiae scientiarum Hungaricae* 8 (1960), 145.

ALFÖLDY, G. (1964), 'Die *Valerii* in Poetovio', *Arheoloski Vestnik* (Ljubljana) 15–16 (1964–5), 137.

ALFÖLDY, G. (1967), *Die Legionslegaten der römischen Rheinarmeen = Epigraphische Studien* 3 (1967).

ALFÖLDY, G. (1968), 'Herkunft und Laufbahn des Clodius Albinus in der Historia Augusta', *Historia-Augusta-Colloquium Bonn* 1966/67 (1968), 19.

ALFÖLDY, G., *Reichsbeamte = Fasti Hispanienses: Senatorische Reichsbeamte und Offiziere in den spanischen Provinzen des römischen Reiches von Augustus bis Diokletian* (1969).

ALFÖLDY, G., *Senat =* 'Septimius Severus und der Senat', *Bonner Jahrbücher* 168 (1968), 112.

ALFÖLDY, G., *HAC =* 'Eine Proskriptionsliste in der Historia Augusta', *Historia-Augusta-Colloquium Bonn 1968/69* (1970), 1.

ALFÖLDY, G., *Sturz =* 'Der Sturz des Kaisers Geta', *Historia-Augusta-Colloquium Bonn 1968/69* (1970).

ALTANER, B., *Patrologie. Leben, Schriften, und Lehre der Kirchenväter*, seventh edition (1966; Eng. trs. of 5th edition, 1960).

AURIGEMMA, S. (1940), 'L'elefante di Leptis Magna e il commercio dell' avorio e delle *ferae Libycae* negli emporii tripolitani', *Africa Italiana* 7 (1940), 67

AURIGEMMA, S. (1950), 'L'avo paterno, una zia, ed altri congiunti dell' imperatore Severo', *Quaderni di archeologia della Libia* 1 (1950), 59

BARBIERI, G. (1936), 'Sulle falsificazioni della Vita di Pertinace negli SHA', *Studi italiani di filologia classica* 13 (1936), 183.

BARBIERI, G., *L'Albo=L'Albo senatorio da Settimio Severo a Carino* (1952).

BARBIERI, G. (1952), 'Aspetti della politica di Settimio Severo', *Epigraphica* 14 (1952), 1.

BARBIERI, G. (1954), 'Mario Massimo', *Rivista di filologia e istruzione classica* 82 (1954), 36; 262.

BARBIERI, G. (1957), 'Un nuovo cursus equestre (Plauziano?)', *Epigraphica* 19 (1957), 93.

BARNES, T. D. (1967a), 'The family and career of Septimius Severus', *Historia* 16 (1967), 87.

BARNES, T. D. (1967b), 'Hadrian and Lucius Verus', *Journal of Roman Studies* 57 (1967), 65.

BARNES, T. D. (1968a), 'Pre-Decian *acta martyrum*', *Journal of Theological Studies*, N.S., 19 (1968), 509.

BARNES, T. D. (1968b), 'Legislation against the Christians', *Journal of Roman Studies* 58 (1968), 32.

BARNES, T. D. (1968c), 'Philostratus and Gordian', *Latomus* 27 (1968), 581.

BARNES, T. D. (1969), ' Tertullian's *Scorpiace*', *Journal of Theological Studies*, N.S. 20 (1969), 105.

BENARIO, H. W. (1958a), 'Rome of the Severi', *Latomus* 17 (1958), 712.

BENARIO, H. W. (1958b), 'Julia Domna mater senatus et patriae', *Phoenix* 12 (1958) 67.

BERSANETTI, G. M. (1938), 'Sulla guerra fra Settimio Severo e Pescennio Nigro in Erodiano', *Rivista di filologia e istruzione classica* 66 (1938), 357.

BERSANETTI, G. M. (1942), 'P. Settimio Geta, fratello di Settimio Severo', *Epigraphica* 4 (1942), 105.

BERSANETTI, G. M. (1946), 'Il padre, la madre, e la prima moglie di Settimio Severo. Con un appendice sull' uso di *Dominus Noster* nelle iscrizioni dell' età Severiana', *Athenaeum* 24 (1946), 28.

BERSANETTI, G. M. (1949), 'Su Pescennio Nigro: Nigro contro Pertinace?', *Aegyptus* 29 (1949), 76.

BERSANETTI, G. M. (1951), 'Perenne e Commodo', *Athenaeum* 29 (1951), 151.

BESCHAOUCH, A., 'Uzappa et le proconsul d'Afrique Sex. Cocceius Anicius Faustus Paulinus', *Mélanges d'archéologie et d'histoire de l'École française de Rome* 81 (1969), 195.

BIRLEY, A. R. (1962), 'The oath not to put Senators to death', *Classical Review*, N.S., 12 (1962), 197.

BIRLEY, A. R. (1963), 'The status of Moesia superior under Marcus Aurelius', *Acta antiqua Philippopolitana. Studia Historica et Linguistica* (1963), 109

BIRLEY, A. R. (1966a), *Marcus Aurelius* (1966).

BIRLEY, A. R. (1966b), 'Two names in the Historia Augusta', *Historia* 15 (1966), 249.

BIRLEY, A. R. (1966c), 'The origins of Gordian I', *Britain and Rome. Essays presented to Eric Birley*, ed. M. G. Jarrett and B. Dobson (1966), 56.

BIRLEY, A. R. (1967a), 'The Augustan History', *Latin Biography*, ed. T. A. Dorey (1967), 113.

BIRLEY, A. R. (1967b), 'The Roman governors of Britain', *Epigraphische Studien* 4 (1967), 63.

BIRLEY, A. R. (1967c), 'Excavations at Carpow', *Studien zu den Militärgrenzen Roms*=Beiheft 10 of the *Bonner Jahrbücher* (1967), 1.

BIRLEY, A. R. (1968a), 'Some teachers of M. Aurelius', *Historia-Augusta-Colloquium Bonn 1966/67* (1968), 39.

BIRLEY, A. R. (1968b), 'The invasion of Italy in the reign of M. Aurelius', *Provincialia. Festschrift für Rudolf Laur-Belart* (1968), 214.

BIRLEY, A. R. (1969), 'The *coups d'état* of the year 193', *Bonner Jahrbücher* 169 (1969), 247.

BIRLEY, A. R., *HAC*='Some notes on *HA Severus* 1-4', *Historia-Augusta-Colloquium Bonn 1968/69* (1970), 59.

BIRLEY, A. R., *Seventh Congress*='Roman frontier policy in the reign of M. Aurelius', *Proceedings of the Seventh International Congress of Roman Frontier Studies* 1967 (forthcoming).

BIRLEY, A. R. (1971), 'VI victrix in Britain', *Soldier and Civilian in Roman Yorkshire*, ed. R. M. Butler (1971).

BIRLEY, E. (1939), 'The Beaumont Inscription, the Notitia Dignitatum, and the garrison of Hadrian's Wall', *Transactions of the Cumberland and Westmorland Antiquarian and Archaeological Society*, 2nd series, 39 (1939), 190.

BIRLEY, E. (1950), 'The governors of Numidia A.D. 193-268', *Journal of Roman Studies* 40 (1950), 60.

BIRLEY, E. (1953a), *Roman Britain and the Roman Army* (1953).

BIRLEY, E. (1953b), 'Senators in the Emperors' service', *Proceedings of the British Academy* 39 (1953), 197.

BIRLEY, E. (1956), 'Hadrianic frontier policy', *Carnuntina. Vorträge beim Internationalen Kongress der Altertumsforscher, Carnuntum*, ed. E. Swoboda (1956), 25.

BIRLEY, E. (1957), 'Beförderungen und Versetzungen im römischen Heere', *Carnuntum Jahrbuch* 1957, 3.

BIRLEY, E. (1959), 'Excavations at Corstopitum, 1906–1958', *Archaeologia Aelina*, 4th series, 37 (1959), 12.

BIRLEY, E. (1961), *Research on Hadrian's Wall* (1961).

BIRLEY, E. (1963), 'Promotions and transfers in the Roman army. 2. The centurionate', *Carnuntum Jahrbuch* 1963–64, 21.

BIRLEY, E. (1966a), '*Alae* and *cohortes milliariae*', *Corolla Memoriae Erich Swoboda Dedicata* (1966), 54.

BIRLEY, E. (1966b), 'The Roman inscriptions of York', *Yorkshire Archaeological Journal* 41.4, (1966), 726.

BIRLEY, E. (1968), 'Some Militaria in the Historia Augusta', *Historia-Augusta-Colloquium Bonn 1966/67* (1968), 43.

BIRLEY, E., *Ep. Stud.* = 'Septimius Severus and the Roman army', *Epigraphische Studien* 8 (1969), 63.

BIRLEY, E. (1971), 'The end of IX Hispana', *Soldier and Civilian in Roman Yorkshire*, ed. R. M. Butler (1971). 81.

BIRLEY, R. E. (1962), 'Excavation of the Roman fortress at Carpow, 1961-2', *Proceedings of the Society of Antiquaries of Scotland* 96 (1962–3), 184.

BIRLEY, R. E. (1963), 'The Roman legionary fortress at Carpow', *Scottish Historical Review* 42 (1963), 126.

BIRT, T., 'Zu Marius Maximus', *Philologus* 76 (1920), 362.

BLOCH, H., 'A dream of Septimius Severus', *Classical World* 37 (1943–4), 31.

BOGAERS, J. E., 'Die Besatzungstruppen des Legionslagers von Nijmegen im 2. Jh. n. Chr.', *Studien zu den Militärgrenzen Roms* = Beiheft 10 of the *Bonner Jahrbücher* (1967), 54.

BOUBE-PICCOT, C., 'Trophée damasquiné sur une statue impériale de Volubilis', *Bulletin d'archéologie marocaine* 6 (1966), 189.

BOWERSOCK, G. W. (1965), Review of F. Millar (1964), *Gnomon* 37 (1965), 469.

BOWERSOCK, G. W. (1969), *Greek Sophists in the Roman Empire* (1969).

BOYCE, A. A., 'The twelfth imperatorial acclamation of Septimius Severus', *American Journal of Archaeology* 53 (1949), 337.

BRAUNERT, H. (1964), *Die Binnenwanderung. Studien zur sozialgeschichte Ägyptens in der Ptolemäer- und Kaiserzeit* (1964).

BRAUNERT, H. (1966), '*Ius Latii* in den Stadtrechten von Salpensa und Malaca', *Corolla memoriae Erich Swoboda Dedicata* (1966), 137.

BRILLIANT, R., *The Arch of Septimius Severus in the Roman Forum* = *Memoirs of the American Academy at Rome* 29 (1967).

BIBLIOGRAPHY

BROUGHTON, T. R. S., *The Romanisation of Africa Proconsularis* (1929).

CALLENDER, M. H., *Roman Amphorae* (1965).

CASSOLA, F. (1956), 'Sull' attendibilità dello storico Erodiano', *Atti dell' Acc.demia Pontaniana*, N.S., 6 (1956–7), 191.

CASSOLA, F. (1957a), 'Sulla vita e sulla personalità dello storico Erodiano', *Nuova rivista storica* 41 (1957), 219.

CASSOLA, F. (1957b), 'Erodiano e le sue fonti', *Rendiconti dell' Accademia delle Belle Arti di Napoli* 32 (1957), 165.

CASSOLA, F. (1965), 'Pertinace durante il principato di Commodo', *La parola del passato* 105 (1965), 451.

CASSOLA, F. (1966), *Ricerche sul II secolo dell' Impero: l'ascesa di Pertinace fino al 180 d. C.=Quaderni di 'Le parole e le idee'* 5 (1966).

CHARLES-PICARD, G. (1949), *Castellum Dimmidi* (1949).

CHARLES-PICARD, G. (1954), *Les religions de l'Afrique antique* (1954).

CHARLES-PICARD, G. (1956), *Le Monde de Carthage* (1956).

CHARLES-PICARD, G. (1957), *Civitas Mactaritana=Karthago* 8 (1957).

CHARLES-PICARD, G. (1959a), *La civilisation de l'Afrique romaine* (1959).

CHARLES-PICARD, G. (1959b), 'Pertinax et les prophètes de Caelestis', *Revue de l'histoire des religions* 155 (1959), 41.

CHARLES-PICARD, G. (1962), 'Origine et sens des reliefs sacrificiels de l'Arc des Argentiers', *Hommages à A. Grenier* (1962), 1254=Collection *Latomus* vol. 58.

CLARKE, G. W., 'Cassius Dio on Britain', *Classical Philology* 63 (1968), 145.

CONDURACHI, E., 'La costizuzione Antoniniana e la sua applicazione nell' Impero romano', *Dacia*, N.S., 2 (1958), 281.

COURTOIS, C. and L. LESCHI, C. PERRAT, C. SAUMAGNE, *Tablettes Albertini. Actes privés de l'époque vandale (fin de Vᵉ siècle)* (1952).

CRAMER, F. H., *Astrology in Roman Law and Politics* (1954).

CROOK, J. (1955), *Consilium Principis* (1955).

CROOK, J. (1968), *Law and Life of Rome* (1968).

DANIELS, C. M., *The Garamantes of Southern Libya* (1970).

DEBEVOISE, N. C., *A Political History of Parthia* (1938).

DE CEULENEER, A., *Essai sur la vie et le règne de Septime-Sévère* (1880).

DEGRASSI, A., *I Fasti consolari dell' Impero romano* (1954).

DEGRASSI, N., 'L'ordinamento di Leptis Magna nel primo secolo e la sua costituzione a municipio romano', *Epigraphica* 7 (1945), 8.

DESANGES, J., 'Note sur la datation de l'expédition de Julius Maternus au pays d'Agisymba', *Latomus* 23 (1964), 713.

DESSAU, H., 'Über Zeit und Persönlichkeit der SHA', *Hermes* 24 (1889), 337.

DI VITA, A. (1964), 'Il "limes" romano di Tripolitania nella sua concretezza archeologica e nella sua realtà storica', *Libya antiqua* 1 (1964), 65.

DI VITA, A. (1969), 'Le date di fondazione di Leptis e di Sabrathra sulla base dell'indagine archaeologia e l'eparchia cartaginese d'Africa', *Hommages offerts à M. Renard* III (1969), 196=vol. 102 of *Collection Latomus*.

DI VITA-ÉVRARD, G. (1963), 'Un "nouveau" proconsul d'Afrique, parent de Septime-Sévère: Caius Septimius Severus', *Mélanges d'archéologie et d'histoire de l'École française de Rome* 75 (1963), 387.

DI VITA-ÉVRARD, G. (1965), 'Les dédicaces de l'amphithéâtre et du cirque de Lepcis', *Libya antiqua* 2 (1965), 29.

DOMASZEWSKI, A. V. (1898), 'Der Staatstreich des Septimius Severus', *Rheinisches Museum für Philologie* 53 (1898), 638.

DOMASZEWSKI, A. V. (1908), *Die Rangordnung des römischen Heeres* (1908); reprinted, with introduction, addenda and corrigenda, and new index, by B. Dobson (1967)=Beiheft 14 of the *Bonner Jahrbücher*.

DOMASZEWSKI, A. V. (1909a), 'Die politische Bedeutung der Religion von Emesa', *Abhandlungen zur römischen Religion* (1909), 197.

DOMASZEWSKI, A. V. (1909b), *Geschichte der römischen Kaiser* (1909).

DOWNEY, G., *A History of Antioch in Syria* (1961).

DUNCAN-JONES, R. P., 'Costs, outlays and *summae honorariae* from Roman Africa', *Papers of the British School at Rome* 30 (1962), 47.

ELIOT, C. W. J., 'New evidence for the speed of the Roman imperial post', *Phoenix* 9 (1955), 76.

FINK, R. O., A. S. HOEY and W. F. SNYDER, 'The *Feriale Duranum*', *Yale Classical Studies* 7 (1940), 1.

FITZ, J. (1959), 'Der Besuch des Septimius Severus in Pannonien im J. 202 u. Z.', *Acta archaeologica academiae scientiarum Hungaricae* 11 (1959), 237.

FITZ, J. (1961), 'Prosopographica Pannonica', *Epigraphica* 23 (1961), 66.

FITZ, J. (1962), 'A military history of Pannonia from the Marcomann wars to the death of Alexander Severus (180–235)', *Acta archaeologica academiae scientiarum Hungaricae* 14 (1962), 25.

FITZ, J. (1963), 'Legati Augusti pro praetore Pannoniae inferioris', *Acta antiqua academiae scientiarum Hungaricae* 11 (1963), 245.

FITZ, J. (1966a), 'Réflexions sur la carrière de Tib. Claudius Candidus', *Latomus* 25 (1966), 831.

FITZ, J. (1966b), *Die Laufbahn der Statthalter in der römischen Provinz Moesia Inferior* (1966).

FITZ, J. (1969), 'La carrière de L. Valerius Valerianus', *Latomus*, 28 (1969), 126.

FLORIANI-SQUARCIAPINO, M., 'Le sculture severiane di Leptis Magna', *VIIIe Congrès International d'archéologie classique Paris 1963* (1965), 229.

FRANK, T., 'Rome and Italy of the Empire'=*Economic Survey of Ancient Rome*, ed. T. Frank, 5 (1940).

FREND, W. H. C., *Martyrdom and Persecution in the Early Church* (1965).

FRERE, S. S., *Britannia* (1967).

GARNSEY, P., 'Adultery trials and the survival of the *quaestiones* in the Severan age', *Journal of Roman Studies* 57 (1967), 56.

GAGÉ, J., 'Les jeux séculaires de 204 ap. J.C. et la dynastie des Sévères', *Mélanges d'archéologie et d'histoire de l'École française de Rome* 51 (1934), 33.

GILLAM, J. P. (1953), 'Calpurnius Agricola and the northern frontier', *Transactions of the Architectural and Archaeological Society of Durham and Northumberland* 10 (1953), 359.

GILLAM, J. P. (1958), 'Roman and Native A.D. 122–197', *Roman and Native in North Britain*, ed I. A. Richmond (1958), 60.

GILLAM, J. P. (1970) and J. C. MANN, 'The Northern British frontier from Antoninus Pius to Caracalla', *Archaeologia Aeliana*, 4th series, 48 (1970), 1.

GILLIAM, J. F. (1958), 'The governors of Syria Coele from Severus to Diocletian', *American Journal of Philology* 79 (1958), 225.

GILLIAM, J. F. (1965), 'Dura rosters and the *Constitutic Antoniniana*', *Historia* 14 (1965), 74.

GNECCHI, F., *I Medaglioni romani descritti ed illustrati* (1912).

GOODCHILD, R. G. (1949) and J. B. WARD-PERKINS, 'The *Limes Tripolitanus* in the light of recent discoveries', *Journal of Roman Studies* 39 (1949), 81.

GOODCHILD, R. G. (1950), 'The *Limes Tripolitanus*—II', *Journal of Roman Studies* 40 (1950), 30.

GRAHAM, A. J., 'The division of Britain', *Journal of Roman Studies* 56 (1966), 92.

GRISET, E., 'Un cristiano di Sabrata', *Rivista di studi classici* 5 (1951), 35.

GROSSO, F. (1964), *La lotta politica al tempo di Commodo* (1964).

GROSSO, F. (1968), 'Ricerche su Plauziano e gli avvenimenti del suo tempo', *Atti dell' Accademia nazionale dei Lincei*, ser. 8, *Rendiconti, Classe di scienze morali, storiche e filologiche* 23 (1968), 7.

GUEY, J. (1946), 'Note sur le Septizonium du Palatin', *Mélanges de la sociéte toulousaine d'études classiques* 1 (1946), 147.

367

GUEY, J. (1948), '28 janvier 98–28 janvier 198, ou le siècle des Antonins', *Revue des études anciennes* 50 (1948), 60.

GUEY, J. (1950), 'Lepcitana Septimiana VI. 1', *Revue africaine* 94 (1950), 51.

GUEY, J. (1951a). 'L'inscription du grand-père de Septime-Sévère à Leptis Magna', *Mémoires de la societé nationale des antiquaires de France* 82 (1951), 161.

GUEY, J. (1951b), 'Au theâtre de Leptis Magna. Le proconsulat de Lollianus Avitus et la date de l'*Apologie* d'Apulée', *Revue des études latines* 29 (1951), 307.

GUEY, J. (1952), 'Lepcitana Septimiana VI. 2', *Revue africaine* 96 (1952), 25.

GUEY, J. (1953), 'Epigraphica Tripolitana', *Revue des études anciennes* 55 (1953), 334.

GUEY, J. (1954), 'L'*Apologie* d'Apulée et les inscriptions de Tripolitaine', *Revue des études latines* 32 (1954), 115.

GUEY, J. (1956), 'La date de naissance de l'empereur Septime-Sévère d'après son horoscope', *Bulletin de la societé nationale des antiquaires de France* 1956, 33.

GUEY, J. (1959), 'Un document sur Septime-Sévère en Égypte (Papyrus Columbia 123)', *Revue des études anciennes* 61 (1959), 134.

GUEY, J. (1962), 'L'aloi du denier romain de 177 á 211 ap. J.-C. (étude descriptive)', *Revue numismatique* 4 (1962), 73.

HAMMOND, M. (1940), 'Septimius Severus, Roman bureaucrat', *Harvard Studies in Classical Philology* 51 (1940), 137.

HAMMOND, M. (1950), Review of G. J. Murphy, *American Journal of Philology* 71 (1950), 193.

HAMMOND, M. (1957), 'The composition of the Senate, AD 68–235', *Journal of Roman Studies* 47 (1957), 74.

HAMMOND, M. (1959), *The Antonine Monarchy* (1959)=*Papers and Monographs of the American Academy in Rome* 19.

HANNESTAD, K. (1944a), 'Solemne sacrum praefecti Aegypti and its historical background', *Classica et Mediaevalia* 6 (1944), 41.

HANNESTAD, K. (1944b), 'Septimius Severus in Egypt. A contribution to the chronology of the years 198–202', *Classica et Mediaevalia* 6 (1944), 194.

HARDEN, D. B., *The Phoenicians* (1962).

HARTKE, W., *Romische Kinderkaiser. Eine Strukturanalyse römischen Denkens und Daseins* (1951).

HARTLEY, B. R., 'Some problems of the Roman military occupation of the North of England', *Northern History* 1 (1966), 7.

HASEBROEK, J. (1916), *Die Fälschung der Vita Nigri und Vita Albini in den SHA* (1916).

HASEBROEK, J. (1921), *Untersuchungen zur Geschichte des Kaisers Septimius Severus* (1921).

HAYNES, D. E. L., *An archaeological and historical guide to the pre-Islamic antiquities of Tripolitania* (revised ed. 1957).

HAYNES, D. E. L. and P. E. D. HIRST, *Porta Argentariorum* (1939).

HAYWOOD, R. M. (1938), 'Roman Africa', *Economic Survey of Ancient Rome*, ed. T. Frank, 4 (1938), 1.

HAYWOOD, R. M. (1940), 'The African policy of Septimius Severus', *Transactions of the American Philological Association* 71 (1940), 175.

HAYWOOD, R. M. (1962), 'A further note on the African policy of Septimius Severus', *Hommages à A. Grenier* (1962), 786=*Collection Latomus* vol. 58.

HELM, R., 'Apuleius Apologie, ein Meisterwerk der zweiten Sophistik', *Das Altertum* 1 (1955), 86.

HERRMANN, L., 'Le procès d'Apulée fut-il un procès de christianisme?', *Revue de l'université de Bruxelles*, N.S., 4 (1951–2), 329.

HEURGON, J., 'Fronton de Cirta', *Receuil de la societé archéologique de Constantine* 70 (1957–8–9), 139.

HÖNN, K., *Quellenuntersuchungen zu den Viten des Heliogabalus und des Severus Alexander im Corpus der SHA* (1911).

HOHL, E. (1913), 'Beiträge zur Textgeschichte der HA', *Klio* 13 (1913), 258; 387.

HOHL, E. (1954), 'Kaiser Commodus und Herodian', *Sitzungsberichte der deutschen Akademie der Wissenschaften zu Berlin. Klasse für Gesellschaftwissenschaften, Jahrgang* 1954, Nr. 1, 3.[7]

HOHL, E. (1956a), 'Kaiser Pertinax und die Thronbesteigung seines Nachfolgers im Lichte der Herodiankritik', *Sitzungsberichte der deutschen Akademie der Wissenschaften zu Berlin. Klasse für Philosophie, Geschichte, usw. Jahrgang* 1956, Nr. 2, 3.

HOHL, E. (1956b), 'Herodian und der Sturz Plautians', *ib.*, 33.

HONORÉ, A. M., 'The Severan jurists', *Studia et documenta historiae et iuris* 28 (1962), 162.

HOWE, L. L., *The Pretorian Prefect from Commodus to Diocletian* (1942).

HUELSEN, C., 'Neue Fragmente der Acta ludorum saecularium von 204 nach Chr.', *Rheinisches Museum für Philologie* 81 (1932), 366.

INSTINSKY, H. U. (1942), 'Studien zur Geschichte des Septimius Severus', *Klio* 35 (1942), 203.

INSTINSKY, H. U. (1944a), 'Senatus in Gemeinwesen peregrinen Rechts', *Philologus* 96 (1944), 201.

INSTINSKY, H. U. (1944b), 'Die Herkunft des L. Fabius Cilo', *Philologus* 96 (1944), 293.

JARDÉ, A., *Étude critique sur la vie et le règne de Sévère Alexandre* (1925).

JARRETT, M. G. (1963), 'The African contribution to the imperial equestrian service', *Historia* 12 (1963), 209.

JARRETT, M. G. (1965), 'Septimius Severus and the defences of York', *Yorkshire Archaeological Journal* 41.3, (1965), 516.

JONES, A. H. M. (1960), *Studies in Roman Government and Law* (1960).

JONES, A. H. M. (1964), *The Later Roman Empire* (1964).

JUDEICH, W., 'Plautianus und Severus', *Festschrift Alexander Cartellieri* (1927), 63.

KAJANTO, I., *The Latin Cognomina* (1965)=vol. 46,2 of the *commentationes humanarum litterarum* of the *societas scientiarum Fennica*.

KEIL, J., 'Ein ephesischer Anwalt des 3. Jahrhunderts durchreist das Imperium Romanum', *Sitzungsberichte der Bayerischen Akademie der Wissenschaften* 1956, Heft 3.

KOLBE, H. G., 'Der Pertinaxstein aus Brühl bei Köln', *Bonner Jahrbücher* 162 (1962), 407.

KOLENDO, J., 'Étude sur les inscriptions de Novae', *Archaeologia* (Sofia) 16 (1965), 124.

KORNEMANN, E., *Weltgeschichte des Mittelmeerraumes* (1949).

KOTULA, T. (1967), 'A propos d'une inscription reconstituée de Bulla Regia (Hammam-Darradji). Quelques municipes "mystérieux" de l'Afrique proconsulaire', *Mélanges d'archéologie et d'histoire de l'École française de Rome* 79 (1967), 207.

KOTULA, T. (1968), *Les curies municipales en Afrique romaine* (1968)= *Travaux de la societé des sciences et des lettres de Wroclaw*, seria A, nr. 128.

KUBITSCHEK, J. W., *Imperium Romanum tributim discriptum* (1889).

KUNKEL, W., *Herkunft und soziale Stellung der römischen Juristen* (1952).

LA PIANA, G., 'The Roman church at the end of the second century', *Harvard Theological Review* 18 (1925), 201.

LUGLI, G., *Roma antica. Il centro monumentale* (1946).

MACKAY, T. S. and P. A., 'Inscriptions from rough Cilicia east of the Calacydnus', *Anatolian Studies* 19 (1969), 139.

MACMULLEN, R. (1963), *Soldier and Civilian in the Later Roman Empire* (1963).

MACMULLEN, R. (1967), *Enemies of the Roman Order: Treason, Unrest and Alienation in the Roman Empire* (1967).

MAGIE, D., *Roman Rule in Asia Minor* (1950).

MANN, J. C. (1961), 'The administration of Roman Britain', *Antiquity* 35 (1961), 316.

MANN, J. C. (1963), 'The raising of new legions during the Principate', *Hermes* 91 (1963), 483.

MANN, J. C. (1967) and M. G. JARRETT, 'The division of Britain', *Journal of Roman Studies* 57 (1967), 61.

MANNI, E., La lotta di Settimio Severo per la conquista di potere', *Rivista di filologia e istruzione classica* 75 (1947), 211.

MCCANN, A. M., *The Portraits of Septimius Severus AD 193–211* (1968)=vol. 30 of the *Memoirs of the American Academy in Rome*.

MIHAILOV, G. 'Septimius Severus in Moesia Inferior and Thrace', *Acta antiqua Philipopolitana. Studia Historica et Linguistica* (1963), 113.

MILLAR, F. (1962), 'The date of the *constitutio Antoniniana*', *Journal of Egyptian Archaeology* 48 (1962), 124.

MILLAR, F. (1964), *A Study of Cassius Dio* (1964).

MILLAR, F. (1968), 'Local cultures in the Roman Empire: Libyan, Punic and Latin in Roman Africa', *Journal of Roman Studies* 58 (1968), 126.

MONCEAUX, P. *Les Africains. Étude sur la littérature latine d'Afrique* (1894).

MORRIS, J. (1963), 'Senate and Emperor', *Γέρας. Studies presented to George Thomson* (1963), 149.

MORRIS, J. (1964), '*Leges annales* under the Principate. 1. legal and constitutional', *Listy filologické* 87 (1964), 316.

MORRIS, J. (1965a), '*Leges annales* under the Principate. Political effects', *Listy filologické* 88 (1965), 22.

MORRIS, J. (1965b), 'Munatius Plancus Paulinus', *Bonner Jahrbücher* 165 (1965), 88.

MORRIS, J. (1968), 'The date of St Alban', *Hertfordshire Archaeology* 1 (1968), 1.

MÜLLER, J. J., 'Der Geschichtsschreiber Marius Maximus', *Untersuchungen zur römischen Kaisergeschichte*, ed. M. Büdinger (1870), 3, 17.

MUNDLE, I., 'Dea Caelestis in der Religionspolitik des Septimius Severus und der Julia Domna', *Historia* 10 (1961), 228.

MURPHY, G. J., *The Reign of the Emperor L. Septimius Severus from the Evidence of the Inscriptions* (1947).

NESSELHAUF, H. (1964), '*Patrimonium* und *res privata* des römischen Kaisers', *Historia-Augusta-Colloquium Bonn 1963* (1964), 73.

NESSELHAUF, H. (1966), 'Die Vita Commodi und die Acta Urbis', *Historia-Augusta-Colloquium Bonn 1964–65* (1966), 127.

NESSELHAUF, H. (1967) and H. V. PETRIKOVITS, 'Ein Weihaltar für Apollo aus Aachen-Burtscheid', *Bonner Jahrbücher* 167 (1967).

NEUGEBAUER, K. A., 'Die Familie des Septimius Severus', *Die Antike* 12 (1936), 155.

OATES, D., *Studies in the Ancient History of Northern Iraq* (1968).

OLIVER, J. H. and R. E. A. PALMER, 'Minutes of an Act of the Roman Senate', *Hesperia* 24 (1955), 320.

PEKÁRY, T., 'Studien zur römischen Währungs- und Finanzgeschichte von 161–235 n. Chr.', *Historia* 8 (1959), 443.

PELLETIER, A., 'Les sénateurs d'Afrique proconsulaire d'Auguste à Gallien', *Latomus* 23 (1964), 511.

PFLAUM, H. G. (1950), *Les procurateurs équestres sous le haut-empire romain* (1950).

PFLAUM, H. G. (1954), Review of E. Hohl (1954), *Revue des études latines* 32 (1954), 450.

PFLAUM, H. G. (1957a), 'À propos de la date de la création de la province de Numidie', *Libyca* 5 (1957), 61.

PFLAUM, H. G. (1957b), 'Les gouverneurs de la province romaine d'Arabie de 193 à 304', *Syria* 34 (1957), 128.

PFLAUM, H. G., *Les carrières procuratoriennes équestres sous le Haut-Empire romain* (1960–1).

PFLAUM, H. G. (1961), 'Les gendres de Marc-Aurèle', *Journal des Savants* 1961, 28.

PFLAUM, H. G. (1962a), 'Deux familles sénatoriales du IIe et IIIe siècles', *Journal des Savants* 1962, 108.

PFLAUM, H. G. (1962b), 'Un nouveau gouverneur de la province de Rhétie, proche parent de l'impératrice Julia Domna, à propos d'une inscription récemment découverte à Augsbourg', *Bayerische Vorgeschichtsblätter* 27 (1962), 82.

PFLAUM, H. G. (1963), 'Du nouveau sur les *agri decumates* à la lumière d'un fragment de Capoue, *CIL* X 3872', *Bonner Jahrbücher* 163 (1963), 224.

PFLAUM, H. G. (1964), 'Les correspondants de l'orateur M. Cornelius Fronto de Cirta', *Hommages à Jean Bayet* (1964), 544=*Collection Latomus*, vol. 70.

PFLAUM, H. G. (1966), *Les sodales Antoniniani à l'époque de Marc-Aurèle* (1966)=*vol.* 15 of *Mémoires présentés par divers savants à l'Académie des inscriptions et belles-lettres.*

PIGANIOL, A., *Histoire de Rome* (4th ed., 1954).

PIGHI, J(ohannes=Giovanni) B., *De ludis saecularibus Romani Quiritium* (1941).

PLATNAUER, M., *The Life and Reign of the Emperor L. Septimius Severus* (1918, reprint 1965).

PLEW, J., *Marius Maximus als direkte und indirekte Quelle der scriptores Historiae Augustae* (1878).

REINMUTH, O. W., 'A working list of the prefects of Egypt 30 B.C. to 299 A.D.', *Bulletin of the American Society of Papyrologists* 4 (1967), 75.

REUSCH, W., *Der historische Wert der Caracallavita in den SHA* (1931)= *Klio*, Beiheft 24.

REYNOLDS, J. M. (1955), 'Inscriptions of Roman Tripolitania. A supplement', *Papers of the British School at Rome* 23 (1955), 124.

REYNOLDS, J. M. (1962), 'Q. Cerellius Apollinaris, *praefectus vigilum* in A.D. 212', *Papers of the British School at Rome* 30 (1962), 33.

RICHMOND, I. A. (1940), 'The Romans in Redesdale', *History of Northumberland* 15 (1940), 63.

RICHMOND, I. A. (1943), 'Roman legionaries at Corbridge. Their supply-base, temples and religious cults', *Archaeologia Aeliana*, 4th series, 21 (1943), 127.

RICHMOND, I. A. (1963), *Roman Britain* (2nd edition, 1963).

RITTERLING, E., *Fasti des römischen Deutschlands unter dem Prinzipat* (1932).

ROMANELLI, P. (1958), 'Fulvii Lepcitani', *Archaeologia Classica* 10(1958),258.

ROMANELLI, P. (1959), *Storia delle province romane dell' Africa* (1959).

ROSTOVTZEFF, M. (1938), *Dura Europos and Its Art* (1938).

ROSTOVTZEFF, M. (1957), *Social and Economic History of the Roman Empire* (2nd edition, 1957).

ST JOSEPH, J. K., 'Air reconnaissance in Britain, 1965–68', *Journal of Roman Studies* 59 (1969), 104.

ŠAŠEL, J., 'Essai d'identification des consuls de l'année 209 après J.-C.', *Historia* 17 (1968), 256.

SASSE, C., *Die Constitutio Antoniniana* (1958).

SCHÖNBERGER, H., 'The Roman frontier in Germany: an archaeological survey', *Journal of Roman Studies* 59 (1969), 144.

SCHWARTE, K. H., 'Der angebliche Christengesetz des Septimius Severus', *Historia* 12 (1963), 185.

SESTON, W. (1966a), 'Sur les traces de Marius Maximus. I. Marius Maximus et les consuls de 209', *Historia-Augusta-Colloquium Bonn* 1964/65 (1966), 211.

SESTON, W. (1966b), 'Marius Maximus et la date de la Constitutio Antoniniana', *Mélanges d'archéologie et d'histoire offerts à Jerome Carcopino* (1966), 877.

SHERWIN-WHITE, A. N., *The Letters of Pliny. A historical and social commentary* (1966).

STANFIELD, J. A. and G. SIMPSON, *Central Gaulish Potters* (1958).

STARK, F., *Rome on the Euphrates* (1966).

STARR, C. G., 'Aurelius Victor, historian of Empire', *American Historical Review* 61 (1955–56), 574.

STAUFFENBERG, A. Graf Schenk v., 'Dorieus', *Historia* 9 (1960), 181.

STEER, K. A. (1958), 'Roman and native in North Britain: the Severan reorganisation', *Roman and Native in North Britain*, ed. I. A. Richmond (1958), 91.

STEER, K. A. (1964), 'John Horsley and the Antonine Wall', *Archaeologia Aeliana*, 4th series, 42 (1964), 1.

STEIN, A. (1940), *Die Legaten von Moesien* (1940).

STEIN, A. (1944), *Die Reichsbeamte von Dazien* (1944).

STEVENS, C. E. (1951), 'Britain between the invasions (54 B.C.–AD 43)', *Aspects of Archaeology in Britain and Beyond. Essays presented to O.G.S. Crawford*, (1951), 332.

STEVENS, C. E. (1966), *The Building of Hadrian's Wall* (1966)=vol. 20 of *Cumberland and Westmorland Antiquarian and Archaeological Society*, Extra Series.

STRAUB, J., 'Die ultima verba des Septimius Severus', *Historia-Augusta-Colloquium Bonn 1963* (1964), 171.

SYME, Sir R. (1939), *The Roman Revolution* (1939 and reprints).

SYME, Sir R. (1958), *Tacitus* (1958).

SYME, Sir R. (1965a), 'Les proconsuls d'Afrique sous Hadrien', *Revue des études anciennes* 67 (1965), 342.

SYME, Sir R. (1965b), 'Hadrian the intellectual', *Les empereurs romains d'Espagne* (1965), 243.

SYME, SIR R. (1968a), *Ammianus and the Historia Augusta* (1968).

SYME, SIR R. (1968b), 'Ignotus, the good biographer', *Historia-Augusta-Colloquium Bonn 1966/67* (1968), 131.

SYME, SIR R. (1968c), 'Not Marius Maximus', *Hermes* 96 (1968), 494.

TEUTSCH, L., *Das römische Städtewesen in Nordafrika in der Zeit von C. Gracchus bis zum Tode des Augustus* (1962).

THOMASSON, B. E., *Die Statthalter der römischen Provinzen Nordafrikas von Augustus bis Diokletian* (1960).

THOMPSON, L. H., 'Roman and native in the Tripolitanian cities in the early Empire', *Proceedings of the Libya in History Conference Benghazi 1968* (forthcoming).

BIBLIOGRAPHY

THOMSEN, P., 'Massilia in Syrien, Ein Beitrag zur Historia Augusta und zur Ortskunde Syriens', *Zeitschrift des deutschen Palästina-Vereins* 67 (1945), 75.

VAN SICKLE, C. E. (1928a), 'The legal status of Clodius Albinus in the years 193–196', *Classical Philology* 23 (1928), 123.

VAN SICKLE, C. E. (1928b), 'The headings of rescripts of the Severi in the Justinian Code', *Classical Philology* 23 (1928), 270.

VERGARA CAFFARELLI, E. and G. CAPUTO, with introduction by R. BIANCHI BANDINELLI, *The Buried City. Excavations at Leptis Magna* (1966).

VITUCCI, G., *Ricerche sulla Prefettura Urbi in età imperiale* (1956).

WALSER, G. and T. PEKÁRY, *Die Krise des römischen Reiches* (1962).

WALSH, P. G., 'Lucius Madaurensis', *Phoenix* 22 (1968), 143.

WARD-PERKINS, J. B. (1948), 'Severan art and architecture at Lepcis Magna', *Journal of Roman Studies* 38 (1948), 59.

WARD-PERKINS, J. B. (1951a), 'The art of the Severan age in the light of Tripolitanian discoveries', *Proceedings of the British Academy* 36 (1951), 295.

WARD-PERKINS, J. B. (1951b), 'The Arch of Septimius Severus at Leptis Magna', *Archaeology* 4 (1951), 226.

WARMINGTON, B. H., *Carthage* (1964).

WATSON, G. R., *The Roman Soldier* (1969).

WELLES, C. B., R. O. FINK and J. F. GILLIAM, *Dura-Europos Final Report V. 1: The Parchments and Papyri* (1959).

WERNER, R., 'Der historische Wert der Pertinaxvita in den SHA', *Klio* 26 (1933), 283.

WESTERMANN, W. L. and A. A. SCHILLER, *Apokrimata. Decisions of Septimius Severus on Legal Matters. Text, Translation and Historical Analysis* (1954).

WHITTAKER, C. R., 'The Revolt of Papirius Dionysius A.D. 190', *Historia* 13 (1964), 348.

WINKLER, G., *Die Reichsbeamten von Noricum und ihr Personal bis zum Ende der römischen Herrschaft* (1969).

WRIGHT, R. P., 'An imperial inscription from the Roman fortress at Carpow, Perthshire', *Proceedings of the Society of Antiquaries of Scotland* 97 (1963–4), 202.

YOUTIE, H. C. and SCHILLER, A. A., 'Second thoughts on the Columbia Apokrimata (P. Col. 123)', *Chronique d'Égypte* 30 (1955), 327.

INDEX

The index covers mainly proper names. Romans are indexed by *nomen*, except in the case of Emperors, authors and one or two others. Rome and Italy are not included.

377

Egnatius Victor, senator, 252, 343
Egypt, 18, 22, 160, 171; Prefects of, 91,
99, 128, 136, 149, 164, 171, 203, 205ff.,
236, 253, 282, 334, 337, 339, 341, 343,
349, 350, 354; visit of Septimius to,
16, 205ff., 222, 326
Elagabalus, Emperor, (Varius Avitus
Bassianus), 8, 17, 275ff., 297f., 304,
317; the god, 117f., 275
Eleusis, 119
Emesa, 117ff., 131f., 177, 274ff., 298, 345
Emona (Ljubljana), 161
Epagathus, see Amelius
Ephesus, 87n., 251, 267
Epiphania, 115
Erucius Clarus, Sex. (cos. II ord. 146), 81
Erucius Clarus, C. (cos. ord. 170), 81
Erucius Clarus Vibianus, C. Julius, (cos.
ord. 193), 145, 199
Etruria, 35ff., 78
Euodus, imperial freedman, 232, 269
Euphrates, river, 64, 66, 110, 115f., 132,
181f., 189, 201ff., 313
Euripides, 113, 204
Eutropius, 5, 14
Eutychianus, actor, 275
Extricatus, see Messius

Fabius Barbarus Valerius Magnus
Julianus, Q. (cos. 99), 343f
Fabius Cilo, L. (cos. II ord. 204), friend
of Septimius, 14n., 158f., 169; from
Spain, 70, 281, 343; his career, 343;
commands legion in Syria, 118; consul designate, 145; consul, 158; commands army in 193, 169, 172; curator
of Nicomedia; governor of Bithynia,
176, 189; governor of Upper Moesia,
189; commands special force, 191;
governor of Upper Pannonia, 193,
201; Prefect of the City, 217; second
consulship, 223; saves life of Macrinus, 233; nearly killed in 212, 271
Fabius Magnus Valerianus, M., senator,
343f
Falco, see Sosius
Fanum Fortunae, in Italy, 84

Faustina I, Empress, 101
Faustina II, Empress, 20, 92, 124, 183n.,
316
Faustina (Annia Aurelia Galeria Faus-
tina), eldest daughter of M. Aurelius,
98n.
Faustina, see Annia, Vitrasia
Faustinianus, see Julius
Faustinus, see Junius
Faustus, see Anicius
Faventia, in Italy, 314
Felix, see Aquilius, Minucius
feriale Duranum, 16, 159n., 162n., 178n.,
202n
Festus, see Valerius
Firminus, see Hostilius
Flaccus, see Septimius, Suellius
Flamma, see Porcius
Flavia Neratia Septimia Octavilla, prob-
able kinswoman of Septimius, 293
Flavia Titiana, wife of Pertinax, 146, 149
Flavius Aper, L., hypothetical kinsman
of Septimius, 294
Flavius Aristus Ulpianus, T., senator,
344
Flavius Athenagoras, senator, 180
Flavius Boethus, senator, 75n
Flavius Genialis, Praetorian Prefect,
163
Flavius Juvenalis, Praetorian Prefect,
162, 164, 296, 344
Flavius Marcianus, Lepcitane, 40f
Flavius Marinus, T., centurion, 219
Flavius Secundus Philippianus, T., sen-
ator, 190
Flavius Septimius Aper Octavianus, L.,
possible kinsman of Septimius, 295,
301
Flavius Sulpicianus, T., father-in-law of
Pertinax, 136, 150, 152, 153f., 199
Flavius Titianus, senator, 344
Flavius Ulpianus, senator, 344
Forth, Firth of, 46, 245, 248, 254, 258ff
Frontinus, see Aemilius
Fronto, M. Cornelius (cos. 143), the
orator, a Numidian, 46; his influence,
71, 74ff.; Septimius might have met

him, 76; anti-Christian writings of, 58n.; a friend of, 61n.; compatriots of, 65, 330; his family, 75ff., 210
Fronto, see Aufidius, Aurelius, Claudius
Frugi, see Licinius
Fulvia Nepotilla, Lepcitane, 295
Fulvia Pia, mother of Septimius, 20, 294
Fulvia Plautilla Augusta, P., daughter of Plautianus, her entourage of eunuchs, 207; betrothed to Antoninus, 212; marriage, 214f., 225; in Africa, 217, 220; hated by husband, 231ff.; no children, 232, 295; divorce and exile, 233, 271; death, 294
Fulvii Lepcitani, 26, 29, 35, 90
Fulvius Dida Bibulianus, Q., Lepcitane, 295
Fulvius Fuscus Granianus, senator, 344
Fulvius Maximus, C., senator, 344
Fulvius Pius, grandfather of Septimius, 294
Fulvius Plautianus, C. (cos. ord. 203), kinsman and Praetorian Prefect of Septimius, 10, 282, 294ff.; supposed homosexual relations with Septimius, 62, 235; sentenced by Pertinax in Africa, 127n., 150, 295; given some post by Pertinax in 193, 150, 295; related to mother of Septimius 150, 295ff.; at Rome in 193, 158; pursues children of Niger, 163, 171; made Prefect of the vigiles, 180n., 295f.; made Praetorian Prefect, 200, 295; with Septimius in east, 201; urges death of Julius Laetus, 203f.; in Egypt, 207ff.; removes rivals, 208, 350; treats Julia Domna badly, 212, 241f.; his daughter betrothed to Antoninus, 212, her marriage, 215, 225; his consulship, 216; in Africa, 217ff.; row with Septimius, 220; returns to Rome, 222; at Saecular Games, 229; his great power, 10, 231, 280; his overthrow and death, 232ff., 238, 252n., 269, 271, 303, 323; his career, 294ff.; Historia Augusta on, 222, 326

Fulvius Plautius Hortensianus, C., son of Plautianus, 233, 296

Gabinius Barbarus, C., possible governor of Upper Moesia, 332
Gabinius Barbarus (?)Vindex Pompeianus, C., senator, 332
Galatia, province of, 10, 177, 186, 191n
Galba, Emperor, 148
Galen, the physician, 5, 14, 75, 138, 286
Gallicus, see Rutilius
Gallienus, Emperor, 11n
Gallitta, see Claudia
Gallus, see Aurelius, Claudius
Garama, desert city, 27, 34
Garamantes, Saharan tribe, 27, 31ff., 34f., 219
Gaul, 2, 66, 186, 191, 194ff., 199, 246
Gavius Cornelius Cethegus, M. (cos. ord. 170), 81
Gemellinus, see Herennius
Geminius Marcianus, see Julius
Genialis, see Flavius
Gentianus, see Cosconius, Hedius
Germany, 197, 217, 245n., 246, 278, 298, 345
Germany, Lower (Germania Inferior), province of, 66, 158; governors of, 12, 104, 159, 190, 196, 247, 314, 325, 331, 344, 354, 355
Germany, Upper (Germania Superior), province of, 64, 75, 77, 123, 136n., 158, 193, 315; governors of, 65, 67, 104, 331, 338, 340, 347, 349, 350, 354
Gessius Marcianus, father of Severus Alexander, 276, 297f
Geta, P. Septimius, younger son of Septimius, vita in the Historia Augusta largely bogus, 11; portraits and inscriptions of defaced, 18, 271; birth of, 125, 303; made Caesar, 202; his tutor, 207f.; called Augustus prematurely in Africa, 219; visit to Africa, 217ff.; his fourteenth birthday, 221; at Saecular Games, 226ff.; consul in 205, 232; 'most noble Caesar', 232; praenomen changed, 232f., 301; quar-

appointed quaestor of Baetica, 85f.;
quaestor of Sardinia instead, 86;
legate in Africa, 87ff.; tribune of the
plebs, 86, 91f.; not regarded as outstanding, 87, 134f.; first marriage, 90;
alleged daughters, 90, 325; praetor,
93f.; in Spain, 94ff.; influenced by
M. Aurelius, 95f., 210f., 289f.; made
legate of IV Scythica and goes to
Syria, 98, 104ff., 106ff., 115ff.; meets
Pertinax, 106; dismissed, 105, 118f.;
meets Julia Domna, 117f.; marries
her, 123f.; at Athens, 119; governor of
Lugdunensis, 122ff., 349; sons born,
124f.; proconsul of Sicily, 127; legate
of Upper Pannonia, 134ff.; hears of
accession of Pertinax, 149; a key figure
under Pertinax, 150; his proclamation as Emperor, 155ff.; march on
Rome, 159ff.; disbands Praetorian
Guard, 164f.; enters Rome, 165f.;
deifies Pertinax, 167f.; goes east
against Niger, 169ff.; raises new
legions, 171, 191; *imperator*, II, III,
176; *imp.* IV, 179; *imp.* V, VI, VII,
182; *imp.* VIII, 187; *imp.* IX, X, 195n.,
imp. XI, 202; *imp.* XII, 202n., 252n.;
pater patriae, 176; Parthicus Arabicus,
Parthicus Adiabenicus, 182; invades
Mesopotamia, 181ff.; calls himself son
of Marcus Aurelius, 184; breach with
Albinus, 184ff.; return to Rome, 191ff.;
at Lugdunum, 194f.; at Rome in 197,
198ff.; deifies Commodus, 186, 198ff.;
goes east again, 200ff.; captures
Ctesiphon, 202; *imp.* XI, Parthicus
Maximus, 202; *imp.* XII, 202n., 252n.;
at Hatra, 203ff.; goes to Egypt, 205ff.;
goes to Syria, 210ff.; *decennalia*, 212,
214f.; inspects Danubian provinces,
212ff.; visits Africa, 216ff.; at Lepcis
Magna, 218ff.; Arch of, at Rome,
222f.; holds Saecular Games, 224ff.;
and fall of Plautianus, 231ff.; activity in
Italy, 235ff.; and Senate, 238ff., 279ff.;
autobiography, 13, 240f., 326; decides
to go to Britain, 244ff.; British expedi-

tion, 253ff.; Britannicus, 255, 264;
death, 268; cremation, 269; and the
Africans, 282ff., 328ff.; army reforms,
283ff.; *stemma*, 307; Marius Maximus's *Life* of, 323ff.
Septimius, senator of Flavian period,
35n.
Septimius, L., murderer of Pompey, 206
Septimius Aper, L. (*cos. ord.* 207), kinsman of Septimius, 295, 301
Septimius Aper, P. (*cos.* 153), kinsman
of Septimius, 21, 44, 60, 64, 293, 301
Septimius Flaccus, legate of III Augusta,
34f., 304
Septimius Geta, P., father of Septimius,
20f., 44f., 302, 312f
Septimius Geta, P. (*cos. II ord.* 203),
brother of Septimius, his *cursus*
inscription, 15, 302f.; his career, 61,
302f.; *Xvir*, 61, 69, 113n.; tribune in
Britain, 61, 68f., 110, 251; perhaps
meets Pertinax, 68, 93, 110; quaestor
in Crete-Cyrenaica, 78f., 340; *curator*
of Ancona, 84, 231; a *fetialis*, 93, 135,
303, 313; legate of I Italica, 93, 125,
174; his name, 125, 231; proconsul of
Sicily, 125; governor of Lusitania,
125; governor of Lower Moesia, 135,
158, 160, 174, 313; governor of Dacia,
174, 189f., 231, 349; his ambitions,
174, 190; second consulship, 216, 219;
death, 231, 234, 296; possible infor-
mant of Marius Maximus, 313f
(Septimius) Macer, *see* Macer
Septi(mius) Petro(nianus), L., procurator, 45, 300
(Septimius) Severus, kinsman of Septimius, 303
Septimius Severus, C., kinsman of
Septimius, 15, 21, 44f., 60, 64, 67, 70,
87ff., 93, 115, 225, 303f
Septimius C. f. Pup. Severus, C., patron
of Praeneste, 304
Septimius Severus, L., grandfather of
Septimius, 15, 20, 35ff., 44, 47n., 60,
67, 74, 78, 250, 304
Sergius Paulus, L. (*cos. II ord.* 168), 75n

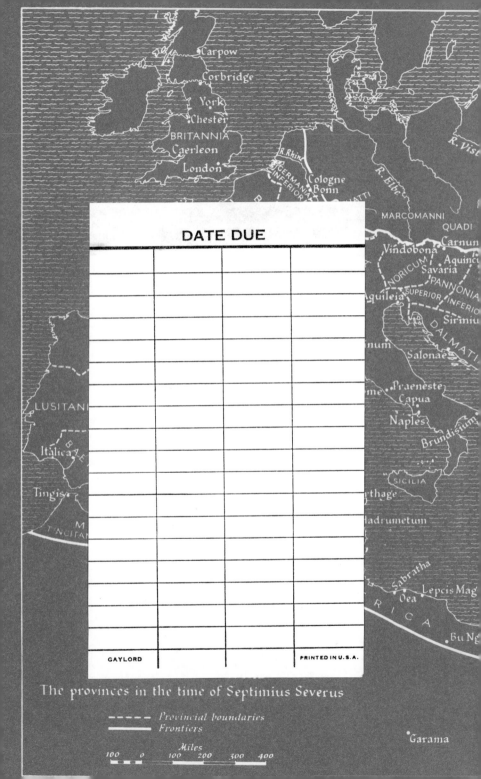

Carpow

Corbridge

York

Chester

BRITANNIA

Caerleon

London

R. Rhin

GERMANIA INFERIOR

Cologne
Bonn

MARCOMANNI

QUADI

Vindobona

Carnun

Aquinc

NORICUM

Savaria

PANNONIA

Aquileia

SUPERIOR

INFERIO

Siriniu

DALMATI

num

Salonae

me

Praeneste

Capua

Naples

Brundisium

SICILIA

rthage

ladrumetum

LUSITANI

Italica

Tingis

M

TINGITAN

R. Vist

R. Elbe

Sabratha

Lepcis Mag

Oea

RICA

Bu Ng

DATE DUE

GAYLORD			PRINTED IN U.S.A.

The provinces in the time of Septimius Severus

- - - - - *Provincial boundaries*
———— *Frontiers*

Miles
100   0   100   200   300   400

Garama